The publisher and the University of California Press Foundation gratefully acknowledge the generous support of the Joan Palevsky Endowment Fund in Literature in Translation.

Bashō

Bashō

The Complete Haiku of Matsuo Bashō

———

Translated, Annotated, and with an
Introduction by Andrew Fitzsimons

UNIVERSITY OF CALIFORNIA PRESS

University of California Press
Oakland, California

© 2022 by Andrew Fitzsimons

Library of Congress Cataloging-in-Publication Data

Names: Matsuo, Bashō, 1644–1694, author. | Fitzsimons, Andrew, translator,
    annotator, writer of introduction.
Title: Bashō: the complete Haiku of Matsuo Bashō / translated, annotated,
    and with an introduction by Andrew Fitzsimons.
Other titles: Poems. English
Description: Oakland, California : University of California Press, [2023] |
    Includes bibliographical references and index.
Identifiers: LCCN 2022001045 (print) | LCCN 2022001046 (ebook) |
    ISBN 9780520385580 (paperback) | ISBN 9780520385597 (ebook)
Classification: LCC PL794.4 .A2 2023 (print) | LCC PL794.4 (ebook) |
    DDC 895.61/32—dc23/eng/20220511
LC record available at https://lccn.loc.gov/2022001045
LC ebook record available at https://lccn.loc.gov/2022001046

Manufactured in the United States of America
28   27   26   25   24   23
10   9   8   7   6   5   4   3

i.m. Gerard Fanning (1952–2017)

In the afterwards
of the moon's setting the four
corners of his desk

CONTENTS

Bashō Chronology   *ix*

Introduction   *xiii*

THE POEMS   1

Acknowledgments   *361*

Glossary   *363*

Bibliography   *369*

Index of Poems in Japanese (Romaji)   *381*

Index of First Lines in Poems in English   *403*

Index of Names   *415*

Except where specified, dates refer to the Gregorian calendar.

1644 Matsuo Kinsaku (Bashō) born at or near Ueno, in the Province of Iga
      (Mie Prefecture), into a family of samurai descent.

1656 His father, Matsuo Yozaemon, dies.

1663 Earliest extant poem. Bashō in the service of Tōdō Yoshitada, a young
      relative of the feudal lord of Iga. Assumes the *haigō* (poetic pen name)
      Sōbō.

1666 Death of Tōdō Yoshitada, at twenty-five. No records of Bashō's life at
      this time. Some poems from this period identify him as "Sōbō of
      Ueno in Iga Province."

1672 Publishes *Kai Ōi* ("The Seashell Game"). The book contains his
      comments on a poetry contest, as well as two of his hokku. Moves to
      Edo (Tokyo).

1675 Under a new pen name, Tōsei ("green peach"), participates in a
      linked-verse gathering with Nishiyama Sōin, founder of the Danrin
      school. Begins to gather students, including Sugiyama Sanpū and
      Takarai Kikaku.

1676 Participates in two Danrin-style linked-verse sequences, with
      Yamaguchi Sodō, published as *Edo Ryōgin Shū* ("Collection of Two
      Edo Poets"). Visits Iga in the summer; returns to Edo with his
      sixteen-year-old nephew, Tōin, in his care.

1677   Begins to work at the waterworks department in Edo; achieves distinction in the poetry contest *Roppyakuban Haikai Hokku Awase* ("The Six Hundred Round Hokku Contest").

1678   Distributes his first *Saitanchō* (New Year's verses), a mark of his status as a haikai master. In the spring, ten thousand verses are composed by a gathering of poets to mark his professional independence.

1679   Shaves his head and becomes a lay monk.

1680   Bashō's circle publishes two major collections: *Tōsei Montei Dokugin Nijikkasen* and *Haikai Awase*, moving away from the Danrin style toward Chinese-influenced poetry. In the winter, moves from central Edo into a hut on the eastern outskirts, in the Fukagawa district.

1681   A disciple, Rika, transplants a bashō plant as a gift for Bashō's new home. The hut becomes known as *Bashō-an* ("the bashō hut") and the poet as "Master Bashō." He practices Zen under Butchō; Zen and Chinese Daoism become influential in his poetry.

1683   On January 25, the Bashō-an destroyed in the *Tenna no Taika* ("The Great Fire of the Tenna period"). Homeless, Bashō accepts an invitation to Kai Province. In early summer, returns to Edo to oversee the anthology *Minashiguri*. In August his mother dies. In the winter, moves into a new Bashō-an in Fukagawa.

1684   In September, begins the journey that will result in *Nozarashi Kikō*, his first travel journal. In Nagoya, leads five linked-verse sequences that later form the book *Fuyu no Hi*, the first major anthology of the *Shōmon*, the "Bashō School."

1685   Visits Iga, to celebrate the lunar New Year. Stays almost two months. His return journey to Edo is marked by haikai gatherings, including at Ōtsu, Atsuta, and Narumi. He arrives in Edo in the summer, after taking the mountainous route through Kai Province.

1686   In January, Bashō and fifteen students compose a sequence of one hundred verses in honor of Kikaku, to mark his new status as a haikai master. Bashō contributes six verses; later, after a request, begins annotating each verse. The comments, published in 1763 as *Hatsukai-shi Hyōchū*, are a key source for Bashō's developing views on poetry.

1687   In September, travels with Sora and Sōha to Kashima Shrine to see the harvest moon, a trip recounted in *Kashima Kikō*. Publishes *Atsume Ku* ("Collected Verses"). In late November, sets off on another long journey to the west, recounted in *Oi no Kobumi*.

1688   Celebrates the lunar New Year in Iga again. After visits to Ise and the Futami Coast, returns to Iga for the thirty-third anniversary of his father's death. Travels with Tokoku to Yoshino, and to Wakanoura, Nara, and historical sites in Suma and Akashi. After a short stay in Kyoto, Tokoku departs. Bashō travels on to Ōtsu and the Nagara River. Prolongs a stay in Nagoya in order to travel to Sarashina village to see the harvest moon, the source of *Sarashina Kikō;* returns to Edo in September.

1689   On May 16 (the twenty-seventh day of the Third Month), leaves Edo, with Sora, on the longest journey of his life, to the north as far as Kisagata, and then down along the western coast of Japan, which becomes the basis for Bashō's most famous work, *Oku no Hosomichi.* In November reaches Iga, where he spends the end of the year.

1690   Visits Nara and stays with Kyorai in Kyoto. Welcomes the lunar New Year at Zeze. Spends three months in Iga. At a haikai gathering in April, speaks of his new poetic ideal of *karumi* ("lightness"). From May until August lives in the Genjū-an ("the Hut of Illusory Dwelling") by Lake Biwa. Writes the haibun *Genjū-an no Ki.* After Genjū-an, spends two months in a hut at Gichū-ji, a temple on the shores of Lake Biwa. Returns to Iga at the end of October, for the rest of the year.

1691   Stays from May to June at Rakushi-sha ("The House of Fallen Persimmons"), a cottage in Saga, in northwest Kyoto. Writes *Saga Nikki,* his last major prose work. Publishes the anthology *Sarumino.* Returns to Edo in December.

1692   Disaffected by the poetic scene in Edo, considers abandoning poetry. A new hut built for him in Fukagawa. Resumes poetic activity.

1693   His nephew, Tōin, becomes ill and moves into Bashō's hut. Bashō supports Jutei and her three children. Tōin dies at the end of April. In August, heartbroken and worn out, Bashō closes his gate to visitors. About a month later, resumes social and poetic activities.

1694   Attends haikai gatherings in Edo, and clarifies *karumi* as poetic ideal. In June, departs for Iga. Jutei and her two daughters move into his hut; her son, Jirōbei, accompanies Bashō. Reaches Iga at the end of June. Revisits the Ōtsu area and stays again at Rakushi-sha. Two anthologies published: *Betsuzashiki* and *Sumidawara.* Eager to propagate *karumi,* enters a period of intense activity, with haikai gatherings in Kyoto and Ueno. Dies on November 28, in Osaka.

Introduction

Bashō is the single greatest figure in the history of Japanese literature, and one of the major figures of world literature. In the selections and versions of his work so far available in English, Bashō has appeared mainly as a philosopher of nature, as a Zen mystic in search of Buddhist enlightenment, and as the refiner and definer of Japanese sensibility, articulated through the brevity of haiku. When we read his haiku in their entirety, however, Bashō emerges as what he most truly was, a poet: the great poet of weather, of the withering and the cooling wind, of the freshening and the lashing rain, of drizzle and hail and sleet, of snow that transforms but can also blind, of the heat-heavy day, of ice cracking water jars in the night. He emerges as the poet of fauna as well as flora, of sex and the erotic, of male love, of friendship and grief, of tetchiness as well as tenderness, of city scenes as well as country, of the indoors and the outdoors, of travel but also of staying put, of lonesomeness as well as the desire to be alone. The dynamic interiority out of which many of these poems emerged has much to say to us in the time of coronavirus; Bashō may, indeed, be *the* poet of a world in lockdown.

Bashō is associated with brevity, restraint, Zen austerity, not with linguistic brio or even fine excess. Yet the range and subtlety of Bashō's language is extraordinary: coming out of the world of *haikai* poetry and its conventions, he mingles high and low diction, elevated literary idioms with a keen ear for the demotic, but he is unique within the *haikai* tradition in the way his work develops in service to a goal of invigorated attention to the extraordinary ordinary of the everyday world. Bashō is not so much a seer as a *see*-er, one of the great lookers and noticers of poetry. There is also Bashō the sociable, involved in the serious fun of the *haikai no renga* social world, at gatherings with friends and followers, with the elite, but also with the rising mercantile class of Edo-period Japan, with doctors, with priests; and through his poems we also catch a glimpse of the Edo demimonde, and the less fortunate: poor farmers, abandoned children, the disregarded and discarded old. Bashō, from the margins of Japanese society himself, a countryman in the city, looks intently, compassionately, at times humorously at the range of Japanese social experience. And in these poems, we see also the famed Bashō of the road, of long journeys into deep country, into nature and the high lonesomeness of the self.

Bashō was born Matsuo Kinsaku in 1644, at or near Ueno, in the province of Iga. Apart from its most famous son, the town, in the west of modern Mie Prefecture, is known chiefly for its connections to the ninja. Visitors to Iga City, as it is now officially called, can see ninja figures, in different shades of their distinctive fighting costume, hanging off lampposts, perched on rooftops, and at various "strategic" commercial points throughout the town. The poet is celebrated by a statue at the bus station plaza in the center of town, and by a memorial hall, built to celebrate his three hundredth anniversary. The Bashō Memorial Museum contains reproductions of objects he may have used and clothes he may have worn on his travels, as well as a modest collection of books, letters, writing materials, drawings, portraits, and scrolls. On an undistinguished street in the town center, you can see a reconstructed version of the small house where he is reputed to have been born. The house is not open to the public, but in another part of town visitors can enter the *Minomushi-an* ("Bagworm Retreat"), the cottage of his disciple Dohō, the only "hermitage" connected to the poet still in existence (see 317). The town's imposing castle, Iga Ueno Castle, with the highest *honmaru* (inner citadel) walls of any castle in Japan, testifies to the turbulence of the province's history.

Though only thirty miles southeast of Kyoto, and even closer to Nara and Ise, the cultural, political, and spiritual centers of the Japanese world, the Province of Iga, surrounded by mountains, was isolated and inaccessible for much of its past. Isolation led to the development of a distinct Iga identity, and eventually a political formation, independent of feudal overlords, known as the *Iga Sōkoku koku Ikki*. During the Sengoku ("Warring States") period, the province was invaded twice, in the Tenshō Iga War: first, unsuccessfully, by Oda Nobukatsu in 1579, and then, devastatingly, by his father Oda Nobunaga in 1581, an event known as *Iga Heitei* ("The Pacification of Iga"). During the early years of the Tokugawa shogunate (1603–1867), Iga became part of the Tsu Domain under the control of the Tōdō clan, members of which were to play a great role in the early life of the poet.

Bashō's father, Matsuo Yozaemon, seems to have been a *musokunin,* a class of landed farmer with some samurai privileges, such as having a family name (Matsuo) and a sword. The family's tenuous samurai status may have been a result of the depredations of the wars of Bashō's great-grandfather's generation. Little is known of Bashō's mother, apart from her parents' having migrated to Iga from Iyo Province (in present-day Ehime, on the island of Shikoku). When Bashō was born, there was already a son and daughter, and there would be three more daughters after him. As the second son, Bashō would not have been in line to inherit his father's property, and his humble origins portended a precarious future, a situation made even more so by the death of his father in 1656, when Bashō was in his thirteenth year.

We have scant information about his childhood and education, but at some point in his late teens, he appears to have entered the service of Tōdō Yoshikiyo, a relative of the *daimyō* (feudal lord), eventually as attendant to his son, Yoshitada, who was two years older than Bashō. By this time, Bashō had assumed the name Munefusa, the custom being to change names at certain stages of life (other names of his childhood and youth include Hanshichi, Tōshichirō, Tadaemon, and Jinshichirō). Like many another socially marginal figure, talent, personal skills, ambition, and the grace and favor of those with influence were necessary for Bashō to get on. He may have come to the attention of Yoshitada, a keen poet known by the *haigō* (poetic pen name) Sengin, because of precocious verbal talent and skill in *haikai no renga,* the composing of "playful" linked verse in groups, a pastime popular among the literate and the socially and culturally ambitious.

During this period Bashō assumed the pen name Sōbō, an alternative reading of the two kanji characters in the name Munefusa. His earliest extant poem, composed when he was nineteen, comes from his time in service to Sengin (see 1). His duties may have included traveling to Kyoto to carry messages to Sengin's mentor, the scholar-poet Kitamura Kigin (see 121), a poet of the Teimon school of haikai, the most influential of the time. Bashō's earliest poems adhere to the Teimon style, with its emphasis on wit, lexical play, and classical parody through the use of vernacular words, and one of the first documented references to him occurs at a renga gathering in late 1665 to mark the death date of Matsunaga Teitoku (1571–1653; see 970), the founder of the Teimon school, presided over by Sengin and to which Kitamura Kigin sent a verse. The following year, the course of Bashō's life changed dramatically. Sengin, barely twenty-five, suddenly and unexpectedly died.

Accounts differ as to what happened next. Some believe that Bashō, heartbroken, resigned and went to Kyoto, then the capital, to study Zen, or to be closer to Kitamura Kigin and the center of Teimon haikai. That he left Iga, at least for a time, is clear: poems surviving from this period identify him as "Sōbō of Ueno in Iga Province." There are rumors of an affair with a woman who later became a nun called Jutei (see 893) and who many years later showed up at his residence in Edo, with children. Yet Bashō's own words (recalling his youth he once wrote: "There was a time when I was fascinated with the ways of *nanshoku* [male love]"), and poems written throughout his life (see 40, 920) indicate more sexual interest in men than in women. The world within which Bashō moved was predominately male. Arashiyama Kōzaburō in *Akutō Bashō* ("Bashō the Rogue," 2006) suggests that Bashō's relationships with some of his disciples included a sexual element. As Paul Gordon Schalow reminds us, this was not unusual, though nanshoku, also known as *wakashudō* ("the way of youth"), "was always supposed to involve an age-based hierarchy between an adult man and an adolescent youth" (p. 3). Neither did it entail social censure: "In seventeenth-century Japan male love was not stigmatized and had been integrated into the literary canon" (p. 2). Indeed in 1676, Kigin himself edited an anthology of male homoerotic poetry and prose titled *Iwatsutsuji* (published in 1713).

Though little is known about the details of this period in Bashō's life, what is certain is that, with the death of his master and the succession of Yoshitada's younger brother as head of the family, Bashō's future had once again become precarious. What is also certain is that he turned aside from a settled life of service, and poetry and the making of poems became the central fact of his existence. Between 1667 and 1671, publication in various haikai anthologies marked Bashō's passage from poetry as avocation to vocation, and then, in 1672, he published his first book under his own name, *Kai Ōi* ("The Seashell Game"), so called after a children's game of comparing seashells. Though only two of his own poems appear in that book (see 39, 40), it contains his comments on the verses of thirty-six poets, participants in a hokku contest of thirty rounds, the matches adjudicated by Bashō. His remarks reveal his wit and imaginative flair, and growing authority within local haikai circles. The book, dedicated to the Tenman-gū shrine in Iga, also marked a kind of farewell to his home province, and worked perhaps as a calling card for the next stage of his life: in the spring of 1672, going on twenty-eight years old, he moved two hundred miles east, to Edo, as Tokyo was then known, not yet the capital of the country, but as the seat of the Tokugawa government, a rapidly expanding commercial and mercantile center.

Why Edo rather than Kyoto or Osaka? The move to Edo indicates not only Bashō's desire to further himself within the haikai world and become a *sōshō*, a haikai master, but also a certain shrewdness. Kyoto and Osaka represented a crowded and well-furrowed field; fast-growing Edo offered a wider range of opportunity. The Tokugawa government's *sankin-kōtai* ("alternate residence") policy stipulated that all daimyō keep a residential estate (*yashiki*) in Edo and spend every other year there, his wife and his heir remaining hostage in Edo when the lord returned to his *han* (domain). The Tōdō clan, therefore, had retainers in Edo, and almost certainly Bashō had acquaintances and contacts in the city before leaving Iga. In his early years in Edo, Bashō relied on Iga connections and on disciples of Kigin who had also moved there. Indeed, throughout his life he maintained connections with the clan, and with Iga friends and acquaintances who had moved to Edo, or made efforts to meet them when they made visits to the city or when on his own travels. The names of Iga connections, whether in Edo or in Osaka and elsewhere, recur throughout his life: as sponsors, as hosts or participants in renga gatherings, and as a support network for Bashō and, most likely, for each other.

Once the preserve of the aristocratic elite, in the sixteenth century haikai no renga had become so popular that *haikaishi*, a class of haikai specialists and teachers, had arisen, one of the many forms of *machi shishō* (town teacher) responding to the demand for instruction in the arts by a monied class of urban commoners (*chōnin*). A haikaishi could earn a living from fees as a *tenja* (marker) of poems, from refereeing at poetry contests, and as master at renga gatherings, and at the level of sōshō could gain students and patrons, and eventually *deshi* (disciples), attracted by professional reputation. These students and patrons came mostly from sections of society which had gained increased access to education as a result of Tokugawa reforms. The han school system, established originally for the education of the children and retainers of the daimyō, and the *terakoya* (temple schools) for commoners, meant that by Bashō's time most samurai, and the better-off among the artisan, farmer, and merchant classes, were able to read, a social change that, along with advances in the printing and availability of books, "transformed haikai, which had been practiced in the medieval period among a limited range of social groups, into a vastly popular form" (Shirane, *Traces,* p. 3).

Bashō's first years in Edo, however, are obscure. He seems to have found work as a scribe and eventually, in 1677, a clerical position in the Edo waterworks department. Despite the necessity for such salaried employment, his first fidelity was to poetry, and by the mid-1670s, having assumed a new pen name, Tōsei ("green peach"), and with his reputation growing, his work began appearing in notable haikai anthologies. Bashō's poems had moved toward the Danrin school, a style of haikai poetry popular in the 1670s and 1680s. Originally founded in Osaka by Nishiyama Sōin (1605–82), with whom, in 1675, Bashō participated in a renga gathering to celebrate his visit to Edo, Danrin differed from the Teimon style in its bolder playfulness with a more limited range of classical antecedents (see Shirane, *Traces,* pp. 59–60). In 1676, Bashō took part in two Danrin-style *hyakuin* (hundred-verse) sequences with Yamaguchi Sodō, later published as *Edo Ryōgin Shū* ("Collection of Two Edo Poets"). Danrin's conventionalized techniques also fostered competitions called *yakazu haikai* ("counting arrows haikai"), in which contestants composed as many solo sequences as possible within a fixed amount of time. Bashō felt little affinity for this aspect of the life of the professional poet, the master of which was his exact contemporary, Ihara Saikaku (1642–93), like Sōin from Osaka, and in later years better-known as a novelist, who in 1677 composed sixteen hundred sequences in twenty-four hours. In 1680, he beat this by composing four thousand, published the following year as *Saikaku Ōyakazu* ("A Great Number of Arrows by Saikaku").

In the summer and autumn of 1676, Bashō made his first return visit to Iga. Something of his feeling for both Iga and Edo can be seen in the poems of this trip:

67

Gazing on something
    so seldom seen from Edo
        The moon-topped mountains

nagamuru ya / Edo ni wa marena / yama no tsuki

By 1676, Edo was one of the largest cities in the world, with a population rapidly approaching one million. The pun on the word Edo (*e-do* can also mean "unclean earth," in the Buddhist sense of a place filled with suffering derived from worldly desires) brings out the contrast with his hometown. This, of course, was early on in his time in Edo, but eventually he would settle into the life of the city, so much so that setting out on a visit to Iga in the autumn of 1684, he could write of it as "home" (see 191). He returned to Edo with his sixteen-year-old nephew, Tōin, in his care, an act and a relationship that reveal much about Bashō's human qualities. Tōin, as well as the family he would go on to raise, would play a large role in Bashō's later life.

Bashō's poems in the mid-1670s typify aspects of the Danrin style (see 71) and yet, as with his earlier Teimon-influenced poems, his work is distinctive even within conventional haikai modes. Steven D. Carter reads Bashō's Danrin period as deriving not from artistic motivations but as "a necessary move for a young poet to achieve professional recognition" (Carter, "On a Bare Branch," p. 62). Professional recognition was forthcoming, and around New Year 1679 Bashō could finally hang out his shingle as a *sōshō* (see 103). He had also by now gathered around him some of the most significant figures in the group of disciples and supporters known later as the *Shōmon*, the Bashō school: Kikaku (1661–1707), Ransetsu (1654–1707), Sanpū (1647–1732), and Ranran (1647–93).

It then seems odd that, having established his professional credentials, Bashō should, in the winter of 1680, choose to turn aside from the main drag of the city's literary life. But this is what he did, and in two major ways. First, and most visibly, he moved from the Nihonbashi area, at the heart of things in Edo, out to the eastern edge of the city, to unfashionable Fukagawa, on the far side of the Sumida River. Second, his poems turned aside from the commercially popular Danrin mode, finding new sources of inspiration in Chinese poetry, in particular in Li Bai and Du Fu, and in poets of the Japanese past, Saigyō and Sōgi. In the headnote to poem 123, written shortly after his move, he makes explicit the connection with a tradition of internal, artistic exile:

> After nine springs and autumns living a lonely, austere life in the city, I have come to the banks of the Fukagawa. "From olden times, Chang-an has been a place of fame and fortune and hard for a wayfarer poor and empty-handed," so someone once said. I am impoverished, probably why I know something of how he felt

He also appears around this time to have taken up the study of Zen with the priest Butchō (see 314, 495), shaved his head, and adopted the attire of a lay monk; he also studied Daoism, and at times called himself Kukusai, from a word found in Zhuangzi (Chuang Tzu). It would not be entirely accurate, however, to read Bashō's turning aside from such worldly concerns as earning a living and making a name for himself as a rejection of his previous life derived from a sense of spiritual deficit religious in origin or remediable within a religious framework. It is true he was now thirty-seven, no longer a young man, and with fifty years the life expectancy in Edo-period Japan, conscious of entering the definitive period of his life. The stakes involved in Bashō's turning aside, however, were poetic as much as spiritual, spiritual as much as poetic, or perhaps it is better to say that Bashō's devotion to poetry as a mode of the spirit had become such that the distinction is meaningless. When Bashō later alluded to this decision, in *Genjū-an no Ki* ("An Account of the Hut of Illusory Dwelling"), it is not correct to say that he made, as Katō Shūichi writes, "no mention of Buddhism, only of retreat from the world" (p. 96). Bashō, in fact, places the decision, just as he places his ideal of a life devoted to poetry, within the larger framework of the "true Buddhist path" (see Shirane, *Traces,* p. 158). Yet there is some truth in what Katō says when he continues: "Indeed it is difficult to find any strong Buddhist influence in his writing. His attitude is rather one that advocated literature as a means of escaping from the turmoil and coarseness of daily life; it was, in a sense, art for art's sake" (p. 96). How central Buddhism was to Bashō's poetic practice is a matter of some debate. Writers such as Katō and Satō Hiroaki (who writes in English as Hiroaki Sato) see little if any influence, while others argue that Bashō's work was entirely informed by Buddhist tenets. Steven D. Carter offers a judicious view: "It can be fairly claimed that Bashō's worldview was Buddhist in its fundamental assumptions about life, death and everything in between, and that those assumptions informed his spiritual life and partially informed his poetics" (*Travel*, p. 181).

Bashō's subjects, to an extent even before this turning point, were unorthodox within the haikai world. Though the teeming, material life of the city, prevalent in the work of Saikaku and others, is, to an extent, present in Bashō, he was more drawn to the mundane and ordinary, to fishermen and farmers going about their work, to a woman tearing salted cod at a roadside shop, and, like W.B. Yeats, to such "liminal figures" as "the beggar, the old man, the outcast, the traveler" (Shirane, *Traces*, p. 11). Even in his personal life, he seems to have been drawn to the socially maladroit and the misfit, figures such as Shadō (see 771) and Tokoku (see 330). The natural world of the poems, too, tends toward the usually disdained: *shigure* (winter drizzle), plumes of miscanthus, skulls, old bones in a field, the gums of a salted sea bream, the *karasu* (crow):

121

On a leafless bough
    the perching and pausing of a crow
    The end of autumn

kareeda ni / karasu no tomarikeri / aki no kure

This, one of his most celebrated poems, can be read as an emblem of Bashō's resolve to place poetry at the spiritual center of his existence. Bashō's precarious social origins may have played a role in his poetic predilections, and also, perhaps, in the fearlessness with which he now embraced the uncertainties and material deprivations of this new life.

The romantic excesses of this view need to be tempered, however, by a knowledge of the tradition to which Bashō, with a kind of restrained demonstrativeness, was now pledging allegiance. In withdrawing from the commercial haikai world, and in a markedly public way, Bashō was aligning himself with a tradition of poetry exemplified by Sōgi and Saigyō: the poet as recluse, weary and wary of the human world, with nature a source of bracing spiritual replenishment, and in so doing, making an artistic claim for himself. As Steven D. Carter has brilliantly put it, for Bashō and for his students, disciples, and patrons, leaving Nihonbashi would have been considered "a step up and not a step out" (Carter, "On a Bare Branch," p. 64): a step up in artistic ambition and seriousness, with a claim on the highest realms of artistic practice, and therefore prestige, among a discerning, if limited, public.

He had left behind, it also has to be said, some of the more onerous, if lucrative, aspects of the haikaishi life, practices that he had been reluctant to follow even in Nihonbashi. In a well-known letter to his disciple Kyokusui, written in 1692, we see Bashō's disdain for the contemporary haikai scene, of the life of the marker, and of poetry as a contest. He divides haikai practitioners into three "grades": the first grade, those completely taken up in the commercial world of the marker, running from poetry session to session, earning a living, feeding their family, and thus, he says, "probably" better than common criminals; the second, a wealthier, dilettantish type, for whom haikai is little more than a diversion, a game of scoring points, winning and losing, but who can also "probably," he says, be included within the ranks of the haikai profession. The third type, and they are few, have an "unswerving devotion to poetry":

> These poets seek the distant bones of Fujiwara Teika, follow the sinews of Saigyō, cleanse the intestines of Po Chü-i [Bai Juyi], and leap into the breast of Tu Fu [Du Fu]. In all the cities and provinces, the number of such individuals is fewer than the fingers of my hands. (qtd. in Shirane, *Traces*, p. 158)

The move to Fukagawa signals that Bashō had achieved a level of recognition and reputation that could both allow for such a move and allow his poetry and life as a poet to continue. Fukagawa, as Carter says, was not up the side of a distant mountain, and he had the support, material and otherwise, of students and patrons close by. An underappreciated aspect of his work, both before his move from its center and even in the years after, is, indeed, how much the life of Edo actually features in his poems. Less than a figure such as Saikaku, certainly, but Bashō did note and evoke the human life of the city around him, with its pleasure quarters at Sakai-chō, flirty wives at blossom viewing, debonair young valets, *wakashu,* Kabuki actors, traders and markets, festivals and feasts, and Dutchmen making obeisance to the shogun.

But it was in Fukagawa that the haikaishi Tōsei became the poet we now know: Bashō. The name derives from a housewarming gift from his student, Rika (see 141), in the spring of 1681: a *bashō* plant. This flowering plant, *Musa basjoo,* in English called the "Japanese banana" or "plantain," is not known for its fruit, which rarely ripens. In Chinese and Japanese tradition, the bashō features chiefly because of its large, broad leaves, some up to two meters long, which are easily torn and, when tattered in the wind and rain of autumn and winter, are symbolic of frailty and impermanence, particularly of the human body (see 148). Bashō loved the plant. He had originally named his residence the *Hakusendō* ("Hall of Moored Boats"), after one of his previous poetic pseudonyms, based on a poem of the same name by Du Fu (see 215). Within a year of planting the bashō in his garden, however, the hut where he lived became known as the *Bashō-an* ("the plantain hut"), and soon the poet began to sign himself *Bashō-an Tōsei* ("Tōsei of the Plantain Hut") or *Bashō Tōsei* (Shively, p. 152). Eventually, he became known simply as Bashō.

The hut itself had been provided to Bashō by his student and chief benefactor, Sanpū (see 185), a wealthy fishmonger, supplier of fish to the shogun's household, the bakufu, and daimyō during their residence in Edo, the hut previously having been used by the caretaker of his carp pond. Most dwellings in Edo were made of wood, and rapid population explosion led to crowding and frequent fires. Bashō had lived there a little over two years when the hut was caught up in the *Tenna no Taika* ("The Great Fire of the Tenna period"), sometimes known as the Yaoya Oshichi Fire,[1] in which up to thirty-five hundred

---

1. The story goes that Yaoya Oshichi ("Greengrocer Oshichi") fell in love with a young man during the great fire. A year later, believing that fire was the way to see him again, she committed arson. She was tried and convicted, and sentenced to burning at the stake. Bunraku and Kabuki plays were written about her, and Ihara Saikaku wrote of her case. So notorious did she become that even a flu outbreak in Edo was named after her.

people perished and which destroyed much of downtown Edo. Bashō made a dramatic escape, but the incident had a lasting effect:

> In the winter of 1682, my grass hut in Fukagawa became enveloped in a sudden fire. I somehow managed to live on by soaking myself in the tidal water, a stick on my shoulder, and surrounded by smoke. That was the beginning of my understanding of the mutability of human life. It was in that incident of a burning home that I understood how we are governed by change, and that my inclination [*kokoro*] for displaced life began. (qtd. in Miner, p. 114)[2]

Bashō was now homeless, a condition given even greater existential weight by the death of his mother later in the same year, whose funeral he was unable to attend. One of the most moving poems in the Bashō canon relates his eventual return to his homeplace, in autumn 1684, when his older brother presented him with the relic pouch containing a lock of their mother's white hair:

201

If held in my hands it would melt
from the hot touch of teardrops
the frost of autumn

te ni toraba kien / namida zo atsuki / aki no shimo

This sense of homelessness and feeling for "displaced life"—his own, that of others, and in the natural world—played a major role in driving Bashō to the travels that dominated the final ten years of his life and led him ultimately to the mature "understanding of the mutability of human life" evinced in the most famous line from his best-known journey, *Oku no Hosomichi*: "Every day is a journey, and the journey itself home."

After the loss of his hut, Bashō accepted an invitation from his sometime student, Biji (Takayama Biji, 1649–1718), to spend time in the Yamura domain in Kai Province (in present-day Yamanashi Prefecture), where he remained for five months. In early summer 1683, he

---

2. The fire took place on the twenty-eighth day of the Twelfth Month, in the second year of Tenna; January 25, 1683, in the Gregorian calendar.

returned to Edo to oversee the publication of *Minashiguri* ("Shriveled Chestnuts"), a two-volume anthology compiled by his disciple Kikaku. In the winter, he moved into a new *Bashō-an* in Fukagawa, which had been built through donations from his students, disciples, and other benefactors (see 170).

Yet this new dwelling could not long contain Bashō's nascent "inclination for displaced life," and in September 1684 he set off on the long journey west that eventually produced his first travel journal, *Nozarashi Kikō* ("The Journey of Weather-Exposed Bones"). Bashō traveled, initially accompanied by Chiri (1648–1716), along the main highway known as the Tōkaidō, from Edo to the Grand Shrines at Ise, to his hometown in Iga, to Nara and Kyoto, then along the southern shore of Lake Biwa, returning to Edo by the Kiso mountains route the following year. This is a key period in the development of his poetry, in which the tension between the claims of what he termed *fūga* ("poetic elegance") and the claims of lived (often distressingly lived) life produced some of his most powerful poems (see 194). The restlessness that manifested itself in travel also manifested itself aesthetically, in a move away from the artifice, overdependence on wordplay, and Chinese-influenced diction of the poems he had been writing.

Part of Bashō's continuing attraction, in Japan and elsewhere, is the image created by these journeys: Bashō the solitary, wandering poet. In fact, Bashō rarely traveled alone. Kanamori Atsuko has calculated that even on his longest journey, the *Oku no Hosomichi* trek, he traveled no more than six *ri* (about 24 km) alone (cited in Carter, *Travel Writings,* p. 86). In making these journeys, Bashō was self-consciously following precedents in the Japanese past, and principally his poetic models Saigyō and Sōgi. The itineraries were planned, among other things, to visit places associated with these figures (see 198, 345), and places resonant within the Japanese literary tradition, the so-called *utamakura.* These travels also had practical poetic purposes. With the anthology *Minashiguri* ("Shriveled Chestnuts"), Bashō and his circle had assumed a publicly available form, and the book "set them distinctly apart from other poets" (Ueda, *Matsuo Bashō,* p. 25). Now the convictions about the "way of poetry" embodied in the maturing Bashō style required the creation of a climate of opinion, or as Wordsworth put it, "the taste," within which these ideas could be better appreciated and understood. This entailed travel.

Poetry was for Bashō, and for those involved in haikai, a communal activity, a practice as well as an art. Many of the poems found in this book are the hokku, the initiating poems, of gatherings convened to welcome Bashō to a particular area during his travels, gatherings that were also occasions at which to spread the poetic word with practical advice, instruction, and example. Such occasions were also a testing ground for ideas, and the accounts and anecdotes handed down by Dohō (1657–1730), Kyorai, and others reveal the centrality of discussion and debate, occasionally rancorous, at these gatherings, often centering around the repercussions of an alternative word, image, or phrase and nuances in the linking of verses. Some of the occasions led to significant publications. During a visit to Nagoya on this journey, Bashō participated in five *kasen* (thirty-six-verse) renga sequences with a local group of haikai poets led by Kakei (1648–1716), who later compiled the sequences into *Fuyu no Hi* ("The Winter Sun," also known as "Winter Days"), the first major anthology of the *Shōmon*, the Bashō School, and the text that marks the beginning of what became known as the *Shōfu*, the Bashō style.

Bashō, of course, was also a countryman, inclined to the rural more than the urban, and journeys through the countryside offered images and scenes and a replenishing resource for both the man and his poems. In the autumn and winter, he visited Iga and celebrated the lunar New Year there for the first time in eight years, meeting old friends, renewing acquaintanceships, and, as we have seen, seeing his brother and his sisters, finally, after the death of their mother. He was now a well-known figure, sought out by local poets and regarded as their teacher. A letter from this time reveals his advice to them and, as Ueda says, Bashō's feelings about "recent poetic trends in Edo" as well as how much his work had moved on: "Anthologies like *Minashiguri* contain many verses that are not worth discussing" (*Bashō and His Interpreters*, p. 122).

And for the next ten years of his life, this remained the pattern: extensive journeys, renga gatherings and visits with local poets, periods of recovery from the exertions of travel, the composition and revision of poems, the collation of material for the travel journals, the supervision of publications, both his own and of the Bashō School. In January 1686, Bashō and fifteen students composed a sequence of one hundred verses in honor of Kikaku, to mark his new status as a haikai master. Bashō contributed six verses, but later, after a request, began annotating each verse. Due to illness, however, the work remained unfinished, but was published eventually in 1763 as *Hatsukaishi Hyōchū* ("Critical Notes on the New Year Sequence"), a key source for Bashō's developing views on poetry, in particular the idea of *atarashimi* ("newness"). The "newness" he extolled, as with the early-twentieth-century Imagist dictum "make it new," was not a rejection of tradition or the classical past, but sought new associations and new perspectives on established topics and sought also a newness in perception that would discover and reveal the hitherto overlooked, disregarded, or unnoticed. Such ideas form the background to Bashō's best-known poem, written in the spring of this year 1686:

270

An olden pond now
    A songfrog springs off into
        the sound of water

furuike ya / kawazu tobikomu / mizu no oto

The poem is, of course, not only Bashō's best-known, it is the single best-known poem in Japanese literature, the significance of which was recognized almost as soon as it was written. That same spring, in April, with the poem as initiating challenge, a gathering of poets was held at which they competed with poems on the subject of frogs, later published as *Kawazu Awase* ("The Frog Contest").

At the *Kawazu Awase,* the story goes, Kikaku suggested *yamabuki ya* ("kerria roses") as an alternative initial five-*on* phrase, invoking the association between the *kawazu* and *yamabuki* established by the classical waka *kawazu naku / Ide no yamabuki / chirinikeri / hana no sakari ni / awamashi mono o* ("At Ide where the / frogs trill kerria roses / already fallen / If only I had been there / when the flowers were in bloom"). Kikaku's suggestion, therefore, fell, somewhat typically, within the parodic mode of haikai. Too typically for Bashō. His rejection of Kikaku's suggestion in favor of his own phrase *furuike ya* ("an old pond") illustrates his move away from haikai as an implied critique of classical tradition. As Hasegawa Kai argues, "By the spring of 1686, for Bashō, obvious criticism of convention had itself become conventional.

It was likely that Bashō was trying to criticize both Kikaku's past think-ing about haikai, as well as his own" (p. 38). Ki no Tsurayuki's *kana* preface to the *Kokinshū* had created a deep association between the *kawazu* and the composition of poetry (see Shirane, *Traces*, p. 14), and among the things the poem is concerned with is poetic tradition itself. In translating the poem, I have tried to capture something of the dia-logue between the present and the past that the poem in Japanese enacts, though it is impossible to convey in English the classical con-notations contained in the word *kawazu*. The *kawazu*, the kajika frog (*Buergeria buergeri*), is a species endemic to Japan. In the main, in Eng-lish, frogs are associated with croaks or "ribbit" sounds, but the *kawazu* makes a pleasant, high-pitched trill. The kanji can be read as *kaeru*, which is more common in modern Japanese, but as *kawazu* we are carried back to the very beginning of a self-conscious Japanese poetic tradition. By using it Bashō was both consciously invoking that tradi-tion and trying to move that tradition, and haikai, forward: the *kawazu*, by convention associated with song, does not sing here; the sound made is from its leap into water (*mizu*).

In September of the following year, Bashō traveled with Sora and with his neighbor, the priest Sōha (see 268), to Kashima Shrine to see the harvest moon, a trip recounted in *Kashima Kikō* ("Kashima Journal"). He published *Atsume Ku* ("Collected Verses"), a selection of thirty-four of his hokku of the previous three years. In late November, he set off on another long journey to the west, recounted in *Oi no Kobumi* ("Journey of a Satchel"). By now his fame was such that many farewell parties were held in his honor, with disciples and other poets writing verses to send him on his way. At one of these gatherings, he composed a poem which sums up the attitude that now governed and guided him:

320

A wayfaring man
    the name I would be called by
      First winter drizzle

tabibito to / waga na yobaren / hatsushigure

On this journey, accompanied by Etsujin, he made a detour to visit his errant disciple Tokoku at Irago, and then traveled back to Nagoya, where he stayed a few weeks. Iga was becoming more and more the center around which he emotionally, and physically, orbited, and he went there to celebrate once again the lunar New Year with old friends and relatives. After visiting friends and attending renga gatherings at the Grand Shrines at Ise (see 364–373), and traveling to the Futami Coast, he returned once more to his hometown in time for the thirty-third anniversary of his father's death. The poems of this time in Iga are some of his most earthy and amusing (see 361), and some of his most emotionally unbuttoned, poems of friendship and remembrance, nods to a shared past, such as the one written on a visit to the son of the long-departed master of his youth, Sengin (see 376).

Tokoku joined him in Iga Ueno, and they stayed together for twenty days, waiting for the opportune time to travel to see the famed cherry blossoms at Yoshino (see 379), after which they traveled on to Wakanoura, Nara, and historical sites in Suma and Akashi, the point at which *Oi no Kobumi* closes (see 410). The journal ends on a note of melancholy awareness of historical violence, that the lost lives of the past, whether prince or servant, call out to poetry to speak of them, and how poetry, most sorrowfully his own, forever falls short. Though the journal ends there, the actual journey continued. After a short stay in Kyoto, Tokoku returned to his home in Irago, and Bashō continued on to Ōtsu and the Nagara River. He prolonged a stay in Nagoya for a month in order to travel to Sarashina village to see the harvest moon, the source of *Sarashina Kikō* ("Sarashina Journal"). He returned to Edo in September.

Bashō was now in his forty-fifth year, by the reckoning of the time an old man, and sickly. He had long been afflicted with intestinal ailments, and had succumbed to illness on his return journey through the Kiso mountains, from which he was still suffering the effects a month into his recuperation in Edo (see 459). And yet by the New Year, he was already turning his thoughts to his next journey (see 475). This would be his most arduous, extensive, and eventually, in its form as the travel account *Oku no Hosomichi* ("The Narrow Road to the Interior"), his most famous. By the end of it, he would have traveled almost 1,500 miles (2,400 km), on foot, on horseback, by palanquin, and by boat, over 156 days, and on the way articulated to himself, and to his disciples, the idea of *fueki ryūkō* ("constancy and change"), first explicated in the summer of 1689, during his time at Mount Haguro (Carter, *Travel Writings*, p. 85), and in the spring of 1690, at a renga gathering in Iga, *karumi*, the term he gave to the plainness in theme and lightness in tone that had become his poetic ideal (see 615, 728, 754, 780, 828, 841, 848, 892).

That Bashō should have taken on such an arduous journey, through territories potentially more hazardous than he had ever traveled before, and at great risk to his already frail health, seems obstinate and reckless. Precisely because he had never been, he wanted to go, he wrote to his old friend, Sōshichi, in Iga, to fulfill a "long-held desire" (Carter, p. 81); and, because it was the five hundredth anniversary of the death of Saigyō, who had journeyed there himself, he wanted also to honor and to emulate a poetic lodestar. At the beginning of *Oi no Kobumi* Bashō singles out the waka of Saigyō, the renga of Sōgi, the painting of Sesshū, and the tea ceremony of Sen no Rikyū, as beating with the same aesthetic pulse: to "follow creation" (*zōka*), the ever-unfolding nature of things. Bashō did not admire the grandiose, and so when, on his *Oku no Hosomichi* journey north, he arrives at the mausoleum of the founder of the Tokugawa shogunate, Ieyasu, at Nikkō, and writes a poem lauding its "resplendence" (see 490) bathing all in its munificent light, we should be aware of the ironies beneath the apparent praise. Bashō's praise resembles the ironic praise of the life of a slave in Randy Newman's "Sail Away." In *Oku no Hosomichi* he writes of being "overawed" by Ieyasu's mausoleum and the shogun's achievement of peace, but we are made aware at the same time that this is an imperial peace, of a kind with the Roman variety, as related by Virgil in the *Aeneid* Book VI, in Dryden's rendering: "But, *Rome*, 'tis thine alone, with awful sway, / To rule mankind, and make the world obey, / Disposing peace and war by thy own majestic way" (ll. 1173–75)

So apparently overawed is Bashō that he says he cannot write, and "sets aside" (*sashiokinu*), he tells us, his "writing brush" (*fude*). Earl Miner reads opposition to the Tokugawa regime in such moments of deliberately enunciated silence. Such a tellingly enunciated silence also occurs in a letter to Ensui, another old friend from Iga, and derives from the same reflections on historical violence with which *Oi no Kobumi* closes: "amid thoughts of life and death, the subservience of the weak to the powerful, mutability and swift time ... Such is the loneliness at the temple of Sumadera that I have composed no poetry" (Miner, p. 262). Konishi Jin'ichi has argued for Bashō as a moral and political writer to rank with Du Fu, placing the "cosmic grandeur" of

Bashō's poem about Sado Island (see 540) within the island's political history as a place of exile and banishment, and thereby implicated the Tokugawa government in that repressive tradition (cited in Miner, p. 262). That Bashō made great efforts, at some personal risk, to visit the banished and disgraced Tokoku "in his distress" (see 330) in a remote village, says something about his compassion, about how important friendship was to him, but also about his attitude to the prevailing political conditions.

Legend, however, prompted by his origins in the ninja capital, says that Bashō may have been in the pay of the Tokugawa government and that his journey north into the Sendai Domain was a cover to spy on the ruling Date clan, who had been charged with the upkeep of Ieyasu's mausoleum, much to their expense and distaste. The legend has little basis in fact. Bashō spent only a day or so at Nikkō, and, rather than noted religious or scenic places, even more than famed Matsushima, Bashō inclined toward the out-of-the-way and the cultivation of "chance experience" (Carter, p. 85). Such lifelong inclinations and sympathies are foundational to the poetics of *fueki ryūkō,* the unchanging that lives within that which changes, and *kōgo kizoku* ("awakening to the high, returning to the low"), with travel a means, in Shirane's words, "of reaching the spiritual and poetic heights" of Saigyō and Nōin and Sōgi, "while returning to and facing the everyday realities of commoner, contemporary life" (p. 252).

After the journey ended, Bashō spent the next two years in and around Iga, traveling to Nara and Kyoto, speaking of karumi, and spending extended periods of time in huts and cottages prepared for him by his students and disciples. At Zeze on Lake Biwa, he stayed from May until August in the Genjū-an ("the Hut of Illusory Dwelling"), where he wrote what is considered the first example of haibun literature, *Genjū-an no Ki* (see Shirane, *Traces,* p. 217). After leaving the Genjū-an, he spent two months in a hut in the precincts of a temple named Gichū, on the shores of Lake Biwa, between Zeze and Ōtsu. In the late spring of 1691, he stayed at the *Rakushi-sha* ("The House of Fallen Persimmons"), a cottage owned by Kyorai in the Saga area in northwest Kyoto, where he wrote *Saga Nikki* ("Saga Diary"), the last of his major prose works. He also busied himself preparing, with Kyorai and Bonchō, *Sarumino* ("The Monkey's Raincoat"), the most important anthology of the Bashō School.

After postponing his return many times because of ill-health, he finally returned to Edo in December 1691. He was so disaffected by the changed poetic scene in Edo—its commercialism, falling standards, and obsession with contests and prizes—that he considered abandoning poetry. So disconsolate was he, indeed, that in the spring he even avoided blossom-viewing. With the support of his followers, in particular Sanpū and Sora, a new hut was built for him in Fukagawa, and the bashō tree, which had been kept by friends in his absence, was transplanted into the yard, and thus this hut became the third Bashō-an. In early 1693, his nephew Tōin, whom he had brought to Edo years earlier, became ill with tuberculosis and moved into the hut. During this period Bashō was also supporting Jutei, who some sources believe to have been Tōin's wife, and her three children, one of whom, Jirōbei, moved into the Bashō-an too, to help care for Tōin. At the end of April, Tōin died, and in August, heartbroken, worn out from haikai gatherings, and "weary of people," Bashō, for a time, closed his gate to visitors (see 807).

In a letter in February 1694, he wrote, "I feel my end is drawing near." Wanting to see his relatives and friends in Iga one last time, and also to heal rifts with his followers in Nagoya (see 866) and settle a dispute between disciples in Osaka (see 914), he began to plan another westward journey. Ill-health delayed his departure, but he attended a number of haikai gatherings in Edo, keen to talk of karumi and encourage new poetic talent. In June, carried in a litter, he departed the city for what turned out to be the last time, leaving the Bashō-an in the care of Jutei and her two daughters, with Jirōbei accompanying him. He reached Iga at the end of June, and stayed two weeks. A family reunion there gave rise to one of the poems that best exemplifies karumi (see 892). During this period, he also revisited the Ōtsu area, and stayed again at Rakushi-sha, where, as if bidding farewell, he received students and friends (see 904). During his stay, word arrived that Jutei had died. Though there is no direct elegy for his nephew Tōin, Bashō's poem on the death of Jutei is remarkable in its emotional candor (see 893).

Bashō's final weeks were filled with activity. Two anthologies of his school, *Betsuzashiki* ("The Detached Room") and *Sumidawara* ("A Sack of Charcoal"), were published and well-received. Despite ill-health, he was keen to engage with a new generation of followers and to instill in them a sense of karumi as a poetic goal. With Jirōbei returned from his mother's funeral in Edo, Bashō traveled incessantly, attending haikai gatherings in Kyoto and Iga and Osaka, only missing an event when too ill to attend, and even then sending on his hokku to the host (see 921). While in Osaka, on the afternoon of the twelfth of the Tenth Month, in the seventh year of Genroku (November 28, 1694), due to illness and the exertions of his last weeks, he died. On his sick bed, three days before his death, his mind was still set on wandering:

922

On a journey stricken
    Dreams a-wandering around
       stalks and stubble-fields

tabi ni yande / yume wa kareno o / kakemeguru

After his death, Bashō's teachings were gathered by his followers, with Dohō's *Sanzōshi* ("Three Booklets") compiled in 1702 and 1703 and Kyorai's *Kyoraishō* ("Kyorai's Gleanings") compiled in 1704, the most important. In the 1730s, the major texts began to be edited and published. The *Haikai Shichibu Shū* ("Haikai Seven Anthologies"), compiled by Ryūkyo (1686–1748) in 1731, collected the principal haikai collections from the different periods of Bashō's work into a set, published in 1756. Bashō's achievements were discussed and debated, with periods of decline in influence alternating with periods of revival. By his centenary, however, he had been deified as a haikai saint, and there were major celebrations of his life and work. On the seventh anniversary of his death, seven Bashō *tsuka* (stone memorials), engraved with either his name or a hokku, had been erected at seven different locations, with the poet's spirit ritually transferred from his burial site in Gichū-ji. By the end of the Edo period in the mid-1860s, there were up to a thousand such memorials dotting the countryside (Shirane, *Traces,* p. 35).

In the late nineteenth and early twentieth century, Bashō began to be known outside Japan. One of the first translations into English was by the Irish writer Lafcadio Hearn ("Old pond—frogs jumped in—sound of water") in his book *Exotics and Retrospectives* (1898), in which he refers to the "famous Bashō" and (erroneously) calls it "the first poem written in the measure called *hokku*" (p. 120). Bashō's influence on Ezra Pound and the Imagists has meant that his work has had a deep and lasting influence on poetry in English since the early twentieth century. In the post–World War II period, the flowering of interest in Zen Buddhism and Japan's economic "miracle" prompted a fascination with things Japanese, with haiku, and with Bashō, fed and fueled by works of explication and translation by R. H. Blyth, Harold Gould Henderson, Kenneth Yasuda, and others. By the 1960s Bashō had become so familiar a marker of Japanese-ness, and "eastern wisdom," that Ian Fleming could include an apocryphal poem "After Bassho" as the epigraph to *You Only Live Twice* (1964). Haiku has since become the most prevalent poetic form in the world, and Bashō's poems the standard by which all others are measured.

NOTES ON THE TRANSLATION

This book translates and annotates the complete haiku of Matsuo Bashō (1644–94), drawing on the authoritative edition by Kon Eizō: *Bashō Ku Shū* ("Collected Hokku of Bashō," Tokyo: Shinchōsha, 1982). The poems are presented in chronological order according to date, or approximate date, of composition. There is still much scholarly debate and disagreement about the dating of the poems. The dating and the numbering system in this book are based on Kon's edition, one of the most authoritative available. In the notes, I have listed the year, the exact date of composition when known, according to the Japanese lunar calendar and era-naming system used in Bashō's time, and have also occasionally included the Gregorian (solar) calendar equivalent, to help with the reader's orientation; I have also listed the season. When Gregorian month names are used in the text, the dates have been converted. Among those for which the exact date of composition is unknown, some winter *hokku* present a particular problem in terms of the modern calendar. In Bashō's day, winter was contained within a continuous three-month stretch of time, and the lunar New Year marked the beginning of spring. In the modern calendar, the winter of the poems can range over two years, and the lunar New Year can occur over a range of dates from late January to late February.

Most, but not all, of the Bashō poems collected here are written in seventeen *on*, in three phrases of 5-7-5. The *on* is the individual sound unit of Japanese poetry, known most commonly, though inaccurately, as "syllable" in English but which linguists refer to as *mora* (plural *morae*). The Japanese writing system consists of three elements: two phonetic *kana* syllabaries, *hiragana* and *katakana,* each of which represents all the sounds of the Japanese language; and Chinese characters called *kanji,* which are used for nouns and the "stem" components of verbs. The word *on* means simply "sound" in Japanese, and each *on* corresponds to a letter or character in *hiragana* (and *katakana*); a single *kanji* may have one or more *on.*

Bashō occasionally writes in what is known as *hachō* ("broken meter") or *ji-amari* ("excess characters") and once said, "Even if you have three or four extra syllables—or as many as five or seven—you need not worry as long as the verse sounds right. If even one syllable stagnates in your mouth, give it a careful scrutiny" (Ueda, *Bashō and His Interpreters,* p. 80). In poem 126, for instance, the count is 10-7-5: *ro no koe nami o utte / harawata kōru / yo ya namida* ("The smacking of these oars upon the waves / shivering through the stomach / The nighttime these tears").

This translation is the first to adhere strictly to form: all 980 of the poems, and the variants and source poems included in the notes, are translated following the *on* count of the original poems. The book also translates for the first time in English a number of Bashō's headnotes (short prose introductions to poems). I have kept to the *on* count of the originals, accepting syllables as a near equivalent: where a poem is written in 5-7-5, or a variation thereof, so is the translation. By doing this, I am not claiming that this is the best, or only, way to translate Bashō's poems. Many wonderful translations have been done quite differently. "Syllable counting," however, is only one of the things I have tried to reproduce out of the Bashō originals. I have also attempted to give a sense in English of the puns, word games, and sound values of the source poems. In poem 540, for instance:

> The t*u*rbulent sea
> > Unf*u*rling over Sado
> > > the Riv*e*r of Stars

*ar*aumi ya / Sado ni yokot*au* / *Amanog*awa

The way the poems now appear in these English versions—three lines, unpunctuated, with a capital letter to indicate the *kireji* ("cutting word"), rather than a dash or other form of punctuation—developed organically, through trial and much error. In order to make the poems work in English to my own satisfaction, I needed a level of linguistic tension, a pressure on the utterance, for which this formal constriction proved useful. Why? To enable, to rephrase Seamus Heaney, the sense that constraint had been overcome and that whatever felicity there is in these poems is an achieved one comparable to the pressures that shaped the original.

The translation is unpunctuated to reflect the fluidity of the Japanese. The three-line form has been taken on its own terms, as part of a tradition of English versions of haiku, and because of the local effect that run-on lines and line-breaks can have, which reflect something of the way "breaks" and "run-on" effects happen even in the single line of the Japanese haiku. Though I have followed this most prominent convention in English-language translations—the three-line division of what, in Japanese, is written as a single, unpunctuated line—there are, of course, many other ways of doing it. Satō Hiroaki (Hiroaki Sato), for instance, has chosen to translate the Japanese into one line of English, with success and with great influence on the practice of English-language haiku; others have used the seventeen-syllable template but vary the spread of the syllables across one, two, three, and sometimes more lines.

Bashō's status meant that his theories on poetry were written down by his disciples and eventually collected in books and anthologies. It was his poetic practice, however, that dictated the poetic lessons he afterwards articulated to these disciples and not the other way around. The poetic ideals of *atarashimi* ("newness"), *karumi* ("lightness"), and a "requirement" such as the use of a *kireji* ("cutting word"), emerged out of a testing of poetic convention, poetic practice, and discovery. There is no one overarching rule dictating the range of Bashō's poetic practice. Bashō was not dogmatic about the "cutting word" (*ka, ya, kana, -keri,* etc.), for instance, which can appear at the end or in the middle of any line, or indeed nowhere in his poems; the juxtaposition of almost independent images can happen, or not, depending on the poem. As Shirane Haruo says, for Bashō "it was the cutting effect rather than the cutting word itself that ultimately mattered" (*Traces,* p. 104). The *karumi* style, perhaps the most famous of Bashō's theories, emerges late in Bashō's work. Even the season word can, at times, be a fiction concocted for the poetic rather than temporal occasion. The haiku as nonnarrative, context-independent, and intent most on a moment of encounter with nature is a set of ideas prominent within contemporary haiku practice in the English-speaking world derived from aspects of Bashō's work, but not reflecting the range and reach of his poetic practice.

One of the most prominent elements in a hokku and in Bashō's poems is the juxtaposition of disparate elements, either with or without a cutting word. The reader is invited to actively participate in the creation of meaning, to move the mind back and forth among the elements, and to complete the work. The temptation for the translator is to fill in gaps so intrinsic to the poem's being, and to explain, and thereby explain away, the poetry. Many translators fill in the "missing" detail or add the nonpoetic information they think "understanding" the poem requires—a prepositional phrase, for instance. I have resisted that temptation as much as possible, and have tried to leave space where there is space in the originals. To give one example:

426

A shaded hillside
    now I will restore myself
      melons in the field

yamakage ya / mi o yashinawan / uribatake

Should relations that are deliberately withheld in the original be made explicit in the translation? The implication in the poem shown above is that the speaker is resting, looking at the melons in the field, which will be a source of replenishment later. Some translations add "with" to the last line, which I believe to be unnecessarily editorial.

I have, however, added notes to the poems, derived from Kon Eizō and various other sources, to illuminate the personal, professional, and cultural contexts of the poems; elucidated some of the puns and wordplay to give a sense of what Bashō is doing with the Japanese language; and noted the many allusions to both classical and popular literary forms to show the capaciousness of Bashō's cultural range and how innovative, and at times radical, his verse was, and is, within the Japanese tradition.

I am not a scholar of classical Japanese or of the Edo period. My specialty is poetry: I write poetry, and write about poetry, in

English—contemporary poetry from Ireland and Britain, mainly— and I have translated Italian poetry: Dante, Montale, and Ungaretti. The work here is a debt of gratitude to Japan: for the family, friends, colleagues, and life that Japan has given me. I have tried to reproduce to the best of my ability the experience of reading Bashō in Japanese. I have relied much on the work of others: translators and scholars, and family, friends, and colleagues. When translating a poem, I read first the Kon edition, which helpfully has an interpretative paraphrase of the poems in contemporary Japanese, as well as copious notes concerning context, allusions, and language. The paraphrase helped me get only so far behind what a poem was doing, however, and so often I consulted my (patient) wife and (very patient) children, to get a sense of how contemporary Japanese people react to, and parse, Bashō's language, which is even more distant from contemporary Japanese than Shakespeare's is from modern English. I consulted other translations into English and, where they existed, translations into other languages, principally Italian and French. I consulted Japanese colleagues and friends, and others in Japan knowledgeable in Japanese poetry. With all of this knowledge, I then tried to produce a poem in English, accurate as far as I could make it to the manner and movement of the original, but which could stand in its own light as a poem.

I traveled to places associated with Bashō: to Iga Ueno, to sites mentioned in his travels, and many times to Fukagawa. I have tried to be as accurate as possible about these places, and about the flora and fauna that Bashō mentions in his poems, for which the Internet has been an invaluable resource. But it is living in Japan for almost a quarter of a century that has afforded me the deepest insight into the rhythms and rituals of Japanese life, the calendar customs that still to a great deal exist from Bashō's day, and the seasons and the plant life of the poems. On one memorable occasion, while translating a poem concerning *yamabuki* ("kerria roses"), I walked out our front door to find *yamabuki* in bloom on our neighbor's fence. I have also tried to be accurate concerning the detail of items referred to in the poems. While researching the previously unpublished headnote to poem 978, I made the memorable discovery, through the Internet, that the vase the poem concerns, the *Kine no Ore* (mistakenly taken to be a wooden mallet in previous translations that relied only on the poem itself), still exists and is held in the Tokugawa Museum in Nagoya.

Because of changes in language and orthography from Bashō's day, there are some inaccurate transliterations of the poems that have become prevalent in English. To give one example: in poem 881, most transliterations write *meshi augu* ("fanning rice") for the first line. In this case, I consulted colleagues in the Department of Japanese at Gakushuin University, who related that, in the Edo period, the word would have been pronounced "awogu," and that a more accurate modern transliteration would be "aogu." There are other inconsistent and misleading versions of the poems available, in book form and on the Internet. I have tried to offer a consistent transliteration of the poems into the Latin alphabet (*romaji*). I use, for example, the dictionary version of words that have been split into two words in other *romaji* renderings. For example, in poem 955, *yanagikage* is usually treated as one word in Japanese, but has been rendered as *yanagi kage* in most romaji transliterations available in English. On other occasions, I have separated words that Japanese usually treats separately but that English versions have conjoined; in poem 944, for instance, *mono ieba* for *monoieba*. The word *shū*, meaning "collection" (of poems), offers its own problems: occasionally in print it is transliterated as part of the preceding word: *Hakusenshū, kushū;* at other times, not. Even the same writer can offer two versions of the same book: Shirane Haruo in *Traces of Dreams* offers *Hakusenshū* (p. 345) but in *Early Modern Japanese Literature* renders it *Hakusen shū* (p. 181). I have decided to be consistent and use *shū* as a separate word for all books containing it. Thus, *Hakusen Shū,* and *Bashō Ku Shū* rather than *Hakusenshū* and *Bashō Kushū,* etc. An exception is made for classical Japanese texts that have acquired standard English transliterations.

HOKKU AND HAIKU

Bashō did not call the poems he was writing *haiku*. Many of the poems collected here are *hokku* ("opening verse"), the initiating poem in *renga* ("linked verse"), a sequence of poems composed by two or more people at a gathering of practicing, if sometimes amateur, poets. The term *haiku* came into use in the early twentieth century, and its prominence in denoting an autonomous poem in the 5-7-5 form is most often credited to Masaoka Shiki (1867–1902). Shiki used the term *haiku* to distinguish the hokku written with no expectation of a follow-up verse from those hokku written at a renga gathering with just such an expectation. Ezra Pound, when discussing his poem "In a Station of the Metro," the poem that, more than any other, initiated English-language interest in the haiku form, famously described his poem as a "hokku-like sentence," showing that in 1913 the term *haiku* had yet to gain currency.

Why did Bashō write hokku? Bashō's profession was master poet, and as such he was guest of honor at renga gatherings, held at the houses of merchants and local dignitaries, and at amateur poetry groups. He would have been required in his capacity as master to write the opening verse for the gathering: to set the theme, to praise the host, to locate the occasion in time and place. This requirement, that the hokku mark the occasion of the gathering, led eventually to the development of the convention that the hokku, and thus the haiku, should contain a season word.

Almost half of the poems in Bashō's travel diaries, it has been estimated, are greetings or expressions of gratitude. Though they may appear to modern readers as lyrical, subjective utterances, Bashō's poems were often composed within a communal context, to fulfill social functions and ritual expectations. As well as greetings and expressions of gratitude, poems functioned as compliments, offerings to the land, consoling words offered to the dead, as farewells to a person or group or place, or to mark, as I have said, the occasion of the gathering itself.

Even before Bashō the hokku had taken on something of an independent life separate from the sequence within which it had initially been composed. At a renga gathering the hokku was written on *kaishi* ("pocket paper"). Later, if particularly memorable, it was inscribed in special calligraphic form on *tanzaku* (pronounced *tanjaku* in Bashō's day) card or on colored decorative paper boards called *shikishi* (see the bibliography of "Original Sources" of Bashō's poems). A hokku could later form part of a *haibun,* surrounded by poetic prose, or form part of a *haiga* ("haikai picture"), a painting/poem combination in which text and drawing complement each other. Bashō, as guest, returned the hospitality of his hosts in the form of his presence as master at gatherings, but also in the material form of kaishi, tanzaku, shikishi and haiga. The hokku, or a revised form of it, the full renga sequence, and haibun might later be compiled in printed haikai collections.

RENGA

Though poets also wrote solo renga sequences (*dokugin*), most sequences were composed in groups of two or more, usually up to six, at a renga gathering. The main guest at the gathering composed the hokku. The length of the sequence was decided in advance: *kasen* (thirty-six verses, the most popular form), *yoyoshi* (forty-four), *gojūin* (fifty), *hyakuin* (one hundred), or *senku* (one thousand). The hokku for a gathering might also be written in advance of the occasion. The host replied to this opening verse with a second verse of fourteen *on* (7-7) called the *wakiku*. Thus, taken together, both verses now formed a *waka,* the thirty-one-*on* poem (5-7-5-7-7) that was the principal form in Japanese classical poetry. The following verse, of 5-7-5, went on then to form a new thirty-one-*on* poem with that preceding 7-7 wakiku verse, and so on. Verses were composed in turn by each participant, in a set order, each succeeding verse (*tsukeku*) linking to the previous (*maeku*) to form new poetic wholes, pushing on one from the other, in mutually illuminating variation. The word *renku* is used for modern linked-verse sequences.

Haikai

The word *haikai* originally referred to certain poems collected in the Heian period (794–1185) anthology of *waka* poetry, the *Kokin Wakashū,* which were termed *haikai-ka* ("humorous poems"). The word later came to be used for a form of lighthearted linked verse, *haikai no renga* ("playful linked verse"), which had developed out of the courtly renga of the Heian cultural elite. In the seventeenth century, haikai no renga became a hugely popular pastime among commoners and samurai. *Haikai* eventually came to denote a spirit of creative play with classical Japanese tradition and convention, and encompassed poetry (*haikai*), painting (*haiga*), and prose (*haibun*). In poetry, both irreverence and reverence were intermingled in the skillful deployment of haikai words (*haigon*) drawn from popular usage, everyday language, and other terms excluded from the classical lexicon. At its broadest, the poet inserted into a well-known line, or a well-known scene from classical literature, a coarse or vulgar word, or bawdy element; in Bashō's hands this became a far subtler affair, with an emphasis on bringing the everyday and the language of common life into a living relationship with the past. It is one of Bashō's achievements to make out of a genre centered initially around wit and parody a vehicle for serious poetry.

The Travel Diaries and Haibun

The most famous of Bashō's works, *Oku no Hosomichi* ("The Narrow Road to the Interior"), is a travel diary, fictionalized to an extent, in the *haibun* form (a mix of prose and poetry), of a journey to the northern provinces and down along the Japan Sea coast, which he began in the late spring of 1689 and which took over five months. In the *Complete Haiku* the poems from the journey are presented in the order of their composition rather than the order in which they appear in *Oku no Hosomichi,* along with other poems written during this period but which Bashō chose not to include in that book. The same holds for the poems from his other travel diaries, and *haibun* sketches, the details of which can be found in the notes to the poems.

Names

Japanese names are given in the order most common in Japan: family name followed by given (or assumed) name. So, Matsuo is the family name, and Bashō his "first" name. Haikai poets are known by their *haigō* (poetic pen name); Matsuo Bashō is known simply as Bashō.

Era Names in Japan

Bashō lived during an era now known as the Edo period (江戸時代, *Edo jidai*), which lasted from 1603 to 1867 and which takes its name from Edo, the seat of the Tokugawa shogunate, known in Japanese as *bakufu,* a form of military government. In 1868, with the fall of the Tokugawa shogunate and the Meiji Restoration, the name of the city became Tokyo ("Eastern Capital").

In contemporary Japan, eras are named according to imperial reign. Before the Meiji period, era names were designated by court officials and changed frequently, to mark the enthronement of a new emperor, the start of a new cycle or particularly significant year in the Chinese zodiac, or to mark disasters such as fires and earthquakes. In Bashō's lifetime there were eleven differently named eras; occasionally in headnotes there is reference to the *nengō* ("year name"), the name of the era, as well as the number of the year within the era.

Era Names during Bashō's Lifetime

Kan'ei	寛永	1624–1644
Shōhō	正保	1644–1648
Keian	慶安	1648–1652
Jōō	承応	1652–1655
Meireki	明暦	1655–1658
Manji	万治	1658–1661
Kanbun	寛文	1661–1673
Enpō	延宝	1673–1681
Tenna	天和	1681–1684
Jōkyō	貞享	1684–1688
Genroku	元禄	1688–1704

In this translation I have attempted to create an English true to the movement and manner of saying of Bashō's poems. Previous translations often present Bashō as a terse proto-imagist, but lesser-known elements in his work include a joyous pleasure taken in punning and innuendo, and a playful relationship with inherited tradition, markers of the *haikai* poetic practice out of which his work first emerged. Rather than a philosopher or spiritual guide, Bashō was a poet, with a poet's concern with the work and world of words. The ambition of the book is to bring us closer to that Bashō, one of the great poets of world literature; I hope readers will enjoy and gain as much from the encounter as I have.

Andrew Fitzsimons, Tokyo

The Poems

1

The Twenty-ninth, yet Risshun is here . . .

Has the springtime come?
       Has the old year gone away?
            Little New Year's Eve

haru ya koshi / toshi ya yukiken / kotsugomori

Winter, 1663. The oldest extant verse by Bashō, who was nineteen at the
time of composition: February 7, 1663. *The Twenty-ninth:* the twenty-
ninth day of the Twelfth Month (February 7, in the Gregorian calen-
dar); *Ōtsugomori* was the last day of the year of the lunar calendar, the
thirtieth day of the Twelfth Month; *kotsugomori:* the twenty-ninth day
of the Twelfth Month. *Risshun:* the first day of spring in the lunar cal-
endar. Because of the disjunction between the lunar and solar calen-
dars, spring could on occasion start one or two days before New Year's
Day, the traditional first day of spring, and this occurred in 1662–63.
Bashō alludes to two poems, one by Ariwara no Motokata (888?–953?),
from the *Kokin Wakashū: toshi no uchi ni / haru wa ki ni keri / hitotose
o / kozo to ya iwamu / kotoshi to ya iwamu* ("In the span of a year / the
springtime has come again / so is it last year / that we are to call this
time / or are we to call it this year?"); and the other from the *Ise Monog-
atari* ("The Tales of Ise"): *kimi ya koshi / ware ya yukiken / omōezu /
yume ka utsutsu ka / nete ka samete ka* ("Was it you who came / Was it
I who went to you? / I do not recall / A dream or reality? / Did I sleep
or did I wake?").

2

The moon now a signpost
       This the way please step inside
            our travelers' inn

tsuki zo shirube / konata e irase / tabi no yado

Autumn, 1663. Alludes to a passage in the Noh play *Kurama Tengu*
("Tengu on Mount Kurama"; see 105): *hana zo shirube naru / konata e
irase tamae ya* ("The blossoms will show you the way / This the way
please step inside"). Bashō puns on *irase tabi* ("kindly deigns to step
inside") and *tabi* ("travel").

3

The rosebud cherry
    flowering for memory
        for the end of age

ubazakura / saku ya rōgo no / omoiide

Spring, 1664. *ubazakura* (literally, "old woman cherry"): *Prunus sub-hirtella,* also known as higan cherry, winter-flowering cherry, or spring cherry. The name *ubazakura* and the tree's association with agedness derive from the tree blossoming before its leaves appear; with *ha* a homonym for both "leaf" and "tooth," the leafless tree can also be said to be "toothless." Bashō alludes to the Noh play *Sanemori* by Zeami Motokiyo (1363–1443), in which the aged warrior Saitō Bettō Sanemori (?—1183), having foreseen his own death, had requested of Munemori, the chief of the Heike, the privilege of wearing into battle a robe of red brocade, a privilege granted only to generals. The return of his dead body to his hometown wearing the robe, he says, will become the finest memory of this old man. See 551.

4

Making everybody
    put on years yet forever
        Ebisu the Young

toshi wa hito ni / torasete itsumo / waka-Ebisu

Spring, 1666. *waka-Ebisu*: a good luck charm with a picture of Ebisu, sold at New Year. Ebisu: one of the *shichifukujin,* the Seven Gods of Fortune; see 831, 832, 960.

5

All Kyoto today all
    the ninety-nine thousand types
        out for hanami

Kyō wa kuman- / kusen kunju no / hanami kana

Spring, 1666. *Kyō* can mean the capital (Kyoto) or "today." *hanami*: cherry blossom viewing. A set phrase of the time said *Kyoto wa kuman hassen-ke* ("Kyoto has 98,000 houses"); Bashō combines this with another common phrase, *kisen kunju* ("a crowd of rich and poor," "all classes of people"), to make *kuman-kusen kunju* (a "ninety-nine thousand crowd"). 7-7-5.

6

A flower visible
    to the eyes of the humble
        The demon thistle

hana wa shizu no / me ni mo miekeri / oniazami

Spring, 1666. The poem alludes to a phrase from Ki no Tsurayuki's (see 16, 359, 844) introduction to the *Kokin Wakashū*: *me ni mienu onikami* ("an invisible fierce god"), and a phrase from the Noh play *Yamamba* ("The Mountain Crone"): *shizu no me ni mienu oni* ("a demon the eyes of the poor do not see"). In the play, the mountain crone, though feared by them, comes to the aid of a poor woodcutter and a weaving woman without their knowing, and these acts are ascribed to an *oni* ("demon") or *kami* ("god"). *oniazami* (*Cirsium borealinipponense*) can be translated "plumed thistle" or "demon thistle." 6-7-5.

7

Rainy season rains
        Excuse my discourtesy
            O face of the moon

samidare ni / onmonodō ya / tsuki no kao

Summer, 1666. *samidare* (literally, "Fifth Month rain"): a set term for the
rainy season. In the current calendar, the rainy season takes place in
late June and July. *onmonodō:* a formal greeting after a long break in
communication.

8

The sounds of downpour
        even ears becoming sour
            in the ume rains

furu oto ya / mimi mo sū naru / ume no ame

Summer, 1666. *ume: Prunus mume:* the "Japanese apricot" or "Chinese
plum." Many translations call the flowers "plum blossom"; in this trans-
lation I use "ume" (pronounced with two syllables, "oo-may") rather
than "plum." The rainy season is called *tsuyu* in Japanese, the two kanji
for which mean "ume rain": the rains that come around the time ume
ripen. See 25.

9

Rabbit-ear iris
        looking like its lookalike
            its water-double

kakitsubata / nitari ya nitari / mizu no kage

Summer, 1666. *kakitsubata: Iris laevigata,* known as Japanese iris, or
rabbit-ear iris. Bashō is alluding to lines from the Noh play *Kakitsubata:*
"they look so alike, the *kakitsubata* and the *ayame*" (*ayame: Iris san-
guinea,* blood iris; see 414).

10

The calabash gourd
  so entrancing its flowers
    my body's floating

yūgao ni / mitoruru ya mi mo / ukari hyon

Summer, 1666. *yūgao* (literally, "evening faces"): *Lagenaria siceraria,* the
calabash, bottle gourd, or white-flowered gourd, the white flowers of
which bloom in the evening; see 146, 421. The larger variety is called
hyōtan, and its fruits when hollowed out were used as containers for
grain and liquid. Out of the common phrase *ukari* hyon ("absent-
minded") Bashō makes a punning relation to a hyō*tan* gourd floating
on water; *ukari* literally means "floating," and is also related to the word
ukare ("gaiety").

11

Rock-azaleas
  dyed by the teardrops of the
    cuckcoochineal

iwatsutsuji / somuru namida ya / hototogishu

Summer, 1666. *hototogishu:* a pun on *hototogi*su (*Cuculus poliocepha-
lus,* the lesser cuckoo), and *shu* (red, vermillion). In Japanese folklore,
the cuckoo sheds "tears of blood." This kind of wordplay, in which one
syllable (in this case *su*) is replaced by another (*shu*), is called *kasuri.*

12

A little while to
  await the call of the cuck-
    oo a thousand years

shibashi ma mo / matsu ya hototogi- / su sennen

Summer, 1666. The poem alludes to the proverb *matsu wa sennen* ("a
pine lives for a thousand years"). The word for pine (*matsu*) can also, as
in English, mean "to wait," or "to yearn for," "to pine." Poets traditionally
waited for the first call of the cuckoo to announce the arrival of the new
season in verse.

13

The autumnal wind
  through the mouthway of a door
    points a piercing voice

akikaze no / yarido no kuchi ya / togarigoe

Autumn, 1666. The wordplay is on yari*do* ("a *sliding* door") and the
homonym *yari* ("a spear"). The word *kuchi* ("mouth") can also mean
"entrance" or "opening."

14

A Tanabata
  heart with rendezvous rained off
    Under the weather

Tanabata no / awanu kokoro ya / uchūten

Autumn, 1666. *Tanabata:* "The evening of the seventh," the Star Festival.
Legend says that the lovers Hikoboshi (represented by the "cowherd"
star, Altair) and Orihime (the "weaver" star, Vega), separated by the
Milky Way, can meet only once a year, on the seventh day of the Sev-
enth Month; see 97, 98, 643, 675. *uchūten:* a pun invented by Bashō as a
negative version of *uchōten* ("rapture," "ecstasy"), combining *u* ("rain"),
chū ("in the middle of"), and *ten* ("the heavens," "sky").

15

Just stay clear and leave
  where I live a capital
    Moon of Kyoto

tanda sume / sumeba miyako zo / Kyō no tsuki

Autumn, 1666. The poem contains a great deal of wordplay in Japanese:
sumeba miyako: a saying that means something similar to "there's no
place like home"; *miyako:* a capital, and also the imperial capital, Kyoto;
Kyō: today, but can also mean Kyoto; *Kyō no tsuki:* the harvest moon.

16

That Celestial light
    the Princess Shitateru?
        The face of the moon

kage wa ame no / Shitateruhime ka / tsuki no kao

Autumn, 1666. *Princess Shitateru:* the "Kana Preface" to the *Kokin Wakashū* by Ki no Tsurayuki (see 6, 359, 844) says that "poetry existed from the time the sky and earth first parted and originated in the skies when Princess Shitateru married Prince Amewaka (Dividing Heaven) to keep him from returning to his celestial home" (Okada, p. 100).

17

Voices in the reeds
    This is the mouth-mimicry
        of the autumn wind

ogi no koe / koya akikaze no / kuchiutsushi

Autumn, 1666. *kuchi utsushi:* a play on words that can mean "mimicry," or "the transfer of food or water from one mouth to another," as in the feeding of an infant.

18

That supine bush-clover
    How impudent-looking her
        and her blooming face

netaru hagi ya / yōgan burei / hana no kao

Autumn, 1666. Another example of *kasuri* wordplay (see 11): *yōgan birei,* a set phrase for "good-looking," changed to *yōgan burei:* "impudent-looking." *hagi: Lespedeza bicolor,* "bush clover," also known as "shrubby bushclover" and "shrub lespedeza"; see 310, 543.

19

In the mirror moon
  of an unseasonal night
    a New Year eyeful

tsuki no kagami / koharu ni miru ya / me shōgatsu

Winter, 1666. *koharu:* unseasonably balmy days in the Tenth Month, an
Indian summer. *kagami* ("mirror"), *miru* ("to see"), and *me* ("eye") are
semantically related words, *engo* ("kindred words"), as are the *haru*
("spring") of *koharu* and shōgatsu ("New Year"). The phrase *me
shōgatsu* ("to enjoy looking at something beautiful") bridges both
groups of words.

20

The winter drizzle
  Irritatedly waited
    for the snow the pines

shigure o ya / modokashigarite / matsu no yuki

Winter, 1666. As seen in 12, the word *matsu* ("pine tree") can also, as in
English, mean "to wait," or "to yearn for," "to pine." *shigure* ("winter driz-
zle") is traditionally thought to be conducive to the foliage of deciduous
trees assuming autumn colors, and so evergreen trees, like the pine, feel
left out.

21

At the Home of a Parent Who Has Outlived a Child

Slumped over bent so low
  The upside-down node-world of
    snow-laden bamboo

shiore fusu ya / yo wa sakasama no / yuki no take

Winter, 1666. *yo:* the node(s) or joint(s) of a bamboo, but can also mean
"world." *yo wa sakasama* ("the world is upside down") is a common-
place phrase. The use of phrases from everyday life was a characteristic
of the Teimon style, but to use the convention to express grief was unu-
sual; see 41.

22

The hailstones commingling
   with the katabira snow
      Such embroidery

arare majiru / katabirayuki wa / komon kana

Winter, 1666. *katabira:* a silk or hemp summer kimono (see 947); *katabira yuki:* large, flat snowflakes.

23

The shriveling frost
      Melancholy the blooming
         in the flower field

shimogare ni / saku wa shinki no / hanano kana

Winter, 1666. Bashō drew the phrase *shinki no hana* ("melancholy flowers") from a *ryutatsu-bushi,* a genre of songs, often erotic, which were highly popular between the 1590s and 1610s.

24

The faces of blossoms
      so bashfully slinks away
         The haze-hidden moon

hana no kao ni / hareute shite ya / oborozuki

Spring, 1667. *oborozuki:* "the moon veiled in haze," a traditional spring season word; see 756. *hana* ("flower") here, as ever, signifies cherry blossoms. 6-7-5.

25

Now fully in bloom
　　So leave the ume untouched
　　　　winnowing breezes

sakari naru / ume ni sude hiku / kaze mogana

Spring, 1667. The *su* of su*de* ("*bare* hands") can also mean "sour" or
"vinegar," and so is associated with ume, a fruit too sour to eat fresh and
which is pickled to make *umeboshi* (see 8). Bashō is playing with the
phrase *sude (o) hiku* ("to leave something untouched").

26

Here's an easterly
　　unraveling the willow
　　　　ruffling through her hair

achi kochi ya / menmen sabaki / yanagi gami

Spring, 1667. The poem has numerous examples of wordplay: *achi
kochi*: "here and there"; *kochi*: "east wind"; *menmen sabaki*: "each person
doing something their own way"; *sabaki* (*sabaku*) can mean "to comb,"
"to loosen hair," "to dispose of," "to sell," "to judge"; *sabaki gami* can
mean "loosened hair"; *yanagi*: "a weeping willow"; *yanagi gami*: the
long branches of a willow tree, or a woman's long hair.

27

Mochi-like snowflakes
　　making stringy rice cakes of
　　　　the willow branches

mochiyuki o / shiraito to nasu / yanagi kana

Spring, 1667. *mochi*: a traditional food at New Year, made from
pounded, glutinous rice, which is also made into cakes of various
shapes.

28

The blossoms unfailing
    My grief this unopening
        pouch of poetry

hana ni akanu / nageki ya kochi no / utabukuro

Spring, 1667. *akanu* can mean both "not weary of" and "not open."
kochi: a slang term for "I" (an earlier version of the poem had the more
usual *ware*), can also be read as "east wind." *utabukuro* (literally, "song
bag"): a container made of *danshi* (strong Japanese paper), cotton, or
other material, into which drafts and manuscripts were placed; also the
name of the balloon-like vocal sac of a frog. The poem rewrites lines
from *Ise Monogatari,* in which Ariwara no Narihira (825–880; see 71,
101, 403, 908) laments his insatiable need for viewing cherry blossoms:
*hana ni akanu / nageki wa itsumo / seshikadomo / kyō no koyoi ni / niru
toki wa nashi* ("The blossoms unfailing / to me ever grievously / That is
so and yet / to this evening of evenings / no other time can compare");
see 52.

29

The springtime breezes
    will make the buds split their sides
        bloomingly let's hope

harukaze ni / fukidashi warau / hana mogana

Spring, 1667. *hana warau* (literally, "flower/s laugh"): the blooming of a
flower.

30

Summer approaching
    Stop up that windsack store up
        blossom-picking winds

natsu chikashi / sono kuchi tabae / hana no kaze

Spring, 1667. In legend, Fūjin, the god of the winds, carries on his
shoulders a large sack containing the winds.

31

To Hatsuse people have come, to see the blossoms

Such merrymakers
　　　here now among Hatsuse's
　　　　　wild cherry blossoms

ukarekeru / hito ya Hatsuse no / yamazakura

Spring, 1667. *Hatsuse:* the old name for Hase, in Sakurai City, Nara. In *kasuri* wordplay Bashō rewrites *uka*ri ("cold-hearted") as *uka*re: ("merry"), based on a poem by Minamoto no Toshiyori (1055–1129) from the *Hyakunin Isshu* (see 879): *ukarikeru / hito o Hatsuse no / yama-oroshi yo / hageshikare to wa / inoranu mono o* ("The one cold to me / as with the winds storming down / from high Hatsuse / fiercer she has become now / Not what it was I prayed for").

32

A Weeping Cherry
　　　As I turn away to leave
　　　　　reeling I'm reeled in

itozakura / koya kaerusa no / ashimotsure

Spring, 1667. *itozakura: Prunus itosakura Sieb.*, a variety of drooping cherry tree, the name of which in Japanese contains the element *ito* ("thread"). *ashimotsure: ashi* ("foot," or "leg"); *motsure* ("to get tangled," "to trip," "to reel").

33

When the breezes blow
　　　tapering off to a wag
　　　　　the Cherry Dogwood

kaze fukeba / obosōnaru ya / inuzakura

Spring, 1667. The poem plays on the words *inuzakura* (literally, "dog cherry tree") and *obosōnaru,* which means "to dwindle," "to lose vigor," "to taper off," "to become lonely," and contains the element *o* (an animal's tail).

34

The blossoming wavecrests
        the snow too the water's out
            of season flowers

nami no hana to / yuki mo ya mizu no / kaeribana

Winter, 1668. *nami no hana* (literally, "wave's flowers"): whitecaps, the
foam on waves. The poem plays on the word *kaeri,* which can mean
both "returning" and, when used with *-bana,* a "flower blooming out of
season."

35

The Katsura Gallant
        where he's living now not clear
            The harvest moon rain

Katsura otoko / sumazu narikeri / ame no tsuki

Autumn, 1669. *Katsura: Cercidiphyllum japonicum,* in legend, a tree on
the moon; *katsura otoko:* a man of incomparable beauty who lives
under a katsura tree on the face of the moon. The wordplay in the poem
centers on *sumazu,* a *kakekotoba* (a word written in hiragana script
rather than kanji, to bring out multiple possible meanings of the homo-
nym), which can mean "not live" or "not clear."

36

At Uchiyama
        the unknown to outsiders
            blossoms in full bloom

Uchiyama ya / tozama shirazu no / hanazakari

Spring, 1670. *Uchiyama:* Uchiyama Kongōjōin Eikyū-ji, a temple in
Nara, which belonged to the esoteric Shingon sect of Buddhism. The
uchi of Uchiyama means "inside," in contrast to *tozama* ("outsider").
The Shingon sect and even the blossoms of its temple were little known
to the outside world.

37

Rainy season rains
      testing the shallows of the
            Minare River

samidare mo / sebumi tazunenu / Minaregawa

Summer, 1670. *Minaregawa:* the Minare River, a tributary of the
Yoshino River, in Gojō City, Nara. The name is related to the verb *min-
areru*, "to get used to seeing something."

38

That the New Year's here
      even striplings realize
            The strawrope-on-doors

haru tatsu to / warawa mo shiru ya / kazarinawa

Spring, 1671. *kazarinawa:* a sacred straw rope in Shinto, put on doors at
New Year. The wordplay centers on *warawa* ("boy," "child") and
waranawa ("straw rope").

39

Come on come and see
      jinbe on as your mantle
            cherish the blossoms

kite mo miyo / jinbe ga haori / hanagoromo

Spring, 1671. Phrases from contemporary popular songs form the
poem's first two phrases. *jinbe ga haori:* a short sleeveless robe for men,
split at the lower back, fashionable at the time. *kite* means both "come"
and "wear," and *haori* means both "robe" and "give oneself up to be
admired." Bashō served as the judge of a contest, eventually published
as his first anthology *Kai Ōi* ("The Seashell Game"), which included this
poem, of which he wrote: "The hokku is poorly tailored, and its words
are badly dyed, too. All this is due to lack of craftsmanship on the poet's
part" (Ueda, *Bashō and His Interpreters*, p. 30; henceforward Ueda).

40

A pair of deer rubbing
　　　hair up against hair each other's
　　　　　hair so hard to please

meotojika ya / ke ni ke ga soroute / ke mutsukashi

Autumn, 1671. Bashō uses the word *ke* ("hair") three times. *ke mutsu-kashi* is a pun on *ki mutsukashi* ("fastidious"). The poem, written when he was twenty-eight, can be read as an allusion to Bashō's love of men. The original has a syllable count of 6-8-7. The second of Bashō's two poems in *Kai Ōi* ("The Seashell Game").

41

As the clouds drift apart
　　　for now friend we separate
　　　　　Wild geese living leave

kumo to hedatsu / tomo ka ya kari no / ikiwakare

Spring, 1672. Written for his friend, Jō Magodayū, before Bashō left Iga for Edo. *kari* can mean both "wild goose" and "temporary": the punning is typical of the Teimon style, but the subject of separation lends the poem a gravity uncommon in Bashō's early verse; see 21. iki*wakare*: separation while living, as distinct from shini*wakare*, separation by death.

42

The summer sward it's
　　　sporting the mountain fastness'
　　　　　short sword on the waist

natsukodachi / haku ya miyama no / koshifusage

Summer, 1672. *kodachi* can mean both "grove" and "short sword."

43

How beautifully
        the princess melon reveals
                the inner Empress

utsukushiki / sono himeuri ya / kisakizane

Summer, 1672. *himeuri* (literally, "princess melon"): *Cucumis melo L. var. makuwa Makino; kisaki*zane: a play on *sane,* the "core of a fruit" or "clitoris," and *kisaki*gane, "empress-to-be." See 145.

44

So much harsher than the
        mouths of the world the mouth of
                the wind for blossoms

hana ni iya yo / sekenguchi yori / kaze no kuchi

Spring, year unknown (44–53 were written in the *Kanbun* period, 1661–73). *hana ni iya yo:* a variation on a set phrase (*iya* yo: "I don't like") from popular songs of the time.

45

I am seeing stars
        Wishes upon the blooms of
                the Weeping Cherry

me no hoshi ya / hana o negai no / itozakura

Spring, year unknown (*Kanbun*). *itozakura* (literally, "string cherry"), also called *shidarezakura* (the weeping cherry). The use of *ito* ("string") in connection with *negai* ("wish") links the poem to the Tanabata Festival (see 14), when people hung poems and wishes to bamboo using a five-colored thread called *negai no ito* ("wishing thread").

46

The life source and seed
    the sprouting taro again
        the mid-autumn moon

inochi koso / imodane yo mata / kyō no tsuki

Autumn, year unknown (*Kanbun*). See 63, 189, 243, 450, 567 for Bashō's
use of the word *inochi* ("life"). *imo* ("taro," or "sweet potato") and *dane*
("seed"): pun on the word *monodane* ("source"); see 613. *kyō no tsuki*:
the harvest moon; at the harvest moon festival on the fifteenth of the
Eighth Month in the lunar calendar, taro were brought to market as a
treat for moonviewers. It was also a custom to boil the sprouts of the
taro and make a soup "to nourish future generations."

47

Not letters loose leaves
    colored sheet upon sheet raked
        burnt after reading

fumi naranu / iroha mo kakite / kachū kana

Autumn, year unknown (*Kanbun*). *iroha*: the first three elements (*i-ro-
ha*) in the Japanese syllabary, thus the rudiments of something (corre-
sponding to ABC, and "ABCs," in English); can also mean "colored
leaves" (*iro*: "color"; *ha*: "leaf"). *kakite*: the verb *kaki* can mean "to write,"
"to scratch," or "to rake." *kachū* ("on fire," "in the fire"): a term people
used at the end of letters to indicate that they wanted the letter
destroyed after reading.

48

In everybody's
    mouth the color of autumn
        a maple-leaf tongue

hitogoto no / kuchi ni arunari / shitamomiji

Autumn, year unknown (*Kanbun*). *shitamomiji*: the colored fallen
leaves under a tree whose foliage has changed in autumn; *shita* can
mean both "under" and "tongue."

49

In setting to plant
　　handle like you would a child
　　　　the Infant Cherry

ūrukoto / ko no gotoku seyo / chigozakura

Spring, year unknown (*Kanbun*). *chigozakura:* a variety of wild cherry
tree; from *chigo*, a child still nursing, also used for young boys who
served at temples. The word also came to mean *catamite*, a young boy
who was the sexual partner of an older man. The homoerotic environ-
ment of Buddhist temples inspired a literary genre called *Chigo Monog-
atari* ("Tales of Acolytes"). See 649, 920.

50

Here's a bamboo shoot
　　Squirt of the slaverings of
　　　　the dewdropping grass

takōna ya / shizuku mo yoyo no / sasa no tsuyu

Summer, year unknown (*Kanbun*). *yo* means both "world" and the
"node" of a bamboo stem (see 21); *yoyo* means "nodes" and also "genera-
tion after generation"; *yoyo* is an adverb describing the dripping of liq-
uid or spittle. The poem parodies a passage in *Genji Monogatari* ("The
Tale of Genji"): *takōna o tsuto nigiri mochite shizuku mo yoyo to kui
nurashi* ("Grabbing a bamboo shoot, he [Kaoru] eats it slobberingly").

51

From the watching them
        so taken I want to take
            the maiden flowers

miru ni ga mo / oreru bakari zo / ominaeshi

Autumn, year unknown (*Kanbun*). *ominaeshi*: "maiden flower" or "lady flower," the Yellow Patrinia (*Patrinia scabiosifolia*), which bears yellow flowers in the autumn; see 448. The name written in kanji can also mean "prostitute flower." A parody of a poem by the priest Henjō (816–90) from the *Kokin Wakashū*: *na ni medete / oreru bakari zo / ominaeshi / ware ochiniki to / hito ni kataru na* ("Because of its name / I have broken off a sprig / of maiden flowers / Of this my depravity / tell no one I beseech you"); see 804.

52

Today comes the nighttime
        of no bedtime no sleeping
            For the moonviewing

kyō no koyoi / neru toki mo naki / tsukimi kana

Autumn, year unknown (*Kanbun*). *kyō no koyoi / neru toki mo naki*: a parody of lines from the passage from *Ise Monogatari* cited in 28: kyō no koyoi *ni* / niru toki *wa* nashi.

53

See the slim figure
        still as yet undeveloped
            The young moon goodness

miru kage ya / mada katanari mo / yoizukiyo

Autumn, year unknown (*Kanbun*). Based on a passage from *Genji Monogatari*: *Hime-gimi wa kiyora ni owase-do* mada katanari *nite* ("The princess is pure, but *not yet grown*"), alluding to the sexual development of the princess Tamakazura. *yoizukiyo*: the young new moon seen only early in the evening and which then disappears (*yoi* can mean both "evening" and "good").

54

For the town doctor
　　a summons to the Big House
　　　A Horse Guard's Parade

machiishi ya / yashikigata yori / komamukae

Autumn, 1675. *machi ishi*: a town doctor, for the common folk rather than the local lord or officials. *komamukae* (literally, "horse welcoming"): before the annual court ceremony called *komahiki,* in which horses from provincial lords were paraded before the emperor, court officials met the horses at the Osaka Barrier in a ceremony called the *komamukae;* see 451. "The humor lies in the sense of incongruity that arises from an imperial ceremony being treated on the same level as plebeian life. Something of the Danrin flavor is beginning to emerge here.—*Shūson*" (Ueda, p. 33).

55

Acupuncturist
　　Upon the shoulder tapping
　　　the bodiless robe

haritate ya / kata ni tsuchi utsu / karakoromo

Autumn, 1675. *karakoromo*: Chinese or Korean style garments; *kara* is an old name for China and Korea, and can also mean "empty"; *koromo* means "robe." In the past, in order to soften fabric and bring it to a shine, *tsuchi* (wooden mallets) were used on clothes placed on a *kinuta* ("fulling block"); see 205.

56

Musashino Plain
　　An inch tall and an inch loud
　　　the deer and its call

Musashino ya / issun hodo na / shika no koe

Autumn, 1675. *Musashino*: "the plain of Musashi Province," an ancient province today comprising the extended Tokyo area, most of Saitama and part of Kanagawa; see 979.

57

Beneath the sake
cup flows a chrysanthemum
on a lacquered tray

sakazuki no / shita yuku kiku ya / kutsukibon

Autumn, 1675. Based on a passage from the Noh play *Yōrō: Natsuyama
no shita yuku mizu no kusuri to naru, geni ya kusuri to kiku no mizu*
("The waters flowing beneath Natsuyama are medicinal, truly the
medicinal chrysanthemum water"). In the legend of the Chrysanthe-
mum Boy, Kikujidō writes the words of the Lotus Sutra on the petals of
a chrysanthemum, the dew from the flower becomes an elixir, and he
remains youthful for seven hundred years; see 108, 234, 552.

58

Weighed upon the scales
Kyoto/Edo balance
eternal springtime

tenbin ya / Kyō Edo kakete / chiyo no haru

Spring, 1676. *Edo*: the name for Tokyo in Bashō's day. *kakete* can mean
both "weigh" and "match equally." Kyoto, the old capital, was still the
residence of the emperor and his court; Edo was the seat of the
shogunate.

59

Seeing these ume
even the cow at Tenjin
would make its first moo

kono ume ni / ushi mo hatsune to / nakitsubeshi

Spring, 1676. Written at the "Tenjin" shrine, Yushima Tenman-gū, in
Tokyo. There is a statue of a cow in front of the shrine, a messenger of
Tenjin, the scholar, poet, politician, and patron of learning, Sugawara
no Michizane (845–903); see 60.

60

And I too at the god's
    treasured firmament gazing
        The ume blossoms

ware mo kami no / hisō ya aogu / ume no hana

Spring, 1676. A reworking of a Chinese-style quatrain written in exile
by Sugawara no Michizane: "Since leaving home, three or four months;
/ I shed tears, a hundred or a thousand lines. / Myriad things are all like
a dream; / Constantly I look up to blue Heaven" (trans. Fraleigh, p. 375).
Just before his departure for Dazaifu, Kyūshū, Michizane composed a
waka expressing his regret that he would never see his favorite ume tree
again. Legend says that the ume tree missed him so much it flew over-
night from Kyoto to Dazaifu to be with him. *hisō* can mean both "treas-
ured" and "firmament."

61

The clouds as its roots
    Fuji assuming a cedar's
        superabundance

kumo o ne ni / Fuji wa suginari no / shigeri kana

Summer, 1676.

62

The Mount of Fuji
    Cover of the tea mortar
        mounted on a flea

Fuji no yama / nomi ga chausu no / ooi kana

Summer, 1676. A parody of a *zokuyō* (popular song): "A flea, carrying a
tea mortar on its back, on its back, jumped over the Mount of Fuji."

63

At Sayo no Nakayama

The life that's given
    The small pool of shade under
        a wickerwork hat

inochi nari / wazuka no kasa no / shitasuzumi

Summer, 1676. *Sayo no Nakayama:* a mountain pass in what is now
called Kakegawa City, Shizuoka. It has many poetical associations (*uta-
makura*), the most well-known being a poem by Saigyō: *toshi takete /
mata koyubeshi to / omoiki ya / inochi narikeri / Saya no Nakayama*
("Never had I dreamed of crossing the Pass of Saya a second time in
ripe old age—this is the span of life I have been vouchsafed!" [McCul-
lough, *Classical Japanese Prose,* p. 571].) The old name was Saya no
Nakayama; see 189. See also 46 and 567 for Bashō's allusions to Saigyō's
use of the word *inochi* ("life").

64

The summertime moon
    from Goyu already come
        to Akasaka

natsu no tsuki / Goyu yori idete / Akasaka ya

Summer, 1676. *Goyu; Akasaka:* two stages on the Tōkaidō road, the dis-
tance between them the shortest on the route, 1.7 km. It is said that
even twenty years later Bashō was still fond of this poem.

65

The wind from Mount Fuji
    borne upon this folding fan
        A gift from Edo

Fuji no kaze ya / ōgi ni nosete / Edo miyage

Summer, 1676. As an elegant gesture, gifts were often placed on fans. In
this case Bashō has only the cool of the air from Fuji to offer. This poem
was the hokku of a linked-verse party held at the home of Takahata
Shiin (?–1722) in Bashō's hometown in Iga.

66

About a hundred ri's
   remove I've come under clouds
      their cooling shadow

hyakuri kitari / hodo wa kumoi no / shitasuzumi

Summer, 1676. *ri* (also transliterated as *li*): a unit of distance, about 4 km; see 218, 388, 508, 514, 900. Bashō wrote this on his return to Iga from Edo.

67

Gazing on something
   so seldom seen from Edo
      The moon-topped mountains

nagamuru ya / Edo ni wa marena / yama no tsuki

Autumn, 1676. Edo, the old name for Tokyo, has a double meaning in the poem in that *e-do* can also mean "unclean earth," in the Buddhist sense of a place filled with suffering derived from worldly desires. Written at a renga party in Iga sponsored by someone called Kuwana at the residence of a man called Watanabe.

68

At long last it's here
   At long last it's here at last
      The end of the year

nari ni keri / nari ni keri made / toshi no kure

Winter, 1676.

69

Kadomatsu

The kadomatsu
>at New Year and overnight
>>thirty years have gone by

kadomatsu ya / omoeba ichiya / sanjūnen

Spring, 1677. *kadomatsu:* a pine decoration placed on both sides of an entrance at New Year. *Ichiya* can mean "one night" or "overnight," but here is also an allusion to the legend of *Ichiya matsu* ("pines put up overnight"), in which a thousand pines appeared overnight at Ukon no Baba at Kitano, Kyoto, a place dear to Sugawara no Michizane (see 59, 60). In Chinese belief, a man "stands firm" at the age of 30. Bashō was 34 when he wrote this poem. 5-7-6.

70

Mist

Across Mount Hiei
>inscribing "shi" at a stroke
>>a lone line of mist

Ō-Hie ya / shi no ji o hiite / hitokasumi

Spring, 1677. The character for "shi" in Japanese orthography: し. *Mount Hiei:* to the northeast of Kyoto, on the southern shore of Lake Biwa; see 420, 666, 715. Enryaku-ji (Enryaku Temple) was founded here in 788 by Saichō, the founder of the Tendai school of Buddhism. In the collection of tales about the priest Ikkyū (*Ikkyū Banashi,* 1668), Ikkyū (1394–1481) was asked by the monks of Enryaku-ji to write something big, so he asked for the monks to join many sheets of paper end to end, spread from the temple to the foot of Mount Hiei, and then ran down along the paper with a brush and ink, drawing the character *shi.* In olden times, the character when drawn quickly resembled a straight line.

71

The Love of the Tomcat's Molly

The tomcat's molly
                through the ruins of a crumbled hearth
                        coming and going

neko no tsuma / hetsui no kuzure yori / kayoikeri

Spring, 1677. Typical of the Danrin school in mocking the mores of
Heian period courtly love, the poem parodies a passage from *Ise*
Monogatari: *tsuiji no kuzure yori kayoikeri* ("through the ruins of a
crumbled earthen wall"), in which Ariwara no Narihira (see 28, 101,
403, 908) surreptitiously visits his secret lover. 5-9-5.

72

Jōshi

Even the Dragon
                Palace with today's low-tide
                        Airing-the-House-Out

Ryūgū mo / kyō no shioji ya / doyōboshi

Spring, 1677. *Jōshi*: March 3, the day when the tide is at its lowest; see 153,
851. *Ryūgū*: *Ryūgū-jō*, the Dragon Palace at the bottom of the sea in the
folktale "Urashima Tarō"; see 201. *doyōboshi*: *doyō* is the hottest period of
summer, and clothes, futon, etc. were put out for airing; see 153, 424.

73

Blooms

Always first to know
                Upon Gichiku's bamboo
                        a snowfall of blooms

mazu shiru ya / Gichiku ga take ni / hana no yuki

Spring, 1677. *Gichiku*: also known as Tōzaburō, a famous player of the
hitoyogiri, an endblown flute made of bamboo. The phrase *hana no yuki*
("a snowfall of blooms") echoes the phrase *hana no fubuki* ("a storm of
blooms") from the popular *hitoyogiri* song "Yoshinoyama"; see 104.

74

Cuckoo

Though unwaited for
> the veg seller's come calling
>> The lesser cuckoo

matanu noni / na uri ni kitaka / hototogisu

Summer, 1677. Many poems in the Japanese tradition concern waiting
in vain for the first call of the *hototogisu* (*Cuculus poliocephalus*, the
lesser cuckoo; see 11), a species of cuckoo native to Japan. Bashō's poem
alludes to a poem by Taira no Chikamune (1144–99): *Ariake no / tsuki
wa* matanu ni *ide nuredo / nao yama fukaki / hototogisu kana* ("The
white morning moon / although unwanted appears / yet deep within
the mountains / remains the cuckoo").

75

Tango no Sekku

Tomorrow chimaki
> leaf-wrappings will dry and die
>> a Naniwa dream

asu wa chimaki / Naniwa no kareha / yume nare ya

Summer, 1677. *chimaki*: steamed dumplings wrapped in leaves (bam-
boo, banana, or reed), served on *Tango no Sekku* ("Boys' Day," nowadays
called *Kodomo no Hi*: "Children's Day"), the fifth day of the Fifth (lunar)
Month. *Naniwa*: a place in Osaka famous for reeds; see 822.

76

Rainy Season

Rainy season rains
> The watchman's lantern lighting
>> the Dragon's candles

samidare ya / ryūtō aguru / bantarō

Summer, 1677. *ryūtō*: a phosphorescence on the sea, in folk belief said
to be an offering of lighted candles by the dragon god, Ryūjin, to the
gods of the sea; the Dragon Palace; see 72, 76, 201. *bantarō*: a municipal
watchman who lived in a guard post on the borders of a town.

77

Mosquito Net

Ōmi mossie-
    net sweat rippling waves breaking
        on the bed tonight

ōmigaya / ase ya sazanami / yoru no toko

Summer, 1677. *Ōmigaya:* a mosquito net made in Ōmi, the province
around Lake Biwa. *sazanami* ("rippling waves") is a word associated with
the Ōmi area; *yoru* can mean both "night" and "to come (rippling waves)."

78

Cicada

From the topmost bough
    emptiness has come falling
        A cicada's husk

kozue yori / ada ni ochikeri / semi no kara

Summer, 1677. The poem alludes to a passage in the Noh play *Sakura-
gawa:* kozue yori ada ni *chirinuru hana nareba, ochite mo mizu no
aware to wa* ("From the tree tops the blossoms scatter in emptiness, fall
into the water to add pathos to the stream").

79

Risshū: Autumn Rising

Autumntime coming on
    Coming to visit my ears
        the pillow-rustling wind

aki ki ni keri / mimi o tazunete / makura no kaze

Autumn, 1677. *Risshu,* the first day of autumn in the lunar calendar; see
1. In this and in the more famous 546, and 130, Bashō alludes to a poem
by Fujiwara no Toshiyuki (?–901) from the *Kokin Wakashū: aki kinu to
/ me ni wa sayaka ni / miene domo / kaze no oto ni zo / odorokarenuru*
("That autumn has come / isn't yet clear to my eyes / so unseeing
though / the sound of the wind makes me / of a sudden realize"). 6-7-6.

80

Ogi

Leaf-sheathed ears of corn
    Under the eaves the green reed
       taken by mistake

tōkibi ya / nokiba no ogi no / tori chigae

Autumn, 1677. *Ogi*: a kind of reed, *Miscanthus sacchariflorus,* the Amur
silvergrass. *nokiba no ogi*: a play on the name of the character and the
episode of mistaken identity involving Nokiba no Ogi (literally, "the
reed under the eaves") in *Genji Monogatari*: Utsusemi, appalled by
Genji's sexual advances, rolls away from him in the night, leaving her
sleeping stepdaughter, Nokiba no Ogi. Mistaking the stepdaughter for
Utsusemi, Genji forces himself on her.

81

Moon

The harvest moon tonight
    Come shine it up Hitomi
       Izumo-no-Kami

koyoi no tsuki / togidase Hitomi / Izumo no Kami

Autumn, 1677. *Hitomi Izumo-no-Kami:* a punning name, something
like "Mr. Seymour Thorogood McCloud" (Hitomi means "person who
sees"; Izumo no Kami can mean "governor of the province of Izumo," or
"to appear from out of the clouds"). Bashō is playing on the names of
two famous mirror makers in Kyoto: Hitomi Sado no Kami and Hitomi
Iwami no Kami.

82

Gazing at the sawn
    end of a freshly felled tree
        Tonight's harvest moon

ki o kirite / motokuchi miru ya / kyō no tsuki

Autumn, 1677. *motokuchi* (literally, "source mouth"): a term from
woodcutting for the end of a log closer to the root.

KOYO

83

Weakening branches
    reddish toushi paper torn
        The wind in autumn

eda moroshi / hitōshi yaburu / aki no kaze

Autumn, 1677. *Koyo:* the changing colors of autumn; *toushi (tōshi):*
decorative paper, imported from Tang China, used initially for painting
and calligraphy. After the Kamakura period (1192–1333), the fragile
paper was exclusively used in *fusuma,* sliding doors.

84

The dyeing begins
    Onto tofu befallen
        a maple-leaf tinge

irozuku ya / tōfu ni ochite / usumomiji

Autumn, 1677. There is a tofu dish called *momiji-dofu,* the pinkish
color of which derives from red pepper. *Momiji* means "red leaves," par-
ticularly of the maple tree, and is another way of referring to the chang-
ing colors of autumn.

WINTER RAIN

85

The scudding of clouds
    A dog running and pissing
        a passing shower

yuku kumo ya / inu no kakebari / murashigure

Winter, 1677. Bashō uses the vulgarism for urine (*bari*).

86

A winter shower
    Pebbles pelting into the
        Koishikawa

hitoshigure / tsubute ya futte / Koishikawa

Winter, 1677. *Koishikawa*: "Pebble River," in present-day Bunkyō Ward, Tokyo.

87

Frost

Swaddled by the frost
    settled to sleep in the wind
        an abandoned child

shimo o kite / kaze o shikine no / sutego kana

Winter, 1677. Alludes to a poem by Fujiwara no Yoshitsune (1169–1206) in the *Shin Kokin-Wakashū*: *kirigirisu / naku ya shimoyo no / samushiro ni / koromo katashiki / hitori kamo nen* ("The cricket crying / In the cold of the frosty / nighttime for my bed / I spread out my padded robes / Will I be sleeping alone?"); see 210. *sutego*: abandoned child; see 194.

88

Snow

Snow on Mount Fuji
　　created in a dream by
　　　　Rosei's pillow

Fuji no yuki / Rosei ga yume o / tsukasetari

Winter, 1677. *Rosei*: Lu Sheng. In the Tang period story "The World inside a Pillow" by Shen Jiji, the meaning and value of life and the uselessness of money are revealed to Lu Sheng in a dream while he sleeps on a pillow offered to him by a Daoist monk. In the dream he saw a silver mountain being constructed.

89

Charcoal

The white of charcoal
　　The Urashima story
　　　　and the age-old box

shirozumi ya / kano Urashima ga / oi no hako

Winter, 1677. *shirozumi*: "white charcoal," a kind of charcoal the preparation of which gives it a whitish surface, and which is used in the tea ceremony. *Urashima*: "Urashima Tarō"; see 72, 76. When Urashima Tarō opened the Tamatebako, the "age-old box" given him in the Dragon Palace, smoke poured out and his hair and eyebrows turned white; see 201.

90

Well so anyway no ado
　　yesterday went and happened
　　　　after fugu soup

ara nani tomo na ya / kinō wa sugite / fukutojiru

Winter, 1677. *fugu* ("globefish") is a potentially lethal food if prepared incorrectly. 8-7-5.

91

Teikin no Ōrai
> Who'll be first to take it out
> this New Year morning?

Teikin no Ōrai / ta ga bunko yori / kesa no haru

Spring, 1678. *Teikin no Ōrai:* a fourteenth-century set of correspondence used as the basis of an educational textbook until the nineteenth century.

92

The Kapitan too
> bows down before the Shogun
> the New Year greeting

kapitan mo / tsukubawasekeri / kimi ga haru

Spring, 1678. *kapitan:* derived from the Portuguese word *capitão* (captain), refers to the head of the Dutch Trading Post at Dejima, Nagasaki, who had to make a formal greeting to the shogun in Edo on New Year's Day every year. *kimi ga haru* is a seasonal expression for the New Year or beginning of spring; the *kimi* refers to the emperor so that *kimi ga haru* literally means "the emperor's spring," but Bashō uses it here to refer to the shogun (see also 132).

93

Dairi-bina
> The Emperor of Dolls holding sway
> over all today

Dairi-bina / ningyō tennō no / gyou toka ya

Spring, 1678. *Dairi-bina:* dolls representing the emperor and empress at *Hinamatsuri* ("The Doll Festival," March 3); see 483. 5-9-5.

94

The first to the blooms
> My life to be longer by
> > seventy-five years

hatsuhana ni / inochi shichijū- / gonen hodo

Spring, 1678. The poem parodies a proverb: "Eat the first produce of the year and live seventy-five *days* longer."

95

Mourning the Death of Fuboku's Mother

Water offerings
> so to console her spirit
> > Dōmyō-ji

mizu mukete / ato toi tamae / Dōmyō-ji

Summer, 1678. *Fuboku:* Ichiryūken Okamura (?–1691), a haikai poet in Edo; see 760. *Dōmyō-ji:* a temple in Osaka which gave its name to a summer dish of dried boiled rice, which was eaten either dry or soaked in cold water. Fuboku himself included this in the haikai anthology *Haikai Edo Hirokōji* (1678).

96

Sweet Flags *calamus* sprouting
    through the skull of a sardine
        weathered under eaves

ayame oi keri / noki no iwashi no / sarekōbe

Summer, 1678. On *Tango no Sekku* ("Boys' Day," the fifth day of the
Fifth Month; see 75, 510), *ayame* ("sweet flags") are displayed to drive
away evil spirits. At *Setsubun*, the last day before spring (nowadays held
on February 3), people throw *daizu* (roasted soybeans), known as *fuku-
mame* (fortune beans), out the doors and windows of houses saying
"Oni wa soto" ("Demons go out!") and scatter beans inside the house
saying "Fuku wa uchi" ("Fortune come in!"). At *Setsubun*, as a charm
against demons, people used to display a sprig of *hiiragi* (a holly-like
plant) speared into the head of a sardine. Though it was *Tango no
Sekku*, this *Setsubun* symbol had still not been removed and so Bashō
saw both. Bashō also alludes to the legend of miscanthus plumes grow-
ing through the eye sockets of the skull of Ono no Komachi, one of the
immortal poets of Japan and a proverbial beauty; see 649, 676, 804, 888.

97

Suigaku please
    provide us now with a boat
        the River of Stars

Suigaku mo / norimono kasan / Amanogawa

Autumn, 1678. *Suigaku*: Suigaku Sōho, a blind scholar, shipbuilder, and
hydraulic engineer, noted for his work on the Sado Island mines in the
1630s. *Amanogawa* (literally, "Heaven's River") is the Japanese term for
the Milky Way (see 540). A Tanabata poem (see 14); the poet is looking
at a river in flood on the evening of the Tanabata festival and asking for
the loan of a boat. At Tanabata, women traditionally placed yarn and
clothes on a shelf for Orihime, the Weaver Princess, to pray for the
improvement of their sewing skills, a practice called *kashi kosode*
("lending a robe").

98

Autumn's here they say
     The Star yearns for his love on
          the coat of a deer

aki kinu to / tsuma kou hoshi ya / shika no kawa

Autumn, 1678. Deer mate in the autumn; Japanese deer maintain the spots on their hide into adulthood. As with 97, this is a Tanabata poem; see 14, 131.

99

So rain-filled today
     The autumn demimonde of
          Sakai-chō

ame no hi ya / seken no aki o / Sakai-chō

Autumn, 1678. *Sakai-chō:* a self-enclosed entertainment district in Edo, with theatres and geisha houses; *sakai* means "boundary" or "border."

100

How precious the moon
     As dear as the price of land on
          Tōri-chō

geni ya tsuki / maguchi senkin no / Tōri-chō

Autumn, 1678. *Tōri-chō:* the main street in Edo (now called Chūo-dōri), which ran north to south from Kanda (Chiyoda ward) to Shiba (Minato ward), with Nihonbashi in the middle.

101

I'll pickle it in salt
    for you to take with you home
        A Capital Bird!

shio ni shite mo / iza kotozuten / miyakodori

Winter, 1678. *miyakodori*: "oystercatcher"; literally, "bird of the imperial
capital," but a bird Bashō often saw on the Sumida River in Edo (at the
time Kyoto was the capital of Japan). Ariwara no Narihira used the
term in *Ise Monogatari*, asking the *miyakodori* for news of his lover in
the capital; see 28, 71, 403, 908.

102

The worry-not herb
    I'll gather for nameshi
        to let go the year

wasuregusa / nameshi ni tsuman / toshi no kure

Winter, 1678. *wasuregusa* (literally, "forget-grass"): *Hemerocallis fulva
var. kwanso,* the orange day-lily; see 353. *nameshi*: steamed rice mixed
with leafy greens.

103

Now for a hokku
    Matsuo Tōsei
        at home at New Year

hokku nari / Matsuo Tōsei / yado no haru

Spring, 1679. *hokku*: the opening poem in a linked-verse sequence,
which later developed into haiku. *Matsuo*: Bashō's family name; *Tōsei*
("green peach"): the *haigō* (poetic pen name) he used prior to Bashō
("banana tree"); see 141. Bashō had now become a *sōshō* (haikai mas-
ter) and had put up his "shop sign."

104

Pining for blossoms
        Tōzaburō's song
            "Yoshinoyama"

matsu hana ya / Tōzaburō ga / Yoshinoyama

Spring, 1679. *Tōzaburō:* the musician Gichiku; *Yoshinoyama:* Mount Yoshino, a mountain famous for its cherry blossoms; see 73.

105

Even Hollanders
        they've journeyed for the blossoms
            Saddles on horses

Oranda mo / hana ni kinikeri / uma ni kura

Spring, 1679. The Dutch would have come all the way to Edo from Dejima, Nagasaki; see 92. The poem adapts lines from the Noh play *Kurama Tengu* (see 2] *hana sakaba tsugemu to iishi yamazato no tsukai wa kitari uma ni kura* ("A messenger from a mountain village came with news of the blossoms, let's saddle the horses"), which in turn had borrowed from a waka by Minamoto no Yorimasa (1104–80): *hana sakaba / tsugeyo to iishi / yamamori no / kuru oto su nari / uma ni kura oke* ("When the blossoms bloom, / please let me know I'd said / The forest ranger's / approach I am hearing now / so go and saddle my horse"). The Dutch, as foreigners, were not permitted to attend blossom-viewing parties.

106

Caught in the Rain

With tucked-in sandal-backs
        I will clip my way homeward
            The mountain cherries

zōri no shiri / orite kaeran / yamazakura

Spring, 1679. The *shiri* ("tails") of the *zōri* ("sandals") were "tucked-in," so as to make the sandals splash less mud on the bottoms of his robes. The pun centers around *orite,* which can refer to "*folding* the tails of the sandals" or "*snapping off* a spray of blossoms."

107

The azure ocean's
　　ripples reeking of sake
　　　　Tonight the full moon

sōkai no / nami sakekusashi / kyō no tsuki

Autumn, 1679. The poem plays on the word *tsuki,* which means "moon,"
but when written in different kanji can mean "wine cup." The phrase
sōkai no nami ("blue sea's waves") alongside the image of the autumn
moon derive from the Noh play *Shari* ("The Sacred Relic").

108

The sake-filled cup
　　with mountain chrysanthemum
　　　　I will drink it dry

sakazuki ya / yamaji no kiku to / kore o hosu

Autumn, 1679. *yamaji no kiku* (literally, "mountain path chrysanthe-
mum"), in Chinese legend the dew from which was drunk for longevity.
In Japan, on *Chōyō no Sekku,* the Chrysanthemum Festival, the ninth day
of the Ninth Month, *kiku no sake* (or *kikuzake*), sake with chrysanthe-
mum, was drunk on the morning of the festival, to wish for long life; see
458, 582, 725, 909. Alludes to a poem by the monk Sosei (c. 844–910):
*nurete hosu / yamaji no kiku no / tsuyu no ma ni / itsu ka chitose o / ware
wa henikemu* ("Did an age slip by / during those fleeting moments / when
I dried my sleeves / drenched by chrysanthemum dew / on the path
through the mountain?" [trans. McCullough, *Kokin Wakashū,* p. 68]).

109

Now I'm surveying
　　now gazing into now seeing
　　　　autumn at Suma

miwataseba / nagamureba mireba / Suma no aki

Autumn, 1679. *Suma:* a beach near Kobe, associated in Japanese litera-
ture with autumnal loneliness; see 404, 405, 574.

110

Taking the Trouble to See Tsuchiya Shiyū Off to Kamakura

Stepping upon the frost
    until where it is crippling
        bidding a farewell

shimo o funde / chinba hiku made / okurikeri

Winter, 1679. *Tsuchiya Shiyū:* a samurai of the Matsue *han* (a domain ruled by the Matsudaira clan), a haikai friend of Bashō. The poem was inspired by the Noh play *Hachi no Ki* (see 815).

111

A snowy morning
    Onion shoots point the way
        into my garden

kesa no yuki / nebuka o sono no / shiori kana

Winter, 1679. *shiori* (literally, "to break off a branch"): originally a broken twig or branch used as a marker on mountain paths.

112

Aha the spring the spring
    so so wonderful the spring
        And the great books say so too

aa haru haru / ōinaru kana / haru to un nun

Spring, 1680. A parody of the words of Mi Fu (Mi Fei, 1051–1107) in praise of Confucius: "Confucius, Confucius great is Confucius. / Before Confucius, there was no Confucius. / After Confucius, there will be no Confucius. / Confucius, Confucius great is Confucius." 6-7-7.

113

How could it be a grief
      for Mozi to see grilled seri
            the color changing?

kanashiman ya / Bokushi seriyaki o / mite mo nao

Spring, 1680. *Bokushi:* Mozi (Mo Tzu, c. 470–c. 391 BCE), Chinese phi-
losopher, who was saddened at the dyeing of pure white silk. *seri:* drop-
wort, which darkens when cooked; see 833.

114

A night under blossoms
      So Hyōtansai
            I can nickname myself now

hana ni yadori / Hyōtansai to / mizukara ieri

Spring, 1680. *Hyōtansai: hyōtan:* a hollowed-out gourd used as a con-
tainer; *sai:* attached to nouns to make a pseudonym.

115

The early summer rain
      the green on the iwahiba
            how long to remain?

satsuki no ame / iwahiba no midori / itsumade zo

Summer, 1680. *iwahiba: Selaginella tamariscina,* a species of spikemoss
that grows in soil or on rocks.

116

Spider what is it
    you voice what is it you cry?
        The wind in autumn

kumo nani to / ne o nani to naku / aki no kaze

Autumn, 1680. Alludes to a passage concerning the *minomushi* ("bag-worm") in *Makura no Sōshi* ("The Pillow Book") by Sei Shōnagon, in which the bagworm is said to cry *chichi-yo! chichi-yo!* ("Father! Father!"); see 317.

117

When to reach safe haven?
    An insect on its journey
        adrift on a leaf

yorube o itsu / hitoha ni mushi no / tabine shite

Autumn, 1680. Alludes to the story of Huo Di, a Chinese soldier in the service of the Yellow Emperor (Huangdi), who is reputed to have come up with the idea for a boat by watching a spider, blown onto a willow leaf by the autumn wind, drifting to safety at the edge of a pond, as recounted in the Noh play *Jinen-Koji* by Kan'ami (Kan'ami Kiyotsugu, also Kanze Kiyotsugu, 1333–84). Kan'ami was the father of Zeami Motokiyo; see 3, 540.

118

Hibiscus flowers
    A garland on the head of
        a naked youngster

hana mukuge / hadaka warawa no / kazashi kana

Autumn, 1680. Alludes to a waka by Yamabe no Akahito (fl. 724–36): *momoshiki no / ōmiyabito wa / itoma are ya / sakura kazashite / kyō mo kurashitsu* ("Those fine courtiers / in the hundred-fold palace / how leisurely they live / Again they have passed the day / cherry blossoms in their hair").

119

Secretly in the night
    in the moonlight a weevil
        bores into a chestnut

yoru hisokani / mushi wa gekka no / kuri o ugatsu

Autumn, 1680. In the Japanese lunar calendar, the autumn harvest moon
is known as *kuri meigetsu* ("the chestnut moon"). Reworks an image by
a Tang Dynasty poet known as Fu Wen: "night rain secretly penetrates
the rock-top moss," from a two-line poem (397) included in the *Wakan
rōei shū* ("Japanese and Chinese Poems to Sing," compiled by Fujiwara
no Kintō, c. 1013; see 122, 352) (Rimer and Chaves, p. 122). Bashō's
poetry had begun to move away from the Danrin style and was becom-
ing more influenced by Chinese poetry in both diction and theme.

120

My humble opinion
    Like so in the world below
        The end of autumn

guanzuru ni / meido mo kaku ya / aki no kure

Autumn, 1680. *aki no kure* can refer to "an autumn evening" or "the
evening of autumn" (meaning late autumn); see 121. *guanzuru ni* was a
measured, scholarly phrase common in annotated volumes.

121

On a leafless bough
　　the perching and pausing of a crow
　　　　The end of autumn

kareeda ni / karasu no tomarikeri / aki no kure

Autumn, 1680. This poem, one of Bashō's most celebrated, has prompted
vast amounts of commentary. "As a leader of the Danrin school Bashō
had been having a hard time, when Kigin [Kitamura Kigin, 1624–1705],
feeling sympathetic, came for a visit and had a talk with him and Sodō
[see 263, 317, etc.] over a cup of tea. The three masters discussed
possible ways in which to soften the excesses of the Danrin style, and in
the end Bashō was urged to take leadership in the matter. Thereupon he
wrote the crow poem, saying it might point in a new direction.—*Ritō*"
(Ueda, p. 57). "It was in Bashō's later years, and after he became more
confident in his art, that he said: 'Poetry of other schools is like a
colored painting. Poetry of my school should be written as if it were
black-ink painting.' Whatever led Bashō to such a position may have
had its origin in this poem.—*Seihō*" (Ueda, p. 59). For the influence of
Saigyō on this poem, see the note to 590. An earlier version reads:
kareeda ni / karasu no tomaritaru ya / aki no kure ("On a leafless bough
/ a crow is just now pausing and perching / The end of autumn").

122

Where the winter shower?
　　Umbrella dangling from his hand
　　　　the returning monk

izuku shigure / kasa o te ni sagete / kaeru sō

Winter, 1680. Alludes to a prose poem by the Chinese poet Chang Tu
(also Zhang Du, 833–89), a Tang era poet and politician known in Jap-
anese as Chōdoku, which Bashō also found in the *Wakan rōei shū*
(poem 403; Rimer and Chaves, p. 124); see 119.

123

After nine springs and autumns living a lonely, austere life in the city, I
have come to the banks of the Fukagawa. "From olden times, Chang-an
has been a place of fame and fortune and hard for a wayfarer poor and
empty-handed," so someone once said. I am impoverished, probably why
I know something of how he felt

To my brushwood door
        fallen tea leaves for my tea
            swept here by the storm

shiba no to ni / cha o konoha kaku / arashi kana

Winter, 1680. The quoted lines are from a poem by Bai Juyi (Po Chü-i,
or Bo Juyi, 772–846; see 164, 213, 458, 765), "Farewell to Hermit Zhang
on His Return to Songyang."

124

Is that the sound of
        cracking wood to make charcoal?
            Ono ax yonder

keshizumi ni / maki waru oto ka / Ono no oku

Winter, 1680. *Ono:* a place in northwest Kyoto noted for Onozumi
("Ono charcoal"), for which the word for "ax" (*ono*) is a homonym. In
the same way the word *oku* can mean both the interior or further
reaches of a territory (as in *Oku no Hosomichi*) and the back of an axe.

125

Ono charcoal-ink
        At handwriting a student
            scratching through ashes

Onozumi ya / tenarau hito no / haizeseri

Winter, 1680. *Onozumi*, see 124, the name of which also calls to mind
Ono no Tōfū, or Michikaze (894?–966), one of the three great calligra-
phers of Japan.

126

Feelings on a Cold Night in Fukagawa

The smacking of these oars upon the waves
    shivering through the stomach
        The nighttime these tears

ro no koe nami o utte / harawata kōru / yo ya namida

Winter, 1680. *Fukagawa:* on the banks of the Sumida River in Edo, to
where Bashō had moved; see headnote to 123. In the haibun *Kotsujiki
no Okina* ("An Old Beggarman"), Bashō prefaces this poem with lines
from Du Fu (see 159, 184, 485, 688): "From my window, I view the snow
of a thousand autumns on the western peaks, and by the gate the ships
waiting to sail toward the east." 10-7-5.

127

The wealthy dine on meat, vigorous youth on vegetable roots. I am poor.

The morning after snow
    I am on my own but able
        to munch dried salmon

yuki no ashita / hitori karazake o / kami etari

Winter, 1680. Based on a passage in the *Caigentan* ("Vegetable Root
Discourse," c. 1590) by the Ming Dynasty scholar Hong Zicheng (also,
Hong Yingming), in turn based on the words of the Sung master Wang
Xinmin (Wang Hsin-min): "If a man can chew the roots of vegetables
(*caigen*), he can do anything." See 830. 6-8-5.

128

The stones have dried up
    the waters shriveled away
        Nothing more winter

ishi karete / mizu shibomeru ya / fuyu mo nashi

Winter, 1680. A play on a phrase in Su Shi (1036–1101; see 160, 534,
797, 823): "water dried up, stones exposed."

129

The morning after
>   Nothing to fret over at
>   cherry blossom time

futsukaei / monokawa hana no / aru aida

Spring, year unknown. Poems 129–135 were written during the Enpō period (1673–81). *futsuka* (literally, "two days" or "second day"): a hangover.

130

The paper-pulp cat
>   even that realizes
>   this morning's autumn

harinuki no / neko mo shirunari / kesa no aki

Autumn, year unknown. Alludes to the Fujiwara no Toshiyuki poem mentioned in 79; see also 546.

131

Surely those lovers
>   in the stars use as a rug
>   the pelt of a deer

sazona hoshi / hijikimono ni wa / shika no kawa

Autumn, year unknown. *those lovers:* see 14, 98.

132

The mochi flowers
>   Ornaments for the hair of
>   long-tailed princess brides

mochibana ya / kazashi ni saseru / yome-ga-kimi

Spring, year unknown. *mochibana:* small pieces of *mochi* (rice cake) used to decorate willow branches at *shōgatsu* (the New Year holiday), to resemble flowers in bloom. *yome ga kimi* (*yome* means "bride" while *ga kimi* is an honorific attached to names): a euphemism for a rodent, used during *shōgatsu*.

133

The Musashino
　　moon a young shoot sprouting from the
　　　　seed of Matsushima

Musashino no / tsuki no wakabae ya / Matsushima-dane

Autumn, year unknown. *Musashino:* see 56. *Matsushima:* a group of
pine-covered islands in Miyagi prefecture; one of the *Three Views of
Japan,* the most famous scenic sights in the country; see 514.

134

Finally the pine
　　Hauled from the receding mistcover
　　　　with a heave a ho

matsu nare ya / kiri eisaraei to / hiku hodo ni

Autumn, year unknown.

135

The Pleasures of Spring at Ueno

Tipsy from the blossoms
　　the haori-wearing woman
　　　　sporting a curved sword

hana ni eeri / haori kite katana / sasu onna

Spring, year unknown. *haori:* a traditional kimono-style jacket; see 639,
705, 965. It was not customary for women to wear *haori.* 6-8-5.

136

New Year Morning, a Feeling in the Heart

Mochi cakes in my dreams
    And the interwoven fern fronds
      this grassy pillow

mochi o yume ni / orimusubu shida no / kusamakura

Spring, 1681. *Urajiro* (fern leaves) are placed under *kagami-mochi* (two round mochi cakes) as part of New Year decorations. For an auspicious *hatsuyume* (first dream of the year; see 330), a picture of the *Takarabune* (the Treasure Ship of the Seven Gods of Fortune; see 4) was placed under pillows before sleep. *kusamakura* (literally, "grass pillow"): an epithet for sleeping outdoors on a journey.

137

The icefish shoaling
    around seaweed would soon vanish
      pooled into my hands

mo ni sudaku / shirauo ya toraba / kienu beki

Spring, 1681. *shirauo* (literally, "whitefish"): an icefish that lives in the waters off China and Japan. Rather than the dense allusions of his earlier poetry, the poem focuses on an object, whitefish, and offers a haikai twist on conventional representations of evanescence.

138

Cherry blossoms in full bloom
    A hippety-hoppety monk
      a wife all flirty

sakarija hana ni / sozoro ukibōshi / numerizuma

Spring, 1681. *sozoro ukibōshi* ("hippety-hoppety monk"), a compound word of Bashō's invention.

139

The scallion fades before the scouring rush, the taro leaf is overcome by the lotus

The dew on mountain roses
      The nanohana
           makes a face almost grimaces

yamabuki no tsuyu / nanohana no / kakochigao naru ya

Spring, 1681. *nanohana*: a Japanese vegetable related to rapeseed. Both the *nanohana* and *yamabuki* ("mountain rose") are yellow in color. 7-5-8.

140

The pickers of tea leaves the
      tree-stripping autumn
          wind though unknowingly so

tsumi ken ya cha o / kogarashi no / aki to mo shirade

Spring, 1681. The picking of tea leaves in spring is, from the point of view of the tea plant, like the *kogarashi,* the "withering wind" of autumn/winter.

141

Rika offered me a bashō tree

The bashō planted
      Now I loathe the sprouting budlife
        of the common reed

bashō uete / mazu nikumu ogi no / futaba kana

Spring, 1681. *bashō: Musa basjoo,* the Japanese banana; *ogi: Miscanthus sacchariflorus,* a common reed. *Rika:* one of his favorite disciples; see 308, 468. Bashō so loved the banana tree, the leaves of which are torn easily in the wind, and became so associated with the tree at this hut, that his *haigō* (poetic pen name) changed from Tōsei; see 103. The wind rustling through the *ogi* is a figure prominent in Japanese classical poetry.

142

Beckon the cuckoo
　　the miscanthus plumes of the
　　　　ripening barley

hototogisu / maneku ka mugi no / muraobana

Summer, 1681. Bashō is here playing with a well-known expression found in waka poetry: "the miscanthus plumes beckon the cuckoo."

143

In the summer rains
　　the legs of the crane
　　　　growing shorter and shorter

samidare ni / tsuru no ashi / mijikaku nareri

Summer, 1681. Alludes to a passage in Zhuangzi: "The duck's legs are short, but to stretch them out would worry him, the crane's legs are long, but to cut them down would make him sad" (trans. Watson, *Zhuangzi,* p. 61). As if to emphasize the theme, the poem has a 5-5-7 syllable count.

144

Such idiocy!
　　In the dark to take a thorn
　　　　for what? A firefly?

gu ni kuraku / ibara o tsukamu / hotaru kana

Summer, 1681. In a manner typical of the Danrin style, Bashō depicts the behavior of a fool for allegorical ends, a device borrowed from Zhuangzi.

145

In the strangeness of the nighttime
a fox crawls along the earth
towards a melon

yami no yo to sugoku / kitsune shitabau / tamamakuwa

Summer, 1681. Another example of *ji-amari* ("excess characters") or
hachō ("broken meter"): the syllable count is 8-7-5. For the sexual over-
tones of Bashō's use of *makuwa* ("melon"), see 43.

146

The whiteness of the moonflowers
Into the nighttime outhouse
carrying a candle

yūgao no shiroku / yoru no kōka ni / shisoku torite

Summer, 1681. *yūgao:* see 10, 421. *kōka* ("hindhouse"): a Zen term for
an outhouse. With the inclusion of an outhouse alongside moonflowers
and a torch, the poem adds a haikai twist to elements taken from the
"Yūgao" chapter of *Genji Monogatari*.

147

In lonesomeness shine
Mr Lonesomemoongazer's
Nara gruel tune

wabite sume / Tsukiwabisai ga / Naracha uta

Autumn, 1681. *wabi:* a feeling akin to loneliness, particularly in relation
to nature, see note to 148. *sume* is the imperative form of the verb *sumu,*
which can mean both "to live" and "to be pure/clear." *Tsukiwabisai:* a
made-up name for himself ("Moon-wabi-sai"; see 114). *Naracha uta*
("*Naracha* song"): a phrase invented by Bashō to mean a song sung to
yourself while eating *Naracha,* a kind of rice gruel, with beans and
chestnuts, cooked in tea.

148

Alone in My Hut

Bashō leaves shred in the gale
rain drips into a basin
All night I listen

bashō nowaki shite / tarai ni ame o / kiku yo kana

Autumn, 1681. Ogata Tsutomu saw in this poem the founding of an
ideal of *wabi* in Bashō's poetry, an inner richness in the face of external
poverty. The bashō plant has large leaves that are easily torn in strong
wind, and in Chinese and Japanese poetry the plant's forlorn appear-
ance in autumn is a symbol of impermanence. In a different headnote
to the poem, Bashō explicitly relates the poem to Chinese poetry and
the motif of the poet alone in the evening listening to the wind and rain
tearing the leaves of the bashō. "As Bashō's references to Chinese recluse
poetry suggest, the speaker in Bashō's hokku hears not just the rain
outside but the evening rain found in the poetry of Tu Fu, Su Tung-p'o
(1037–1101), and other noted Chinese poets. Instead of listening to the
raindrops fall on the plantain [bashō] leaves, however, the recluse, in a
haikai twist, hears the sound of the rain falling into a "tub" (*tarai*), a
vernacular word that brings the world of the Chinese recluse down to
everyday, commoner life" (Shirane, *Traces*, p. 65). Su Tung-p'o (Su Shi):
see 128, 160, 534, 797, 823.

149

A mountain temple's
kettle screeching in the frost
The cold in that voice

hinzan no / kama shimo ni naku / koe samushi

Winter, 1681.

150

At This Hut I Need to Buy Water

The bitter taste of ice
    A mole moistening to quench
        the thirst in its throat

kōri nigaku / enso ga nodo o / uruoseri

Winter, 1681. Bashō uses the unusual Chinese word *enso* to refer to the small Japanese mole (*Mogera imaizumii*). Some translations mistakenly construe *enso* as a "sewer rat," but Bashō is invoking a passage in Zhuangzi concerning Yao, a legendary Chinese monarch who wanted to cede his kingdom to the recluse Xu You, to which Xu replies: "You are ruling all under heaven and everything is already in order. If I were to take your place now, would I be doing it for the name? A name is subordinate to the reality. Would I be a subordinate? A wren nests in the forest using no more than a branch. A mole drinks from the river taking no more than a bellyful. Please return and forget about this, my lord. I have no use with all that under heaven" (Richey, p. 188). Zhuangzi: see 143, 144, 163, 172, 173. The water in Fukagawa (see 123, 126) was not potable, so residents had to buy it from water-sellers who came by boat.

151

The end of year ends
    Mochi-pounding echoing
        into lonesome sleep

kure kurete / mochi o kodama no / wabine kana

Winter, 1681. *Mochi-pounding:* at New Year rice is pounded using mallets to produce *mochi* for rice cakes and *ozoni* (a soup with *mochi* eaten at New Year).

152

Ume and willow
   A lithesome young man maybe
      Maybe a woman

ume yanagi / sazo wakashu kana / onna kana

Spring, 1682. *wakashu:* a boy between the ages of eleven and sixteen, before *genpuku* (the coming-of-age ceremony), slang for a homosexual boy; see 49.

153

Jōshi

They're muddying up their sleeves
   the collectors of mud-snails
      time to spare no more

sode yogosuran / tanishi no ama no / hima o na mi

Spring, 1682. *Jōshi:* March 3, also Girls' Day; the day when the tide is at its lowest (see 72), and so the best time for clam-digging at the seashore. Bashō is comparing farmers collecting mud-snails in rice fields (*tanishi no ama*) to actual *ama* (fishermen) by the shore.

154

A debonair young valet
   beating around the blossoms
      chants a Come-All-Ye

en naru yakko / imayō hana ni / Rōsai su

Spring, 1682. *yakko:* a male servant charged with the care of his master's straw sandals. *Rōsai:* a form of semi-improvised song popular in the Edo period. Bashō is playing on *Rōsai* and the phrase *rōei-su* ("to chant"); *imayō:* modern, contemporary, fashionable, trendy; and *imayō-uta:* a form of song popular from the eleventh to the thirteenth century. 7-7-5.

155

A globefish in snow
       Left side the winner
               the sliced carp of Midsummer

yuki no fuku / hidari kachi / minazuki no koi

Summer, year unknown. In *ku-awase,* a hokku verse contest between
poets, the pairs were divided into "Left" and "Right," with a judge decid-
ing the winner. *minazuki:* the traditional name for the Sixth Month in
the Japanese lunar calendar; see 524, 706, 763. The dish referred to is *koi
no arai,* thinly sliced raw *koi* (carp), often served cool or iced.

156

Responding to Kikaku's Knotweed and Firefly Poem

At morning glories
       gawping munching on boiled rice
               That's the man I am

asagao ni / ware wa meshi kū / otoko kana

Autumn, 1682. *Kikaku:* Takarai Kikaku, also known as Enomoto
Kikaku (1661–1707), a disciple of Bashō, see 299, 759. Kikaku's poem:
kusa no to ni / ware wa tade kū / hotaru kana ("At the grassy door / I am
as a firefly / munching on knotweed"). Kikaku is alluding to the proverb
tade kū mushi mo suki zuki ("Some worms choose to feed on knot-
weed"), which means something akin to "there's no accounting for
taste." "In answer to Kikaku, who said he enjoyed night and preferred a
bitter taste, Bashō stated that he could not live that kind of abnormal
life, that he was an ordinary man who slept at night, awoke early in the
morning, and took a plain meal instead of liquor. His statement has
a savage, biting sarcasm. Even someone like Kikaku must have been
nonplussed.—*Ebara*" (Ueda, p. 81).

157

The moon at crescent
    A morning glory at nighttime
        the bud readying

mikazuki ya / asagao no yūbe / tsubomuran

Autumn, 1682. 5-8-5.

158

The moon of the Fourteenth night
    Tonight I'm a thirty-nine-year-old
        juvenile

tsuki jūyokka / koyoi sanjūku no / warabe

Autumn, 1682. Reworks a passage in *The Analects* of Confucius: "At fifteen I set my heart on learning; at thirty I took my stand; at forty I came to be free from doubts; at fifty I understood the Decree of Heaven; at sixty my ear was attuned; at seventy I followed my heart's desire without overstepping the line" (Confucius, trans. D. C. Lau, p. 63). 7-9-3.

159

Remembering Du Fu

With his beard blowing in the wind
    and lamenting the late autumn
        Whose child is this?

hige kaze o fuite / boshū tanzuru wa / ta ga ko zo

Autumn, 1682. The poem derives from a line in Du Fu (also Tu Fu, 712–70): "Whose child / Propped on a goosefoot cane lamenting this world?" "K'Uei-Chou's Highest Tower" (Hinton, p. 75). In David R. McCraw's rendering, "With goosefoot cane, sighing the world—who are you, fellow?" (McCraw, p. 43). See 126, 184, 485.

160

Tilting his hat, Su Shi would look at the cloudy heavens, and Du Fu, his hat covered in snow, would rove far and wide. In this grass hut I have time, and so with my own hands have made a rainproof hat out of paper, imitating the hat Saigyō wore in his lonely wanderings

> To live is to fall
> > away as Sōgi says
> > > of a rain shelter

yo ni furu mo / sarani Sōgi no / yadori kana

Miscellaneous (no season), 1682. *Sōgi:* Iio Sōgi (1421–1502), a renga (linked-verse) poet admired by Bashō; see 345, 583. Bashō substitutes one word, *shigure* ("winter shower"), with Sōgi's name in this poem by Sōgi: *yo ni furu mo / sarani shigure no / yadori kana.* Sōgi (and Bashō) pun on the word *furu,* which means both "to fall (rain/snow, etc.)" and "to pass time." *Su Shi* (also Su Tung-p'o; see 128, 148, 534, 797, 823): one of the most eminent figures in Chinese classical literature, often depicted admiring a snow scene in Chinese and Japanese art, wearing a traveler's hat, riding a donkey. *Du Fu:* see 126, 159, 184, 485, 688. *Saigyō:* see 197, 198.

161

> The weight of these bedclothes
> > In the skies of Wu the snow
> > > will be seen and soon

yogi wa omoshi / Go-ten ni yuki o / miru aran

Winter, 1682. *Go-ten:* the skies (*ten*) of Wu, an ancient Chinese state during the Western Zhou Dynasty and Spring and Autumn period, corresponding roughly to modern Jiangsu. The poem plays on lines from the Chinese poet Ka Shi: "My hat is heavy with snow, under the skies of Wu."

162

At New Year

New Year's Day today
    The lonesome remembering
        of autumn's evening

ganjitsu ya / omoeba sabishi / aki no kure

Spring, 1683. Bashō's cultivation of ambiguity can give rise to conflict-
ing interpretations: "The hokku's last two phrases indicate that the poet
made a distinction between the loneliness of the New Year and that of
late autumn. It is quiet on New Year's Day [after the hustle and bustle of
the end of the year], but there is something happy in that quietness.—
Shūson"; "The hokku's middle phrase implies, not that New Year's Day
is lonely, but that late autumn is lonely. [. . .] As a contrast to the gaiety
and liveliness of New Year's Day, he thought of a late autumn day and
felt that that was what human life was all about. He wrote this hokku to
give form to that feeling.—*Komiya*" (Ueda, p. 87).

163

Is the bush warbler
    the slumbering soul within
        the comely willow?

uguisu o / tama ni nemuru ka / taoyanagi

Spring, 1683. Bashō alludes to Zhuangzi's dream (see 172) but in haikai
manner changes the butterfly into a bush warbler. *taoyanagi* ("comely wil-
low") is Bashō's coinage, derived from *taoyame* ("gentle/demure lady").

164

Only when in sorrow do we know the holy power of sake
Only when we become poor do we realize the godlike power of wealth

Amid the flowers flush
    The whiteness of my sake
        the dark of my rice

hana ni ukiyo / waga sake shiroku / meshi kuroshi

Spring, 1683. The headnote quotes two lines from "Recommending Wine" (in Chinese, with Japanese reading) by Bai Juyi (Po Chü-i; see 123, 213, 458, 525, 765): *Ureitewa masani sake no hijiri o shiri / hinshitewa hajimete zeni no kami o satoru* (see also 389).

165

Cuckoo O cuckoo
    By January ume
        already blooming

hototogisu / mutsuki wa ume no / hana sakeri

Summer, 1683. *mutsuki* ("month of harmony"): the First Month of the lunar calendar, a traditional name for January. *Ume* is the harbinger of spring, *hototogisu* (cuckoo), the harbinger of summer. See 12 for the traditional impatience of Japanese poets awaiting the cuckoo.

166

I will hear clearly now
    my ears cleansed by burning incense
        the cuckoo calling

kiyoku kikan / mimi ni kō taite / hototogisu

Summer, 1683. In Japanese, the verb *kiku* ("to hear") rather than *kagu* ("to smell") is used of incense. Bashō also plays on a Chinese poem which says that only the purified of heart can truly appreciate the delicate scent of incense.

167

The mulberry's fruit
  A flowerless butterfly's
    wine for a hermit

kuwa no mi ya / hana naki chō no / yosutezake

Summer, 1683. Mulberry wine is called *sōchinshu.* The word *sōmon* ("mulberry gate") is a euphemism for a Buddhist priest and could also be read as *yosute-bito* ("person who has abandoned the world"). In the word *yosutezake,* Bashō has changed *bito* ("person") to *zake* (sake).

168

These bluegreen crackers
  ear-like from kusamochi
    exfoliating

aozashi ya / kusamochi no ho ni / idetsuran

Summer, 1683. *kusamochi* ("grass mochi"): a dish eaten in spring, made from mochi (see 151) and Japanese mugwort; see 265, 759.

169

A Painting

That monk in the hat on horseback, where is he from, where is he going? The painter says it's a portrait of me on my journey. Well then, poor horseman of the Three Realms, mind now you don't fall off

The horse ambling along
  I see me in a picture
    a moor in summer

uma bokuboku / ware o e ni miru / natsuno kana

Summer, 1683. The poem was not inspired by seeing a picture; the head-note, in fact, was inscribed on a painting at a later date than the poem. *the Three Realms:* in Buddhist cosmology, corresponding to the world of desire, the world of form and the world of formlessness. *bokuboku* (sometimes *hokuhoku*): onomatopoeia for the sound of a horse's hooves, as in clip-clop in English, though here it connotes a slow, quiet movement.

170

In Bashō-an Again after Being Rebuilt

Listening to the hail
> This body now as before
> > an old deadleafed oak

arare kiku ya / kono mi wa moto no / furugashiwa

Winter, 1683. The original Bashō-an (hut) had been destroyed by fire in January 1683; the new dwelling was built through donations from his disciples and friends in the autumn and winter of 1683. The oak referred to is the *Quercus dentata,* known as the daimyo oak, or Japanese emperor oak. Though deciduous, dead leaves are retained on the tree into winter.

171

See how the cuckoo
> has colored the bonito
> > At least so it looks

hototogisu / katsuo o some ni / keri kerashi

Summer, year unknown (171 through 185 were written during the *Tenna* period, 1681–84). For another reference to the cuckoo shedding "tears of blood," see 11.

172

Rise and shine rise and shine
> I want to make you my friend
> > sleeping butterfly

okiyo okiyo / waga tomo ni sen / nuru kochō

Spring, year unknown (*Tenna*). Zhuangzi (Chuang Tzu) dreamt he was a butterfly, and after he awoke was not sure whether he was a man dreaming he was a butterfly or a butterfly dreaming it was a man. See 163, 173, 630.

173

Seeing an Image of Zhuangzi

Butterfly Butterfly
> Would I could ask you
>> about Chinese poetry

chō yo chō yo / morokoshi no / haikai towan

Spring, year unknown (*Tenna*). *Zhuangzi*: Zhuang Zhou, also Chuang Tzu, fourth-century-BCE Taoist. Another version of the poem reads: *morokoshi no / haikai towan / tobu kochō* ("About the poems / of China I'd like to ask / flying butterfly"). *morokoshi*: an old word for China, which can be found in the *Nihon Shoki* ("The Chronicles of Japan"), the second oldest book of Japanese history (after the *Kojiki*), completed in the eighth century. 6-5-7. Handwritten on his own drawing.

174

By a Morning Glory, Sleep Talking

Ought there be laughter ought there be tears
> seeing my morning glory
>> withering away

warau beshi naku beshi / waga asagao no / shibomu toki

Autumn, year unknown (*Tenna*). 9-7-5.

175

The Bravery of the Bindweed

In the midst of the snow
the bindweed unwithering
the light of the sun

yuki no naka wa / hirugao karenu / hikage kana

Summer, year unknown (*Tenna*). *hirugao* ("noon face"): Japanese bind-
weed, *Calystegia japonica;* see 422, 423. Based on a *Ch'an* (Zen) poem
found in the *Zenrin kushū* ("Zen Forest Anthology"), a compilation of
writings used in the Rinzai sect of Zen: "The bashō in the snow / The
picture painted by Mojie / Ume under the burning sun / The poem
composed by Chen Yuyi." Mojie was the courtesy name of the poet and
painter Wang Wei (701–61), whose painting (now lost) of "Yuan An
Lying in Bed after a Snowfall" initiated the motif of the "bashō [banana
plant] in snow" as emblem of resilience. Chen Yuyi (1090–1138), poet
and politician during the Song Dynasty.

176

By the bindweed blooms
a rice huller cooling off
The pity in that

hirugao ni / kome tsuki suzumu / aware nari

Summer, year unknown (*Tenna*). The original poem, titled "The Lowli-
ness of the Moonflower" [moonflower: *yūgao;* see 10, 146], read: *yūgao
ni / kome tsuki yasumu / aware kana* ("By the moonflowers / a rice
huller takes a rest / The pity in that"). Bashō changed *yūgao* to *hirugao*
(see 175) and *yasumu* ("to take a rest") to *suzumu* ("to cool off").

177

White chrysanthemum white chrysanthemum
      with the shamelessly long hair
          with straggly long hair

shiragiku yo shiragiku yo / haji nagakami yo / nagakami yo

Autumn, year unknown (*Tenna*). Based on a line in passage 7 of *The Tsurezuregusa* ("Essays in Idleness") of Yoshida Kenkō (c. 1283–c. 1350; see 303, 713, 714, 927, 980): "The longer you live, the greater your share of shame" (McKinney, p. 24). 10-7-5.

178

Cat Mountain

The Cat of the Mount
      licking and licking the snow
          from its crevices

yama wa neko / neburite iku ya / yuki no hima

Spring, year unknown (*Tenna*). The Japanese title is "Nekoyama" ("Cat Mountain"), but the place is actually called Nekomagadake, the western peak of Mount Bandai.

179

The Doorway

Upon the inn door
      on the tablet be announced
          cuckoo yon cuckoo

to no kuchi ni / yadofuda nanore / hototogisu

Summer, year unknown (*Tenna*). The title in Japanese, "To no Kuchi," means "doorway" but was also the name of a pier on the shores of Lake Inawashiro. When a member of the nobility stayed at an officially sanctioned inn, a tablet bearing the noble's name was put on the door indicating the dignitary's presence.

180

Ogashima

1

With a flick of fin
    skipjack move closer still to
        the Isle of Oga

2

Fluttering her scarf
    the doe approaches the stag
        on Oga Island

hire furite / mejika mo yoru ya / Oga no Shima

Autumn, year unknown (*Tenna*). Ogashima: *Oga:* stag; *shima:* island.
The poem is an example of Bashō's use of double-meaning wordplay:
hire, written in hiragana script in the original, can mean either a fin or
a lady's decorative neck scarf of the Nara and Heian periods; *mejika,*
again written in hiragana script, can mean a young tuna or skipjack fish,
or a female deer. Deer wave the white underside of their tails to indicate
readiness to mate.

181

Kuromori

So now Black Forest
    who will be calling you that
        this snowy morning?

kuromori o / nani to iu tomo / kesa no yuki

Winter, year unknown (*Tenna*). *Kuromori* ("black forest"): there are
many forests with this name in northern Honshū, and the one consid-
ered the most likely source of this poem is near Sakata, in Yamagata
Prefecture.

182

All these white poppies
    the blossoming flowers of
        a winter shower

shirageshi ya / shigure no hana no / sakitsuran

Summer, year unknown (*Tenna*).

183

Nowadays cuckoo
    nary a haiku master
        in the world for you

hototogisu / ima wa haikaishi / naki yo kana

Summer, year unknown (*Tenna*). *haikaishi:* a professional poet who performed the role of master at renga (linked-verse) gatherings. Interpretations of the poem vary: no poet could make a poem to rival the cuckoo's song in beauty; before the beauty of the cuckoo's song poetry falls silent.

184

Ishikawa Hokukon's young brother, Santen, came here to tear me from my idleness with rice and parsley. The same parsley, perhaps, as that grown on the banks of the Qing ni Fang mentioned in that poem by Du Fu, and now I realize the value of his simple, elegant taste

Is it for my sake
    the crane has left half-eaten
        rice mixed with parsley?

waga tame ka / tsuru haminokosu / seri no meshi

Spring, year unknown (*Tenna*). Both Ishikawa Hokukon and his brother Santen are unknown. *Du Fu:* see 126, 159, 160, 485, 688.

185

In Grief for Senpū

I've come and offered
    tubers instead of lotus
        Lookalikes they say

tamukekeri / imo wa hachisu ni / ni taru tote

Autumn, year unknown (*Tenna*). *Senpū:* Sugiyama Senpū, the father of
Bashō's chief benefactor and noted poet, Sanpū (1647–1732); see 304.
imo: a general name for potato-like vegetables, for instance, *sato-imo*
(taro) or *satsuma-imo* (sweet potato). *hachisu: Nelumbo nucifera,* the
lotus, symbol of the Western Pure Land in Buddhism. Lotus leaves were
used as plates for food offerings at the graves of the dead. In offering the
leaves of the *imo* rather than the lotus leaves they resemble, Bashō may
be alluding to similarities between father and son, as in their names.

186

The spring arising
    In a new year the old rice
        about five shō

haru tatsu ya / shinnen furuki / kome goshō

Spring, 1684. Written on February 16, New Year's Day in the lunar cal-
endar in 1684. *shō:* a unit of volume, about 1.8 litres; see 688. The
expression *go shō* ("five shō"), or sometimes *go to* ("five to"), meant "just
the right amount" (*to* is a measure equivalent to ten *shō*); see 779.

187

Asakusa, at Chiri's House

The elegance of
    seaweed soup arrayed in an
        Asagi-wan bowl

norijiru no / tegiwa misekeri / asagiwan

Spring, 1684. *Asakusa:* an area in Edo (and modern Tokyo); *Chiri:* Nae-
mura Chiri (1648–1716), a disciple of Bashō, and companion for the ini-
tial part of the seven-month journey recounted in *Nozarashi Kikō* ("The
Journey of Weather-Exposed Bones"); see 190, 202. *nori* ("seaweed"): see
187. *asagi-wan:* a lacquered bowl decorated with flowers and birds.

188

Bunrin sent me an image of Shussan Shaka, and I placed it on an altar

Praise be to Buddha
        On a pedestal of grass
            in the cooling air

namo hotoke / kusa no utena mo / suzushi kare

Summer, 1684. *Bunrin:* Torii Bunrin, a disciple who presented Bashō
with a statue of *Shussan* (or *Shutsuzan*) *Shaka:* "Buddha coming forth
from the mountains," a scene from the historical Buddha's life depicted
often in Zen art. Before he died, Bashō gave the statue to Shikō (see
432, 751).

189

If you don't forget
        Sayo no Nakayama
            take the cool air there

wasurezuba / Sayo no Nakayama / nite suzume

Summer, 1684. *Sayo no Nakayama:* see 63; Bashō is reminding his
friend, Fūbaku, who was setting off on a journey to Ise, of poem 63.

190

*It was autumn, the Eighth Month of the first year of Jōkyō, as I set out
from my tumbledown hut by the river the sound of the wind was chilling*

Old bones in a field
    Into the mind on the wind
        into the body

nozarashi o / kokoro ni kaze no / shimu mi kana

Autumn, 1684. *Jōkyō*: name for the period from February 1684 to September 1688. This is the opening of Bashō's travelogue *Nozarashi Kikō* ("The Journey of Weather-Exposed Bones"), the first of his four major journeys. Bashō set out from Edo in September 1684 and traveled along the Tōkaidō road, from Edo to Ise and Kyoto, then along the southern shore of Lake Biwa, returning to Edo by the Kiso mountains route the following year.

191

Ten autumns it's been
    Now I think of Tokyo
        when I talk of home

aki totose / kaette Edo o / sasu kokyō

Autumn, 1684. In fact, it was Bashō's thirteenth year living in Edo, but Bashō is alluding to a poem by Jia Dao (779–843; see 715) that uses the phrase "ten frosts." Written as he was setting out from Edo to journey to his actual hometown in Iga. *kaette* can mean "rather, instead, on the contrary" but also "having returned"; *sasu* can mean "refer to something" and also "head for somewhere."

192

*The day I crossed the Barrier, it was raining and the mountains were
hidden by clouds*

A mist-rain in Fall
    A no-sign-of-Fuji day
        Glamoured and gladdened

kirishigure / Fuji o minu hi zo / omoshiroki

Autumn, 1684. *the Barrier*: the government checkpoint at Hakone. For barriers, see 210.

193

The clouds and the mist
    And a hundred scenes created
        moment to moment

kumo kiri no / zanji hyakkei o / tsukushikeri

Autumn, 1684.

194

You who listen to monkeys
    To this waif in the autumn
        wind what would you say?

saru o kiku hito / sutego ni aki no / kaze ikani

Autumn, 1684. Written in 7-7-5, *jiamari* ("hypermeter," a number of syllables in excess of the standard). The poem has given rise to a great deal of commentary: "Bashō here saw a deserted child crying in the autumn wind; he did not hear a monkey's cry. Yet, during the phase of his career that immediately preceded the present journey, he had shown a great deal of interest in Chinese poetry. It was natural that his grief at hearing the child's cry at this time should remind him of a shrieking monkey. And to Tu Fu [Du Fu], Li Po [Li Bai], Po Chü-i [Bai Juyi], and all the other poets who had been so touched by a monkey's cry, he asked, almost in protest, which of the two cries would sound more pathetic. In other words, he contrasted his genuine pity for the deserted child with the imaginary grief that Japanese poets put into their poems about the monkey's cry. It also meant that he became aware of a conflict within himself, a conflict between the spirit of *fūga* [poetic elegance], which he had hitherto cherished, and the humane feeling of pity aroused by the sight of an abandoned child.—*Yamamoto*"; "In later years Bashō said: 'My *fūga* is like a fireplace in summer and a fan in winter.' He was alluding, with both modesty and pride, to the power-lessness of poetry in the practical sphere of life. The germ of that idea is already seen in this hokku.—*Imoto*" (Ueda, pp. 103–4). In Chinese legend, homesick travelers passing through the Three Gorges region of the Yangtze River weep at the third cry of the monkeys on the cliffs. *sutego* (abandoned children) were not a rare sight in a period of Japanese history when famine was common; see 87.

195

On Horseback

Along a byroad
    the hibiscus meets my horse
        chomping and chewing

michi no be no / mukuge wa uma ni / kuwarekeri

Autumn, 1684. *mukuge: Hibiscus syriacus*, occasionally translated as rose
mallow, or rose of Sharon. This poem has given rise to a great deal of
commentary, particularly around its relation to Zen; see Ueda, pp. 105–7.

196

*In a lingering dream of Du Mu's "Early Departure," as I arrived at Sayo
no Nakayama I wakened with a start*

On horseback sleeping
    The dregs of dreams the far-off moon
        smoke from the tea stoves

uma ni nete / zanmu tsuki tōshi / cha no keburi

Autumn, 1684. *Du Mu* (also Tu Mu, 803–52): a poet of the late Tang
dynasty. The poem Bashō refers to, in Sam Hamill's translation: "My
quirt dangles freely. / I trust my horse // Traveling mile after mile /
without as much as a cock crow, // dozing off as I / pass through the
woods, / I wake with a start / when leaves begin to fly" (Hamill, p. 201).

197

As night fell, I visited the Outer Shrine. Here and there in the dim darkness around the first torii sacred lanterns were visible. The "pine wind from the peak" pierced me through, filling me with awe

> The end of the month moonless
> > Cedars a thousand years old
> > > embraced by the storm

misoka tsuki nashi / chitose no sugi o / daku arashi

Autumn, 1684. The Outer Shrine at Ise is worshipped as a moon deity. *torii:* the gate that marks the entrance to a Shinto shrine. In the headnote Bashō is referring to a poem by Saigyō (see 198): *fukaku irite / kamiji no oku o / tazunureba / mata ue mo naki / mine no matsukaze* ("I made my way into / the deeps of Mount Kamiji / searching everywhere / and high above everything / pine wind from the mountain peak"). Kamiji is the name of the mountain at the Grand Shrine of Ise; see 374. Another interpretation of lines 2 and 3 reads Bashō as embracing one of the cedars.

198

At the bottom of Saigyō Valley there is a stream. I gazed at women cleaning potatoes

> You women scrubbing potatoes
> > if Saigyō were here
> > > there'd be poetry

imo arau onna / Saigyō naraba / uta yoman

Autumn, 1684. *Saigyō* (Satō Norikiyo, 1118–90): a poet Bashō admired greatly, and on his journeys he visited places associated with Saigyō's poems (see 585). *Saigyō Valley:* considered to refer to Uji in Ise, where Saigyō is said to have built a hermitage (see 591 for the other area in Ise purported to be the location of Saigyō's hut). The poem is based on the story of *Eguchi no Kimi,* in which Tae, a prostitute from Eguchi, Osaka, refuses Saigyō shelter during a storm but relents after he composes a poem of protest. There are differing interpretations of the poem: in one reading, it is Saigyō who would compose a poem; in the other, the women; and in a third reading, poems are exchanged between them.

199

When I dropped in at a tea-house, a woman called Chō (Butterfly) asked me for a poem mentioning her name. She produced a piece of white silk on which I wrote

> The scent of orchid
>> On Lady Butterfly's wings
>>> a hint of incense

ran no ka ya / chō no tsubasa ni / takimono su

Autumn, 1684. *takimono su:* the practice of scenting robes. Bashō's disciple Dohō (see 231, 243, 288, 615, 683, 895), in *Sanzōshi,* relates that the woman handed Bashō paper rather than silk.

200

Visiting the hut of a hermit

> The creeping ivy
>> and four or five bamboo stalks
>>> gathering the storm

tsuta uete / take shi go hon no / arashi kana

Autumn, 1684. A greeting poem to his host, Roboku of Ise, who at one time may have been a professional haikai poet and had retired into seclusion. tsuta (ivy) is an autumn season word indicating *tsuta-momiji* (russet-tinged ivy).

201

At the beginning of the Ninth Month, I went back home. The grass by my mother's room had withered in the frost, and everything had changed. The locks at the sides of my brother's and sisters' heads were white and there were wrinkles around their eyes. "We are still alive," was all we could say. My older brother opened the relic pouch and said, "Pay your respects to Mother's white hair. Like Urashima Tarō with his jeweled box, your brow has aged." For a little while, we wept

> If held in my hands it would melt
> > from the hot touch of teardrops
> > > the frost of autumn

te ni toraba kien / namida zo atsuki / aki no shimo

Autumn, 1684. Bashō had an older brother and four sisters. After saving a turtle, the fisherman Urashima Tarō was invited to *Ryūgu-jō* (the Dragon Palace; see 72, 76) by the Princess Otohime. Upon leaving, after a number of days of being fed and entertained, he was given a Tamate-bako (a jeweled treasure box) with the warning to never open it. When he returned home, his parents had died and there was no one now he recognized. Ignoring the princess's instructions, he opened the box, whereupon a white puff of smoke escaped and he was transformed into a white-haired old man; see 89. 8-7-5.

202

Continuing our journey into Yamato, we came to a place called Take-no-uchi in Katsuge District. This was Chiri's native village, so we rested our feet here a few days

> The willowing bow
> > The sweet sound of the biwa
> > > deep in the bamboo

watayumi ya / biwa ni nagusamu / take no oku

Autumn, 1684. *Yamato:* a province corresponding to present-day Nara prefecture. *watayumi:* a bow-like apparatus to make cotton yarn; *biwa:* see 213; *Chiri:* see 187.

203

Visiting Futakamiyama Taimadera, we saw a pine tree about a thousand years old in the temple's precincts. It was large enough to hide oxen, as in Zhuangzi's story. Though said to be devoid of sense and feeling, it was still fortunate for this tree that, under the protection of the Buddha, it had avoided the woodcutter's axe

> Priests and morning glories
>> how many the redyings?
>>> The Law and the pine

sō asagao / iku shinikaeru / nori no matsu

Autumn, 1684. *Futakamiyama Taimadera:* Taimadera, a temple on Mount Nijō, a mountain with twin peaks known locally as *Futakamiyama* ("twin mountain") and worshipped as a gateway to heaven. *nori:* the Law of Nature in Zhuangzi's Taoist philosophy, "dharma" in Buddhism; see 287, 530, 791. In Zhuangzi's story the tree was an oak so large that it could cover thousands of oxen, and had lived long because it served no purpose, illustrating thus the usefulness of the useless. *Zhuangzi:* see 163, 172, 173.

204

> The house that knows no
>> winter resounds with the hail
>>> of the rice hulling

fuyu shira nu / yado ya momi suru / oto arare

Autumn, 1684. The poem features at the end of a text sometimes known as *Momi suru oto* ("The Sound of Hulling Rice"), in which Bashō praises the sensitivity and care for his mother of a prosperous man in the mountain village of Nagao, in the province of Yamato.

205

Lodging for the night at a temple hostel

> Now pound upon that cloth
> to let me listen to the sound
> wife of the temple

kinuta uchite / ware ni kikaseyo ya / bō ga tsuma

Autumn, 1684. *kinuta:* a "fulling block"; see 55. By Bashō's day a method of smoothing out and softening clothes associated with the distant past, and in the poetic tradition a sound (of the wooden mallet striking the clothes on the block) evoking loneliness. 6-8-5.

206

The site of Saigyō's thatched hut was a few hundred yards to the right of the Inner Cloister, reached along a barely trodden woodcutter's path. Facing the opposite hillside across a steep gorge, the view was stunning. The "clear, dripping water" trickles down even now, seeming unchanged from of old

> The dew drip-drops drip-drops
> I would this transitory world
> rinse out if I could

tsuyu toku toku / kokoromi ni ukiyo / susugabaya

Autumn, 1684. Bashō quotes from a poem attributed to Saigyō: *tokutoku to / otsuru iwama no / koke shimizu / kumihosu hodo mo / naki sumai kana* ("Drop by drop dripping / On down through the mossy rocks / the clear spring water / yet still enough to draw from / for this life as a hermit").

207

Paying Respects at the Tomb of the Emperor Go-Daigo

The emperor's tomb grown old
>   What is it you have endured
>   yon enduring ferns?

gobyō toshi hete / shinobu wa nani o / shinobugusa

Autumn, 1684. Emperor Go-Daigo (1288–1339) overthrew the
Kamakura shogunate in 1333 and established the Kenmu Imperial Res-
toration, the last time an emperor had any political power until the
Meiji Restoration in 1868, but in turn was overthrown by Ashikaga
Takauji in 1336. The emperor died in the mountains of Yoshino, and his
mausoleum is located in the hills behind Nyoirin-ji Temple, Nara. The
Tokugawa government did not support the maintenance of the struc-
tures in Yoshino. *shinobu* means both a fern (*Davallia mariesii*, squir-
rel's foot fern) and "to recall" or "to endure"; see 221. 7-7-5.

208

*Late autumn, wanting to see the changing colors of the cherry trees, I
entered the mountains of Yoshino, but my feet were sore from my straw
sandals so I stopped and stood, leaning on my walking stick awhile*

The cherry trees' leaves
>   falling so lightly upon
>   my hinoki hat

konoha chiru / sakura wa karoshi / hinokigasa

Autumn, 1684. *hinoki*: a kind of cypress, *Chamaecyparis obtusa. hinoki-
gasa*: a hat made from strips of cypress; see 214.

209

Beyond Imasu and Yamanaka, I came to the grave of Lady Tokiwa.
Moritake of Ise once wrote "the autumn wind resembles Yoshitomo" and
I wondered what the resemblance was he found. And I too wrote

'Twas Yoshitomo's
heart and mind resembled so
the wind in autumn

Yoshitomo no / kokoro ni nitari / aki no kaze

Autumn, 1684. *Yoshitomo:* Minamoto no Yoshitomo (1123–60), head of
the Minamoto clan and father of Yoritomo (1147–99), the first shogun
of the Kamakura shogunate, and Yoshitsune (1159–89), one of the most
legendary figures in all of Japanese history. *Lady Tokiwa:* Yoshitomo's
mistress, and Yoshitsune's mother. Captured by Taira no Kiyomori (see
694), she was forced to be his concubine in exchange for the safety of
her children. She is also known as "Hotoke Gozen" ("Lady Buddha").
Moritake of Ise: Arakida Moritake (1473–1549), a waka, renga, and
haikai poet who, at sixty-nine, became head priest of the Inner Ise
Shrine; see 249.

210

Fuwa

Now the autumn wind
through the thickets and the fields
The Gate at Fuwa

aki kaze ya / yabu mo hatake mo / Fuwa no seki

Autumn, 1684. *Fuwa no seki:* the Barrier of Fuwa, at Sekigahara-chō,
Gifu, about 4 km from Imasu, abandoned in the eighth century. The
barriers were government checkpoints along the main highways. Seki-
gahara was the site of a major battle, in 1600. The allusion is to a waka
by Fujiwara no Yoshitsune (see 87): *hito sumanu / Fuwa no sekiya no /
itabisashi / arenishi nochi wa / tada aki no kaze* ("Nobody lives here / At
the Fuwa Barrier / the eaves made of wood / all fallen into decay / all
except the autumn wind").

211

At the Grave of Tomonaga in the Province of Mino

Buried under moss
the world of the ivy of
the Nembutsu chant

koke uzumu / tsuta no utsutsu no / nebutsu kana

Autumn, 1684. *Tomonaga:* Minamoto no Tomonaga (1144–60), the second son of Yoshitomo. Following their defeat in the Heiji Rebellion of 1159, Yoshitomo fled with Tomonaga and his two brothers, Yoshihira and Yoritomo. In the most well-known version of events, the wounded Tomonaga asked his father to kill him so he would not fall into enemy hands. Yoshitomo (see 209) was killed shortly after, in Owari. *nebutsu:* the Nembutsu (also transliterated *nenbutsu*) prayer in Pure Land Buddhism entails the ritual incantation of the name of Amida Buddha (Amitābha); see 973.

212

When I set off from Musashino, my mind foresaw weather-exposed bones in a field, and now . . .

Dying not yet done
after all this journey's nights
the end of autumn

shini mo senu / tabine no hate yo / aki no kure

Autumn, 1684. *Musashino:* see 56. Written at the house of Bokuin (see 215). He had originally planned this to be the end of the journey recounted in *Nozarashi Kikō. aki no kure* can mean either "autumn evening" or "the end of autumn."

213

"Song of the Biwa"
  in the night the shamisen
    a downpour of hail

Biwakō no / yo ya shamisen no / oto arare

Winter, 1684. *Song of the Biwa*: a poem by Bai Juyi (Po Chü-i; see 123, 164), also known as "Song of the Lute," which Ezra Pound used in an early version of Canto II. The *biwa* (called the *pipa* in China) and *shamisen* are stringed musical instruments. Bashō's poem reworks a line of Bai Juyi: "The big strings plang-planged like swift-falling rain." See Watson, *Po Chü-i,* p. 79.

214

Ceremonious
  the sound of hailstones upon
    my hinoki hat

ikameshiki / oto ya arare no / hinoki-gasa

Winter, 1684. *hinoki-gasa* ("hinoki hat"): see 208.

215

The scribbles at the sacred oratory of Tado Gongen Shrine at Ise. The aged Bashō, hermit-owner of the Hakusendō cottage at Fukugawa in Bushū, and Tani Bokuin, master of Kansuiken at Ōgaki, Nōshū, poem-vendors, on a journey to Ise and Owari, offer to you these poems of the four seasons

> The Ise poets'
> > poems we would rescue from
> > > the River of Leaves (Bokuin)

Isebito no / hokku sukuwan / ochibagawa

> *In Disgust at the Scribbles Mentioned Above*

> Warden of the shrine
> > sweep my name away into
> > > the River of Leaves

miyamori yo / waga na o chirase / konohagawa

Winter, 1684. *Hakusendō* ("Hall of Moored Boats"): the old name for the Bashō-an in Fukugawa, taken from one of Bashō's previous pseudonyms and based on a poem of the same name by Du Fu (see 126, 159, 160, 184). *Bushū:* another name for the province of Musashi. *Tani Bokuin:* Bokuin (1646–1725), of Ōgaki, was a wealthy shipper; see 212, 584.

216

> *At Hontō-ji in Kuwana*

> Winter peonies
> > and the plovers over there
> > > cuckoos of the snow

fuyubotan / chidori yo yuki no / hototogisu

Winter, 1684. *Hontō-ji:* Hontō Temple. *botan:* peony; see 798, 853.

217

In the darkness before dawn, I went out along the shore

> The light of sunrise
>> A whitefish's iciness
>>> its oneinchness of white

akebono ya / shirauo shiroki / koto issun

Winter, 1684. Written on the beach at Kuwana. 5-7-6. Toyama Susumu identifies an allusion to lines by Du Fu (see 126, 159), translated by Burton Watson as "White-little, one among the teeming species, / Heaven-destined two-inch fish" (Watson, *Du Fu*, p. 149).

218

After a good time at Kuwana, I have come to Atsuta

> To have a good time
>> and to angle for globefish
>>> seven ri I've come

asobi kinu / fuku tsurikanete / shichi ri made

Winter, 1684. *ri:* a unit of distance, about 4 km; see 66. In the legend of Urashima Tarō (see 72, 76, 89, 201), he went fishing and enjoyed it so much he did not return for seven days.

219

The owner of the house, Tōyō, because his kindness was not small, I've decided to stay with him a while

> Into this ocean
>> I'll throw away my sandals
>>> Cold rain on my hat

kono umi ni / waranji suten / kasashigure

Winter, 1684. *Tōyō:* Hayashi Tōyō (?–1712), a leading figure in haikai circles in Atsuta. Bashō stayed at his home twice; see 254.

220

Seeing a Traveler

And even a horse
    lingering on in the eyes
        this snowy morning

uma o sae / nagamuru yuki no / ashita kana

Winter, 1684. Composed at Tōyō-tei ("Tōyō's house") in Atsuta, as with
219, as a gesture of thanks.

221

Paying Respects at Atsuta Shrine

The fernstalks withered
    The mochi cakes I have bought
        at a wayside inn

shinobu sae / karete mochi kau / yadori kana

Winter, 1684. As in 207, as well as meaning "fern," *shinobu* has connota-
tions of longing and endurance. Atsuta Shrine had long been dilapi-
dated by the time of Bashō's visit.

222

Caught in a Shower on the Road

Hatless so I am
    and under a winter shower
        Sure that's how it goes

kasa mo naki / ware o shigururu ka / ko wa nanto

Winter, 1684. In an earlier version of the poem, the last line is *nan to
nan to* ("what's what"). 5-8-5.

223

My hat had been worn through by the rains on my long journey, and my paper coat had creased and crumpled in the storms along the way. I looked such a state even I looked on myself as a wretched vagabond. I suddenly recalled that many years ago a kyōka *writer of talent had visited this province, and so I wrote*

1

With witty waka in the wind
    I must look a little like
        Chikusai now

2

Comic Verse

The withering wind
    makes me look a little like
        Chikusai now

(kyōku) kogarashi no / mi wa Chikusai ni / nitaru kana

Winter, 1684. *Chikusai:* a poor, quack doctor in a comic novel story of the time who sets off for Edo, making up *kyōka* (a comic style of waka) as he makes his way. Like Bashō here, he arrives in Nagoya with his clothes in tatters. It is a well-known crux in Bashō studies whether the word *kyōku* ("comic, or mad, verse") is the title or part of the poem proper.

224

The grassy pillow
    that dog getting rained upon too?
        The bark of the night

kusamakura / inu mo shigururu ka / yoru no koe

Winter, 1684. *kusamakura:* a conventional poeticism for a journey; see 136, 250, 541, 622.

225

Walking to View the Snow

Yo marketgoers
    I will sell you this straw hat
        a snow umbrella

ichibito yo / kono kasa urō / yuki no kasa

Winter, 1684. *kasa* appears twice in the poem and can mean both hat and umbrella. Composed at the home of a man named Hōgetsu, a haikai poet in Nagoya.

226

Snow against the snow
    On this December evening
        harvest of the moon?

yuki to yuki / koyoi shiwasu no / meigetsu ka

Winter, 1684. Written at a renga gathering at the house of Tokoku (see 252, 328–32, 379), as a way of mediating a disagreement between two members.

227

All Day by the Sea

The sea has darkened
    A mallard calling
        a whiteness I barely hear

umi kurete / kamo no koe / honoka ni shiroshi

Winter, 1684. Written at Atsuta. 5-5-7.

228

Taking off my straw sandals here, putting down my walking stick there,
I spent the days and nights on my journey until the year came to a close

> The end of the year
>> Wearing a hat still wearing
>> a pair of sandals

toshi kurenu / kasa kite waraji / haki nagara

Winter, 1684. "This poem can be said to condense Bashō's entire life.—
Higuchi" (Ueda, p. 125).

229

Welcoming the New Year at My Native Place

> Whose bridegroom is this
>> bearing mochi cakes on ferns?
>> The Year of the Ox

ta ga muko zo / shida ni mochi ou / ushi no toshi

Spring, 1685. It was the custom in Bashō's home province, Iga, for a new
bridegroom to bring a rice cake decorated with fern leaves on the back
of an ox to his bride's parents at New Year. In the Chinese zodiacal sys-
tem, 1685 was a Year of the Ox.

230

> This Day of the Rat
>> I will go to Kyoto
>> Would I had a friend

nenohi shi ni / Miyako e ikan / tomo mogana

Spring, 1685. *nenohi:* the Feast of the Day of the Rat, a custom begun
among the Heian aristocracy, by Bashō's day an outing on the first zodi-
acal "rat" day of the year to pick pine seedlings (a symbol of longevity)
and wild young greens.

231

A wandering crow's
      old nest now turning into
          blossoms of ume

tabigarasu / furusu wa ume ni / narini keri

Spring, 1685. *tabigarasu* ("wandering crow"), an epithet for a bird of
passage, a wanderer, or stranger. Dohō (see 199, 243, 895) relates that
the poem was composed when Bashō saw a screen with a painting of
ume blossoms and a crow at the house of his host, Sakuei, an old friend
in Iga who had become prosperous. *ume:* in this poem (and in 841 and
964) Bashō wrote hiragana characters for *ume* that can also be read as
mume, though in Bashō's time these characters were still actually pro-
nounced *ume.*

232

On the Road to Nara

So spring's really come
      The mountains nameless within
          diaphanous mist

haru nare ya / na mo naki yama no / usugasumi

Spring, 1685. In its not naming of the mountains, the poem is consid-
ered to exemplify haikai, in contrast to classical waka's celebration of
famous mountains.

233

Retreat at Nigatsu-dō

O-mizutori
      The icy sound of the monks
          their wooden sandals

mizutori ya / kōri no sō no / kutsu no oto

Spring, 1685. *O-mizutori:* the Water-Drawing Ceremony, a Buddhist
rite held annually, in March, at Tōdai-ji, Nara. *Nigatsu-dō:* "The Hall of
the Second Month," one of the main halls at Tōdai-ji.

234

In Kazuraki at Takenouchi there lived a man. He took good care of his family, took on workers to plough his fields in spring and to harvest the rice in autumn. His house was filled with the scent of apricot flowers, which boosted and consoled sorrowful poets. In summer with irises, in autumn it goes with chrysanthemums, this sake could compare to even Jidō's dewdrops

The first of springtime
      The aroma of selling
          ume-tinged sake

shoshun mazu / sake ni ume uru / nioi kana

Spring, 1685. In the Noh play *Makura-Jidō*, Jidō copies verses from a sutra onto a chrysanthemum leaf and the dew that forms there becomes an immortal elixir; see 57, 108, 552.

235

At Takenouchi, the House of One Branch

Let scent fill the world
      On a single ume branch
          the contented wren

yo ni nioe / baika isshi no / misosazai

Spring, 1685. "The wren builds its nest in the dense forest, but needs only one branch" (Zhuangzi). *Isshi-ken* ("The House of One Branch") was the pseudonym of Bashō's host, the doctor Akashi Genzui.

236

Ume Grove

I went to Kyoto, to visit the mountain villa of Mitsui Shūfū at Narutaki

White ume blossoms
>Yesterday did someone steal
>>the crane from the field?

ume shiroshi / kinō ya tsuru o / nusumareshi

Spring, 1685. *Mitsui Shūfū* (1646–1717): a wealthy merchant and patron of poetry, compared in this poem to the Chinese recluse, Lin Hejing (also Lin Bu, 967–1028), a poet of the Northern Song dynasty, who amused himself by planting ume and feeding cranes.

237

How the ring-cupped oak
>pays no heed to the blossoms
>>What a way to be

kashi no ki no / hana ni kamawanu / sugata kana

Spring, 1685. Written at Mitsui Shūfū's mountain villa in the Narutaki area of Kyoto, where Bashō stayed for several weeks; see 236.

238

Meeting the Priest Ninkō at Fushimi-Saigan-ji

Drip down on my robes
>a dribble of dewdrops from
>>Fushimi peaches

waga kinu ni / Fushimi no momo no / shizuku seyo

Spring, 1685. *Ninkō:* Ninkō Shōnin (Saint Ninkō, 1606–86), the third head priest at Fushimi Saigan Temple, Kyoto, and also a poet. In the fable by Tao Yuanming (Enmei in Japanese; see 458, 803), "Peach Blossom Spring" is a utopian abode where people live in idyllic harmony with nature, oblivious to the outside world. Fushimi was noted for its peach groves, and the dew from its peaches was said to confer good health.

239

Along the Mountain Road to Ōtsu

On a mountain path
    what a wonderful something
      A wild violet

yamaji kite / nani yara yukashi / sumiregusa

Spring, 1685. *sumiregusa:* wild violet; see 793.

240

A View of the Lake

The Karasaki
    pine more so than the blossoms
      hidden in the haze

Karasaki no / matsu wa hana yori / oboro nite

Spring, 1685. *Karasaki:* on the western shores of Lake Biwa, famous in poetry for a pine tree that inspired many waka poets. The cherry blossoms on nearby Mount Nagara had also inspired poetry. Bashō alludes to a waka poem by the emperor Go-Toba (1180–1239): *karasaki no / matsu no midori mo / oboro nite / hana yori tsuzuku / haru no akebono* ("At Karasaki / the greenness of the pine tree / hidden in the haze / beyond even the blossoms / in the dawn on a spring day"). Masaoka Shiki (1867–1902), in his essay "Bashō Zatsudan" ("Conversations about Bashō"), accused Bashō of "a worse crime than plagiarism."

241

Stopping to Eat at a Roadside Shop

In the shade of a pail
    of azaleas
        a woman tearing salted cod

tsutsuji ikete / sono kage ni / hidara saku onna

Spring, 1685. "This might appear to be a purely descriptive poem, which is rare for Bashō. But the flowers are azaleas, and the fish is a dried codfish. These images create a rustic, *wabi*-type impression. It is likely that Bashō wanted to produce that mood of *wabi* here rather than write a merely descriptive poem.—*Ebara*" (Ueda, p. 132). 6-5-8.

242

Journey Poem

In the colza field
  making hanami faces
    a host of sparrows

nabatake ni / hanamigao naru / suzume kana

Spring, 1685. *nabatake* (*na*: "colza"; batake: "field"): *Brassica campestris*, Chinese colza, a plant of the mustard family, similar to rape or rapeseed.

243

At Minakuchi, I met a friend again after twenty years

In the midst of our own two
  lives lives the flowering life
    of the cherry tree

inochi futatsu no / naka ni ikitaru / sakura kana

Spring, 1685. *a friend*: Dohō (Hattori Dohō, 1657–1730) of Iga Ueno, a disciple who wrote *Sanzōshi* (1702), one of the principal sources of information about Bashō's life; see 199, 231, 288, 615, 683, 895. In this poem of friendship, Bashō draws on imagery of the interlinked lives of parent and child from the Noh play *Shichikiochi* ("Seven Warriors in Flight").

244

A View of Narumigata

Even the headway
  of a boat at times pauses
    Peach blooms on the beach

funa ashi mo / yasumu toki ari / hama no momo

Spring, 1685. *Narumigata*: Narumi Bay, a smaller inlet within Ise Bay, Owari; see 322, 323, 335, 438.

245

A Sunlit Field

A lone butterfly
    aflutter over a field
        over its shadow

chō no tobu / bakari nonaka no / hikage kana

Spring, 1685. *chō* (butterfly) can be either singular or plural; *hikage* can mean "sunlight" or "shadow in the sun." A more literal rendering: "Only butterflies / aflutter over a field / in the bright sunlight."

246

Rabbit-ear iris
    stirs in me an idea
        another *hokku*

kakitsubata / ware ni hokku no / omoi ari

Summer, 1685. Based on the word-game waka from *Ise Monogatari* mentioned in the note to 403.

247

On a Fan with a Picture of a Birdcatching Rod

The birdcatcher too
    sets aside his bamboo rod
        seeing the cuckoo

torisashi mo / sao ya suteken / hototogisu

Summer, 1685.

248

On a portrait of a monk with his back turned is written: "With my back to the secular world I have lived, now I've come to a mountain village in the black robes of a priest. Drawn and written by the ascetic, Bansai." I think of him and his ways with a kind of nostalgia

> With a folding fan
>> I'll send air to the man with
>>> his back to the world

uchiwa mote / aogan hito no / ushiromuki

Summer, 1685. *Bansai:* Katō Bansai (1621–74), a poet and scholar, who produced annotated editions of Sei Shōnagon and Kenkō, among others.

249

These venerable three were gifted with great poetic talent and expressed the heart in poems of eternal value. Whoever loves their poems, honors poetry

> Of moon and flowers
>> behold these the truly great
>>> the poet masters

tsuki hana no / kore ya makoto no / aruji tachi

No season, 1685. *These venerable three:* Matsunaga Teitoku (1571–1654), see 970; Yamazaki Sōkan (c. 1465–c. 1553), see 413; Arakida Moritake, see 209.

250

A monk from Hiru-ga-kojima in Izu, on pilgrimage alone since last autumn, heard tell of me and has come to Owari to join my journey

> So together now
>> let's graze on ears of barley
>>> on pillows of grass

iza tomo ni / homugi kurawan / kusamakura

Summer, 1685. *A monk:* Rotsū (Inbe Rotsū, 1649–1738), one of Bashō's most eccentric followers (see 471, 605, 622); *kusamakura* ("grass pillow"): a poetic epithet for travel; see 136, 224, 541, 622.

251

The Abbot of Engaku-ji, Daiten, passed away early in the First Month. Although I could scarcely believe it, I sent on word from the road to Kikaku

Longing for ume
    I bow to the deutzia
        with eyes full of tears

ume koite / unohana ogamu / namida kana

Summer, 1685. *Daiten* (1629–85): the 164th Abbot of Engaku-ji. *Kikaku:* see 156, 814. When Bashō composed the poem (in the Fourth Month) the *unohana* (deutzia) was in bloom; the ume blooms in the First Month.

252

Given to Tokoku

From a white poppy
    a torn wing the butterfly's
        remember-me-by

shirageshi ni / hane mogu chō no / katami kana

Summer, 1685. A farewell present to *Tokoku:* Tsuboi Tokoku (d. 1690), a favorite disciple of Bashō's, a merchant from Nagoya who died around the age of 30; see 226, 328–32, 379.

253

I'll arise and go
    to Kiso to April of
        the cherry blossoms

omoitatsu / Kiso ya shigatsu no / sakuragari

Summer, 1685. *Kiso:* the name of a river and mountainous area in central Japan. Because of the altitude, the cherry trees bloom later.

254

I stayed with Tōyō again, and now I set out for the east

> From the depths of a peony
>   a bee crawling out letting go
>   hesitatingly

botan shibe fukaku / wake izuru hachi no / nagori kana

Summer, 1685. *Tōyō:* see 219, 220. *botan* ("tree peony"), sometimes called *fūkigusa,* the "plant of wealth"; see 216, 798, 853. Another example of *hachō* ("broken meter"): the syllable count is 8-8-5, emphasizing the sorrow of parting from a friend.

255

Stopping a While in the Mountains of Kai

> The journeying horse
>   taking comfort in barley
>   A traveler's rest

yuku koma no / mugi ni nagusamu / yadori kana

Summer, 1685. *Kai:* Kai Province, the area now known as Yamanashi Prefecture. In legend, Prince Shotoku rode a horse called the *Kai no Kurokoma* ("the Black Horse of Kai") to the top of Mount Fuji.

256

In the Mountains of Kai

> The poor woodcutter
>   ever buttoning his lip
>   The mouth-high cleavers

yamagatsu no / otogai tozuru / mugura kana

Summer, 1685. *mugura:* cleavers, or bedstraw (*Galium spurium var. echinospermon*), a tall wild plant. On his way to Edo, Bashō met a woodcutter who didn't reply when asked a question.

257

At the end of the Fourth Month, I arrived back at my hut and recuper-
ated from my long journey

> From my summer robes
>> I still haven't quite done with
>>> picking out the hoppers

natsugoromo / imada shirami o / tori tsukusazu

Summer, 1685. The concluding poem in *Nozarashi Kikō*.

258

> Clouds now and now again
>> offering people a break
>>> from viewing the moon

kumo oriori / hito o yasumeru / tsukimi kana

Autumn, 1685. Alludes to a waka by Saigyō: *nakanaka ni / tokidoki
kumo no / kakaru koso / tsuki o motenasu / kazari narikere* ("The clouds
appearing / now and every so often / to cover it up / enhance the beauty
of the / moon, provide embellishment").

259

Three people living in Reiganjima came to my thatched hut late at night.
They happened to all have the same name: Shichirobei. I recalled Li Bai's
poem about drinking alone and playfully wrote

> In my sake cup
>> the three names I'll be drinking
>>> this moonlit evening

sakazuki ni / mitsu no na o nomu / koyoi kana

Autumn, 1685. *Li Bai's poem:* "Drinking Alone with the Moon": "I take
my wine jug out among the flowers / to drink alone, without friends. //
I raise my cup to entice the moon. / That, and my shadow, make us
three" (Hamill, p. 83). Li Bai (also Li Po, 701–62); see 194, 383, 538.

260

Eating what I've been given, what was begged for, surviving without starving till the end of the year

> Soon I will be included
>> among the fortunate ones
>>> The end of old age

medetaki hito no / kazu ni mo iran / oi no kure

Winter, 1685. At that time forty was considered the beginning of old age; Bashō, now in his forty-second year, had ceased being a *tenja,* one who commented on poems for a fee, and was dependent on his disciples. He rejected that former life, despite the hardships the decision entailed, saying: "It is better to become a beggar [than a *tenja*]" (Shirane, p. 319).

261

> How many the frosts
>> testing the mettle of my
>>> New Year plantain-pine

ikushimo ni / kokorobase o no / matsu kazari

Spring, 1686. The poem puns on Bashō's name: just as matsu *kazari* (the pine decoration placed on doors at New Year) suggests Matsuo, so *kokoro*base o suggests the older way of writing Bashō.

262

> An old patch of land
>> nazuna a-gathering
>>> a clatter of men

furuhata ya / nazuna tsumi yuku / otoko domo

Spring, 1686. *nazuna:* shepherd's purses. *nanakusa gayu* ("Seven Herb Rice Porridge," which includes nazuna) is eaten on January 7; see 263, 354, 789, 840. *nazuna tsumi* ("nazuna a-gathering"): the poem is playing on the traditional image of the aristocratic spring outing called *wakaba tsumi* ("gathering young leaves").

263

When I look closer
    I see nazuna blooming
        underneath the hedge

yoku mireba / nazuna hana saku / kakine kana

Spring, 1686. Based on a line in "Impromptu on an Autumn Day" by
Cheng Hao (also Cheng Mingdao, 1032–85), as reflected also in the
postscript to his friend Sodō's "Minomushi no setsu" ("Comment on
the Bagworm," 1687), where Bashō writes: "When in quiet we reflect, we
see everything is self-at-ease." See 317.

264

Is Mafukuda
    wearing that hakama now?
        A field horsetail shoot

Mafukuda ga / hakama yosou ka / tsukuzukushi

Spring, 1686. *Mafukuda*: Mafukudamaru, in *Konjaku Monogatari*
("Tales of the Distant Past"), a page who decides to become a monk, so
impressing the daughter of the family she makes him a pair of *hakama*
(a trouser-like pleated garment worn over a kimono). *tsukuzukushi*: the
fertile shoots of a field horsetail (*Equisetum arvense*); the top of the
shoot reminds Bashō of the shaved head of a monk and the lower part
the pleats of a *hakama*.

265

I am in bed sick
    no way I'll stomach mochi
        The blooming peach trees

wazuraeba / mochi o mo kuwazu / momo no hana

Spring, 1686. *mochi*: Bashō intends *kusamochi* (a sweet made of mochi
and Japanese mugwort; see 168, 759), which is eaten on *Hinamatsuri*
(March 3; see 93), a time when peach trees bloom.

266

The rooftiles of the
    Kannon visible among
        the clouds of blossoms

Kannon no / iraka miyaritsu / hana no kumo

Spring, 1686. *Kannon:* the Kannon Temple at Asakusa, Tokyo, known officially as Sensō-ji, visible across the Sumida River from Bashō's hut in Fukagawa; see 123, 294.

267

    Impromptu, On the Twentieth of the Third Month

The flowers blooming
    And a crane seen seven days
        where the hill rises

hana sakite / nanuka tsuru miru / fumoto kana

Spring, 1686. Cherry trees bloom for about seven days, and a crane is said to stay for seven days where it has alighted.

268

On the occasion of my neighbor, the priest Sōha, leaving his hut on a journey

The old nest emptied
    How lonely it will be now
        the next-door neighbor's

furusu tada / aware narubeki / tonari kana

Spring, 1686.

269

Mourning the Priest Tandō

Falling to the ground
    coming closer to the roots
        the flower's farewell

chi ni taore / ne ni yori hana no / wakare kana

Spring, 1686. When a flower dies, it is said "to return to its roots"; see also 687.

270

An olden pond now
    A songfrog springs off into
        the sound of water

furuike ya / kawazu tobikomu / mizu no oto

Spring, 1686. Bashō's most celebrated poem, and the single most famous poem in Japanese literature. There have been countless versions of the poem in English. Another possible translation: "An ancient pond now / A songfrog takes off into / the sound of water." *kawazu*: the kajika frog or Buerger's frog (*Buergeria buergeri*), a species endemic to Japan. The name *kajika* (literally, "river deer") comes from its cry, which is said to resemble the belling of a buck (*Ojika*).

271

The east and the west
    the melancholy all one
        the autumnal wind

higashi nishi / awaresa hitotsu / aki no kaze

Autumn, 1686.

272

The autumn full moon
　　　round and round the pond I walked
　　　　　all the nighttime through

meigetsu ya / ike o megurite / yomosugara

Autumn, 1686. In this year the full moon was on October 2.

273

"One of the blind ones?"
　　　how other people see me
　　　　　when viewing the moon

zatō ka to / hito ni mirarete / tsukimi kana

Autumn, 1686. *zatō*: a member of a guild of blind men who worked as
musicians, masseurs, and acupuncturists. Like Buddhist monks, and
like Bashō, they shaved their heads.

274

With the only thing
　　　I possess my life is light
　　　　　This hisago gourd

mono hitotsu / waga yo wa karoki / hisago kana

Autumn, 1686. *hisago*: a hollowed-out gourd used as a container;
see 10.

275

Heading off somewhere, I passed the night in a boat. At sunrise, raising my head from the rush mat cover, I saw a beautiful waning moon

> The dawn coming on
> > On the twenty-seventh too
> > > see a crescent moon

akeyukuya / nijūshichiya mo / mika no tsuki

Autumn, 1686. *nijūshichiya*: the twenty-seventh night of the lunar calendar; *mika no tsuki*: the moon of the third night of the lunar calendar, a crescent moon; see 157, 434, 767, 813.

276

A Deserted Garden

> The withering of flowers
> > the sorrow in the shedding
> > > of the grass's seed

hana mina karete / aware o kobosu / kusa no tane

Autumn, 1686.

277

The Priest Genki gave me a gift of sake, so I sent this in reply

> The water so cold
> > to lie down to sleep so hard
> > > and for a seagull

mizu samuku / neiri kane taru / kamome kana

Winter, 1686.

278

Cold Night

A water jar cracks
  in the ice of the nighttime
   in bed awoken

kame waruru / yoru no kōri no / nezame kana

Winter, 1686.

279

*Wanting to see the first snow of the year from my hut, many times
in vain I rushed back there whenever the skies clouded over. On the
eighteenth of the Twelfth Month, snow finally began to fall and I was
overjoyed*

First snow of the year
  what happiness to be here
   in my own small hut

hatsuyuki ya / saiwai an ni / makariaru

Winter, 1686.

280

First snow of the year
  The leaves of the narcissus
   beginning to bend

hatsuyuki ya / suisen no ha no / tawamu made

Winter, 1686. Bashō emphasizes the leaves rather than the flowers of
the narcissus. In the painting Bashō did to accompany this poem, the
narcissus flowers are white.

281

A Snowy Night in Fukagawa

I'm drinking sake
　　incapable now of sleep
　　　　at nighttime the snow

sake nomeba / itodo nerarene / yoru no yuki

Winter, 1686. A famous conundrum: is Bashō being kept awake by the alcohol, by the loveliness of the scene, or some inner turmoil?

282

A man named Sora has made temporary residence near my hut, and we visit each other often. When I cook, he helps feed the fire; at night when I make tea, he breaks ice for water. By nature a man who likes quiet and solitude, he has become a dear friend. One evening, after a snowfall, he dropped by

Friend of mine make the fire
　　I will show you something great
　　　　a snowball this big

kimi hi o take / yokimono misen / yukimaruge

Winter, 1686. *Sora:* Kawai Sora (also Sōgorō, 1649–1710), who later accompanied Bashō on the journey recounted in *Oku no Hosomichi* ("The Narrow Road to the Interior"); see 471, 557, 587, 705, 797. 6-7-5.

283

The sheen of the moon
　　in December see Shiro
　　　　awaken again

tsuki shiroki / shiwasu wa Shiro ga / nezame kana

Winter, 1686. *Shiro:* Zilu (also Zhong You, 542–480 BCE), one of most accomplished and well-known disciples of Confucius. He was noted for his valor and died in battle. His name in Japanese is a homonym for white (*shiro*).

284

The year-end bazaar
  Couldn't I get up and go
    and buy some incense?

toshi no ichi / senkō kai ni / idebaya na

Winter, 1686. Incense sticks were a relatively new product in Bashō's time, having come into Japan from China in the mid-sixteenth century, with domestic production beginning in the mid-seventeenth century.

285

Writing "moon" and "snow"
  how I have indulged myself
    the end of the year

tsuki yuki to / nosabari kerashi / toshi no kure

Winter, 1686.

286

Who is this person
  What form has "I" taken on
    this New Year morning?

tare yara ga / katachi ni nitari / kesa no haru

Spring, 1687. Bashō had received a *shōgatsu kosode* (a kimono for the New Year) from his Edo disciple Ransetsu (Hattori Ransetsu, 1654–1707; see 309, 749, 759), and was delighted but felt awkward wearing such a fine garment.

287

Old and Weary

Rather than oysters
sheets of nori you should sell
when you get older

kaki yori wa / nori o ba oi no / uri mo se de

Spring, 1687. *nori:* thin sheets of edible dried seaweed; see 187, 690. Bashō is also playing on the meaning of *nori* as law (dharma); see 203, 530, 791. The poem is a joke on the stimulation provided by oysters. Life expectancy in the Edo period was about fifty; Bashō was forty-four when he wrote this poem.

288

Village Ume

Kids of the village
don't break every ume branch
Goad sticks for cattle

sato no ko yo / ume orinokose / ushi no muchi

Spring, 1687. In *Sanzōshi* ("Three Booklets"), compiled by Dohō after his death, Bashō says that in the past cattle sticks made from ume were prized by literary people.

289

When I went to visit my friend at his hut, he was not there. The old care-taker told me he had gone off to a temple. The ume tree by the fence was in bloom, and I said, "They are like the master of the house." The man said, "They belong to his neighbor"

My friend's not at home
even the ume blossoms
belong to next door

rusu ni kite / ume sae yoso no / kakiho kana

Spring, 1687.

290

Try not to forget
        in the midst of the thicket
            the ume blossoms

wasuruna yo / yabu no naka naru / ume no hana

Spring, 1687. The original first line read *mata mo toe* ("please visit again") in the version in the text sometimes known as "Plum in a Thicket," in which a monk Bashō had met the previous year comes to visit him. The poem is a parting gift.

291

All Things are Self-at-Ease

Flitting among flowers
        don't gobble up the horsefly
            Sparrows you are friends

hana ni asobu / abu na kurai so / tomosuzume

Spring, 1687. The title alludes to Cheng Hao's "Impromptu on an Autumn Day"; see 263, 295, 317. *tomosuzume* means "a flock of sparrows"; Bashō is literalizing the meaning of *tomo* ("friend").

292

The nests of white storks
        visible through the blossoms
            the cherry tree's leaves

kō no su mo / miraruru hana no / hagoshi kana

Spring, 1687.

293

A Mountain Cottage

By the white stork's nest
        beyond the reaches of storm
            the cherry blossoms

kō no su ni / arashi no hoka no / sakura kana

Spring, 1687.

294

My Thatched Hut

A cloud of blossoms
          That tolling from Ueno?
                    from Asakusa?

hana no kumo / kane wa Ueno ka / Asakusa ka

Spring, 1687. *Ueno, Asakusa:* districts of Edo still so-named in contemporary Tokyo. Each district contains a large temple. See 266.

295

Even a long day
          can never be long enough
                    for the skylark's song

nagaki hi mo / saezuri taranu / hibari kana

Spring, 1687.

296

Above the meadow
          clinging to nothing at all
                    a skylark calling

haranaka ya / mono ni mo tsukazu / naku hibari

Spring, 1687. Written on the same day as 295.

297

On Hearing Someone Talk of the History of the Temple

At Kasadera
    an Unleaking Grotto too
      in the springtime rain

Kasadera ya / moranu iwaya mo / haru no ame

Spring, 1687. *Kasadera:* Kasadera Kannon, also known as Ryūfuku-ji ("hat-covering temple") in Nagoya, part of the Owari Thirty-three Kannon temples in Aichi Prefecture. Legend says that the temple was once so dilapidated a woman offered her hat (*kasa*) to cover the Buddha's head from the rain leaking through its roof. After making a fortune, the woman later donated funds for a new building. *moranu iwaya* ("unleaking grotto"): Bashō derives this phrase from poems by Gyōson (1055/57–1135) and Saigyō. The "Unleaking Grotto" is on Mount Kunimi, a place sacred to the Shugendō sect of ascetic Buddhism.

298

A cuckoo flying
    calling flying and calling
      busybodily

hototogisu / naku naku tobu zo / isogawashi

Summer, 1687.

299

Go-shichi-nichi, the Memorial

Deutzia flowers
    In a house with no mother
      drearsomely blooming

unohana mo / haha naki yado zo / susamajiki

Summer, 1687. *Go-shichi-nichi:* the thirty-fifth day after someone's death. The memorial was for Kikaku's mother, Myōmuni, who had died aged fifty-seven. Kikaku; see 156, 251, 299.

300

Tsuyu

Rainy season rains
    the hoop on the bucket cracks
      the voice of the night

samidare ya / oke no wa kiruru / yoru no koe

Summer, 1687. *Tsuyu:* the rainy season; see 8. *samidare:* see 7.

301

Self-Portrait of a Miserable Man

My hair growing out
    a blue pallor to my face
      the long summer rains

kami haete / yōgan aoshi / satsukiame

Summer, 1687. *yōgan aoshi* ("a blue pallor to my face"): "a Japanese translation of an idiom used in Chinese poetry—*Handa*" (Ueda, p. 158).

302

Rainy season rains
    the floating nest of the grebe
      I'll go and visit

samidare ni / nio no ukisu o / mi ni yukan

Summer, 1687. One text of the poem has the headnote "To Lord Rosen," which refers to Naitō Yoshihide (1655–1733), whose pen name was Rosen ("Dew Wet"). He was the son of Naitō Yoshimune (1619–85), known as Fūko ("Wind Tiger"), both of whom were keen patrons of haikai (see 952). *nio:* the little grebe; Lake Biwa was known as *Nio no Umi* ("the Sea of the Little Grebe"), see 623, 677; a grebe's nest is made from waterweeds and floats on the water. "What the poem embodies is not the lukewarm *fūryū* of a bystander who would stay home and write an imaginary poem on a grebe's nest. The spirit of *fūkyō*—and of haikai—lies in going out in the rain and not minding if one gets soaked.—*Imoto*" (Ueda, p. 160).

303

Bonito seller
> who is it now you're going
> > to intoxicate?

katsuouri / ikanaru hito o / yowasu ran

Summer, 1687. Based on passage 119 in *The Tsurezuregusa* of Kenkō:
"The fish called 'bonito' [*katsuo*] is the finest caught in the seas around
Kamakura, and is much prized nowadays. An old man in Kamakura
told me, 'This fish was never served to the elite until the time we were
young. Even the servants wouldn't eat the head, but cut it off and threw
it away.' In these decadent times, such things have penetrated even to
the upper echelons" (McKinney, p. 79); see 117, 713, 714, 927, 980.
Drunkenness was said to be caused by poison, and the bonito thought
to be poisonous, but by Bashō's day people no longer believed these
things and the bonito was a popular dish.

304

My disciple Sanpū sent me a hemp kimono as a summer gift

Now I am attired
> in a well-fitting garment
> > cicada-patterned

ide ya ware / yoki nuno kitari / semigoromo

Summer, 1687. *Sanpū*: Bashō's chief benefactor, a wealthy fishmonger;
see 185, 459. *hemp kimono: katabira;* see 22, 947.

305

Coolness

I'd drunkenly sleep
> among these fringed pinks blooming
> > my pillow a stone

youte nen / nadeshiko sakeru / ishi no ue

Summer, 1687. *nadeshiko* ("fringed pinks") are often found by riverbanks
and hence are also known as *kawaranadeshiko* (*kawara:* "riverside").

306

This man had gone into seclusion; I visited his old hut, overgrown with cleavers

> Dear melon-grower
> > would you were here this evening
> > > in the cooling breeze

uri tsukuru / kimi ga are na to / yūsuzumi

Summer, 1687. Based on a poem by Saigyō: *matsu ga ne no / Iwata no kishi no / yūsuzumi / kimi ga are na to / omohoyuru kana* ("By the pine tree's roots / by the Iwata river's / cool evening breezes / O how I wish you were here / that is what I am thinking").

307

> A small river crab
> > creepy-crawling up my leg
> > > in the clear water

sazaregani / ashi hainoboru / shimizu kana

Summer, 1687.

308

Given to Rika

> A flash of lightning
> > grasped by the hand in the dark
> > > a paper candle

inazuma o / te ni toru yami no / shisoku kana

Autumn, 1687. *Rika:* one of Bashō's most talented disciples, who had given him the bashō tree from which he took his name; see 141, 468.

309

Ransetsu painted a morning glory, and asked would I write a poem about it

A morning glory
            even one painted poorly
                        blossoms with feeling

asagao wa / heta no kaku sae / aware nari

Autumn, 1687. *Ransetsu:* a disciple in Edo; see 286, 749, 759.

310

Field of bush clover
            one night at least give refuge
                        to the mountain dogs

hagihara ya / hitoyo wa yadose / yama no inu

Autumn, 1687. *hagi: Lespedeza bicolor,* bush clover; see 18, 543. In waka poetry, wild boar are said to rest on bush clover. An earlier version, included in the anthology *Hakusenshū,* uses *ōkami* ("Japanese wolf"), the implication being that bush clover can pacify even the wildest animals.

311

In the Country

Cranes stalking across
            a half-harvested rice field
                        The village autumn

karikakeshi / tazura no tsuru ya / sato no aki

Autumn, 1687.

312

A country youngster
    removing the husks from grain
        looks up at the moon

shizu no ko ya / ine surikakete / tsuki o miru

Autumn, 1687.

313

Leaves of the taro
    Moon-waiting in the village
        of fire-fallowed fields

imo no haya / tsuki matsu sato no / yakibatake

Autumn, 1687. *imo* here signifies *satoimo* ("taro"), eaten during the harvest moonviewing of the Eighth Month. *yakibatake:* the slash-and-burn method of cultivation.

314

The traveling moon
    the treetops still holding on
        to the nighttime's rain

tsuki hayashi / kozue wa ame o / mochi nagara

Autumn, 1687. Written at Chōkō-an, the cottage of his friend and Zen teacher, Butchō (full Zen name Butchō Kanan, 1642–1716; see 495) in the grounds of Konpon-ji at Kashima. The weather had been bad so Bashō had gone to bed without seeing the moon. He was awakened near dawn as the sky cleared.

315

A temple night's sleep
How solemnly I now turn
my face to the moon

tera ni nete / makotogao naru / tsukimi kana

Autumn, 1687. As with 314, written at Konpon-ji in Kashima.

316

Shinzen

This pine a seedling
during the Age of the Gods
Autumn at the shrine

kono matsu no / mibae seshi yo ya / kami no aki

Autumn, 1687. *Shinzen*: "Before the Altar of (the) God/s." Written at
Kashima Jingū, one of the oldest Shinto shrines. *yo ya kami* ("the Age of
the Gods"); *kami*: god, or the gods; the god enshrined in Kashima Jingū is
Takemikazuchi, a god of thunder, who is also known as Kashima-no-kami.

317

Listening to Quiet

Come listen with me
to the song of the bagworm
in my grass retreat

minomushi no / ne o kiki ni koyo / kusa no io

Autumn, 1687. See 116, 263, 291. The bagworm makes no sound, but in
Sei Shōnagon's *The Pillow Book* it is said to cry *Chichiyo! Chichiyo!*
("Father! Father!"). "In response to this hokku by Bashō, Yamaguchi
Sodō (1642–1716), a scholar of Chinese literature and a *kanshi*
[Chinese-style haikai] poet, wrote the haibun essay 'Comment on the
Bagworm' ('Minomushi no setsu'), which in turn caused Bashō to com-
pose 'Postscript to "Comment on the Bagworm,"' in which he praised
the beauty of Sodō's poetic prose. The result is an extended prose dia-
logue, like that of linked verse, in which Bashō and Sodō alternately
meditate on the nature of reclusion" (Shirane, *Traces*, p. 173). See 263.

318

Hermitage Rain

Beginning to rise
    faintly the chrysanthemum
        after the waters

okiagaru / kiku honokanari / mizu no ato

Autumn, 1687. *mizu* means "water" but in this context denotes heavy rain.

319

Thin at the same time
    somehow the chrysanthemum
        in bud yet again

yase nagara / warinaki kiku no / tsubomi kana

Autumn, 1687. In a famous reading of the poem, Yamamoto Kenkichi explored the poem's romantic connotations, considering it a poem of abandoned love, with the chrysanthemum emblematic of a pregnant woman enduring, and accepting, the harshness of fate.

320

A wayfaring man
    the name I would be called by
        First winter drizzle

tabibito to / waga na yobaren / hatsushigure

Winter, 1687. Written at a farewell party for Bashō as he prepared to depart on the journey recounted in *Oi no Kobumi* ("Journey of a Satchel"), in which he prefaces the poem with the remark: "Early in the month when there are no gods, with the sky uncertain, as I set out on my journey, I too felt unsure of my future, like a leaf in the wind." Bashō used the old name for the Tenth Month, *kannazuki* (literally, "the month when there are no gods"); in Shinto tradition, during *kannazuki* it was believed the eight million gods of Japan congregated annually at Izumo Taisha; see 746, 748, 831. Bashō set off on the twenty-fifth of the Tenth Month (November 29, 1687).

321

Fuji

One of its ridges
    darkening with drizzling cloud
      On Mount Fuji snow

hitoone wa / shigururu kumo ka / Fuji no yuki

Winter, 1687.

322

To the "capital"
    about half the sky to go
      Clouds heavy with snow

Kyō made wa / mada nakazora ya / yuki no kumo

Winter, 1687. Bashō was staying in Narumi at the home of Terashima
Bokugen (1646–1736), who showed him a waka written by Asukai
Masaaki (1611–79) at the same lodging twenty-five years earlier: *Kyō
wa nao / miyako mo tōku / Narumigata / harukeki umi o / naka ni heda-
tete* ("Now the capital / seems even further away / at Narumi Bay /
looking across the vast sea / separating me from home").

323

Stopping at Narumi

At the Cape of Stars
    look at the darkness they say
      the plovers' voices

Hoshizaki no / yami o miyo to ya / naku chidori

Winter, 1687. *Hoshizaki* ("The Cape of Stars"), on Narumi Bay, is
famous for plovers. Composed at the house of Yasunobu in Narumi on
the seventh day of the Eleventh Month.

324

As cold as it is
        we two sleeping here tonight
            an enheartening

samukeredo / futari nuru yo zo / tanomoshiki

Winter, 1687. *we two:* Bashō and Etsujin (see 327), on their way to visit
Tokoku (see 252, 328–32, 379) at Cape Irago, stayed at an inn in Yosh-
ida (now Toyohashi) on the eleventh day of the Eleventh Month.

325

Travelers' Inn

A pine-needle fire
        I dry my tenugui
            in the bitter cold

go o taite / tenugui aburu / samusa kana

Winter, 1687. *go:* the local name for dried pine needles in the province
of Mikawa, between Toyohashi and Nagoya; see 743. *tenugui:* a hand
towel.

326

In the winter sun
        I am on horseback frozen
            become my shadow

fuyu no hi ya / bashō ni kōru / kagebōshi

Winter, 1687. A pun on his own name, *bashō ni* means "on horseback";
kagebōshi: kage means "shadow" and *bōshi* is a suffix that can denote a
priest, priest-like person, or person in general.

327

On the road to Irago, Etsujin gets drunk and gets on a horse

Onto snow or sand
>> may you tumble off that horse
>>> sake-drunk rider

yuki ya suna / muma yori ochiyo / sake no yoi

Winter, 1687. *Etsujin:* Ochi Etsujin (1656–c. 1739), a favored disciple,
from Nagoya, who later accompanied Bashō to Sarashina; see 470.

328

Solitary hawk
>> Such a vision to behold
>>> at Cape Irago

taka hitotsu / mitsukete ureshi / Iragozaki

Winter, 1687. *Iragozaki:* Cape Irago. The hawk of the poem is often
taken as a metaphor for Tokoku (see 330), whose exile at Irago recalled
the exile of Prince Omi, who features in two poems in the *Man'yōshū*
(vol. 1: 23, 24).

329

Since Cape Irago was nearby, we went to see it

The Irago cape
>> not a thing comparable
>>> the call of the hawk

Iragozaki / niru mono mo nashi / taka no koe

Winter, 1687. Bashō was accompanied by Etsujin and Tokoku.

330

Visiting Tokoku in his distress at Cape Irago, every now and then I heard the call of a hawk

Better than a dream
    the hawk of reality
        An enheartening

yume yori mo / utsutsu no taka zo / tanomoshiki

Winter, 1687. The most auspicious first dream of the year (*hatsuyume*) is of Mount Fuji, the second best, of a hawk, and third, of an aubergine (eggplant). Tokoku (see 252) had been sentenced to death for market speculation. The sentence was commuted, but he was expelled from Nagoya, and was living in the vicinity of the village of Hobi, near Cape Irago. Bashō made a detour of over 90 km to see him.

331

As I knew to fear
    In the wrack and ruins of
        a frost-crusted shack

sareba koso / aretaki mama no / shimo no yado

Winter, 1687. Composed on Bashō's visit to Tokoku's house in exile.

332

The barley sprouting
    a good place to retreat to
        Hatake Village

mugi haete / yoki kakurega ya / Hatake Mura

Winter, 1687. In his exile, Tokoku had first lived in Hatake. The word *hatake* ("field of cultivated land") is an *engo* ("kindred word") for *mugi* ("barley").

333

The origin of the name of this village, Hobi, comes from long ago when a retired Emperor is said to have said "praise its beauty" [hō bi]. This is what one of the villagers told me. I do not know in which book this is written, but the sentiment and story are inspiring

Ume winter rose
      praise be the early blooming
           in Hobi village

ume tsubaki / hayazaki homen / Hobi no sato

Winter, 1687. *tsubaki: Camellia japonica,* sometimes called the "rose of winter."

334

Given to a Man Hidden Away a While

First of all rejoice
      in the ume in the heart's
           winter reclusion

mazu iwae / ume o kokoro no / fuyugomori

Winter, 1687. *fuyugomori:* staying indoors during winter; see 465, 598, 821.

335

Narumi, at the House of Dewa no Kami Ujikumo

So interesting
      the snow it will turn into
           the rain in winter

omoshiroshi / yuki ni ya naran / fuyu no ame

Winter, 1687. *Dewa no Kami Ujikumo:* Okajima Sasuke, a swordsmith and poet.

336

To drink medicine
    bad enough with no journey
        no pillow of frost

kusuri nomu / sarademo shimo no / makura kana

Winter, 1687.

337

Atsuta Shrine, Rebuilt

Now it's repolished
    the mirror's clarity shows
        the flower-like snows

togi naosu / kagami mo kiyoshi / yuki no hana

Winter, 1687. Bashō was visiting the Shinto shrine at Atsuta, which had been repaired after eighty years. He had seen it in its neglected state three years earlier (see 221). A circular mirror, representing the *kami* (god/s), stands on the altar at Shinto shrines. White is the symbol of purity in Japan.

338

At Someone's Party

Smoothing out wrinkles
    attending the snow-viewing
        in my paper robe

tametsukete / yukimi ni makaru / kamiko kana

Winter, 1687. The greeting hokku of a *kasen* (thirty-six-verse sequence) party at the house of Shōheki in Nagoya, on the twenty-eighth day of the Eleventh Month, the "snow party" of Derek Mahon's poem "The Snow Party."

339

1

So farewell for now
　　　we're off to look at the snow
　　　　　till we all fall down

iza saraba / yukimi ni korobu / tokoro made

2

Let's get up and go
　　　view the snow till we come to
　　　　　wherever we fall

iza yukan / yukimi ni korobu / tokoro made

Winter, 1687. Written on a different day and at a different place from 338, at the home of Sekidō in Nagoya, on the third of the Twelfth Month.

340

Crossing Hakone
　　　some travelers surely there
　　　　　in the morning snow

Hakone kosu / hito mo aru rashi / kesa no yuki

Winter, 1687. *Hakone:* Hakone Pass was an important post station on the main Tōkaidō highway between Edo and Kyoto. The Tokugawa government established an official checkpoint here, the *Hakone sekisho* ("Hakone Barrier"), for all travelers entering and leaving Edo. The poem was composed at the villa of Chōsetsu in Atsuta, on the fourth day of the Twelfth Month. Bashō had passed the Hakone Barrier a month before and was thinking of the ordeal of winter travelers while he was ensconced with companions (Chōsetsu, Jokō, Yasui, Etsujin, and Kakei) enjoying the snow from indoors.

341

The ninth day of the Twelfth Month, a party at Issei-tei

A journey's good rest
at an inn a December
Evening-Moon evening

tabine yoshi / yado wa shiwasu no / yūzukiyo

Winter, 1687. *Issei-tei:* Issei's house, a haiku poet in Nagoya. *yūzukiyo:*
an evening with the moon bright only at evening time.

342

At This Man's Party

On the scented trail
of ume see a warehouse
the span of the eaves

ka o saguru / ume ni kura miru / nokiba kana

Winter, 1687. A greeting hokku to the host, a wealthy man called Bōsen.
kura: a warehouse or storehouse, and here signifying Bōsen's wealth (an
earlier version used *ie* ["house"]). It was a custom to visit a new warehouse,
to celebrate its completion. A *tanbai* ("searching for *ume*") poem; see 784.

343

The dewdrops frozen
the writing brush drawing up
the clear spring water

tsuyu itete / fude ni kumihosu / shimizu kana

Winter, 1687. An allusion to the Saigyō waka quoted in 206; see 391.
Composed at a gathering at the home of Shōkei in Nagoya.

344

Breaking my journey
    I look on the fleeting world
        at its housecleaning

tabine shite / mishi ya ukiyo no / susuharai

Winter, 1687. *susuharai* (literally, "sweeping the soot away"): the annual housecleaning in preparation for the New Year, on the thirteenth day of the Twelfth Month in this period; see 668. *ukiyo:* "the floating world," the life of the city, in particular the life of transitory pleasure-seeking; see 455, 753.

345

"From Kuwana I had come with nothing to eat," in the village of Hinaga mentioned in that poem I hired out a horse to ride up So-Take-a-Walking-Stick-Hill, but my pack-saddle overturned and I was thrown from the horse

Had I only walked
    So-Take-a-Walking-Stick-Hill
        no fall from a horse

kachi naraba / Tsuetsukizaka o / rakuba kana

Miscellaneous (no season), 1687. The poem Bashō quotes is by Sōgi (see 160, 583). *Tsuetsukizaka:* a steep slope on the Tōkaidō road near Yokkaichi, so called from a legend in the *Kojiki* concerning Yamato Takeru, who was so tired he used his sword as a stick to walk up the hill. In *Oi no Kobumi* ("Journey of a Satchel") Bashō relates that he was so annoyed by what happened that he forgot to include a season word.

346

At the homecoming
    I weep to see my birth cord
        the end of the year

furusato ya / heso no o ni naku / toshi no kure

Winter, 1687. On this visit to his native town in the winter of 1687–88, Bashō was given his umbilical cord. A portion of an umbilical cord was, and sometimes still is, kept as a family memento.

347

Into the gusting
　　wind a fish jumps a rite of
　　　　purification

fuku kaze no / naka o uo tobu / misogi kana

Summer, year unknown (347–356 were written during the *Jōkyō* era,
1684–87). *misogi:* an abbreviation of *misogiharae,* also called *ōharae* or
ōharai, a Shinto rite purification in sacred rivers, waterfalls, or lakes;
conducted twice a year on the last day of the Sixth and Twelfth Months.
According to Kon Eizō, the one depicted in this poem is the one on the
last day of the Sixth Month.

348

This work is not quite a travel journal, but more a record of the move-
ment of the heart as it encounters mountain bridges and shops and tea
stalls in the country. Upon this picture scroll Nakagawa Jokushi has
applied his colors, making up for my inability to paint the scenes with
words. When others see his pictures, I will feel ashamed

Spend nights on the road
　　to understand my poems
　　　　The autumnal wind

tabine shite / waga ku o shire ya / aki no kaze

Autumn, year unknown (*Jōkyō*). *Nakagawa Jokushi* (dates unknown): a
samurai from Ōgaki who painted the illustrations for *Nozarashi Kikō.*

349

The temple bell fades
　　The fragrance of flowers strikes
　　　　into the evening

kane kiete / hana no ka wa tsuku / yūbe kana

Spring, year unknown (*Jōkyō*).

350

Curiosity
      Upon odorless grass a
         butterfly alights

monozuki ya / niowanu kusa ni / tomaru chō

Spring, year unknown (*Jōkyō*).

351

Scooped into my hands
      the spring water surprises
         my teeth with its cold

musubu yori / haya ha ni hibiku / izumi kana

Summer, year unknown (*Jōkyō*).

352

The sound so cleanly
      echoing off to the Plough
         from the fulling block

koe sumite / hokuto ni hibiku / kinuta kana

Autumn, year unknown (*Jōkyō*). *fulling block:* see 205. Alludes to a Chinese poem (number 346) by Liu Yüan-shu in the *Wakan rōei shū;* see 119, 122), which mentions both the Great Bear constellation and a wife beating clothes on a fulling block.

353

A melon flower's
　　dripping water to forget
　　　　what in the grasses?

uri no hana / shizuku ikanaru / wasuregusa

Summer, year unknown (*Jōkyō*). Bashō was invited to a tea ceremony
by the tea master Kōno Shōha. Shōha had placed a melon flower in a
vase made from an old cracked gourd from which water dripped slowly
onto a stringless *biwa* lute; see 202, 213, 930. Bashō admired the ele-
gance of his host's taste. *wasuregusa* (literally, "forget-grass"): the orange
day-lily; see 102.

354

Jinjitsu

Coming from all sides
　　the wallop-chop-walloping
　　　　of shepherd's purses

yomo ni utsu / nazuna mo shidoro / modoro kana

New Year, year unknown (*Jōkyō*). *Jinjitsu*: the seventh day of the New
Year; *nazuna*: shepherd's purses. As in 262, poem concerns the gather-
ing of ingredients for *nanakusa gayu*. *shidoro modoro*: a colloquial
expression meaning "in a confused manner," e.g., *shidoro modoro ni
aruku*: "to stagger like a drunken man." In modern Japanese, *shidoro
modoro* most often describes an incoherent way of talking.

355

In Mourning for the Old Priest, Dokukai

To whatsoever
　　the beckoning now grown still
　　　　plumes of miscanthus

nanigoto mo / maneki hatetaru / susuki kana

Autumn, year unknown (*Jōkyō*). Dokukai died at Bashō's hut, where the
poet had tended to him.

356

Someone gave me some rice

> Out there in the world
>   it's time to harvest the rice
>   I'm in my thatched hut

yo no naka wa / ine karu koro ka / kusa no io

Autumn, year unknown (*Jōkyō*).

357

On New Year's Eve, not willing to let go of the year, I drank deep into the night and missed the sunrise on New Year's morning

> This year's second day
>   I'll not make the same mistake
>   the Spring blossoming

futsuka ni mo / nukari wa seji na / hana no haru

New Year, 1688. It is still a tradition in Japan to greet the dawn on the first day of the year.

358

Early Spring

> The spring arisen
>   only the ninth day of it
>   in the hills and fields

haru tachite / mada kokonoka no / noyama kana

Spring, 1688. A greeting poem for Fūbaku, a samurai of the Iga-Tōdo clan, praising the warmth of his welcome. Included in *Oi no Kobumi* ("Journey of a Satchel").

359

Akokuso's heart
    I will never really know
        the ume blossoms

Akokuso no / kokoro mo shirazu / ume no hana

Spring, 1688. *Akokuso*: the childhood name of Ki no Tsurayuki (c. 872–945), poet, anthologist and court noble, who wrote the following waka to which Bashō alludes: *hito wa isa / kokoro mo shirazu / furusato wa / hana zo mukashi no / ka ni nioikeru* ("The hearts of people / I will never really know / In my native town / the ume blooms still give off / the fragrance of times long gone"); see 6, 16, 844.

360

An area near the castle in Iga produces something they call "uni." The smell is revolting

Let your fragrance waft
    ume blossoms on the hill
        they dig for uni

ka ni nioe / uni horu oka no / ume no hana

Spring, 1688. *uni*: the word in Iga dialect for both "peat" and "lignite"; brown coal.

361

In a House in the Iga Mountains

Allow the sound of
    a farmer's blow the ume's
        fully blossoming

tebana kamu / oto sae ume no / sakari kana

Spring, 1688. *tebana*: to blow one's nose with one's fingers, usually onto the ground.

362

Above the dead grass
    the warm air's shim-shimmering
        one two inches high

kareshiba ya / yaya kagerō no / ichi nisun

Spring, 1688. *kagerō:* waves of heat, an image of spring; *kareshiba:* dead grass, an image of winter.

363

About five meters
    the height of the shimmering
        above the stone plinth

jōroku ni / kagerō takashi / ishi no ue

Spring, 1688. Composed on the site of Shin-Daibutsu (New Great Buddha) Temple at Awa, in the province of Iga, which had been destroyed by a landslide in 1635. Originally built by the monk Chōgen of Tōdai-ji, Nara, famous for its Daibutsu (Great Buddha), from which the temple's name derived. *jōroku* (approximately 4.85 meters): the standard height of statues of the Buddha. The air above the plinth is shimmering in the heat to about the height of the Buddha statue that is no longer there.

364

Ise Yamada

What tree is this that
    blossoms so? I do not know
        Such an aroma

nani no ki no / hana to wa shirazu / nioi kana

Spring, 1688. Yamada is the location of the Grand Shinto Shrines of Ise, and this poem was composed at the Outer Shrine on the fourth day of the Second Month as the first verse of a thirty-six-verse sequence presented to the shrine. Bashō alludes to a waka by Saigyō: *nanigoto no / owashimasu ka wa / shirane domo / katajikenasa ni / namida koboruru* ("What divinity / resides within and graces / this place I know not / but my gratitude makes these / teardrops begin to flow").

365

1

The Shrine Maidens' House
　　　So graceful with the one tree
　　　　　the ume blossoms

okorago no / hitomoto yukashi / ume no hana

2

In the shrine's precincts there's not even a single ume tree to be seen, so I asked a man why this was so. "There's no reason, but since olden days there's never been a tree here except for the one behind the Shrine Maidens' House," he said

One ume alone
　　　So graceful in the garden
　　　　　of the Shrine Maidens

ume mare ni / hitomoto yukashi / Kora no Tachi

Spring, 1688. The second is an earlier version of the poem. *okorago* (and *Kora*): the old name for a shrine maiden at the Grand Shrine of Ise.

366

Ichiyū's Wife

Beyond the curtain
  beyond the deep inner room
    a north-wing ume

nōren no / oku monofukashi / kita no ume

Spring, 1688. A greeting poem for Sonome (Shiba Sonome, 1664–1726; see 919), regarded as Bashō's most accomplished female disciple, the wife of a doctor (Shiba Ichiyū), and represented here by the *kita no ume* ("north-wing ume"): "Between the southern guest room and the northern 'inner room' (*okunoma*) hangs a *nōren* (a hanging curtain; modern Japanese *noren*), beyond which the speaker can glimpse a plum tree in bloom. The word *oku* (inner, within), which suggests 'depth,' refers not only to the inner room but to *oku niwa* (inner garden) as well as to *okusan* ('wife' or 'person within'). *Kita* (north) similarly implies *kita no kata* (literally, 'lady of the northern quarters'), a classical word for principal wife. The description of the setting thus becomes a tribute to the quite [sic] refinement and 'depth' (*monofukashi*) of the lady of the house, represented by the plum blossoms [ume]" (Shirane, *Traces*, p. 165).

367

Meeting Ajiro Minbu's Son, Setsudō

From the ume tree
  another sprout emerging
    The ume blossoms

ume no ki ni / nao yadorigi ya / ume no hana

Spring, 1688. *Ajiro Minbu* (1640–83): a poet and Shinto priest at Ise Shrine, and his son Hirokazu (1657–1717), who wrote poetry using the name Setsudō.

368

Ryū no Shōsha

The name of these things
    may I first of all ask you
        these freshleafed grasses?

mono no na o / mazu tou ashi no / wakaba kana

Spring, 1688. *Ryū no Shōsha:* the pseudonym of Tatsuno Hirochika (1616–93), a priest at the Outer Shrine of the Ise Grand Shrine, as well as a Shinto scholar and poet.

369

A Gathering in a Thatched Hut

The tubers planted
    And now growing by the gate
        the cleavers' fresh leaves

imo uete / kado wa mugura no / wakaba kana

Spring, 1688. *mugura:* cleavers; see 256. Composed at Nijōken, in the precincts of Taikō-ji, a temple at Ise.

370

Bodai-san

Tell the mountain's tale
    the sadness of its story
        old digger of yams

kono yama no / kanashisa tsuge yo / tokorohori

Spring, 1688. *Bodai-san:* literally "Buddhahood Mountain," the site in Ise province of a temple built in the eighth century by the emperor Shōmu (701–56) but had fallen into disrepair by the Kamakura period (1185–1333). *tokorohori: tokoro (tororo* in modern Japanese), *Dioscorea polystachya,* or Chinese yam; *hori:* "dig out." Alludes to a poem by Ono no Takamura (802–53): *watanohara / yasoshima kakete / kogiidenu to / hito ni wa tsuge yo / ama no tsuribune* ("To the wide ocean's / five hundred islands and more / I have now headed out / Tell that to my family / you fisherfolk in your boats").

371

Kusube

Into my sake
> don't go dolloping your dirt
> > yon gulp of swallows

sakazuki ni / doro na otoshi so / muratsubame

Spring, 1688. *Kusube:* a town about 2 km north of the Ise Grand Shrine, where Bashō rested a while on his journey. *muratsubame:* the prefix *mura* is an older form of *mure* ("flock"), but it can also mean "village." Other versions of the poem end with *tobu-tsubame* ("flying swallows") and *mau-tsubame* ("fluttering swallows").

372

At Rosō's House

Though my paper robes
> get wet I'll snap a sprig of
> > blossoms in the rain

kamiginu no / nuru tomo oran / ame no hana

Spring, 1688. *Rosō:* a high-ranking priest of the Outer Shrine at Ise.

373

On the fifteenth, at Tachi in the precincts of the Outer Shrine

Within the shrine's bounds
> against all expectation
> > Buddhist nirvana

kamigaki ya / omoi mo kakezu / nehanzō

Spring, 1688. *Tachi:* a residential quarter for priests on the northern side of the shrine. Seeing *nehanzō* (an image of the Buddha's death and achievement of nirvana: *nehan,* nirvana; *zō:* image) within a Shinto shrine is highly unusual. The fifteenth of the Second Month commemorates Buddha entering Nirvana; see 845 (1).

374

On the seventeenth day of the Second Month, departing from Mount Kamiji

To walk naked now?
> More than enough time still for
>> February's storms

hadaka ni wa / mada kisaragi no / arashi kana

Spring, 1688. Alludes to the story of Zōga Hijiri (917–1003), a Buddhist holy man (*hijiri*), who received a message from the gods at Ise to throw off fame and wealth, and gave all his clothes to beggars. The traditional name for the Second Month, *Kisaragi*, means "wear another layer of clothes." Mount Kamiji is near Ise; see 197.

375

At Yakushi-ji, the First of the Monthly Haikai Meetings

The cherry's first blooms
> And luckily today is
>> a beautiful day

hatsuzakura / orishimo kyō wa / yoki hi nari

Spring, 1688.

376

The Honorable Tangan held a blossom-viewing party at his villa; there I found everything as it had been in the old days

So so many things
> open in the memory
>> the blossoms again

samazama no / koto omoidasu / sakura kana

Spring, 1688. *Tangan* (1666–1710): the son of Sengin (Tōdō Yoshitada, 1642–66), the master whom Bashō had served until his early death.

377

Staying at Hyōchiku-an, with my traveler's heart at peace

The blossoms a refuge
from beginning to their end
twenty days or so

hana o yado ni / hajime owari ya / hatsuka hodo

Spring, 1688. *Hyōchiku-an* ("Gourd Bamboo Hut"): belonged to
Okamoto Taiso, a samurai and poet from Iga. Blossoms were said to last
twenty days, between opening and falling. 6-7-5.

378

The Day of Departure

For my time spent here
I give thanks to the blossoms
and bid you farewell

kono hodo o / hana ni rei iu / wakare kana

Spring, 1688.

379

Two Travelers with No Abode in Heaven and Earth

There at Yoshino
I'll show you cherry blossoms
my hinoki hat

Yoshino nite / sakura mishō zo / hinokigasa

Spring, 1688. *Two Travelers . . .*: the pilgrim's motto; see 557. The phrase
evokes the Buddha as the traveler's companion. *Yoshino*: the most
famous place in Japan for cherry blossoms; see 104. Bashō had been
joined on his journey by Tokoku; see 226, 252, 328–32.

380

Hatsuse

A spring evening-time
the charm of a retreatant
a temple corner

haru no yo ya / komorido yukashi / dō no sumi

Spring, 1688. *Hatsuse:* see 31. Hasedera (Hase Temple) had been a place
of pilgrimage since the Heian period, and court ladies spending days in
retreat here feature in *The Tale of Genji* and *The Pillow Book*. The
Senjūshō, a collection of Buddhist tales once attributed to Saigyō, also
relates the tale of Saigyō encountering his wife, who had become a nun,
praying in the Kannon Hall at Hasedera. *komorido:* a person in retreat
who spends the whole night in prayer.

381

At Hoso Tōge, on the road from Tō-no-mine to Ryūmon

Higher than the larks
up in the blue I'm resting
the mountains the pass

hibari yori / sora ni yasurau / tōge kana

Spring, 1688. *Hoso Tōge* ("Hoso Pass"): on the way from Hatsuse to
Yoshino.

382

Ryūmon

Ryūmon Falls
The blossoms a souvenir
for my drinking friend

Ryūmon no / hana ya jōgo no / tsuto ni sen

Spring, 1688. *Ryūmon* (literally, "Dragon's Gate"): an abbreviation of
Ryūmon no Taki (Ryūmon Falls), a waterfall about ten meters high on
Mount Ryūmon in the north of Yoshino; see 383.

383

With my drinking friend
        I'll chat about cascading
                waterfall blossoms

sakenomi ni / kataran kakaru / taki no hana

Spring, 1688. The Chinese poet Li Bai (Li Po; see 194, 259, 538) was known for his love of both drinking and waterfalls.

384

On my ramble through Yamato Province, I lodged a night at a farmhouse. The master of the house was kind-hearted and showed me warm hospitality

Shaded by blossoms
        so resembling a Noh play
                A rest on the road

hana no kage / utai ni nitaru / tabine kana

Spring, 1688.

385

With fan unfolded
        I mime imbibing sake
                The falling blossoms

ōgi nite / sake kumu kage ya / chiru sakura

Spring, 1688. In Noh plays the drinking of sake is imitated by using a fan.

386

Were my voice better
  I'd recite the poem of
    the blossoms falling

koe yokuba / utaō mono o / sakura chiru

Spring, 1688. A more literal rendering: "Were my voice better / I would
recite songs from Noh / the blossoms falling."

387

Nijikō

Petal by petal
  kerria roses at fall
    the sounding waters

horohoro to / yamabuki chiru ka / taki no oto

Spring, 1688. *Nijikō* ("West River"): a swift section on the upper reaches
of the Yoshino River. *horohoro* can mean "one by one" and describes
tears or petals falling or fluttering down quietly; it also describes a gur-
gling bird sound, and is onomatopoeia for the cry of a pheasant; see 394.

388

To see the blossoms
  I scarcely believe each day
    I walk five six ri

sakuragari / kidoku ya hibi ni / go ri roku ri

Spring, 1688. *ri*: a unit of distance, about 4 km; see 66.

389

"Tomorrow a hinoki," the old tree in the valley once said. Yesterday is gone, tomorrow yet to come, and only for the pleasures on earth of a cask we indulge ourselves with the excuse "tomorrow" and "tomorrow," until at the end we are held to account by a sage

> The blossom-filled day
> > darkens the sadness of the
> > > asunaro tree

hi wa hana ni / kurete sabishi ya / asunarō

Spring, 1688. In the headnote, Bashō alludes to Po Chü-i's (Bai Juyi) poem "Recommending Wine" (see also 164). *asunarō:* asunaro, a tree of the cypress family, *Thujopsis dolabrata,* also known as the false arborvitae. The name *asunarō* means "tomorrow I will become," the implication being "become a hinoki cypress" (the tree looks like a smaller version of the hinoki).

390

The Mossy Spring

> The spring rain trickling
> > along the lower branches
> > > this clear spring water?

harusame no / koshita ni tsutau / shimizu kana

Spring, 1688. An allusion to the Saigyō waka quoted in the note to 206; see also 343.

391

The Mossy Spring

> So the thaw begins
> > the writing brush drawing up
> > > the clear spring water

ite tokete / fude ni kumihosu / shimizu kana

Spring, 1688. Considered a revised version of 343; see also 206.

392

Yoshino

Blossoms at their peak
    And the mountain as always
      at the break of day

hanazakari / yama wa higoro no / asaborake

Spring, 1688. *Yoshino:* see 104, 379.

393

Mount Kazuraki

Still I wish to see
    as dawn dapples the blossoms
      the face of the god

nao mitashi / hana ni akeyuku / kami no kao

Spring, 1688. The god is Hitokotonushi. When the ascetic En no Gyōja ("En the Ascetic"; see 497), a semilegendary seventh-century priest and founder of the mountain-worshipping Shugendō sect, prayed to the gods for a bridge to be built between Mount Kazuraki and Mount Yoshino, Hitokotonushi responded and began constructing a bridge of rocks, which he failed to finish. So ugly he didn't want his face to be seen, he worked only at night and disappeared at dawn. "To complement this hokku, Bashō drew a portrait of a mountain priest sleeping under a tree, adding the note: 'This is what the priest said in his sleep'" (Ueda, p. 193).

394

Mount Kōya

My father mother
    so very much I miss them
        A kiji calling

chichi haha no / shikirini koishi / kiji no koe

Spring, 1688. *Mount Kōya:* the site of the mausoleum of Kukai (774–835), founder of the Shingon ("True Word") school of Buddhism, and the graves of Bashō's ancestors. Based on a waka by the priest Gyōki (668–749; see 506): *yamadori no / horohoro to naku / koe kikeba / chichi ka to zo omou / haha ka to zo omou* ("The copper pheasant's / 'horohoro' crying call / as I'm listening / I wonder is it my father? / is it my mother I wonder?"). *kiji:* a green pheasant, *Phasianus versicolor,* the national bird of Japan; in classical poetry symbolic of love for one's family; "kiji" is a homophone also for "abandoned child." See 481, 621.

395

Wakanoura

With the fleeing spring
    here at Wakanoura
        at last I am in step

yuku haru ni / Waka-no-ura nite / oitsukitari

Spring, 1688. *Wakanoura:* literally, "bay of waka (poems)," on the coast of Wakayama, praised for its beauty in poetry since the *Man'yōshū,* the oldest extant anthology of waka poetry, compiled during the Nara period, at some point after 759.

396

Koromogae

A layer taken off
    and thrown over my shoulder
        Seasons and their clothes

hitotsu nuide / ushiro ni oinu / koromogae

Summer, 1688. *Koromogae:* the changing of clothes according to season. The first day of the Fourth Month was the day for changing from spring to summer clothing.

397

The Buddha's birthday
    and coincidentally
        first dawn for this fawn

kanbutsu no / hi ni umareau / kanoko kana

Summer, 1688. *kanbutsu:* the Buddha's birthday, celebrated on the eighth day of the Fourth Month, nowadays on April 8; see 845 (2). In the *kanbutsu-e* ceremony, scented water or hydrangea tea is poured over a small statue of the Buddha. Friends had arrived from Iga Ueno to visit Bashō on this day; see 399.

398

Ganjin of Shōdai-ji in coming to Japan from China had to suffer seventy adversities, and the salt wind is said to have blown the sight from his eyes. Worshipping his sacred image

With the freshest leaf
    the tears brimming from your eyes
        I would wipe away

wakaba shite / onme no shizuku / nuguwabaya

Summer, 1688. Ganjin (Jianzhen, or Chien-chen, 688–763), the Chinese founder of Tōshōdai-ji in Nara, attempted to come to Japan five times in ten years, and was prevented by shipwreck or intervention by Chinese authorities. He finally reached Japan in 753. His life is the subject of Inoue Yasushi's novel *Tempyō no Iraka* ("The Roof Tile of Tempyō"). A dry-lacquer statue of the blind Ganjin made shortly after his death can still be seen in Tōshōdai-ji.

399

Parting from Old Friends at Nara

Now the deer's antlers
      begin to branch into beams
            A separation

shika no tsuno / mazu hitofushi no / wakare kana

Summer, 1688. *Old friends:* Ensui (see 870), Takutai (see 684), Baiken, Risetsu, friends from his hometown in Iga; see 397. The phrase *hito fushi* can mean "the joint of a horn where it branches into two," or "a juncture in life, a point of transition at which a new stage in life begins," which here refers to the poet's parting from his friends.

400

Wearied traveling
      I arrive where I will stay
            Wisteria blooms

kutabirete / yado karu koro ya / fuji no hana

Spring, 1688. The poem was written on the eleventh of the Fourth Month (May 10 in the solar calendar), at Yagi in the province of Yamato, and originally the first line was *hototogisu* ("cuckoo"), a season word for summer. In changing the first line, the remaining season word became that of spring, *fuji no hana* ("wisteria flowers").

401

The lotus is known as the Prince of Flowers. Among the blossoms, the tree peony is said to be the wealthy noble. Rice seedlings rise from the mud but are purer than the lotus; in autumn, the yield is fragrant rice, richer than the tree peony. This one plant combines the virtues of both, being both pure and rich

The villagers sing
      planting rice chanting poets
            of the capital

satobito wa / ine ni uta yomu / miyako kana

Summer, 1688. See 505.

402

The ume trees have shed their blossoms, the bush warbler has sung amid the bamboo, the cherry trees have bloomed, and now the rainy season sky has cleared, and now the cuckoo urges the farmer to take rice seedlings in hand. Along a country road at dusk, astride a heavy ox, I have come, my pipe the light of a firefly. Taking refuge from the heat under a gourd pergola, I'll not forget the songs I sing, drunk from moon-reflecting cups from this gourd of sake worth its weight in gold

So pleasureable
　　　The cool air of a rice field
　　　　　the sound of water

tanoshisa ya / aota ni suzumu / mizu no oto

Summer, 1688.

403

At a House in Osaka

Rabbit-ear iris
　　　Merely to chit and chat one
　　　　　joy of the journey

kakitsubata / kataru mo tabi no / hitotsu kana

Summer, 1688. The house of Isshō (Yasukawa Yaemon), a paper merchant and old friend from Iga who had moved to Osaka. Alludes to the word-play poem in *Ise Monogatari* (chapter 9) where Ariwara no Narihira (see 28, 71, 101, 908) composes a waka in which each line begins with a syllable from the word *kakitsubata* ("rabbit-ear iris"); see 246.

404

Suma

Although the moon is here
    the air of an empty house
      Suma in summer

tsuki wa aredo / rusu no yō nari / Suma no natsu

Summer, 1688. Suma, a beach in the west of Kobe, features prominently
in Japanese literature, in waka, in Noh, and in Kabuki. In *Oi no Kobumi,*
Bashō quotes from a passage in *Genji Monogatari* which refers to the
"matchless beauty" of autumn in Suma; Royall Tyler, *The Tale of Genji,*
p. 244, renders the passage thus: "At Suma the sea was some way off
under the increasingly mournful autumn wind, but night after night
the waves on the shore, sung by Counsellor Yukihira in his poem about
the wind blowing over the pass, sounded very close indeed, until
autumn in such a place yielded the sum of melancholy"; see 109. 6-7-5.

405

Though I see the moon
    something seems to be missing
      Suma in summer

tsuki mite mo / monotarawazu ya / Suma no natsu

Summer, 1688. An earlier version of 404.

406

*At the time when the first cuckoo sings, light from the east began to fall
on the sea and, as it strengthened, on the high plain the ears of wheat
were tinged reddish-brown, and among the white poppies the fishermen's
huts could be seen*

A fisherman's face
    the first of all to flesh forth
      the poppy flowers

ama no kao / mazu miraruru ya / keshi no hana

Summer, 1688.

407

Fisherman of Suma
　　in flight from your arrowheads
　　　　the cuckoo crying?

Suma no ama no / yasaki ni naku ka / hototogisu

Summer, 1688. In *Oi no Kobumi*, Bashō writes of fishermen drying
their fish-catch on the sands and trying to scare off with bows and
arrows the crows swooping to snatch the fish away. He wonders if such
cruelty is the lingering effect of Suma being the site of a bloody battle
between the Taira and Minamoto clans (see 408, 409). The poem sug-
gests the fishermen with this "sinful" method might hurt an innocent
cuckoo. 6-7-5.

408

At Suma Temple
　　Listen to the unblown flute
　　　　in the greeny shade

Sumadera ya / fukanu fue kiku / koshitayami

Summer, 1688. *Suma Temple:* Suma-dera, also known as Jōya-san
Fukushō-ji, a Shingon Buddhist temple founded in 886. In the *Heike
Monogatari* ("The Tale of the Heike"), the epic account of the war
between the Taira clan and Minamoto clan for control of Japan, the
warrior Taira no Atsumori (1169–84), a "youth in his seventeenth year,"
is reluctantly killed by Kumagai Naozane, who has a son the same age,
and who later in guilt for the deed becomes a Buddhist monk. Atsumori
had carried the flute known as *Aoba no Fue* ("the flute of green leaves")
on his waist into battle. The flute can still be seen at Suma-dera.

409

Cuckoo yon cuckoo
  disappearingwards going
    The only island

hototogisu / kieyuku kata ya / shima hitotsu

Summer, 1688. The view is from Tekkai-ga-mine ("Tekkai Peak"), in the western part of Kobe and overlooking the site of the Battle of Ichi-no-Tani between the Minamoto clan and the Taira clan in the *Heike Monogatari*. The island is Awaji. The poem alludes to, and borrows from, various waka: in the *Senzai Wakashū* (vol. 3, no. 161), by Fujiwara no Sanesada (1139–92), better known to posterity as Tokudaiji Sanesada, or Later Tokudaiji Minister of the Left; and by the emperor Gomizuno-o (1596–1680): see Ueda, p. 199; Shirane, p. 208.

410

Spending the Night at Akashi

An octopus pot
  How fleet the dreaming under
    the moon in summer

takotsubo ya / hakanaki yume o / natsu no tsuki

Summer, 1688. *takotsubo* ("octopus pot"): an unglazed earthenware pot used to trap octopus. The traps were put out in the evening and the catch was hauled out by rope in the morning. The connotation of *natsu no tsuki* ("the summer moon") is with *akeyasui* ("early/easy daybreak"; see 412): night is short in summer and day breaks early, thus the moon is short-lived. The headnote and theme of uneasy sleep allude to "Staying Overnight at Maple Bridge," by the Tang Dynasty poet Zhang Ji. Bashō actually stayed on this night (the twenty-second) at Suma rather than Akashi. By using Akashi, he invokes the mistakenly secure sleep of the Taira clan before their defeat in the Battle of Ichi-no-Tani.

411

It is said, "You could crawl from Suma to Akashi," and now I understand what that means

O dear little snail
    stretch those tiny horns across
        Suma Akashi

katatsuburi / tsuno furiwakeyo / Suma Akashi

Summer, 1688. The distance between Suma and Akashi is approximately 12 km.

412

I washed my feet and then
    all of a sudden the dawn
        A sleep with clothes on

ashi arōte / tsui akeyasuki / marone kana

Summer, 1688. Apart from Kon Eizō, most anthologizers consider this an unconfirmed part of the Bashō canon. 6-7-5.

413

At the site of Yamazaki Sōkan's residence, Konoe-dono's poem "Sōkan here / cuts such a skinny figure / Rabbit-ear iris" came to mind

The venerable
    figure I will bow down to
        Rabbit-ear iris

arigataki / sugata ogaman / kakitsubata

Summer, 1688. *Yamazaki Sōkan:* penname of Shina Norishige or Norinaga (c. 1465–c. 1553), a poet from Ōmi Province; see 249. *Konoe-dono:* Konoe Sakihisa (1536–1612), an influential court noble from a prominent branch of the Fujiwara clan. His poem: *Sōkan ga / sugata o mireba / gakitsubata* (*gaki*tsubata rather than *kaki*tsubata, for the pun on *gaki:* the Buddhist "hungry ghost").

414

A townsman invited me, on the fourth day of the Fifth Month, to see a performance by Yoshioka Motome. On the fifth he died. This is a memorial for him

>Overnight the blood
>>iris flower has withered
>>>Motome alas

hana-ayame / ichiya ni kareshi / Motome kana

Summer, 1688. *hana-ayame* ("flower of the *ayame*"); *ayame*: blood iris, *Iris sanguinea; Yoshioka Motome:* a *wakashu-Kabuki* actor (young man who played female roles).

415

>In the summer rains
>>only one thing unhidden
>>>The bridge at Seta

samidare ni / kakurenu mono ya / Seta no hashi

Summer, 1688. The Chinese Bridge at Seta, on the southern shore of Lake Biwa, famed for its beauty at sunset, is one of the *Eight Views of Ōmi,* scenic spots in what is now called Shiga Prefecture; see 609, 627, 720.

416

While I was thinking about the journey I would soon undertake on the Kiso Road, I stayed at Ōtsu and went to see the fireflies at Seta

>These flitting fireflies
>>to the Rice-Terrace-Moonlight
>>>I'd like to compare

kono hotaru / Tagoto no Tsuki ni / kurabemin

Summer, 1688. *Tagoto no Tsuki:* the moon reflected in each field of a rice terrace at Obasute-tanada, in Sarashina, Nagano Prefecture; see 474.

417

Fireflies

My eyes filling with
    Yoshino looking at the
      fireflies at Seta

me ni nokoru / Yoshino o Seta no / hotaru kana

Summer, 1688. *Yoshino*: see 104, 379.

418

From a blade of grass
    dropping then flying upward
      a firefly afloat

kusa no ha o / otsuru yori tobu / hotaru kana

Summer, 1688.

419

At Ōtsu

The world in summer
    drifting upon on the lake
      on the rippling waves

yo no natsu ya / kosui ni ukamu / nami no ue

Summer, 1688. The headnote to another, later edition of the poem
reads, "Having a pleasant time at the house of Ikari Sakuboku." Bashō's
host, about whom little is known, had a house at Ōtsu, on Lake Biwa.

420

The end of the Fifth Month, I've climbed a certain man's lake-viewing tower

Clear sky over the lake
    still raining on Mount Hiei
      The weather in May

umi wa harete / Hie furinokosu / satsuki kana

Summer, 1688. *Mount Hiei*: see 70, 666, 715. 6-7-5.

421

The Cool Air

Calabash flowers
    Come autumn become so many
      shapes of bottle gourd

yūgao ya / aki wa iroiro no / fukube kana

Summer, 1688. *yūgao* ("evening faces"): Calabash gourd flowers, also known as moonflowers; see 10, 146; the plant produces similar-looking flowers but different shapes of gourd in the autumn. The poem was written on a charcoal container made out of a gourd and, unusually, uses both *ya* and *kana*: *ya* for the flowers being looked at, and *kana* for the gourds they will become in the autumn.

422

The first year of Genroku, a gathering on the fifth day of the Sixth Month

The noonfaced flowers
    after a night's sleep too short
      drowsing at midday

hirugao no / mijikayo neburu / hiruma kana

Summer, 1688. *Genroku*: the period from 1688 to 1704; the headnote was written at some stage after the change of era name. *hirugao* ("noon face"): bindweed flowers; see 175.

423

By noonfaced flowers
    I would lay me down to nap
      The mountain my bed

hirugao ni / hirune shō mono / Toko no Yama

Summer, 1688. *Toko no Yama*: near Hikone on the Nakasendō Road, a place often mentioned in connection with sleep in waka poems (*toko* means "bed" and *yama* "mountain"). The *hiru* in both *hirugao* and *hirune* ("midday nap") means "midday" or "noon."

424

Hearing that Chine had passed away, I sent a message to Kyorai from Mino

The robes of the dead
    need also now to be aired
        The Doyō season

naki hito no / kosode mo ima ya / doyōboshi

Summer, 1688. *Chine:* the sister of Kyorai (Mukai Kyorai, 1651–1704), Bashō's disciple; see 603, 625, 703, 705, 792, 871, 872, 875. *doyōboshi:* "Doyō season airing"; see 72.

425

I will lodge here till
    the goosefoot plant grows into
        a stick to walk with

yadori sen / akaza no tsue ni / naru hi made

Summer, 1688. Bashō was staying at Myōshō-ji, Kajikawa, in modern Gifu, at the temple home of the monk, Kihaku. Buddhist monks, among others, ate the young leaves of a goosefoot (*akaza*), which when fully grown becomes a hardy but light walking stick.

426

Accepting an invitation from a certain Rakugo, I enjoy the cool shade of the pine trees on Mount Inaba, and recuperate from the hardships of my journey

A shaded hillside
    now I will restore myself
        melons in the field

yamakage ya / mi o yashinawan / uribatake

Summer, 1688. *Rakugo:* Yasukawa Suke'emon (1652–91), a wealthy cloth merchant in Gifu; see 427. *Mount Inaba:* the old name of Mount Kinka (also Kinkazan), in the center of the modern city of Gifu, and the location of several temples; see 428.

427

I'd liken a flower
     to a fragile child but none
          in the summer field

moroki hito ni / tatoen hana mo / natsuno kana

Summer, 1688. A poem of condolence to Rakugo, whose child had died shortly before Bashō's visit. *hana mo natsuno* conflates two expressions: hana *mo* na*i* ("with not a flower") and na*tsuno* ("a summer field").

428

Mount Inaba

The temple bell too
     about to reverberate
          The cicada's song

tsukigane mo / hibiku yōnari / semi no koe

Summer, 1688. *Mount Inaba*: see 426.

429

A certain Kisaburo invited me to his quiet home at the foot of Mount Inaba to enjoy the cool breezes

The castle's ruins
     But first I will go visit
          the ancient wellspring

shiroato ya / furui no shimizu / mazu towan

Summer, 1688. Alludes to a waka by Saigyō: *sumu hito no / kokoro kumaruru / izumi kana / mukashi o ika ni / omoiizuran* ("The heart of the one / living here clear as the spring / waters being drawn / O now how my thoughts turn to / the long-gone days of the past").

430

I was invited to see the famed cormorant fishing as the dark drew in. People were seated under the trees at the foot of Mount Inaba, raising their sake cups

Nothing of the kind close
       to the Nagara river's
              vinegared sweetfish

mata ya tagui / Nagara no kawa no / ayunamasu

Summer, 1688. *cormorant fishing: ukai,* a traditional method of catching river fish such as *ayu* (sweetfish) using trained cormorants. The fishermen on the Nagara River still have official patronage from the emperor. *namasu:* vegetables and raw fish in vinegar; see 615, 657.

431

On the Nagara River in Mino, going to see fishermen using cormorants to fish

So alluring indeed
       but soon a sadness follows
              The cormorant boats

omoshirōte / yagate kanashiki / ubune kana

Summer, 1688.

432

In the Same Place, Enjoying a Water Tower

Looking all around
    everything that comes to the eye
        a freshening breeze

kono atari / me ni miyuru mono wa / mina suzushi

Summer, 1688. In *Oi Nikki* ("Backpack Diary"), a posthumous collection
edited by his disciple Shikō (Kagami Shikō, 1665–1731; see 751, 755) in
1695, the poem appears at the end of the *haibun* "An Account of Eighteen
View Tower." The poem was written to thank his host, Kashima, who
owned a tower with panoramic views of the Nagara River in Mino (Gifu);
see 431. Bashō dubs Kashima's tower "Eighteen View Tower" because it
calls to his mind the Chinese "Eighteen Views": the Eight Views of Xiaox-
iang (also Hsiao-hsiang) and the Ten Scenes of West Lake; see 568.

433

Though summer has come
    only one frond on the fern
        the one Creeping Fern

natsu kite mo / tada hitotsuba no / hitoha kana

Summer, 1688. *hitotsuba* (literally, "one leaf"): *Pyrossia lingua,* tongue
fern, felt fern, or creeping fern. The plant has olive green blade-like
fronds, about 45 cm long and 6 cm wide, which rise singly from slender
surface-creeping rhizomes.

434

The Third Day

No simile to
    capture nothing to compare
        to the crescent moon

nanigoto no / mitate ni mo nizu / mika no tsuki

Autumn, 1688. *The Third Day:* the third day of the seventh lunar month.
In classical poetry, the crescent moon has inspired comparison to,
among other things, a sickle, a bow, the prow of a boat, and the eyebrow
of a woman. See 157, 275, 767, 813.

435

At Hōzō-ji, in the Rice Fields

The harvest half done
On the side with the stubble
the call of a snipe

kariato ya / wase kata kata no / shigi no koe

Autumn, 1688. Alludes to a famous waka by Saigyō: *kokoro naki / mi ni mo aware wa / shirarekeri / shigi tatsu sawa no / aki no yūgure* ("Even a person / with no feeling could not help / being touched and moved / seeing a snipe flying up / on an evening in autumn").

436

That cloudshape a sign?
Pining for a lightning flash
the rice god's message

ano kumo wa / inazuma o matsu / tayori kana

Autumn, 1688. Lightning was considered a good omen for the rice harvest.

437

On a Newly Built House

Such a splendid house
Out the back sparrows delight
in the millet field

yoki ie ya / suzume yorokobu / sedo no awa

Autumn, 1688. The house of Saburōzaemon, younger brother of Shimosato Chisoku, a disciple of Bashō in Narumi.

438

A View of Narumi

The first of autumn
> The sea and the rice fields too
> > all the one green hue

hatsuaki ya / umi mo aota no / hitomidori

Autumn, 1688. *Narumi:* see 244, 322, 323, 335.

439

Risshū, the First Day of Autumn

Tired of journeying
> how many days is it now?
> > The autumnal wind

tabi ni akite / kyō ikuka yara / aki no kaze

Autumn, 1688. *Risshū*, the first day of autumn, fell on August 5.

440

A pond of lotus
> Unplucked blossoms left just so
> > Tama Matsuri

hasuike ya / orade sonomama / Tama Matsuri

Autumn, 1688. *Tama Matsuri:* a festival to pray to and for the souls of the dead, and when the souls revisit the world. In the past, beginning on July 13 of the lunar calendar until July 16, nowadays held in mid-August. Cut lotus blossoms are used as decorations at this time. See 545, 644.

441

On the twentieth day of the Seventh Month, the fifth year of Jōkyō, I went to the gathering hosted by Chōkō at Chikuyō-ken

Millet on millet
　　　Nothing at all to want for in
　　　　　this grass-roofed cottage

awa hie ni / toboshiku mo arazu / kusa no io

Autumn, 1688. *Chōkō:* the priest at Yakushidō Temple in Nagoya. *Jōkyō:* see 190. *awa:* foxtail millet; *hie:* Japanese millet, also known as barnyard millet. Bashō is praising Chōkō for his self-sufficiency.

442

Chrysanthemum Blossom Butterfly

Autumn deepening
　　　A butterfly too licking
　　　　　chrysanthemum dew

aki o hete / chō mo nameru ya / kiku no tsuyu

Autumn, 1688. See 108, 234 and 552 for the story of Jidō and chrysanthemum dew. A butterfly in autumn is considered old and weak.

443

This house doesn't hide
　　　its vegetable soup and
　　　　　Fushimi peppers

kakusanu zo / yado wa najiru ni / tōgarashi

Autumn, 1688. A poem in praise of the simple life of his host, a doctor named Usō. Fushimi peppers are long peppers eaten as a vegetable rather than used as a spice.

444

Yasui, Setting Off on a Journey

The back and shoulders
    at farewell a loneliness
        The autumnal wind

miokuri no / ushiro ya sabishi / aki no kaze

Autumn, 1688. *Yasui:* Okada Yasui (1658–1743): a merchant and disciple in Nagoya; see 867.

445

1

The being-seen-offs
    the farewells come to an end
        Autumn in Kiso

okuraretsu / wakaretsu hate wa / Kiso no aki

2

The being-seen-offs
    the seeings-off at an end
        Autumn in Kiso

okuraretsu / okuritsu hate wa / Kiso no aki

Autumn, 1688. The first version appears in *Sarashina Kikō;* the second version in *Arano,* an anthology compiled by Kakei, supervised by Bashō, in 1689. Bashō was leaving Kiso (see 253), in Shinano Province (modern-day Nagano and Gifu), for Sarashina, on the journey that would become *Sarashina Kikō* ("Sarashina Journal").

446

The various grasses
    singularly showing off
        brilliant blossoms

kusa iroiro / ono ono hana no / tegara kana

Autumn, 1688. Another poem of farewell to his disciples as he set off for Sarashina. The disciples had given him a collection of their poems. 6-7-5.

447

People came to see me off at the edge of town, and we had a few drinks together

> The morning glories
>> ignoring all this drinking
>>> In full bloom themselves

asagao wa / sakamori shiranu / sakari kana

Autumn, 1688. *asagao* ("morning face"): morning glory. Bashō was leaving, with Etsujin (see 327, 470), to go view the moon over Mount Obasute in Sarashina; see 452.

448

> Slivery slender
>> Even dew a burden for
>>> the patrinia

hyoro hyoro to / nao tsuyukeshi ya / ominaeshi

Autumn, 1688. *ominaeshi*: literally, "lady flower" or "maiden flower," *Patrinia scabiosifolia;* see 51. It has a long history in Japanese poetry as one of the *aki no nanakusa* ("seven grasses of autumn"). In the Noh play *Obasute* (see 452), the ghost of the abandoned old woman compares herself to a patrinia whose bloom has passed its prime.

449

> I'd like to sprinkle
>> there a picture in lacquer
>>> the moon at this inn

ano naka ni / maki-e kakitashi / yado no tsuki

Autumn, 1688. *maki-e:* literally, "sprinkled picture," a design on the surface of lacquerware. The moon is frequently compared to a round lacquered sake cup or tray.

450

A ladder-like bridge
And clinging on for dear life
these tightening vines

Kakehashi ya / inochi o karamu / tsutakazura

Autumn, 1688. *Kakehashi*: a suspension bridge along a riverside cliff on
the Kiso Road near Agematsu in Shinano Province, about which poems
had been written for centuries. It was about 160 meters long and origi-
nally made from boards tied with chains and wisteria vines, but by
Bashō's day it had been rebuilt with sturdier materials and was no
longer dangerous; see 451.

451

The Kiso swing bridge
The first thing that springs to mind
the horses crossing

Kakehashi ya / mazu omoiizu / umamukae

Autumn, 1688. *uma mukae*: a version of *komamukae* (see 54), the cer-
emony at which horses were presented at the Imperial Court in Kyoto.
The area around Kiso was famous for horse-rearing, and on the journey
to the Court the horses had to cross the Kakehashi bridge.

452

Mount Obasute

The vestigial trace
    of an old woman crying
        moon companion

omokage ya / oba hitori naku / tsuki no tomo

Autumn, 1688. *Mount Obasute:* in folklore, a mountain on which old
women were abandoned; associated most often with Mount Kamuriki
in Nagano Prefecture. Legend says that the practice was broken by a
man who, seeing the moon over the mountain, returns at dawn the next
morning to take his mother (in some versions, his aunt), whom he had
reluctantly abandoned, back home. Bashō may also have in mind the
Noh play *Obasute,* which includes the phrase *tsuki no tomo* (literally,
"friend of the moon"). In the play, a man from Kyoto and his attendants,
like Bashō and his companion, go to view the moon at Sarashina. They
climb Mount Obasute and there they learn the tale of the man who, at
the behest of his wife, abandoned the aunt who had raised him. In
regret for his actions, he had returned to the mountain, to find her
already dead and turned into a boulder.

453

Staying at Sakaki in Shinano Province

The Sixteenth-night moon
    and I too lingering on
        in Sarashina

izayoi mo / mada Sarashina no / kōri kana

Autumn, 1688. *izayoi:* the "hesitating" moon, on the sixteenth night of
the month; see 458, 717, 718, 811. There is a play on the name *Sarashina*
and *saranu* ("not leaving"). As the poem by Etsujin immediately follow-
ing this one in *Sarashina Kikō* ("Sarashina Journal") attests, they spent
three days, from the fifteenth to the seventeenth, traveling the area to
view the moon from different vantages.

454

My body run through
    with the hot tang of daikon
      The wind in autumn

mi ni shimite / daikon karashi / aki no kaze

Autumn, 1688. The *karami* daikon (white radish) of the Kiso region
was known to be particularly pungent.

455

Kiso horse-chestnuts
    For the weary in the world
      some such souvenirs

Kiso no tochi / ukiyo no hito no / miyage kana

Autumn, 1688. *tochi: Aesculus chinensis,* a variety of horse-chestnut
that grows in remote mountains, in this case in the Kiso region in Shi-
nano Province. The eating of horse-chestnuts, ground into a gruel or as
cakes, is associated with hermits and monks. Bashō sent this poem and
some chestnuts to Kakei (see 340, 445, 866) in Nagoya. *ukiyo:* "the float-
ing world," the life of the city, in particular the life of transitory pleas-
ure-seeking; see 164, 206, 344, 753, 959.

456

Zenkō-ji

The light of the moon
    The Four Gates and the Four Sects
      All one and the same

tsuki kage ya / shimon shishū mo / tada hitotsu

Autumn, 1688. The Four Gates of Zenkō-ji, Nagano. In fact, the temple
embraced three Buddhist sects (Tendai, Jōdo, and Ji), and Kon Eizō
argues that Bashō made it four as a poetic expedient.

457

Tossing and turning
   the stones on Mount Asama
      an autumn windstorm

fuki tobasu / ishi wa Asama no / nowaki kana

Autumn, 1688. *Mount Asama:* an active volcano between Shinano and
Kōzuke Provinces (Nagano and Gunma Prefectures today). *Sarashina
Kikō* ends with this poem. *nowaki:* a typhoon in autumn, the literal
meaning is "field parting (wind)"; see 148, 646, 927.

458

*The old host of the lotus pond loves chrysanthemums. Yesterday he held
a party for the Chrysanthemum Festival like that one at Longshan, and
today we drink what remains of the sake while we make our poems.
Who of us will be in good health when we gather again next year?*

   At Sodō-tei, Chrysanthemums on the Tenth

The Sixteenth-night moon?
   Or on the morning after
      the chrysanthemums?

izayoi no / izure ka kesa ni / nokoru kiku

Autumn, 1688. *Sodō-tei:* the residence of Sodō (Yamaguchi Sodō; see
121, 263, 317), a poet and Bashō's friend. The Chrysanthemum Festival
(*Chōyō no Sekku*) is held on the ninth day of the Ninth Month (see 108,
582, 725, 909), so the "Tenth" is the day after the peak of the blossoms.
Longshan: a mountain in China, where the poet Tao Yuanming's
(Enmei; see 238, 803) maternal grandfather attended a gathering
hosted by the Jin Dynasty general, Huan Wen (312–73), and acciden-
tally dropped his hat, whereupon all present derided him for his lack of
manners. His response surprised everyone: as he continued to drink
nonchalantly, he composed fine poems. *The Sixteenth-night moon:* the
day after the full moon; see 453.

459

The thinning at Kiso
        I'm still not quite over yet
                the late harvest moon

Kiso no yase mo / mada naoranu ni / nochi no tsuki

Autumn, 1688. Written on October 6, a month after Bashō had returned
to Edo from his arduous journey to the west, and he was still suffering
from the effects of illness on the road. In the lunar calendar it was the
thirteenth of the Ninth Month, prized as the day of the "late harvest
moon" (the harvest moon occurred in the Eighth Month), and Bashō
hosted a moonviewing party, attended by Etsujin, Sanpū, and six other
poets.

460

Leaves of the ivy
        bring a tinge of long ago
                The autumn colors

tsuta no ha wa / mukashi mekitaru / momiji kana

Autumn, 1688.

461

Autumn departing
        Scrunching my body under
                the bedding too small

yuku aki ya / mi ni hikimatou / minobuton

Autumn, 1688. *minobuton:* the smallest futon mattress; literally, a
"three-*no* futon" (*no* was a measurement of width, about 36 cm). A
minobuton is usually used as a *shikibuton* (mattress), but Bashō here is
pulling it over himself like a *kakebuton* (duvet), which is usually wider,
from four to five *no* in width.

462

The Emperor Nintoku's "When I climb to a high place and look about me," that considerate poem is remembered even now

> By the Emperor's
> > grace the people got to glow
> > > by their cooking fires

eiryo nite / nigiwau tami no / niwakamado

Spring, 1688. An allusion to a poem by the emperor Nintoku (the six-teenth Emperor of Japan, traditionally, if inaccurately, considered to have reigned from 313–99). After climbing the tower of his palace and seeing no cooking fires, he realized the poverty of the people and exempted them from taxes for three years. Three years later, from the tower he saw cooking smoke everywhere and wrote the waka Bashō quotes from. *niwamakado:* a temporary cooking range built in the earth near the door, or in the garden. It was a custom in Nara in olden days for it to be used on the first three days of the New Year, and for the people of the house and servants to gather to eat and drink; a season word for spring. This poem (and 463) are examples of *daiei* (poems on set themes, these particular ones on rulers and exemplary subjects in the past), and a *daiei* poem need not stick to the season within which it was composed.

463

Musashi-no-Kami Yasutoki, he put benevolence first, and threw off personal desire in governing the country

> The full moon shining
> > The Fifty-One Article
> > > Law's resplendent light

meigetsu no / izuru ya Gojū- / ichi kajō

Autumn, 1688. *The Fifty-One Article Law:* the *Goseibai (Jōei) Shikimoku*, the administrative code of the Kamakura shogunate, promulgated in 1232 by the third Regent Hōjō Yasutoki ("Musashi-no-Kami Yasutoki").

464

Cut all chrysanthemums
　　cockscombs to commemorate
　　　　Nichiren's decease

kiku keitō / kiri tsukushikeri / Omeikō

Winter, 1688. *Omeikō*: memorial service for the priest Nichiren (1222–82), founder of the Nichiren sect of Buddhism; see 540, 779. Bashō said: "This hokku is mediocre, but here I have tried, in my own clumsy way, to use a season word [*Omeikō*] no one has used in the fifty-year history of haikai. If the holy priest's soul is still around, I'd like him to take note of my name. That's the joke I tell people" (Ueda, p. 214). Unlike most critics, Kon Eizō categorizes the season of this poem as winter. *Omeikō* is now a season word for autumn, but it used to be a season word for winter, since the ceremony was held on the thirteenth day of the Tenth Month (mid-November in the solar calendar).

465

Wintering indoors
　　I will lean my back again
　　　　against this pillar

fuyugomori / mata yorisowan / kono hashira

Winter, 1688. *fuyugomori*: see 334, 736, 821, 822.

466

Five or six of us
　　spread out around the tea cakes
　　　　The hearth in the floor

itsutsu mutsu / cha-no-ko ni narabu / irori kana

Winter, 1688. *irori*: a square, stone-lined pit in the floor, for heating the home and cooking.

467

The late Dōen of Daitsū-an, whose name I knew well, we'd promised to meet some day, but alas before that day could come he passed away, like the overnight frost of early winter. Today, I hear, is the first anniversary of his death

That figure I long
        to see his walking stick made
                from a withered tree

sono katachi / mibaya kareki no / tsue no take

Winter, 1688. *Dōen:* a Zen monk about whom little is known.

468

Mourning Rika's Wife

The futon pulled up
        over the head the freezing
                night's desolation

kazuki fusu / futon ya samuki / yo ya sugoki

Winter, 1688. Rika had gifted Bashō the tree from which his pen name derived; see 141, 308.

469

At a Memorial

The brazier's banked
        ashes extinguishing to
                the hiss of your tears

uzumibi mo / kiyu ya namida no / niyuru oto

Winter, 1688. Rakugo's son had died; see 426, 427. Another text has the headnote "In sympathy for a person who has lost a young son."

470

Jūzō of Owari Province is known as Etsujin, after the place where he was born. Now he earns his living in the city, in order to get food and fuel. After working two days, he enjoys himself for the next two; if he works three days, the next three he spends at his ease. He loves a drink, and he sings from the "Tales of the Heike" when he's drunk. He is a man I call a true friend

> The snows we have seen
> > have they again this year too
> > > fallen now anew?

futari mishi / yuki wa kotoshi mo / furikeru ka

Winter, 1688. *Etsujin:* see 324, 327, 329.

471

Playfully seeking a theme, I bags the two words "rice buying" on a snowy evening

> Off to buy the rice
> > in the snow this empty bag
> > > I'll use as a hood

kome kai ni / yuki no fukuro ya / nagezukin

Winter, 1688. The Eight Poor Poets of Fukagawa: Bashō, Isui, Taisui, Deikin, Sekigiku, Yūgo, Sora, and Rotsū drew lots to decide on the themes (*dai*, as in *daiei*, see note to 462) of their poems. The preset themes were "rice buying," "sake buying," "firewood buying," "charcoal buying," "tea buying," "tōfu buying," "drawing up water," and "boiling rice." *yuki* can mean both "snow" and "outward journey."

472

Are you a friend to
        the self-secluding cleavers
                winter greens seller?

sashikomoru / mugura no tomo ka / fuyuna uri

Winter, 1688. *mugura*: cleavers; see 256. In winter seclusion in his creeper-covered hut in Fukagawa, Bashō occasionally saw farmers from nearby Komatsugawa selling their meagre winter produce. *komatsuna*, a near synonym for *fuyuna* ("winter greens"), derives its name from Komatsugawa.

473

Everyone please pray
        to Futami's sacred rope
                the end of the year

mina ogame / Futami no shime o / toshi no kure

Winter, 1688. *Futami*: at Futami-ga-ura in Ise Bay there are a pair of rocks known as *Meoto-iwa* (the "Wedded Rocks") connected to each other by a *shimenawa*, a ceremonial rope of entwined and twisted rice straw.

474

On this New Year's Day
        sunlight on rice terraces
                what I yearn to see

ganjitsu wa / Tagoto no hi koso / koishikere

New Year, 1689. Written on January 21, the lunar New Year. *Tagoto no*: most usually refers to the *moon* shining on each field of a rice terrace, especially the rice terraces in Sarashina; see 416.

475

Such expectations!
>This year in the spring again
>>the skies of the road

omoshiro ya / kotoshi no haru mo / tabi no sora

Spring, 1689. Bashō was beginning to plan the journey recounted in
Oku no Hosomichi ("The Narrow Road to the Interior").

476

Morning and evening
>pining at Matsushima
>>A one-sided love

asa yosa o / taga Matsushima zo / kata-gokoro

No season, 1689. *Matsushima* ("Pine Island/s"): see 133, 514. As in Eng-
lish, *matsu* can mean both pine tree and to "pine for" a loved one.

477

Genroku, Second Year, Second Month, at Tōzan's Inn

A shimmer rises
>off of me from the shoulders
>>of my paper robe

kagerō no / waga kata ni tatsu / kamiko kana

Spring, 1689. *Genroku:* the period from the Ninth Month of 1688 to the
Third Month of 1704. The poem was written in March, 1689, at the *kasen*
party at the inn where Tōzan, a poet from Ōgaki, was staying; see 979.

478

Red ume blossoms
>The unseen love created
>>by elegant blinds

kōbai ya / minu koi tsukuru / tamasudare

Spring, 1689. *tamasudare:* decorated bead blinds, used by court ladies.

479

Looking Respectfully at a Picture of Futami

Succumb not to doubt
    The flowering waves tell of
        Spring at Futami

utagau na / ushio no hana mo / Ura no haru

Spring, 1689. *Ura:* Futami-ga-ura; see 473. *utagau na* ("doubt not"): a phrase used in religious discourse.

480

Even the cleavers'
    young leaves lovely and tender
        A tumbledown house

mugura sae / wakaba wa yasashi / yabureie

Spring, 1689. *mugura:* cleavers; see 256. Shikin, a samurai from Ōgaki, had asked Bashō to write a poem on a painting of a ramshackle house; see 736.

481

Into the skylark's
    song a rhythm intervenes
        The kiji calling

hibari naku / naka no hyōshi ya / kiji no koe

Spring, 1689. *kiji:* a green pheasant; see 394, 621. *naka no hyōshi:* a technical term for rhythm in Noh.

482

Looking at a Picture of a Man Drinking

The moon and blossoms
    lacking just a man drinking
        sake all alone

tsuki hana mo / nakute sake nomu / hitori kana

No season, 1689.

483

Even a thatched hut's
　　world replaced with another
　　　　A hina doll house

kusa no to mo / sumikawaru yo zo / hina no ie

Spring, 1689. The first hokku in *Oku no Hosomichi*. There is a slightly
different version (with *ya* instead of *zo*) written on a piece of paper in
Bashō's own hand, with a headnote which reads "Turning My Hut Over
to a Man with Daughters." Before he set out, Bashō passed his hut on to
a man named Heiu (or Heiuemon). *hina doll*: see 93; at *Hinamatsuri*
(the third day of the Third Month in Bashō's day; March 3 after the
adoption of the Gregorian calendar), hina dolls are displayed on a red-
carpeted stand for the young girls in a family. The dolls are passed
down from generation to generation. The word *yo* (*sumikawaru yo*) can
mean "world," "period," or "generation."

484

The youngster sweetfish
　　seeing off an old icefish
　　　　That kind of farewell

ayu no ko no / shirauo okuru / wakare kana

Spring, 1689. Written as Bashō was departing on the *Oku no Hosomichi*.

485

Springtime departing
　　Birds cry and the eyes of fish
　　　　brim over with tears

yuku haru ya / tori naki uo no / me wa namida

Spring, 1689. Both 484 and 485 were written as Bashō set off from Fuk-
agawa on the *Oku no Hosomichi* journey, but only 485 was included in
the final version. The poem alludes to "Looking at the Springtime" by
Du Fu (Tu Fu; see 126, 159, 184): "In fallen States / hills and streams are
found, / Cities have Spring, / grass and leaves abound; // Though at such
times / flowers might drop tears, / Parting from mates, / birds have hid-
den fears" (Cooper, p. 171). See also 515.

486

Muro no Yashima

Threads of heated air
    interweaving intertwined
        with signals of smoke

itoyū ni / musubitsukitaru / kemuri kana

Spring, 1689. *Muro no Yashima:* a Shinto shrine mentioned often in
poetry, now called Ōmiwa Jinja in Sōja, Tochigi. Poems concerning the
shrine conventionally mention smoke, an allusion to the tale of Kono-
hana Sakuya Hime who, to prove the divinity of her pregnancy to her
consort Ninigi no Mikoto, gave birth in a burning room. *itoyū* (literally,
"thread play"): a heat shimmer; see 487. *musubi:* "to tie" laces, etc.

487

The sun about to
    set the last shimmering to
        the heat of the day

iri kakaru / hi mo itoyū no / nagori kana

Spring, 1689.

488

A town with no bell
    to ring what is there for them
        the springtime passing?

kane tsukanu / sato wa nani o ka / haru no kure

Spring, 1689. Likely refers to Kanuma, in Shimotsuke Province (Tochigi
Prefecture). Even today all over Japan, at 5 P.M. or 6 P.M., bells are rung.
As in 489, the phrase *haru no kure* can mean either "an evening in
spring" or "the passing of spring."

489

Feeling Lonely on a Spring Evening in a Village

The bell at sunset
Even that unlistened to
the springtime passing

iriai no / kane mo kikoezu / haru no kure

Spring, 1689. *iriai no kane:* a temple bell at sunset.

490

Ah the resplendence
on evergreen on young leaves
the light of the sun

ara tōto / aoba wakaba no / hi no hikari

Summer, 1689. Written at Nikkō, the site of the Tōshōgū Shrine, the mausoleum of the first Tokugawa shogun, Ieyasu (1543–1616), and a Buddhist temple founded by Shōdō Shōnin (735–817). Nikkō means "light of the sun," as does *hi no hikari.*

491

Confined for a while
in behind the waterfall
The retreat begins

shibaraku wa / taki ni komoru ya / ge no hajime

Summer, 1689. The waterfall, at Nikkō, is called *Urami no Taki* ("View-from-Behind Falls"; see 492). *ge* means a period of time, and is an abbreviation of *ge-ango* or *ge-gomori,* with both *ango* and *komori* meaning "retreat": the Buddhist practice of confinement and seclusion for ninety days beginning on the sixteenth day of the Fourth Month.

492

A cuckoo calling
>> at the View-from-Behind Falls
>>> out front I'm behind

hototogisu / Urami no Taki no / ura omote

Summer, 1689. *Urami no Taki:* "View-from-Behind Falls"; see 491. Written with different kanji characters, *urami* can also mean "resentment": Bashō resents not being able to hear the cuckoo clearly from behind the waterfall.

493

Visiting Suitō of Yoze in Nasu Province

A hay-shouldering
>> man marked the way here across
>>> the summer farmlands

magusa ou / hito o shiori no / natsuno kana

Summer, 1689. *Suitō:* Kanokobata Toyoakira, a follower of Bashō, the younger brother of Jōbōji Zusho Takakatsu (1661–1730), whose pen name was Shūa; see 494.

494

On the Beautiful Views at Master Shūa's House

The mountain itself too
>> moving into the garden
>>> the cool summer room

yama mo niwa ni / ugokiiruru ya / natsuzashiki

Summer, 1689. The summer room was a tatami room with sliding doors that opened to the outdoors, allowing views into the distance.

495

Even though its ground
*   cover less than five feet square*
to build this grass hut
*   is still something to regret*
*   If only there were no rain*

I knew the Priest Butchō wrote this poem about his hut, but seeing it is
more moving than hearing about it and my soul feels purified

Even woodpeckers
        leave this hut inviolate
                in the summer grove

kitsutsuki mo / io wa yaburazu / natsukodachi

Summer, 1689. Bashō had studied Zen meditation with Butchō (see
314), and on the *Oku no Hosomichi* journey visited the hut where
Butchō had once lived, behind Ungan-ji in Kurobane, Tochigi. Butchō's
poem in Japanese reads: *tateyoko no / goshaku ni taranu / kusa no to o /*
musubu mo kuyashi / ame nakariseba.

496

Rice fields and barley
        and above all the sound of
                the summer cuckoo

ta ya mugi ya / naka ni mo natsu no / hototogisu

Summer, 1689. Written on the seventh day of the Fourth Month, at
Kurobane, in anticipation of a journey to the Shirakawa Barrier, which
was famous in poetry for scenes of spring, autumn, and winter.

497

In the summer hills
        I pray to these wooden clogs
                starting my journey

natsuyama ni / ashida o ogamu / kadode kana

Summer, 1689. Bashō visited the Gyōja-dō at Kōmyō Temple in Kurobane, and saw the statue of En no Gyōja (see 393). He is typically represented as wearing a white hooded robe and a pair of unusually high wooden clogs with one support instead of the usual two, for walking in the rain.

498

On a Painting of a Bashō Tree and a Crane

The call of a crane
        That voice would tatter the leaves of
                the bashō tree

tsuru naku ya / sono koe ni bashō / yarenubeshi

Autumn, 1689. Written at Kurobane. "There are lines of a Chinese poem that say: 'As the crane screeches in a deep valley / Its voice reaches as high as heaven.' Or the hokku may allude to the unbearably pathetic sound of a crane crying for its child at night. In either case, the image of a banana plant [*bashō*] is irreplaceable here.—*Tosai*" (Ueda, p. 233).

499

The chief steward of the mansion lent me a horse as I departed. The groom leading me asked "Can you write me a poem card?" I was touched by the refinement of his request

Across the wide plain
        pull my horse's reins toward
                the cuckoo calling

no o yoko ni / uma hiki mukeyo / hototogisu

Summer, 1689. Bashō was traveling across the Nasu Plain in Shimot-suke. A poem card is a rectangular sheet of stiff paper on which a poem is written to give as a gift.

500

Two priests on pilgrimage together to the north country visited Shino-hara in Nasu and then hurried to see the Sesshōseki, the Killing Stone, but on the way it started to rain, so they decided to stay here

> From on high falling
> > the cuckoo's calling at the
> > > inn at Takaku

ochikuru ya / Takaku no shuku no / hototogisu

Summer, 1689. *Sesshōseki:* see 502. The word *taka* ("high") is embedded in the place name Takaku, northwest of Kurobane. The poem, in particular the phrase *ochikuru ya,* alludes to the Noh play *Sesshōseki.*

501

The gods of Yuzen Daimyōjin are enshrined here with the gods of Iwash-imizu Hachimangū, and when we pray here we pray to the gods of both shrines

> The hot waters scooped
> > the covenant all the same
> > > the spring from the rocks

yu o musubu / chikai mo onaji / iwashimizu

Summer, 1689. The *yu* of *Yuzen* means "hot water," and *Iwashimizu* means "spring water from rocks." *chikai* means "pledge," and in this case the pledge is on the part of the gods to save mortals; *chikai mo onaji* means "the divine favor will be the same," or "you will be saved either way."

502

The Killing Stone

The stench of the stone
>   The summer grasses burn red
>   the dewdrops boiling

ishi no ka ya / natsukusa akaku / tsuyu atsushi

Summer, 1689. *The Killing Stone: Sesshōseki,* a large rock located near Nasu, in present-day Tochigi Prefecture, said in Japanese mythology to kill anyone who approaches due to the noxious gases that emanate from around it (Nasu is the site of sulphurous hot springs). Legend says that the stone is haunted by the spirit of a nine-tailed fox who had transformed into Tamano-no-Mae, a beautiful woman intent on seducing and killing Emperor Toba (1103–56). Exposed by the exorcist Abe no Yasuchika, the fox fled to Nasu Plain, where later it was killed by Miura-no-suke.

503

The willow "where the spring water flows" was there still at Ashino village, by a rice field. The district chief, a man I called The Registrar, had often said "I want to show you the willow," and I always wondered where it might be. Today I stand in the shade of that tree

A rice field planted
>   And off I departed from
>   the willow tree's shade

ta ichimai / uete tachisaru / yanagi kana

Summer, 1689. Bashō alludes to a waka by Saigyō: *michinobe ni / shimizu nagaruru / yanagi kage / shibashi tote koso / tachidomaritsure* ("Beside the roadway / the spring water flows in the / shade of a willow / Rest a little while I thought / Yet I have lingered so long"). "The Registrar": the man's name was Ashino Minbu Suketoshi, with *minbu* originally the name of a Chinese government office, later renamed *kohō.* In the headnote, Bashō nicknames the man *Kohō-bō,* something like "Mr. Registrar."

504

To the west? Or to the east?
  Yet first through the rice seedlings
    the sound of the wind

nishi ka higashi ka / mazu sanae ni mo / kaze no oto

Summer, 1689. Bashō had reached the Shirakawa Barrier, and is allud-ing to a poem by the priest Nōin: *Miyako o ba / kasumi to tomoni / tachishikado / akikaze zo fuku / Shirakawa no Seki* ("In the springtime mist / I had left the Capital / with the haze rising / now the autumn wind blows at / Shirakawa Barrier"). Though it is summer, and so Bashō cannot feel the autumn wind that Nōin felt, the first thing he feels at the Shirakawa Barrier is the wind.

505

Crossing the Shirakawa Barrier

Here's where art begins
  In a rice-field in the wilds
    the rice-planting chants

fūryū no / hajime ya oku no / taueuta

Summer, 1689. Actually written at Sukagawa, as a greeting hokku to the host of the *kasen* party, Sagara Tōkyū (1638–1715). The Shirakawa Bar-rier was the entrance to the northern provinces. *fūryū* (literally, "drift-ing on the wind"): a term for aesthetic taste; see 401.

506

*The Chinese written character "chestnut" is formed by combining "west"
and "tree," and so it is that the chestnut tree is associated with the West-
ern Pureland of Amida Buddhism. Hence the Bodhisattva Gyōki, so they
say, used the wood of the chestnut for his staff and for the pillars of his
house*

> By worldly people
>> unregarded the chestnut
>>> blossoms by the eaves

yo no hito no / mitsukenu hana ya / noki no kuri

Summer, 1689. A greeting hokku for Kashin, a Buddhist monk who had
a chestnut tree by the eaves of his house. Gyōki (see 394) was a monk
who wandered the country helping to build bridges and dams, and
roads. He also played a role in raising funds for the Great Buddha at
Tōdai-ji, Nara.

507

*I missed hearing your poems in Shirakawa. I feel so full of regret I am
writing a letter from the road in Sukagawa*

> The border guard's house
>> Would I had only asked the
>>> water rail to knock

sekimori no / yado o kuina ni / toou mono

Summer, 1689. A greeting poem in a letter to Ka-un written at Sagara
Tōkyū's house in Sukagawa. Bashō had only found out about Ka-un
from Tōkyū (see 505). The water rail's call is often compared to knock-
ing on a door; see 934.

508

About two ri east of the post-town of Sukagawa is the Ishikawa Water-fall, which for a long time I'd planned to go and see. Alas, the heavy rains of the last few days had swollen the waters of the river so much it was impossible to cross

Rainy season rains
      outpouring even the Falls
         An overflowing

samidare wa / taki furiuzumu / mikasa kana

Summer, 1689. *ri:* a unit of distance, about 4 km; see 66, 218, 388.

509

Picking rice seedlings
      by hand and olden times rub
         again on the stone

sanae toru / temoto ya mukashi / shinobuzuri

Summer, 1689. *shinobuzuri:* in *Oku no Hosomichi,* Bashō writes of coming to the village of Shinobu to look for a large rock on which the local custom had been to dye cloth by rubbing (*zuri*) ferns (*shinobu*) against rough stone. The verb *shinobu* also means "to recall"; see 207, 221, 726.

510

A satchel and a sword
      on these May days fly them too
         by paper banners

oi mo tachi mo / satsuki ni kazare / kaminobori

Summer, 1689. *satsuki:* the Fifth Month of the lunar calendar. On and around *Tango no Sekku* ("Boys' Day," the fifth day of the Fifth Month; see 75), *kaminobori* (a paper banner on which a god, legendary figure, or samurai warrior is painted) are flown from poles. Bashō was visiting Iō-ji, a temple that held the sword of the military commander Minamoto no Yoshitsune (1159–89; see 209, 515, 545, 682), and the traveling chest of his loyal retainer, the warrior monk Benkei (d. 1189).

511

The Takekuma
        Pine let it be shown to him
            late-blooming cherries

takekuma no / matsu misemōse / osozakura

Kyohaku gave that poem to me as a farewell gift, so I wrote

From the cherry blooms
        to the double-trunked pine tree
            a three-month longing

sakura yori / matsu wa futaki o / mitsuki goshi

Summer, 1689. *The Takekuma Pine*: a famous pine tree with a trunk that forked just above the base, and which was long celebrated in poetry. Kyohaku (?–1696), a disciple of Bashō's in Edo. As in 12 and 20, the word *matsu* ("pine tree") can also, as in English, mean "to wait," or "to yearn for," "to pine"; and the *mi* in *mitsuki* can mean both "three" and "see."

512

Where's Kasashima?
        What I wonder as I walk
            the mud roads of May

Kasashima wa / izuko satsuki no / nukarimichi

Summer, 1689. *Kasashima*: the name means "hat island," the "hat" being one worn on a rainy day. Bashō was attempting to visit the grave of the poet Fujiwara no Sanekata (d. 999), who died in exile in Kasashima.

513

Sweet Flags *calamus*
  I will bind them to my feet
      as my sandal-cord

ayamegusa / ashi ni musuban / waraji no o

Summer, 1689. Bashō was visiting the woodblock cutter, Kaemon
(?–1746), in Sendai: "When Kae'mon, the eccentric painter [sic] and the
traveler's host, gives the parting visitor a pair of straw sandals (*waraji*)
with dark blue thongs (*o*), which echo the color of the iris (*ayame* or
ayamegusa), the traveler responds with [the poem above]. During the
Iris Festival, *ayame*, a seasonal word for summer, were placed on the
eaves of each house to ward off illness and evil. In a *fūkyō*-esque twist,
the poet ties the irises to his feet, as a prayer for safety on the road. The
journey, in short, becomes his dwelling" (Shirane, *Traces,* p. 246).
Shirane defines *fūkyō* as "poetic madness": "The behavior and thought
of a poetic persona so devoted to the pursuit of poetic beauty and ide-
als that he or she appears mad to the outside world" (p. 294). In Kon
Eizō's reading, Bashō is simply comparing the dark blue thongs dyed by
Kaemon to sweet flags. *ayame:* see 96, 761.

514

Matsushima is said to be the most beautiful place in this land of beauty.
Artists of the past and present have been enchanted by these islands,
have concentrated their hearts and minds and been moved to write and
paint. Here the sea spreads for three ri, with island after island of various
shapes and sizes, as if sculpted by the hand of heaven, each covered with
flourishing pines, all lovely, a beauty beyond words

Islands and islands
  A thousand pieces shattered
      on the summer sea

shimajima ya / chiji ni kudakite / natsu no umi

Summer, 1689. *Matsushima:* see 133, 476. *ri:* about 4 km; see 66, 218, 388.

515

At Takadachi in Ōshū Province

The summer grasses
   For warriors of the past
      glory's aftermath

natsukusa ya / tsuwamono domo ga / yume no ato

Summer, 1689. *Takadachi:* Takadachi Castle, in Hiraizumi, where Yos-
hitsune (see 209, 510, 545, 682) and his retainers died after a fierce bat-
tle. See 485 for Du Fu's "Looking at the Springtime," which Bashō quotes
in the lead-up to this poem in *Oku no Hosomichi.* "As with most of
Bashō's most noted poems, this hokku depends on polysemous key
words: *ato,* which can mean 'site,' 'aftermath,' 'trace,' or 'track,' and *yume,*
which can mean 'dream,' 'ambition,' or 'glory.' The summer grasses are the
'site' (*ato* as a spatial marker) of a former battlefield and of the dreams
of glory of the many noted warriors who fought here in the distant past.
Ato (literally 'after') also refers to the passage of time: the summer
grasses are the 'aftermath' of the dreams of glory" (Shirane, *Traces,* p.
238). "For the first time in the history of haikai, an idea has become the
subject of a poem.—*Konishi*" (Ueda, p. 243). Ōshū Province, also known
as Mutsu Province: included present-day Miyagi and Fukushima Pre-
fectures, and parts of Akita, as well as Aomori and Iwate Prefectures.

516

Rainy season rains
   leaving undimmed the brightness
     of the Hall of Light

samidare no / furinokoshite ya / Hikaridō

Summer, 1689. *Hikaridō:* the Hall of Light or Shining Hall, built in
1124, a pavilion with gilded walls in Chūson-ji, a temple near Hirai-
zumi. As well as rain, *furi* ("fall"/"falling") can also refer to the passing
of time; more than five hundred years had passed since the completion
of the *Hikaridō.*

517

The firefly at noon
    A light dim in the daylight
        behind a pillar

hotarubi no / hiru wa kietsutsu / hashira kana

Summer, 1689. Also written at the Hikaridō in Chūson-ji.

518

From Narugo Onsen we wanted to enter the province of Dewa through Shitomae Barrier. Few travelers come along this road, so the border guards were suspicious and interrogated us at length before they finally allowed us to pass. As the sun set, we reached the summit of a large mountain and saw a border guard's house where we asked for a night's lodging. Heavy rain and wind for the next three days confined us to this dismal place

The fleas and the lice
    and a horse having a pee
        at my pillowside

nomi shirami / uma no shitosuru / makuramoto

Summer, 1689. Bashō plays on the place name Shitomae: the kanji for *shito* is the same as that in the verb *shitosuru,* which refers to a child's urination. *the province of Dewa:* present-day Akita and Yamagata Prefectures.

519

A cooling freshness
    I have made my dwelling place
        now all is cushty

suzushisa o / waga yado ni shite / nemaru nari

Summer, 1689. A greeting hokku to Suzuki Seifū (1651–1721), a wealthy safflower merchant, of whom Bashō said, "despite his wealth, he has no meanness in his heart." *nemaru:* a dialect word of the area, meaning "at ease."

520

Come on crawl on out
        From under the silkworm shed
            the croak and its toad

haiide yo / kaiya ga shita no / hiki no koe

Summer, 1689. A play on a poem from the *Man'yōshū* (no. 2265): *asagasumi / kaiya ga shita ni / naku kawazu / koe da ni kikaba / ware koime ya mo* ("A morning of mist / and under the silkworm shed / the song of a frog / If I could but hear your voice / none of this yearning for you").

521

Seeing Safflowers in Bloom at Mogami

An eyebrow brush forms
        an image come to the mind
            Safflowers in bloom

mayuhaki o / omokage ni shite / beni no hana

Summer, 1689. *Mogami:* in the province of Dewa. *beni no hana:* safflowers, literally "rouge flowers," *Carthamus tinctorius,* from which rouge was made. The Mogami River was important to the region's economy and safflowers were transported from here to Kyoto; see 523, 525, 533.

522

Hear the quietness
       Entering into the rocks
             cicada refrain

shizukasa ya / iwa ni shimiiru / semi no koe

Summer, 1689. Written at Ryūshaku-ji, also known as Yamadera ("mountain temple"), in Yamagata. The temple is now called Risshaku-ji (or Rissyakuji). There is another version of the poem, with the title "Ryūshaku-ji": *Yamadera ya / ishi ni shimitsuku / semi no koe* ("The mountain temple / Ingraining into the rocks / cicada refrain"). Another version reads: *sabishisa ya / iwa ni shimikomu / semi no koe* ("The lonesomeness here / Permeating the rockslabs / cicada refrain"). Since the word can be both singular and plural, a famous conundrum concerns the number of *semi* (cicada/s): "If my sensibility is reliable, there should not be many cicadas here—*Mizuho*. I disagree. The whole mountain is filled with the cicadas' screech.—*Watsuji*" (Ueda, p. 249). Bashō may be alluding to "Entering Ruoye Creek," one of only two surviving poems by Wang Ji (fl. 500): "With the chirping of cicadas, the woods are even quieter; / With the singing of birds, the mountains are more tranquil"; see Yang, p. 149.

523

Rainy season rains
       gather in spate harry the
             Mogami River

samidare o / atsumete hayashi / Mogamigawa

Summer, 1689. *Mogamigawa:* the Mogami River; see 521, 525, 533. Originally a greeting poem for Takano Ichiei, a shipping agent, who owned a boathouse on the eastern shore of the river, at Ōishida. The original's *suzushi* ("cool") has been changed to *hayashi* ("fast," or "swift"); see Shirane, *Traces*, pp. 171–73, for a discussion of the revision process.

524

At the Home of Fūryū

Upstream a little
>I could well find an icehouse
>>beyond this willow

mizu no oku / himuro tazunuru / yanagi kana

Summer, 1689. On *Himuro no Sekku* ("The Ice Room Festival"), held on
the first day of *Minazuki,* the traditional name for the Sixth Month in
the Japanese lunar calendar, people ate a special dish of preserved rice
cakes. *himuro:* an ice hut where snow was sealed at the end of January,
for use during the summer months.

525

At Seishin's House

A scent on the breeze
>from the south from the flowing
>>Mogamigawa

kaze no ka mo / minami ni chikashi / Mogamigawa

Summer, 1689. *Seishin:* Shibuya Kurobei (or Kurōbei), a wealthy mer-
chant in Shinjō. Written at a gathering on the second day of the Sixth
Month (July 1). Bashō compliments Seishin for the coolness of his resi-
dence by invoking the local river with an allusion to a line from Bai Juyi
(Po Chü-i): "Scented wind comes from the south."

526

How thankful I am
>to breathe this snow-scented air
>>Minamidani

arigata ya / yuki o kaorasu / Minamidani

Summer, 1689. *Minamidani:* on Mount Haguro (see 527). This was a
greeting hokku to his host, the priest Ekaku (d. 1707), of Nyakuōin-ji,
of which there had been a branch temple at Minamidani.

527

What cooling freshness
      A sliver of moon over
            holy Haguro

suzushisa ya / hono mikazuki no / Haguroyama

Summer, 1689. *Haguroyama:* Mount Haguro, one of the Three Holy
Mountains of Dewa Province, along with Mount Gassan and Mount
Yudono. *mikazuki:* a crescent moon on the third day of a lunar month.

528

The summit-like clouds
      how many have crumbled now?
            The Mount of the Moon

kumo no mine / ikutsu kuzurete / Tsuki no Yama

Summer, 1689. *Tsuki no Yama:* Mount Gassan, literally "mount of the
moon." There is also wordplay on *tsuki,* which as well as "moon" sug-
gests the verb *tsuku:* "to be exhausted," or "to be gone."

529

Forbidden to tell
      of Yudono and my sleeves
            wringing wet with tears

katararenu / Yudono ni nurasu / tamoto kana

Summer, 1689. "In contrast to the first two mountains, Hagurosan and
Gassan, which had never appeared in classical poetry, Yudono (literally,
Bathhouse) was an *utamakura,* referred to in classical poetry as Koi no
yama [sic], Mountain of Love. The body of the Yudono deity was a huge
red rock that spouted hot water and was said to resemble sexual organs.
'Forbidden to speak' (*katararenu*) refers to the rule, described in *Nar-
row Road to the Interior,* that all visitors to Yudono, the holiest of the
Three Dewa Mountains, were forbidden to talk about the appearance of
the mountain to others" (Shirane, *Traces,* pp. 229–30).

530

That jewel his soul
    returns to Mount Haguro
        The Law of the Moon

sono tama ya / Haguro ni kaesu / nori no tsuki

Autumn, 1689. A poem to commemorate the High Priest Tenyū, of
Mount Haguro, who had been exiled to Izu, where he died. The moon is
here a symbol of enlightenment and the teachings of Buddha. "Tama" can
mean both "jewel" and "soul." *nori:* the Law of Nature; see 203, 287, 791.

531

I had wanted to ask
    about the moon and flowers
        The Four Sleepers snored

tsuki ka hana ka / toedo shisui no / ibiki kana

Miscellaneous, 1689. *The Four Sleepers:* a theme in *Ch'an* (Japanese:
Zen) painting, depicting Hanshan (Kanzan), Shide (Jittoku), and Feng-
gan (Bukan) with his pet tiger; see 781. 6-7-5.

532

A singular treat
    Down from the mountain to meet
        the first aubergine

mezurashi ya / yama o ideha no / hatsunasubi

Summer, 1689. A greeting hokku for Nagayama Shigeyuki, who had
served him the first aubergine (eggplant) of the season after Bashō's
seven-day stay on Mount Haguro. *ideha* means "on departing," but is
also an alternative way of reading the name of the province Dewa.

533

The heat of the day
    emptying into the sea
        Mogamigawa

atsuki hi o / umi ni iretari / Mogamigawa

Summer, 1689. *atsuki hi* can mean both "hot day" and "hot sun." Origi-
nally written as part of a *kasen* (linked-verse sequence) at the residence
of Terajima Hikosuke, a merchant at Sakata. As with 523, this poem was
revised, with *suzushisa ya* ("The coolness here") replaced by *atsuki hi o*
and *umi ni iretari* replacing *umi ni iretaru* ("to empty into the sea"), for
inclusion in *Oku no Hosomichi;* see Shirane, *Traces,* pp. 170–71.

534

In Kisagata
    in the rain Seishi in
        the silk tree's flowers

Kisagata ya / ame ni Seishi ga / nebu no hana

Summer, 1689. *Kisagata* (or Kisakata): a lagoon area to the northeast of
Sakata (in present-day Akita Prefecture), and the most northerly point
of Bashō's journey in *Oku no Hosomichi.* "The hokku includes a play on
words, as *nebu* means both 'silk tree' and 'to sleep.' Hsi Shih (Seishi in
Japanese) was a Chinese woman of ancient times who was noted for
her beauty. The defeated king of Yüeh offered her to his conqueror, the
king of Wu, who subsequently became so infatuated with her that he
came to neglect affairs of state. It was said that she looked most charm-
ing when she was in grief" (Ueda, p. 257). Bashō alludes to a poem by
Su Tung-p'o (Su Shi; see 128, 148, 168) that compares Lake Hsi ("West
Lake"; see 432) to the beauty of Hsi Shih.

535

The evening rain ended, and a local showed us around the area by boat

The clear evening sky
    At ease under the cherry
        the waves blossoming

yūbare ya / sakura ni suzumu / nami no hana

Summer, 1689. On the seventeenth of the Sixth Month, Bashō took a
boat trip around the Kisagata inlet to Nōinjima, to visit a famous old
cherry tree known as the *Saigyō-zakura* ("Saigyō cherry tree"), men-
tioned in a poem attributed to Saigyō: *kisagata no / sakura wa nami ni
/ uzumorete / hana no ue kogu / ama no tsuribune* ("The Kisagata /
cherry blossoms in the waves / deeply embedded / Rowing over the
flowers / the boats of the fishermen").

536

At Shiogoshi
    the crane's legs dipping into
        the cool of the sea

Shiogoshi ya / tsuruhagi nurete / umi suzushi

Summer, 1689. *Shiogoshi:* both the name of a place to the west of Kisa-
gata, and a noun referring to the shallows at the entrance of a bay.

537

From Atsumiyama
    all the way to Fuku Bay
        the airish evening

Atsumiyama ya / Fukūra kakete / yūsuzumi

Summer, 1689. A greeting hokku to Bashō's host, Itō Fugyoku (1648–
97), the doctor of the lord of Sakata. *Atsumiyama:* Mount Atsumi,
which is about 40 km south of Sakata, and Fukūra about 20 km north.
The name Atsumi is related to the word *atsui* ("hot"), and Fukūra is
related to *fuku* ("to blow [cool air]"). 6-5-7.

538

At the house of Ōmiya Gyokushi, a cool makuwa melon was served as we enjoyed the evening air. The host asked us to compose a poem, saying playfully: "No poem, no melon!'

> The year's first melon
>> Will I cut it into four
>>> or carve round slices?

hatsumakuwa / yotsu ni ya tatan / wa ni kiran

Summer, 1689. *Ōmiya Gyokushi:* a wealthy merchant in Sakata; his phrase "No poem, no melon" alludes to an episode in which Li Bai (see 194, 259, 383), when hosting a gathering, said: "No poem, three glasses!" *makuwa* ("melon"): see 43, 145, 640.

539

> The Star Festival
>> Even its eve leaving the
>>> usual behind

fumizuki ya / muika mo tsune no / yo ni wa nizu

Autumn, 1689. *The Star Festival: Tanabata,* the seventh day of the Seventh Month; see 14. *fumizuki:* the old name for the Seventh Month; *muika:* the sixth day (of the month). Composed for a twelve-verse linked sequence at Naoestu in Echigo Province; see 540.

540

At a post town called Izumozaki in the province of Echigo, looking out toward Sado Island

The turbulent sea
    Unfurling over Sado
        the River of Stars

araumi ya / Sado ni yokotau / Amanogawa

Autumn, 1689. *The River of Stars*: *Amanogawa* ("Heaven's River"), the Japanese for the Milky Way; see 97. As well as gold mining, Sado, off the Niigata coast in the Sea of Japan, was from the eighth century until Bashō's day associated with banishment, and significant poets, priests, and political figures, including Nichiren (see 464, 779) and the Noh playwright Zeami (see 3), had been exiled there. In *Oku no Hosomichi* this poem is also placed after 539, thereby linking it to the Star Festival, Tanabata.

541

At Dr. Hosokawa Shun-an's House

From the herb garden
    which flower will I pick for
        a makeshift pillow?

yakuran ni / izure no hana o / kusamakura

Autumn, 1689. A greeting hokku to a medical doctor in Takada whose pen name was Tōsetsu, and who owned an herb garden. *kusamakura*: literally, "grass pillow," an epithet for sleeping outdoors on a journey; see 136.

542

These tiny sea bream
　　skewered with cool willow twigs
　　　　the fisherman's house

kodai sasu / yanagi suzushi ya / ama ga ie

Summer, 1689. The season word *suzushi* ("cool") places the poem in
summer, but it was actually written in the autumn of 1689. There is
another version, titled "Nishihama," which reads: *kodai sasu / yanagi
suzushi ya / ama ga tsuma* ("These tiny sea bream / skewered with cool
willow twigs / the fisherman's wife"). Kon Eizō chooses the *ama ga ie*
version as it is the one in Bashō's own handwriting.

543

Under this one roof
　　courtesans too have rested
　　　　bush clover the moon

hitotsuya ni / yūjo mo netari / hagi to tsuki

Autumn, 1689. This encounter with prostitutes at an inn in Ichiburi is
related in *Oku no Hosomichi* and is commonly held to be fictitious. *bush
clover: Lespedeza bicolor;* see 18, 310, 765.

544

Through the aroma
　　of ripened rice to the right
　　　　the Ariso Sea

wase no ka ya / wakeiru migi wa / Arisoumi

Autumn, 1689. "Arisoumi (Rocky Coast Sea), which the traveler views
from a distance, is a famous *utamakura* (poetic toponym) from the
Man'yōshū. Together, the two expansive and felicitous images—the
waves of ripening rice plants and the waves of Arisoumi—suggest the
grandeur and richness of Kaga Province" (Shirane, *Traces,* p. 178).

545

Having entered the Province of Kaga

> Thief Kumasaka
>> When do his descendants do
>> Tama Matsuri?

Kumasaka ga / yukari ya itsu no / Tama Matsuri

Autumn, 1689. *Kumasaka:* Kumasaka Chōhan, a notorious bandit in the twelfth century, from Kumasaka in Kaga Province (see 549). He was killed by Yoshitsune (see 209, 510, 515, 682) and features in many kabuki plays. *Tama Matsuri:* the Bon Festival, when the souls of the dead are consoled; see 440, 644, 893.

546

On the Road

> Red on red on red
>> unrelenting the sun yet
>> the wind of autumn

akaaka to / hi wa tsurenaku mo / aki no kaze

Autumn, 1689. The poem "captures the feeling of lingering summer heat (*zansho* [see 711]), an early autumn topic, and was originally written in 1689, during the journey to the Interior [*Oku no Hosomichi*], on the road between Echigo and Kanazawa" (Shirane, *Traces,* p. 280). See 79.

547

I was invited to a grass hut

> The cool of autumn
>> With our own hands let us peel
>> melons aubergines

aki suzushi / tegoto ni muke ya / uri nasubi

Autumn, 1689. A greeting hokku to his host, Issen, for the renga gathering at Shōgen-an in Kanazawa on the twentieth of the Seventh Month.

548

A man called Isshō had become well-known for his devotion to poetry, but he died last winter. His brother held a haikai gathering in his memory

Arouse the gravemound too
    the wail of my grief-filled cry
      the wind in autumn

tsuka mo ugoke / waga naku koe wa / aki no kaze

Autumn, 1689. *Isshō:* Kosugi Isshō (1653–88), a tea dealer and the most famous poet in Kanazawa. Isshō had longed to meet Bashō; Bashō did not know of his death until he arrived in Kanazawa. The memorial gathering was held on the twenty-second of the Seventh Month at Gannen-ji in Kanazawa, where this poem is now inscribed on a monument at the gate of the temple. 6-7-5.

549

At a Place Called Komatsu

The genteelness of
    the name Komatsu blowing
      clovers silvergrass

shiorashiki / na ya Komatsu fuku / hagi susuki

Autumn, 1689. *Komatsu:* "Little Pine," part of the ancient Kaga Province, in present-day Ishikawa Prefecture. *hagi:* bush clover, *Lespedeza bicolor; susuki:* silvergrass, *Miscanthus sinensis.* Composed at a gathering on the twenty-fifth of the Seventh Month as a greeting poem for his host, the Shinto priest Kosen (Fujimura Izu) of Hiyoshi Shrine. Behind the shrine was the site of the Ataka Barrier, the setting for one of the most famous of all kabuki plays, *Kanjinchō,* itself based on the Noh play *Ataka,* and also the basis for Kurosawa Akira's film *The Men Who Tread on the Tiger's Tail* (1945).

550

At Kansei's House

Sopping wet as they pass
    these people beguiling too
      Bush clover in rain

nurete yuku ya / hito mo okashiki / ame no hagi

Autumn, 1689. *Kansei:* the leading haikai poet in Komatsu. Composed at a gathering held the day after the one in 549, at which Kansei and his circle had been participants. *hagi:* "bush clover"; see 18, 310, 543.

551

The pity of it
    Underneath a war helmet
      a creaker-cricket

muzan ya na / kabuto no shita no / kirigirisu

Autumn, 1689. At Tada Shrine in Komatsu, Bashō saw the helmet of Saitō Bettō Sanemori (see 3). Sanemori features in book 7 of *Heike Monogatari,* from which Bashō has adapted the first line of the poem. Sanemori was over seventy when he fought in the battle at Shinohara; to conceal his age, he had dyed his hair black. After the battle, Higuchi Jirō (?–1184), examining the old warrior's severed head, exclaims, "How awful!" (in Royall Tyler's translation, *The Tale of the Heike,* p. 370). *kirigirisu:* in Bashō's day, and in classical Japanese, *kirigirisu* refers to a "cricket" (*Grylloidea*). In modern Japanese the *kirigirisu* refers to the "bush cricket" or "katydid" (*Tettigoniidae*), sometimes translated as "grasshopper." The word *kirigirisu* literally means "*kirigiri*-maker," *kirigiri* being onomatopoeia for the insect's sounds. In this translation, I have returned to the onomatopoeic etymology of the word "cricket," literally "little creaker," from the Old French *criquer* (or *crikier*), meaning "to creak" or "to grind [one's teeth]"; see 648, 660, 713, 911, 967.

552

At Yamanaka
the chrysanthemums unsnipped
The hot waters' scent

Yamanaka ya / kiku wa taoranu / yu no nioi

Autumn, 1689. In the legend of the Chrysanthemum Boy, Kikujidō
writes the words of the Lotus Sutra on the petals of a chrysanthemum,
the dew from the flower becomes an elixir, and he remains youthful for
seven hundred years (some sources say eight hundred); see 57, 108,
234. A greeting hokku for Bashō's host, Kumenosuke, who was fourteen
years old. Yamanaka was, and is, a place known for its therapeutic hot
springs.

553

Don't give up those leaves
peach tree let them not scatter
The wind in autumn

momo no ki no / sono ha chirasu na / aki no kaze

Autumn, 1689. Bashō gave Kumenosuke (see 552) the pen name Tōyō.
Tō (also *momo*, "peach") had been part of Bashō's previous pseudonym,
Tōsei (see 103, 141), and *yō* derived from *momo no yōyō* ("the young
beauty of a peach") in *The Shijing* (*The Book of Songs*), the oldest collec-
tion of Chinese poetry.

554

The Ten Sights of Yamanaka: Fishing Fires at Takase

In the fish-luring
light the kajika sobbing
beneath the ripples

isaribi ni / kajika ya nami no / shitamusebi

Autumn, 1689. *kajika: Cottus pollux,* the Japanese fluvial sculpin, a bot-
tom-dwelling fish of mountain streams. The fish are attracted to light
and were caught at night by torchlight.

555

Hot springs leavetaking
    Tonight I will get gooseskin
      suffering the cold

yu no nagori / koyoi wa hada no / samukaran

Autumn, 1689. Another greeting poem for Kumenosuke; Bashō was
leaving the hot springs at Yamanaka.

556

Hot springs leavetaking
    Looking back how many times
      into the mist-steam

yu no nagori / ikutabi miru ya / kiri no moto

Autumn, 1689.

557

From today the words
    written there will disappear
      The dew on my hat

kyō yori ya / kakitsuke kesan / kasa no tsuyu

Autumn, 1689. Bashō and Sora had written on their bamboo hats the
pilgrim's motto: *kenkon mujū dōgyō ninin* ("between heaven and earth,
without fixed abode, two wayfarers"; see 379). Due to illness, Sora had
decided to travel ahead to a relative's home in Nagashima; see 587.
Bashō's poem also responds to Sora's *yuki yukite / taorefusutomo / hagi
no hara* ("Onwards and onwards / no matter if I fall down / bush clover
meadow"), a poem that was the source of the title for Kazuo Hara's film
Yuki Yukite Shingun ("The Emperor's Naked Army Marches On," 1987).
The first line of Sora's poem had originally read *izuku ni ka*; Bashō
edited it to read *yuki yukite*.

558

Visiting the Kannon Temple at Nata

A whiteness whiter
     than the stones of Stone Mountain
          The wind in autumn

Ishiyama no / ishi yori shiroshi / aki no kaze

Autumn, 1689. Autumn is traditionally associated with the color white,
and the word *hakufū* (literally, "white wind") is another way of saying
"the autumn wind." "Bashō visited Nata Temple in Komatsu on Septem-
ber 18. The temple was dedicated to the bodhisattva Kannon and situ-
ated on top of a hill, which was composed of quartz trachyte, a whitish
rock. Ishiyama, literally meaning 'stone-mountain,' may refer to this hill
or to Ishiyama in Ōmi Province, which was renowned for its white
rocks" (Ueda, p. 266). See 672.

559

Leaving this temple
     I'd sweep the garden of its
          fallen willow leaves

niwa haite / idebaya tera ni / chiru yanagi

Autumn, 1689. Bashō stayed at Zenshō-ji for the night, and as he left
was asked for a poem by the young monks. It was customary for a
traveling monk who had stayed overnight at a temple to clean the bed-
chamber, and so forth, before leaving.

560

I scribbled something
     tore the folding fan in two
          Leavetaking again

mono kaite / ōgi hikisaku / nagori kana

Autumn, 1689. Bashō was parting from his disciple, Hokushi (d. 1718),
who had accompanied him from Kanazawa to Matsuoka.

561

Fukui, Inviting Tōsai

Those places famous
>for views of the Harvest Moon
>>Let's be on our way

meigetsu no / midokoro towan / tabine sen

Autumn, 1689. *Tōsai*: a disciple of Bashō's in Fukui, whom he had met in Edo about ten years earlier. Bashō stayed in his house for two nights and then both of them traveled to Tsuruga.

562

Crossing the bridge at Asamuzu, popularly known as "Asōzu," I recall the "bridge" passage of The Pillow Book by Sei Shōnagon where this very place is written as "Asamutsu"

Asamutsu Bridge
>On our moonviewing journey
>>dark gives way to dawn

Asamutsu ya / tsukimi no tabi no / akebanare

Autumn, 1689. *Asamuzu-no-hashi* (or *Asōzu-no-hashi*), "the bridge at Asamuzu," south of Fukui, is an *utamakura* (a place with poetical associations). *Asamutsu* is a homonym for the word denoting the sixth hour of the morning, or between 5 A.M. and 7 A.M. in the modern way of reckoning the hours.

563

Tamae

Go view the moon there
>the leggy Tamae reeds
>>before they get cut

tsukimi seyo / Tamae no ashi o / karanu saki

Autumn, 1689. *Tamae* ("Jewel Bay"): to the south of Fukui; noted for how its reeds complement the viewing of the moon, especially when flowering in the Eighth Month. *ashi* is a homonym for both "leg" and "reed."

564

Hina-ga-dake

Tomorrow night's moon
> Are the auguries for rain
>   Hina-ga-dake?

asu no tsuki / ame uranawan / Hina-ga-dake

Autumn, 1689. *Hina-ga-dake:* Mount Hino, in Fukui Prefecture. A play
on words: the *hi* in "Hina" means "sun," and can also mean "to compare."

565

Yu-no-o

In the moonlight his
> name no longer hideable
>   the God of Smallpox

tsuki ni na o / tsutsumikanete ya / imo no kami

Autumn, 1689. *Yu-no-o:* a mountain pass at Imajō, in Fukui Prefecture,
where the teahouse sold amulets against smallpox. The eating of *imo*
(taro) is associated with moonviewing (see 46), and the Chinese char-
acters for smallpox can also be read as "imo."

566

Hiuchi Castle

Did Yoshinaka
> awake and see this mountain?
>   The sorrowing moon

Yoshinaka no / nezame no yama ka / tsuki kanashi

Autumn, 1689. *Yoshinaka:* Minamoto no Yoshinaka (1154–84), also
known as Kiso Yoshinaka, or Lord Kiso, after his home region. He was
a cousin of Yoritomo and Yoshitsune, became shogun, but was soon
killed by Yoritomo's men. He features in *Heike Monogatari* ("The Tale of
the Heike"). See 644, 680.

567

On the Koshi Road, at Nakayama

Ah Nakayama
On the Koshi Road the moon
Life alive again

Nakayama ya / Koshiji mo tsuki wa / mata inochi

Autumn, 1689. *Nakayama*: a mountain pass called Kinome Tōge, on the
route along the Japan Sea coast, reminded Bashō of the mountain pass
at Sayo no Nakayama and the famous poem by Saigyō; see 63, 189.

568

The Kehi Sea

The Eight Sights of so
many provinces and now
the moon at Kehi

kuniguni no / hakkei sara ni / Kehi no tsuki

Autumn, 1689. *Kehi*: or Kei, the old name for Tsuruga. The "Eight Sights"
comes from the Chinese tradition of the Eight Views of Xiaoxiang; see
432. See 654 for Bashō's allusion to the Eight Famous Scenes of Ōmi.

569

*In the second year of Genroku, viewing the moon at Tsuruga Bay, I vis-
ited the Kehi Shrine, and heard of the tradition of the Yugyō priests*

The cool clear moonlight
On the sands once carried here
by Priest Yugyō

tsuki kiyoshi / Yugyō no moteru / suna no ue

Autumn, 1689. *Yugyō*: the title of the chief priest of Yugyō-ji in Fuji-
sawa, and of the Ji sect of Buddhism. Legend says that the second
Yugyō, Taa Shōnin (1237–1319), carried sand and stones to dry the
marshes around the shrine at Kehi, which became an annual ritual
called *sunamochi* ("sand-carrying"). *the second year of Genroku:* 1689.

570

The Fifteenth, as the innkeeper had predicted, it rained

The Harvest Moon night
        the weather in the northlands
                unpredictable

meigetsu ya / hokkoku biyori / sadamenaki

Autumn, 1689. *The Fifteenth*: The fifteenth of the Eighth Month in the lunar calendar (September 28), the night of the harvest moon. In *Oku no Hosomichi,* the moon had shone brightly the night before.

571

On the same night, the innkeeper told a story, "Sunken in the sea here, there's a temple bell. The governor of the province once sent divers to go down for it, but its dragon-headed hook lay buried upside down, so there was no way to pull it up"

The moon's whereabouts?
        And the temple bell sunken
                to the sea bottom

tsuki izuku / kane wa shizumeru / umi no soko

Autumn, 1689.

572

Beach

Not only the moon
        in the rain the sumo too
                an unhappening

tsuki nomi ka / ame ni sumō mo / nakarikeri

Autumn, 1689. *Beach*: Kehi Beach, at Tsuruga.

573

Bay

The olden name of
    Tsunuga that loveliness
        the moon in autumn

furuki na no / Tsunuga ya koishi / aki no tsuki

Autumn, 1689. *Tsunuga* ("antler deer"): the port city now called Tsu-ruga, named for Tsunuga Arashito, who had a horn on his forehead, according to the classical chronicle *Nihon Shoki;* his origins were in Korea, and Tsunuga was a hub port connecting not just to other Japa-nese ports along the Sea of Japan coast, but to the Korean peninsula and the Asian continent.

574

Here is lonesomeness
    surpassing even Suma
        the strand in autumn

sabishisa ya / Suma ni kachitaru / hama no aki

Autumn, 1689. *Suma:* near Kobe on the Seto Inland Sea, a place famous in classical literature as a place of exile and desolation; see 109, 404. Bashō is writing of Iro-no-hama ("Color Beach"), a beach to the north-west of Tsuruga; see 576.

575

In the combers' folds
    tiny seashells mingle with
        shreds of bush clover

nami no ma ya / kogai ni majiru / hagi no chiri

Autumn, 1689. Iro-no-hama was noted for a kind of clam with a small, pink shell; see 576.

576

Drawn to Iro-no-hama

Small bush clover fall
      the small Masuho seashells
            a small sake cup

kohagi chire / Masuho no kogai / kosakazuki

Autumn, 1689. *Masuho seashells*: small red seashells found on Iro-no-hama. Bashō was "drawn to Iro-no-hama" by a famous waka by Saigyō: *shio somuru / masuho no kogai / hirou tote / iro-no-hama to wa / iu ni ya aruran* ("The sea water dyed / by the small crimson seashells / which are gathered here / This must be the reason why / people call it the colored beach").

577

Iro-no-hama

In priestly garments
      I'll go gather small seashells
            The moon at Iro

koromo kite / kogai hirowan / Iro no tsuki

Autumn, 1689. As with 576, based on the poem by Saigyō, for whom with the phrase *koromo kite* ("In priestly garments") Bashō expresses respect.

578

Not yet a butter-
      fly and autumn deepening
            A worm of the fields

kochō ni mo / narade aki furu / namushi kana

Autumn, 1689. Written after his arrival at Ōgaki. "It may seem that the poet is reflecting on his life and deploring the fact that he has put on years in vain. Implicit in his reflection, however, is the nobility of mind that has brought him peace in his nonutilitarian pursuit. The poem faintly echoes the story of Chuang-tzu's [Zhuangzi's] butterfly.—*Tosai*" (Ueda, p. 271). For Zhuangzi's butterfly, see 163, 172.

579

At the Akasaka Kokuzō, on the twenty-eighth day of the Eighth Month, Oku-no-in

> The cry of a dove
>> pierces and fills the body
>>> The cave opening

hato no koe / mi ni shimiwataru / iwato kana

Autumn, 1689. An image of Kokuzō Bosatsu (the "Bodhisattva of All-Encompassing Wisdom," the wisdom that permeates the universe) is enshrined in a cave in the Inner Temple (*Oku-no-in*) of Myōshōrin-ji (or Myōjōrin-ji), on Mt. Kinshō, at Akasaka, near Ōgaki, Gifu Prefecture.

580

When I open the door, to the west is a mountain called Ibuki. There are no flowers, there is no snow, there's only the dignity of this lone mountain

> Just the way it is
>> Even the moon unneeded
>>> Ibukiyama

sonomama yo / tsuki mo tanomaji / Ibukiyama

Autumn, 1689. *Ibukiyama*: Mount Ibuki, to the northeast of Lake Biwa. See 263, 291, 317, for the idea of the "self-at-ease."

581

Written impromptu, at the villa of Josui

> Secluded in here
>> what the trees and grasses shed
>>> would I could gather

komoriite / ko no mi kusa no mi / hirowabaya

Autumn, 1689. *Josui*: Toda Gondayū, chief retainer of the Toda clan in the Ōgaki Domain.

582

Come on now blossom
Nearly the ninth of the Ninth
chrysanthemum blooms

hayaku sake / kunichi mo chikashi / kiku no hana

Autumn, 1689. *the ninth of the Ninth*: *Chōyō no Sekku,* the Chrysanthe-
mum Festival, held on the ninth day of the Ninth Month; see 108, 458,
725, 909.

583

*A man named Sogyū, who lives in Seki, came to visit me at my lodging
in Ōgaki. Those "White Wisteria Slope" flowers of which Sōgi had sung
had glowed in those olden days and now before us in autumn were not
the flowers but the beans*

Wisteria beans
to make a haikai
The trace of blossoms

fuji no mi wa / haikai ni sen / hana no ato

Autumn, 1689. *Sogyū*: Hirose Gennojō (?–1711), later known as Izen.
Sōgi: see 160, 345. When Sōgi passed the Ōsaka no Seki (the Osaka Bar-
rier), he compared the white wisteria he saw in bloom on a nearby slope
to the Fujishiro Misaka (White Wisteria Slope) in Kii Province, a place
famed in old poetry, and wrote: *seki koete / koko mo Fujishiro / Misaka
kana* ("The barrier crossed / And here too another White / Wisteria
Slope"). Bashō alludes to Sōgi's poem also through the use of a pun on
the place-name *Seki* and *seki,* the Japanese word for barrier. "Wisteria
beans have neither practical use nor poetic elegance, yet they dangle
down in a way that suggests detachment from worldly things, and are
therefore a fitting subject for haikai. The poem is intended to teach the
true purpose of haikai to Sogyū, who had become Bashō's student only
a short time earlier.—*Yamamoto*" (Ueda, p. 272). *ato*: "trace," "vestige,"
"aftermath," as in 515.

584

At Bokuin's House

Such a hideaway
    The moon the chrysanthemums
        an acre of rice

kakurega ya / tsuki to kiku to ni / ta santan

Autumn, 1689. *Bokuin:* Tani Bokuin, of Ōgaki; see 212, 215. *ta santan:*
"a rice field of three *tan*"; *tan* is a unit of area, approximately 991.7
square meters.

585

Inscription on a Painting

Let Saigyō's
    sandals dangle alongside
        the dew on the pine

Saigyō no / waraji mo kakare / matsu no tsuyu

Autumn, 1689. *Saigyō:* see 63, 198, 206. The sandals are Bashō's imag-
ined addition to a painting of a pine tree wet with dew.

586

A clam from its shell
    To Futami departing
        An autumn farewell

hamaguri no / Futami ni wakare / yuku aki zo

Autumn, 1689. This is the poem with which *Oku no Hosomichi* ends.
"Bashō's hokku turns on a series of homophones: *wakaru* [the root
form of *wakare*] means both 'to depart for' and 'to tear from,' and
Futami refers to a noted place on the coast of Ise Province (the traveler's
next destination and a place known for clams) as well as the shell (*futa*)
and body (*mi*) of the clam (*hamaguri*). The passing of the season
becomes an implicit metaphor not only for the sorrow of parting,
which lies at the heart of travel, but also the ceaseless passage of time,
the traveler's constant companion" (Shirane, *Traces,* p. 247).

587

Staying two nights at Daichi-in, at Nagashima in the Province of Ise

I'm a misery
>> So now bring on lonesomeness
>>> temple in autumn

uki ware o / sabishigarase yo / aki no tera

Autumn, 1689. Priest Seishū of this temple was the uncle of Sora (see 282, 471, 557), Bashō's companion on the *Oku no Hosomichi* journey. This poem was later rewritten (see 698) and draws on a poem by Saigyō: *tou hito mo / omoitaetaru / yamazato no / sabishisa nakuba / sumiukaramashi* ("People no longer / think of coming to visit / this mountain village / Were there no lonesomeness here / living would be wretchedness").

588

I stayed at the house of Yūgen in the Province of Ise. His wife, in keeping with her husband's deepest wishes, worked attentively to ease this traveler's weary heart. The wife of Hyūganokami cut off her hair, to ready a renga gathering, so let us now remember her selfless act

Moon do lonesome now
>> I want to tell the story
>>> of Akechi's wife

tsuki sabiyo / Akechi ga tsuma no / hanashi sen

Autumn, 1689. *Yūgen* (1671–1742), of Ise. *Hyūganokami*: Akechi Mitsuhide (1528–82), a general during the Sengoku era. When he was an impoverished young man his wife cut off and sold her hair to pay for the expense of hosting a renga gathering. Akechi promised that within fifty days he would rise in power and she would be the wife of a general, a vow that he fulfilled.

589

The Inner Shrine had already been moved; I worshipped at the Outer Shrine during the Re-Enshrinement Ritual

> Nearing the holy
>> everyone pushes and shoves
>>> The Re-Enshrinement

tōtosa ni / mina oshiainu / go-sengū

Autumn, 1689. Every twenty years both the Inner and Outer Shrines at the Grand Shrine of Ise are rebuilt. After completing the *Oku no Hosomichi* journey, Bashō went to Ise to see the *go sengū* ceremony (the ritual of re-enshrining the gods from the old to the new shrine). He arrived on the eleventh of the Ninth Month, one day late for the ceremony for the Inner Shrine but in time for the Outer Shrine ceremony, held on the thirteenth.

590

A Place called Nakamura in the Province of Ise

> The autumnal wind
>> the Ise cemetery
>>> even more chilling

aki no kaze / Ise no hakahara / nao sugoshi

Autumn, 1689. In Ise, a province under the strong influence of Shinto, there were strict taboos related to the "pollution" of death, and human corpses were regarded as "impure." Bashō may be alluding to the local practice of *hayagake* ("early disposal"), where a dying person was taken to the grave before the point of death. The poem also carries echoes of Saigyō's use of *sugoki* ("desolate"): *furuhata no / soba no tatsu ki ni / iru hato no / tomo yobu koe no / sugoki yūgure* ("On a tree rising / from a cliff by an old field / a dove is calling / for a friend in a voice so / desolate in the evening"). Saigyō's poem also influenced 121.

591

Futami

Saigyō's inkstone?
    I pick up a hollowed-out
        dewy-damp pebble

suzuri ka to / hirou ya kuboki / ishi no tsuyu

Autumn, 1689. When Saigyō lived in Futami (see 586), he is said to
have used a naturally hollowed-out stone as his inkstone. There are two
theories as to the location of Saigyō's hut in Ise: Futami, as in this poem,
or Uji, as in 198.

592

Shuei-in

Entering the gateway
    The sago palm giving off
        the orchid's fragrance

mon ni ireba / sotetsu ni ran no / nioi kana

Autumn, 1689. *Shuei-in:* a Pure Land Buddhist temple in Ise; the tem-
ple no longer exists. *sotetsu:* cycad, or Japanese sago palm (*Cycas revo-
luta*). 6-7-5.

593

The shape of the tree
    changing each and every day
        Cotton rosemallows

edaburi no / higoto ni kawaru / fuyō kana

Autumn, 1689. This poem was inscribed on a painting of cotton rose-
mallows. The flowers bloom in the morning and wilt in the evening; the
next day a new flower blooms at a different point on the shrub.

594

First winter drizzle
    Even monkeys look in want
        of a straw raincoat

hatsushigure / saru mo komino o / hoshigenari

Winter, 1689. *hatsushigure:* the first winter shower, a stock theme in Japanese poetry. One of Bashō's best-known poems, written while he was on his way from Ise to his hometown in Iga.

595

Let the drizzle come
    drizzle the folk in this house
        no matter the cold

hitobito o / shigure yo yado wa / samukutomo

Winter, 1689. Written at a haikai party at the house of Hairiki, the pen name of Sugino Kanbei (1653–1732), a samurai of the Tōdō clan in Bashō's hometown in Iga. The implication is that the cold rain will bring a feeling of *wabi* (poetic desolation) to the gathered poets.

596

Gathering mushrooms
    Perilously close to the
        cold evening showers

takegari ya / abunaki koto ni / yūshigure

Winter, 1689.

597

A winter garden
    The moon too thinned to a thread
        an insect singing

fuyuniwa ya / tsuki mo ito naru / mushi no gin

Winter, 1689. The hokku for a *han kasen* (eighteen-stanza linked-verse)
party held at the house of Yamagishi Hanzan, Bashō's nephew, a samu-
rai in Iga.

598

On the folding screen
    a mountaintop depicted
        The wintering in

byōbu ni wa / yama o egaite / fuyugomori

Winter, 1689. *fuyugomori:* staying indoors during winter; see 334, 465,
736, 822. For a revision of this poem, see 821.

599

Playing with Children in the Mountains

In the year's first snow
    from the pelt of a rabbit
        let's make us a beard

hatsuyuki ni / usagi no kawa no / hige tsukure

Winter, 1689. Bashō's hometown in Iga is in a basin surrounded by
mountains. Opinions differ as to what to make of this poem. Included
in a letter to Mangikumaru (Tokoku); see 226, 252, 328–32, 379.

600

The first day of the Eleventh Month in the second year of Genroku, for a linked verse at Ryōbon's house

> Come along children
>> Let's go and gallivant in
>>> this shower of hail

iza kodomo / hashiriarikan / tamaarare

Winter, 1689. *Ryōbon:* the pen name of Tomoda Kakuzaemon (1666–1730), a samurai serving at Iga Castle. The date of the poem equates to December 12, 1689.

601

Visiting the Southern Capital, yearning for the rebuilding of the Buddha Hall to be completed

> The year's first snowfall
>> And the Great Buddha's columns
>>> when will they go up?

hatsuyuki ya / itsu daibutsu no / hashiradate

Winter, 1689. In 1689, when Bashō visited Tōdai-ji in Nara, the old capital, the bronze Great Buddha in the temple was still in disrepair, headless after a battle between Matsunaga Hisahide and the Miyoshi clan in 1567, and exposed to the elements. The head was finally repaired in 1691, and the hall that houses the image was completed in 1709.

602

Song on a Journey

To Yamashiro
    a rented Ide litter
        The winter drizzle

Yamashiro e / ide no kago karu / shigure kana

Winter, 1689. *Yamashiro:* a province that corresponds to the southern half of present-day Kyoto Prefecture, and which included the city of Kyoto. Bashō had just crossed from the province of Yamato into the province of Yamashiro, and was passing through the town of Ide when he was caught in the rain (*Ide* can also mean "to go out"). A *kago* was a type of litter used for transportation by the nonsamurai class from feudal times up to the Meiji period.

603

Chōshō's grave
    Maybe they've gone up there too?
        The alms-bowl beaters

Chōshō no / haka mo meguru ka / hachitataki

Winter, 1689 (1690). *Chōshō:* Kinoshita Chōshōshi (1569–1649), a feudal lord who, after defeat at the Battle of Sekigahara in 1600, lived as a poet in seclusion in Kyoto. As part of the ritual to commemorate the Buddhist saint Kūya (903–72), lay monks (*Kūya-sō:* "Kuya's monks") walked through Kyoto and its environs chanting and beating bowls for forty-eight nights, beginning on the thirteenth day of the Eleventh Month. Bashō stayed with his disciple Kyorai, on the twenty-fourth of the Twelfth Month (February 3, 1690 in the Gregorian calendar), in order to listen to the hachitataki, the mournful beating of the bowls, but the monks didn't pass Kyorai's house until almost dawn. Bashō's poem echoes Chōshō's *hachitataki / akatsukigata no / hitokoe wa / fuyu no yo sae mo / naku hototogisu* ("The alms-bowl beating / at the breaking of the dawn / the voices as one / even on a winter night / the calling of the cuckoo"). See 670, 671.

604

*In Ōtsu, visiting the Nun Chigetsu, it is said that Ono-ga-ne-no-Shōshō
in her later years lived in seclusion nearby*

The Shōshō-
no-Ama story retold
the snow in Shiga

Shōshō-no- / ama no hanashi ya / Shiga no yuki

Winter, 1689. *Shōshō-no-Ama:* the Nun of Shōshō, the lady-in-waiting
to the second consort to the emperor Go-Horikawa (1212–34), after
which she became a nun, living in seclusion at Ōgi, Shiga. *the Nun
Chigetsu:* Kawai Chigetsu (c. 1633–1718), a poet and friend of Bashō,
one of the contributors to the *Sarumino* anthology. Though ten years
older than Bashō, she outlived him and, along with her brother Otoku-
ni's wife, made the garment for his body at his funeral rites and per-
formed services at his grave; see 678.

605

This the world has left
unblemished and unbegrimed
An old wooden bowl

kore ya yo no / susu ni somaranu / furugōshi

Winter, 1689. The poem refers to a wooden bowl Bashō's disciple Rotsū
(see 250, 471, 622) had left in Osaka, and which was returned seven
years later undamaged.

606

Many people visit my Zeze grass hut, so

> I wish it would hail
>> I'd boil and serve up icefish
>>> from a wicker weir

arare seba / ajiro no hio o / nite dasan

Winter, 1689. Bashō's hut was at Gichū-ji, a temple in Zeze, on the southern shore of Lake Biwa. *ajiro* ("wicker weir"), translated by Arthur Waley as "fish-weirs," were fishing traps made of reeds or bamboo. *Hio* (or *hiuo*): the young of *ayu* (sweetfish), the kanji for which literally means "ice fish."

607

> Wherefore and what for
>> to the end-of-year market
>>> this on-the-go crow?

nani ni kono / shiwasu no ichi ni / yuku karasu

Winter, 1689. In speaking of this poem, Bashō emphasized the force of its opening phrase. The *karasu* ("crow") has been read as referring to Bashō.

608

Greeting the New Year Near the Capital

> Wrapped in a straw mat
>> a man of some importance
>>> The New Year blooming

komo o kite / tarebito imasu / hana no haru

Spring, 1690. The lunar New Year fell on February 9. Bashō uses the honorific verb *imasu* to refer to the man. "Five hundred years ago Saigyō, in *Senjūshō,* cited many examples of sages living beggarly lives. With my uninitiated eyes, I am not able to distinguish a sage from a beggar. Sadly remembering Saigyō, I wrote this hokku. I hear, however, people in Kyoto are saying what an abominable poet I am to refer to a beggar in a verse celebrating the New Year. How silly of them!—*Bashō*" (Ueda, p. 284).

609

To One Heading Off to Zeze

Make sure to go see
    the Festival of Otters
        The Seta margins

kawauso no / matsuri mite koyo / Seta no oku

Spring, 1690. *Seta:* a river and town at the southern end of Lake Biwa;
see 415, 720. The Festival of Otters, from the sixteenth to the twentieth
of the First Month.

610

A bush-warbler's hat
    come fluttering from the tree
        A camellia

uguisu no / kasa otoshitaru / tsubaki kana

Spring, 1690. Bashō plays with the literary convention of *uguisu* (bush
warblers) improvising rain hats from ume blossoms, as in this waka by
Minamoto no Tokiwa (812–54): *uguisu no / kasa ni nuu chō / ume no
hana / orite kazasan / oikakuru ya to* ("The bush warbler makes / a hat
for itself out of / blossoms of ume / I'll take a spray for my hat / to cover
my aged face").

611

*In my hometown, in my brother's garden, I planted three kinds of vegeta-
ble seed*

Spring showers again
    The sprouting beginning in
        the aubergine seeds

harusame ya / futaba ni moyuru / nasubidane

Spring, 1690. The three kinds of vegetable: aubergine (eggplant), red
chili pepper, and taro. See 612, 613.

612

These minuscule seeds
　　I would never belittle
　　　　The pepper reddens

kono tane to / omoikonasaji / tōgarashi

Spring, 1690. *tōgarashi: Capsicum annuum.*

613

The Year of the Horse, in the mountains of Iga, a spring scene

The taro-seed man
　　with the blossoms in full bloom
　　　　vending his way round

taneimo ya / hana no sakari ni / uri aruku

Spring, 1690. The third year of Genroku (1690) was the "Year of the Horse" in the Chinese zodiac. Taro was traditionally planted in the Second Month. See the note to 46 for the significance of *imodane,* the meaning of which is the same as *taneimo* ("taro seed").

614

At Kyōboku's

Pines on a raised bank
　　and blossoms a lord's mansion
　　　　deep in the forest

dote no matsu / hana ya kobukaki / tonozukuri

Spring, 1690. *Kyōboku:* Tōdō Shuri, the nineteen-year-old chief retainer at Iga Castle, who had a mansion on its grounds.

615

Hanami

Underneath the tree
some soup and namasu some
cherry blossoms too

ki no moto ni / shiru mo namasu mo / sakura kana

Spring, 1690. *Hanami:* blossom viewing. *namasu:* vegetables and raw fish in vinegar; see 430, 657. "When he wrote this hokku, Master Bashō said: 'Having learned something about writing a verse on blossom viewing, I gave a tone of *karumi* (lightness) to this hokku.'– *Dohō*" (Ueda, p. 286). *shiru mo namasu mo:* an idiom (no longer used) which meant "the whole lot, anything and everything," as in the English "from soup to nuts." *karumi:* see 728, 754, 780, 841, 848, 856.

616

So appropriate
beanflour-dusted rice balls for
the Blossom Hunting

niawashi ya / mame no komeshi ni / sakuragari

Spring, 1690. *sakuragari:* "Blossom Hunting," another name for blossom viewing. To Bashō, the simplicity of the food matches the occasion of blossom viewing in the mountains.

617

The sounds of tilling
in the field a storm rising
through the blossom-hemp

hatake utsu / oto ya arashi no / sakura-asa

Spring, 1690. Bashō's note to the poem reads, "The eleventh of the Third Month, at the shrine of Shirahige in Araki Village." Combining *arashi* ("storm") and *sakura* ("cherry blossoms") is a conventional literary trope. *sakura-asa* is the male hemp plant. The farmers, preparing to plant hemp, evoke a spring storm through blossoms. Bashō is also playing on *arashi* and *arai* ("harsh" [sound of tilling]).

618

A shimmer of heat
      Slender shoots of saiko
            in the hazy light

kagerō ya / saiko no ito no / usugumori

Spring, 1690. *saiko:* a medicinal herb, with long thin stalks and yellow blossom.

619

The butterfly's wings
      flitting how often over
            the fence with the roof?

chō no ha no / ikutabi koyuru / hei no yane

Spring, 1690.

620

This townland "Hanagaki no Shō," it is said, was created to protect the double-petalled cherry tree of Nara

The villagers here
      Are they all descendants of
            the blossom watchmen?

hitosato wa / mina hanamori no / shison ka ya

Spring, 1690. The thirteenth-century collection of Buddhist parables *Shasekishū* ("Sand and Pebbles Collection") relates the tale of the empress Ichijō (988–1074), who so loved a cherry tree at Kōfuku-ji in Nara that she wanted to transplant it to Kyoto. The monks opposed the plan. Impressed by their passion and taste, she gave the small local village of Yono no Iga to the temple, naming it Hanagaki no Shō ("Village with a Flower Fence"). When the blossoms were in full bloom, guards were stationed by the tree for seven days. See 951.

621

Hearing they eat snakes
        how chilling to overhear
            the kiji calling

hebi kū to / kikeba osoroshi / kiji no koe

Spring, 1690. *kiji*: a green pheasant; see 394, 481.

622

On the Departure of Rotsū for Michinoku

The grassy pillow
        Go and learn the proper way
            to view the blossoms

kusamakura / makoto no hanami / shite mo koyo

Spring, 1690. *kusamakura* ("grass pillow"): a conventional epithet for travel. Rotsū (see 250) was setting off to follow Bashō's *Oku no Hosom-ichi* route. Rotsū was a shiftless, irresponsible character, who had tried to put the blame for losing the valuable tea chest of a wealthy family in Zeze onto his friend, Inkei. Bashō was furious, but before Bashō's death they reconciled. Rotsū attended Bashō's funeral at Gichū-ji.

623

An Account of Sharaku-dō

From four directions
        blossoms blowing into the
            waves of Lake Biwa

shihō yori / hana fukiirete / nio no nami

Spring, 1690. *nio*: an abbreviation of *Nio no Umi* (the "Sea of the Little Grebe"), another name for Lake Biwa; see 302. A greeting poem written at Sharaku-dō, the home of Hamada Chinseki, a physician in Zeze later known by the haikai name Shadō; see 771, 773, 822, 871, 910, 911, 914. Sharaku-dō had broad views of Lake Biwa and its surroundings. Bashō later wrote the haibun *Sharaku-dō no Ki* ("An Account of Sharaku-dō," 1690) for Shadō.

624

Mountain cherry trees
    And first here's the two buildings
        with rooftop tiling

yamazakura / kawara fukumono / mazu futatsu

Spring, 1690. The poem alludes to a phrase by Chōshō (see 603): "in the place where I usually live, there are two buildings with tiled roofs."

625

By the lakeside, lamenting the end of Spring

The spring departing
    The people of Ōmi
        us all lamenting

yuku haru o / Ōmi no hito to / oshimikeru

Spring, 1690. Ōmi, the province around Lake Biwa. "Master Bashō asked me, 'Shōhaku criticized this hokku and said that "Ōmi" could be replaced by "Tanba," and "spring" by "year." What do you think?' I answered, 'Shōhaku's criticism misses the point. The image of Ōmi province, with mist spreading over the large lake, helps to enhance sorrow over spring's departure. Besides, the hokku expresses how the poet actually felt at that time.' The Master replied, 'You're right. People in the old days felt just as much regret at spring's departure in this province as they did in Kyoto.' I said, 'I'm deeply moved by what you have said. If you were in Ōmi at the end of the year, how could you feel as truly sad as you did? If you were in the mountainous province of Tanba when spring ended, you wouldn't have felt that way either. How true an emotion is when it arises from the heart of someone moved by an actual scene from nature!' The Master was very pleased and said, 'Kyorai, you are someone I can talk poetry with.'—*Kyorai*" (Ueda, p. 288).

626

A nun all alone
     in a straw-thatched hut a clipped
          white azalea

hitori ama / waraya sugenashi / shirotsutsuji

Spring, 1690.

627

Staying overnight at Seta, I worshipped at Ishiyama-dera at dawn, and saw the Genji Room

At the break of day
     as lavender light lingers
          a cuckoo calling

akebono wa / mada murasaki ni / hototogisu

Summer, 1690. *Seta:* see 415, 609, 720. *The Genji Room:* so called because, it is said, Murasaki Shikibu wrote *Genji Monogatari* in this room. Murasaki means "purple," or as Edward Seidensticker translates it in his version of the tale, "lavender."

628

Missing the wife's love
     deep within the bamboo grass ——
Unfinished

tsuma koute / nezasa kazuku ya / ——

Written on the same sheet of paper as 626 and 627.

629

Up behind Ishiyama-dera, entering the Illusory Dwelling

Ever first looked to
    the pasania here too
        in the summer grove

mazu tanomu / shii no ki mo ari / natsukodachi

Summer, 1690. After completing the *Oku no Hosomichi* journey, Bashō stayed for three months at the Genjū-an ("the Hut of Illusory Dwelling"), offered to him by his disciple, Kyokusui (see 630, 652, 658, 729, 782, 785, 880, 881), and where he wrote his best-known haibun, *Genjū-an no Ki* ("An Account of the Hut of Illusory Dwelling"). *shii: Pasania cuspidata,* an evergreen of the beech family, which features often in waka poetry as a source of shelter or of nourishment.

630

You the butterfly
    and I the sage Zhuangzi
        the dream-mind mind-dream

kimi ya chō / ware ya Sōji ga / yumegokoro

Spring, 1690. *Sōji:* Zhuangzi (Chuang Tzu). For the story of the butterfly and Zhuangzi, see 172, 173. This hokku was included in a letter Bashō sent to his disciple, Dosui, the brother of Kyokusui; see 658.

631

In the summer grass
    slough it off in rich display
        the skin of the snake

natsukusa ni / fūki o kazare / hebi no kinu

Summer, 1690. Written at the Genjū-an. In a letter to Otokuni (see 678), Bashō wrote that "many snakes and centipedes bother me here."

632

Through the summer grass
        I would gladly walk ahead
                chase the snakes away

natsukusa ya / ware sakidachite / hebi karan

Summer, 1690. Bashō was alone for three months in the Genjū-an, and
this poem expresses his wish for a visitor.

633

Belonging neither
        to the night nor to morning
                the melon flowers

yūbe ni mo / asa ni mo tsukazu / uri no hana

Summer, 1690. The *yūgao* (literally, "evening faces"; see 10, 146, 421)
blooms in the evening, the *asagao* ("morning faces") in the morning,
but the yellow flowers of the melon bloom in daytime. *uri* usually refers
to the *makuwauri;* see 43, 145, 353, 640.

634

The path of the sun
        Where the hollyhock inclines
                in the summer rain

hi no michi ya / aoi katamuku / satsukiame

Summer, 1690.

635

Fragrant oranges
        In what year in what farmfield
            the cuckoo calling?

tachibana ya / itsu no nonaka no / hototogisu

Summer, 1690. The oranges are associated with the late Fourth Month,
and the cuckoo with the Fifth. Based on an anonymous waka included
in the *Kokinshū* and the *Ise Monogatari: satsuki matsu / hana tachibana
no / ka o kageba / mukashi no hito no / sode no ka zo suru* ("As the fra-
grances / rise from the orange blossoms / that await the Fifth / Month I
recall the scent on / the sleeves of one long ago").

636

Firefly-viewing at Seta

Watching the fireflies
        And the boatman now tipsy
            the boat unsteady

hotarumi ya / sendō youte / obotsukana

Summer, 1690. Seta: see 415, 609, 627. *Firefly-viewing at Seta:* see 416.
The custom of viewing fireflies developed in the mid-seventeenth cen-
tury in the Seta and Ishiyama districts of Ōtsu (present-day Shiga Pre-
fecture). When the fireflies were at their peak in early summer, *hotarub-
une* ("firefly boats") would take people on eating and drinking
excursions to the best places to see them. The Chinese-style bridge at
Seta was one of the most popular spots, along with Uji, near Kyoto.

637

Each by their own light
        the fireflies make of the trees
            a blossomy lodge

onoga hi o / kigi no hotaru ya / hana no yado

Summer, 1690.

638

In Kyoto too
          a yearning for Kyoto
                    Cuckoo cuckooing

Kyō nite mo / Kyō natsukashi ya / hototogisu

Summer, 1690. *Kyō:* Kyoto. The second Kyō is considered to refer to the Kyoto of the past; the cuckoo is emblematic of nostalgia in Japanese poetry.

639

Taking the evening air by the river at Shijō, Kyoto. From the moon at the beginning of the Sixth Month to the moon at mid-month, a platform is set up and people drink and eat all night long. Women wear large, showy obi sashes, and men wear long haori jackets. Monks and old folks mingle in the crowd, with apprentices to coopers and blacksmiths, carefree, row-dily singing. Such indeed the life of the capital!

The riverside breeze
          Wearing pale persimmon robes
                    the airish evening

kawakaze ya / usugaki kitaru / yūsuzumi

Summer, 1690. *usugaki* ("pale persimmon robes"): light summer kimono made from hemp. *haori:* see 135, 705, 965.

640

From the Naniwa area a hermit named Tōko came to see this talentless teacher

> Do not take after me
> > In two halves on the table
> > > the cut muskmelon

ware ni niru na / futatsu ni wareshi / makuwauri

Summer, 1690. *Tōko:* Emoto Tōko (1659?–1708), also known as Shidō (see also the note to 914, and 921), a young merchant from Naniwa (Osaka) who wanted to be Bashō's student. "A melon cut in half" is a Japanese idiom for two people who are almost identical. "Probably Tōko was such an ardent admirer of Bashō that he had done nothing but imitate his poetry. Accordingly, alluding to a melon that happened to be there, Bashō advised that Tōko should not be like one half of a melon, that he should become aware of his own individuality. Or it may be that Bashō was warning Tōko against becoming a wanderer like him.—*Kōseki*" (Ueda, p. 295).

641

> In my tiny hut
> > the mosquitos so tiny
> > > a tiny mercy

waga yado wa / ka no chiisaki o / chisō kana

Summer, 1690. Written when Akinobō (d. 1718) of Tsurugi, Kaga (now Hakusan, Ishikawa), visited the Genjū-an.

642

Life Transient and Brief

> Soon to be dying
> > yet giving away no sign
> > > the cicada sings

yagate shinu / keshiki wa miezu / semi no koe

Summer, 1690. The Japanese title is *Mujō Jinsoku: Mujō,* the transience of life; *Jinsoku:* quick, swift.

643

At Tanabata

Don't peep at the glee
　　　through the leaves of the silk tree
　　　　　The light of the stars

nebu no ki no / hagoshi mo itoe / hoshi no kage

Autumn, 1690. *Tanabata:* see 14, 97, 539. The *nebu* of the phrase *nebu no ki* ("silk tree"), when written in kanji, can also mean "taking pleasure together, sharing pleasure."

644

At the grass hut near Kiso Yoshinaka's grave, my heart drawn to the cemetery

Tama Matsuri
　　　Even today cremation
　　　　　smoke curls through the air

Tama Matsuri / kyō mo yakiba no / kemuri kana

Autumn, 1690. *Tama Matsuri:* see 440, 545, 893. Composed at Gichū-ji in Zeze. *Kiso Yoshinaka:* see 566, 680.

645

Here's a dragonfly
　　　clinging in vain to the air
　　　　　above the grasses

tonbō ya / toritsukikaneshi / kusa no ue

Autumn, 1690.

646

Even the wild boar
        buffeted and blown about
                The grass-parting wind

inoshishi mo / tomo ni fukaruru / nowaki kana

Autumn, 1690. *nowaki:* an autumn typhoon; see 148, 457, 927.

647

The monk Unchiku of Kyoto had painted what was perhaps a self-portrait, a monk with his face turned away. Unchiku asked me for a verse for the picture, and thereupon I wrote: You are over sixty, and I nearly fifty. We are both in a world of dreams, and this painting is of a man in a dream. Here now I add the words of another such man talking in his sleep:

Turn your face this way
        I am a lonesome one too
                The autumn evening

kochira muke / ware mo sabishiki / aki no kure

Autumn, 1690. *Unchiku:* Kitamuki Unchiku (1632–1703), of Tō-ji Kanchi-in, a famous calligrapher of the Daishi School who was also Bashō's calligraphy teacher.

648

Plucking out white hairs
        And underneath my pillow
                a creaker-cricket

shiraga nuku / makura no shita ya / kirigirisu

Autumn, 1690. The opening hokku of a *han kasen* (eighteen-stanza linked verse) composed at Gichū-ji in Zeze with Chinseki (see 623) and Shidō (Emoto Tōko had changed his name to Shidō when he visited Bashō at the Genjū-an in June, 1690; see 640). *kirigirisu:* a cricket; see 551, 660, 713, 911, 967.

649

At an old temple, moonviewing

> At the moonviewing
> > among all that gathering
> > > no beautiful face

tsukimi suru / za ni utsukushiki / kao mo nashi

The poem has three previous versions:

> At the Harvest Moon
> > the temple page boys lined up
> > > on the veranda

meigetsu ya / chigotachi narabu / dō no en

> At the Harvest Moon
> > turning to face the sea the
> > > Seven Komachis

meigetsu ya / umi ni mukaeba / nana-Komachi

> At the Harvest Moon
> > among all that gathering
> > > no beautiful face

meigetsu ya / za ni utsukushiki / kao mo nashi

Autumn, 1690. Written at a moonviewing party at Gichū-ji. *Komachi:* Ono no Komachi, a poet who was also a proverbial beauty; see 96, 676, 804, 888. *nana Komachi* ("Seven Komachis") is a poeticism for the effect of changes of the moon on the landscape.

650

At Masahide's House, for the first haikai party

The white of the moon
Hands placed and poised on laps in
the house of evening

tsukishiro ya / hiza ni te o oku / yoi no yado

Autumn, 1690. *Masahide:* Mizuta Masahide (1657–1723), an uncle of
Suganuma Kyokushi (see 629). He was a merchant or a high-ranking
official in the Zeze Domain, and later became a physician in the village
of Matsumoto.

651

A paulownia
The calls of quail traveling
over garden walls

kiri no ki ni / uzura nakunaru / hei no uchi

Autumn, 1690. In Bashō's day the wealthy kept quail to hear their calls,
which were considered poignant; see 722.

652

*A learned monk once said, "Superficial Zen is the foundation of deep
flaws," and I am grateful for his words*

In a lightning storm
who sees no enlightenment
that's one to admire

inazuma ni / satoranu hito no / tattosa yo

Autumn, 1690. Contained in a letter written at Gichū-ji to his disciple
Kyokusui (see 629) in Edo, criticizing disciples in Ōmi (see 625) for the
complacent conventionality of their poetry and their dissolute social
lives.

653

You will know my hut
    by the flowering knotweed
        and the red peppers

kusa no to o / shire ya hotade ni / tōgarashi

Autumn, 1690.

654

In Katada

An ailing wild goose
    fallen in the nighttime cold
        A kip on the road?

byōgan no / yosamu ni ochite / tabine kana

Autumn, 1690. *Katada* (or Katata): on the western shore of Lake Biwa, included in the *Ōmi Hakkei* ("Eight Famous Scenes of Ōmi") as a place where wild geese alighted. At the invitation of local disciples, Bashō visited Katada in October 1690 and fell ill.

655

In the fisher's house
    mingling among the small shrimp
        a camel cricket

ama no ya wa / koebi ni majiru / itodo kana

Autumn, 1690. As with many of the poems, it is up to the reader to judge whether singular or plural suits the situation best; some translators infer more than one *itodo* ("camel cricket").

656

At Shōzui-ji in Katada

Drinking morning tea
the monk coming to silence
and chrysanthemums

asacha nomu / sō shizukanari / kiku no hana

Autumn, 1690. *Shōzui-ji:* a Zen temple.

657

While I was staying for quite a while at Awazu, I was invited by a man who loved the tea ceremony and served chrysanthemums gathered from a nearby beach

A butterfly comes
to sup on the namasu
of chrysanthemums

chō mo kite / su o sū kiku no / namasu kana

Autumn, 1690. *Awazu:* the name for the area that includes the castle town of Zeze and the village of Baba. Gichū-ji (see 644) is located in Baba; *namasu:* a vinegared salad, usually of daikon, carrot and fish; see 430, 615.

658

To hear the wild geese
the capital of autumn's
where I need to go

kari kiki ni / miyako no aki ni / omomukan

Autumn, 1690. *miyako:* the ancient imperial capital, Kyoto. In a letter to Dosui, a disciple at Zeze, the brother of Kyokusui; see 629, 630.

659

On the Road to My Hometown

A winter drizzle
  Enough to darken the fields
    the freshcut stubble

shigururu ya / ta no arakabu no / kuromu hodo

Winter, 1690.

660

A creaker-cricket
  a voice almost forgotten
    at kotatsu time

kirigirisu / wasurene ni naku / kotatsu kana

Winter, 1690. *kotatsu:* a hearth with a wooden frame raised around it with a quilt placed on the frame, where people could sit with legs underneath the quilt to stay warm in winter. *kirigirisu:* the cricket is associated with autumn in classical Japanese poetry; see 551, 648, 713, 911, 967.

661

Remembering Olden Days

And after the frosts
  a wild fringed pink blossoming
    on a brazier

shimo no nochi / nadeshiko sakeru / hioke kana

Winter, 1690. *hioke:* a wooden *hibachi* (brazier) decorated with pictures, in this case of flowers. In Bashō's time a *hioke* decorated with images of *nadeshiko* (*Dianthus superbus:* fringed pink) would have called to mind the distant past; see 305, 766, 939.

662

A withering wind
> The pain in the swollen cheeks
> of a human face

kogarashi ya / hōbare itamu / hito no kao

Winter, 1690. *kogarashi:* see 140, 223, 740.

663

A Journey

The year's first snowfall
> The color of the backbox
> of a pilgrim monk

hatsuyuki ya / hijirikozō no / oi no iro

Winter, 1690. *hijirikozō* (or *kōyahijiri*): a monk from Mount Kōya, who travels the country to preach and to raise funds for the temple by selling prayer beads and other goods from his *oi,* a lacquered box carried on his back.

664

Traveling along the Shinano Road

The snow falling now
> on susuki grass uncut
> for the shrine hut's roof

yuki chiru ya / hoya no susuki no / karinokoshi

Winter, 1690. *hoya:* a temporary hut for the Suwa Shrine festival in Shinano (Nagano), still held in August (the Seventh Month in Bashō's day). The poem is a fiction, as Bashō did not travel to Shinano in 1690. He visited there in 1688, but not in winter.

665

Only the First of the Twelfth Month . . .

When Sekizoro
　　Players come Poetry too
　　　　seeing off the year

Sekizoro no / kureba fūga mo / shiwasu kana

Winter, 1690. *Sekizoro:* a group of entertainers who would come near
the end of the year, and go from door to door asking for money; see
786. *shiwasu:* an old name for the Twelfth Month; see note to 677.

666

Plovers taking off
　　Evening deepens and departs
　　　　to winds down Hiei

chidori tachi / fukeyuku shoya no / hieroroshi

Winter, 1690. *Hiei:* Mount Hiei, the site of a Tendai Buddhist monastery
to the northeast of Kyoto; see 70, 420, 715. *hieroshi:* cold winds blow-
ing from Mount Hiei.

667

*Even though I've been asked to leave, I stay on in this inn eating away,
beginning to feel uneasy*

Wandering heartmind
　　the alighting nowhere long
　　　　A moveable hearth

sumitsukanu / tabi no kokoro ya / okigotatsu

Winter, 1690. *okigotatsu:* while a *horigotatsu* is a *kotatsu* (see 660) that
is a permanent part of a room, an *okigotatsu* is a brazier that can be
moved from place to place.

668

A Journey

The Year-End Cleaning
    Through the crannies of cedars
        the branch-clearing storm

susuhaki wa / sugi no konoma no / arashi kana

Winter, 1690 (1691). *susuhaki:* "sweeping the soot from the house," the
housecleaning done at the end of the year, usually on the thirteenth day
of the Twelfth Month, to welcome the New Year; see 344, 836. The thir-
teenth day of the Twelfth Month equates to January 11, 1691.

669

A Year-End Poetry Gathering

For this half a day
    the gods our companions
        Throwing the year off

hanjitsu wa / kami o tomo ni ya / toshiwasure

Winter, 1690. Written at the home of Ogurusu Yūgen, known as Jiyū,
the chief priest of Kami-Goryō-sha in northwest Kyoto, whose house
was within the shrine's precincts. *toshiwasure:* a "year-forgetting" party,
held at the end of the year; see 678, 751, 945.

670

Resting from my journey in Kyoto, I heard each night the melancholy
sound of pilgrims making their rounds beating the alms bowls

Dried salted salmon
      and a Kūya monk's thinness
         The dead of winter

karazake mo / Kūya no yase mo / kan no uchi

Winter, 1690. For "Kūya monk" and beating the alms bowl, see 603; *kan:*
the coldest thirty days of winter; monks practiced especially rigorous
spiritual exercises during this period. "The arctic internal landscape of
the poet, who was painfully aware of his aging body as well as of his
destiny as a wanderer, was made here into an abstract painting that sug-
gests the coldest season through the images of a dried salmon and a
Kūya pilgrim. Probably this hokku shows the highest point reached by
Bashō in his art of poetry during the *Sarumino* period, a period when
he tried to body forth the colors of his mind through objects and scenes
in nature.—*Ogata*" (Ueda, p. 307).

671

These natto-slicing
      sounds please cease a little while
         The alms-bowl beating

natto kiru / oto shibashi mate / hachitataki

Winter, 1690. *nattō:* fermented soybeans. In Japanese the word *nattō*
usually has a four-*on* pronunciation, but can also be pronounced with
three *on*. Bashō adopts the three-*on* pronunciation in this poem. *hachi-*
tataki: see 603, and above.

672

Upon the stones of
> Stone Mountain comes pelting down
>> a hailstone shower

Ishiyama no / ishi ni tabashiru / arare kana

Winter, 1690. *Ishiyama*: Ishiyama-dera, a Shingon Buddhist temple near the southern shore of Lake Biwa, which was built on an outcropping of wollastonite, a white stone; see 558. Bashō may have been inspired by the following waka by Minamoto no Sanetomo (1192–1219), the third shogun of Kamakura: *mononofu no / yanami tsukurou / kote no e ni / arare tabashiru / nasu no shinohara* ("As the warrior / repositions his arrows / the hailstone shower / pelts down upon his gauntlet / The bamboo field at Nasu"). Legend says that Murasaki Shikibu conceived *Genji Monogatari* while staying at Ishiyama-dera; see also 627.

673

So hated on most days
> yet even the crow snowy
>> this snowy morning

higoro nikuki / karasu mo yuki no / ashita kana

Winter, 1690. 6-7-5.

674

In Ōtsu

Even the three-foot
> mountain set upon by the
>> leaf-scattering storm

sanjaku no / yama mo arashi no / konoha kana

Winter, 1690. *shaku*: a Japanese unit of length, about 30 cm; "three-foot mountain," a coinage meaning small hill.

675

Hira Mikami
> Across the mountains the snow
> a white egret bridge

Hira Mikami / yuki sashiwatase / sagi no hashi

Winter, 1690. *Hira Mikami:* the Hira Mountains, on the western shore of Lake Biwa, the snow scene of which was one of the *Ōmi Hakkei* ("Eight Famous Scenes of Ōmi"; see 654); Mount Mikami, on the eastern shore. The snow connecting both mountains transforms the Tanabata legend in which a bridge of magpies connect the stars; see 14.

676

In Response to a Request from the Priest Jōko

Ah magnificent, so magnificent. The hat precious, the straw coat precious too. Who told us her tale, who has rendered this image so, this vision of a thousand years, here before us now? When the form is here, the spirit too is here again. The straw coat precious, the hat precious too

> So very precious
> > even on a snowless day
> > the straw coat the hat

tōtosa ya / yuki furanu hi mo / mino to kasa

Winter, 1690. Concerning a painting of Ono no Komachi, the early Heian period poet numbered among the *Thirty-Six Poetry Immortals* chosen by Fujiwara no Kintō, whose beauty became proverbial; see 96, 649, 804, 888. In the painting she was depicted in old age as a wandering crone, based on a story by Kan'ami (see 117). *Priest Jōkō:* the head priest at Mii-dera (see 679).

677

Into hiding now
    the grebes on the brimming lake
        as the year runs down

kakurekeri / shiwasu no umi no / kaitsuburi

Winter, 1690 (1691). "The hokku, which Bashō composed late in the
Twelfth Month of Genroku 3 (Jan. 1691), probably at Ōmi, describes
the grebes (*kaitsuburi*), small birds that float on the surface of Lake
Biwa [see 302, 623] and occasionally dive beneath the water, 'hiding'
(*kakurekeri*) before popping up in an unexpected location. The larger
context suggested by 'Twelfth Month' (*shiwasu*, literally, 'teacher
running')—a seasonal word for winter and for the end of the year,
when everybody is running about cleaning up and settling their finan-
cial accounts—implies that the observer is a carefree, reclusive person,
someone who has the leisure to observe the grebes at the busiest time
of the year" (Shirane, *Traces*, p. 49).

678

At Otokuni's New House

Now I've got someone to
    buy a house to let me get
        to throw the year off

hito ni ie o / kawasete ware wa / toshiwasure

Winter, 1690. *Otokuni*: Kawai Otokuni, a wealthy patron in Ōtsu, the
brother (and adopted son) of Kawai Chigetsu (see 604), who invited
Bashō to stay in his recently bought house over the New Year holiday.
Bashō is mocking his own impudence in jocularly describing having
had Otokuni buy him a house. 6-7-5.

679

Closing my mouth for three days, on the fourth day of the New Year a theme

From Ōtsu-e
    brushes to begin the year
        what kind of Buddha?

Ōtsu-e no / fude no hajime wa / nani botoke

Spring, 1691. *Ōtsu-e:* "Ōtsu pictures," folk art sold at roadside stalls, popular as souvenirs for pilgrims to Mii-dera ("Temple of Three Wells"); see 715. *botoke* (*hotoke*): an image of the Buddha.

680

The Kiso spirit
    Arising out of the snow
        the springtime grasses

Kiso no jō / yuki ya haenuku / haru no kusa

Spring, 1691. Written at the grave of Kiso Yoshinaka at Gichū-ji in Ōtsu (see 566, 644) where Bashō requested also to be buried. Kiso is also the name of a river, gorge, highway, and town.

681

For Otokuni, leaving for Edo

Ume and young greens
    at the Mariko station
        the tororo soup

ume wakana / Mariko no shuku no / tororojiru

Spring, 1691. *Otokuni:* see 678. *Mariko no shuku:* Mariko-juku, the twentieth (counted from Edo) of the fifty-three staging posts, and one of the smallest, along the Tōkaidō road, one of the "Five Routes" of Edo-period Japan; now part of Shizuoka City; *tororo:* a soup of grated yam, for which the Mariko-juku was renowned. Along the route Otokuni would be traveling at that time of the year, ume trees would be in bloom, and young greens abundant.

682

Fragrance of ume
    Shirara Ochikubo
      Kyōtarō

ume ga ka ya / Shirara Ochikubo / Kyōtarō

Spring, 1691. *Shirara, Ochikubo, Kyōtarō:* the names of stories mentioned in *Jōruri Monogatari,* a popular fifteenth-century tale of the love between the young Ushiwakamaru (Minamoto no Yoshitsune; see 209, 510, 515, 545) and a young woman named Lady Jōruri. The allusion is to a line in the tale in which Lady Jōruri, in the springtime, is asked which of the stories she has read.

683

In the Mountains of Iga, Early Spring

A mountain village
    Manzai dancers late
      The ume blossoms

yamazato wa / manzai ososhi / ume no hana

Spring, 1691. *Manzai:* a troupe of itinerant players who sang and danced door to door at New Year. "A hokku involves a movement of the mind that advances and then returns. It can be illustrated by this verse on Manzai dancers. The poet first proceeded to assert that the dancers were late in coming to the mountain village, and then he came back to observe that the plum blossoms were in bloom. Such 'advancing' and 'returning' of the mind is what makes a hokku—*Dohō*" (Ueda, p. 309).

684

Waiting for the Moon
        The ume at full tilt of
            a young mountain monk

tsukimachi ya / ume katageyuku / ko-yamabushi

Spring, 1691. Bashō had been invited to a *tsukimachi* ("waiting for the moonrise") party at the home of Takutai (see 399) in Iga; see 817 for a *kagemachi* ("waiting for the sunrise") poem. *ko-yamabushi*: a *yamabushi* still in training, who passed by carrying a sprig of ume blossoms. *yamabushi*: mountain ascetic, follower of the Shugendō branch of Buddhism.

685

Utter laziness
        being shaken-awakened
            A springtime shower

bushōsa ya / kakiokosareshi / haru no ame

Spring, 1691. An earlier version reads *bushōsa ya / dakiokosaruru / haru no ame* ("Utter laziness / shaken out of the scratcher / A springtime shower"). Bashō was staying in his brother's house in Iga.

686

At a Farmhouse

Thin from boiled barley
        or emaciating love?
            The tomcat's molly

mugimeshi ni / yatsururu koi ka / neko no tsuma

Spring, 1691.

687

Each and every year
    nourishing the cherry tree
        the fallen blossoms

toshidoshi ya / sakura o koyasu / hana no chiri

Spring, 1691. Echoes a proverb that says "flowers return to the roots";
see 269.

688

Once we've drunk it dry
    let's make a flower vase of
        this fourlitre cask

nomi akete / hanaike ni sen / nishō daru

Spring, 1691. Inspired by a line in Du Fu (see 126, 159, 160, 184, 215,
485, 515): "a sake bottle now made into a flower vase"; *nishō:* two shō, a
shō is about 1.8 litres; see 186.

689

For a little while
    floating above the blossoms
        the moon of tonight

shibaraku wa / hana no ue naru / tsukiyo kana

Spring, 1691. It was a matter of debate in renga circles whether verses
on the moon or on flowers were of more importance.

690

The weakening years
    My teeth bite into and hit
        sand in the seaweed

otoroi ya / ha ni kuiateshi / nori no suna

Spring, 1691. *nori:* thin sheets of edible dried seaweed, used to wrap
boiled rice to make *norimaki.* An earlier version reads: *kami atsuru / mi
no otoroi ya / nori no suna* ("My teeth bite into / the body's aged weak-
ness / Sand in the seaweed"); see 287.

691

Kerria roses
    So right to stick in a hat
        the cut of that spray

yamabuki ya / kasa ni sasubeki / eda no nari

Spring, 1691.

692

On a Picture

Kerria roses
    The aroma of tea roast-
        ing time at Uji

yamabuki ya / Uji no hoiro no / niou toki

Spring, 1691. *Uji:* a town to the south of Kyoto, famous for the cultiva-
tion of green tea.

693

In the night's darkness
    bewildered as to its nest
        the plover calling

yami no yo ya / su o madowashite / naku chidori

Spring, 1691.

694

Melancholy nub
    The nodes of a bamboo shoot
        the end of a life

uki fushi ya / takenoko to naru / hito no hate

Summer, 1691. *fushi:* the nodes or joints of a bamboo stem, which in Japanese culture figuratively evokes an important juncture in time and space; see 399. While walking in the bamboo grove at Sagano, near Kyoto, Bashō came across the grave of Kogō no Tsubone, a favorite concubine of the emperor Takakura (1161–81) but who fell afoul of Taira no Kiyomori (1118–81) and was forced to become a nun. The emperor fell ill and died, and Kogō committed suicide by throwing herself into the Ōi River.

695

Arashiyama
    Through the thickets of bamboo
        the lines of the wind

Arashiyama / yabu no shigeri ya / kaze no suji

Summer, 1691. *Arashiyama* ("storm mountain"): the hills to the west of Kyoto, along the southern banks of the Ōi River and a famous scenic spot. Both 694 and 695 were written on the same day, the nineteenth day of the Fourth Month.

696

Blossoms of yuzu
    Let's recollect olden days
        the Food Setting Room

yu no hana ya / mukashi shinoban / ryōri no ma

Summer, 1691. *yuzu:* Chinese lemon, a citrus used in various dishes; *ryōri no ma* ("food room"): a floored room between the dirt-floored kitchen and the dining area where food was arranged before serving. In classical Japanese poetry, the smell of citrus flowers evokes the distant past. The poem concerns Rakushi-sha; see 699, 703.

697

Cuckoo cuckooing
    Into the bamboo forest
        the moonlight leaking

hototogisu / ōtakeyabu o / moru tsukiyo

Summer, 1691.

698

I'm a misery
    So now bring on lonesomeness
        yon mountain cuckoo

uki ware o / sabishigarase yo / kankodori

Summer, 1691. *kankodori: Cuculus canorus,* the mountain cuckoo, in contrast to the *hototogisu* (*Cuculus poliocephalus,* the little, or lesser, cuckoo), is rare and prized for its lonely song; the two kanji characters for *kankodori* can be read as "solitude" and "old." This poem is a revision of 587. Bashō quotes two waka of Saigyō in *Saga Nikki* (*Saga Diary,* 1691): *tou hito mo / omoitaetaru / yamazato no / sabishisa nakuba / sum-iukaramashi* ("People no longer / think of coming to visit / this mountain village / Were there no lonesomeness here / living would be wretchedness"); *yamazato ni / tare o mata kowa / yobukodori / hitori nomi koso / sumamu to omou ni* ("A mountain village / who on earth is it calling / the mountain cuckoo? / All by myself for certain / I had thought I would be living"). However, he misquotes the second waka as *yamazato ni / kowa mata tare o / yobukodori / hitori sumanto / omoishi mono o,* and makes it 5-7-5-7-7 rather than the 5-7-5-7-8 of the original. "We can see Bashō's desire to be immersed in the world of *sabi.* The hokku's beginning phrase implies his dissatisfaction with his own self, which is not yet merged with that world of solitude.—*Ebara*" (Ueda, p. 316).

699

The clapping of hands
    in the echoes the dawning
        the moon in summer

te o uteba / kodama ni akuru / natsu no tsuki

Summer, 1691. Written at Rakushi-sha; see 696, 703. Another version of
the poem appears in *Saga Nikki: natsu no yo ya* / kodama *ni akuru / geta
no oto* ("The summer evening / the dawn in the echoes of / the sound
of the clogs"). "With the clapping, echoes. With the echoes, the summer
dawn. At dawn, the summer moon. Through a skillful use of words, the
poet has linked these three things in such a way that one flows into
another. The technique has enabled the poet to condense the language
of the poem on the one hand and to create a harmonious relationship
among the images on the other. In my opinion, the way in which the
poetic material is given form here illustrates the ultimate art of haiku.—
Watsuji" (Ueda, p. 317). In Japan there is a custom of clapping hands to
greet the morning sun, and of clapping at the altar of a Shinto shrine to
gain the attention of the gods.

700

Shoots of wild bamboo
    The playthings of the drawings
        of my childish days

takenoko ya / osanaki toki no / e no susabi

Summer, 1691.

701

Day after day by day
    barley in the field reddens
        and the skylark sings

hitohi hitohi / mugi akaramite / naku hibari

Summer, 1691. 6-7-5.

702

The drowsy noddings-
　　　off of this ne'er-do-well me
　　　　　nixed by reed warblers

nōnashi no / nemutashi ware o / gyōgyōshi

Summer, 1691. *gyōgyōshi*: a word that can mean both "reed warbler" and "too loud."

703

Reluctantly leaving the House of Fallen Persimmons tomorrow, I go inside, cast my eyes over each and every room

The Rainy Season
　　　The shikishi boards peeled off
　　　　　traces on the wall

samidare ya / shikishi hegitaru / kabe no ato

Summer, 1691. *House of Fallen Persimmons*: Rakushi-sha, a cottage owned by Kyorai (see 424) in Sagano, where Bashō stayed in the spring of 1691 and where he wrote *Saga Nikki; shikishi*: a square card with a poem or painting on it.

704

Making chimaki
　　　Onehandedly dealing with
　　　　　the fall of her hair

chimaki yū / katate ni hasamu / hitaigami

Summer, 1691. *chimaki*: see 75.

705

On a Portrait of Jōzan

Summer on the breeze
    That haori coat's lapel
        he'll not straighten too

kaze kaoru / haori wa eri mo / tsukurowazu

Summer, 1691. *Jōzan:* Ishikawa Jōzan (1583–1672), a scholar of Chinese and poet in the Tang style, whose hermitage in Kyoto, Shisen-dō, later became a Sōtō Zen sect temple. Bashō, with Kyorai, Sora, and Jōsō, visited Shisen-dō in June 1691. *haori:* see 135, 639, 965.

706

The swelter of June
    The temperature of one
        taken with ague

minazuki wa / fukubyōyami no / atsusa kana

Summer, 1691. *minazuki:* the traditional name for the Sixth Month in the Japanese lunar calendar; see 155, 524, 763. *fukubyō:* an old word for the common cold derived from *Genji Monogatari*. The word in *Genji Monogatari* is, in fact, *fubyō*, which was also pronounced *fūbyō*. According to Yamamoto Kenkichi, it was later erroneously changed to *fukubyō*. In contemporary Japanese, *fubyō* (or *fukubyō*) equates to *kanbō* or *kaze*, the common cold.

707

Early Autumn

In early autumn
    a folded mosquito net's
        a bedcover now

hatsuaki ya / tatami nagara no / kaya no yogi

Autumn, 1691.

708

Now a begonia's
    bloomed into the colors of
        a watermelon

shūkaidō / suika no iro ni / sakinikeri

Autumn, 1691. *shūkaidō: Begonia grandis Dryand,* a hardy variety of begonia, bearing pink flowers. 6-7-5.

709

The autumn wind blows
    To the burrs on the chestnut
        the bluegreen still hews

akikaze no / fukedomo aoshi / kuri no iga

Autumn, 1691.

710

In the autumn of the Iron Sheep Year, at my ease strolling, on the Ninth Street of Kyoto, I passed by the Rashōmon gate

The miscanthus plumes
    grabbing at heads at the gate
        Rashōmon

ogi no ho ya / kashira o tsukamu / Rashōmon

Autumn, 1691. *Iron Sheep Year:* 1691, in Japanese *kanotohitsuji,* or *shinbi;* based on the sexagenary cycle of reckoning time in China and other East Asian cultures. *Rashōmon* (also *Rajōmon*): the main gate to the (partially) walled city of Heijō-kyō, or Heian-kyō, built at the southern end of Suzaku Ōji ("Suzaku Avenue"), the avenue leading to the Imperial Palace from the south in Japanese capitals. At the northern end of Suzaku Ōji was *Suzakumon,* which was the main entrance to the palace. In the Noh play *Rashōmon* by Kanze Nobumitsu (1435–1516), a demon resides at the top of the gate. The demon grabs Watanabe no Tsuna by the back of his helmet, and the samurai cuts off the demon's arm with his sword. In 1915, the play was reworked as a horror story by Akutagawa Ryūnosuke (1892–1927). The gate provided the title and some details of the 1950 Kurosawa Akira film, which is based mainly on another Akutagawa story, "Yabu no naka" ("In a Bamboo Grove," in Jay Rubin's translation).

711

In the cattle-shed
     mosquito voices dusky
         The last of summer

ushibeya ni / ka no koe kuraki / zansho kana

Autumn, 1691. *zansho:* the heat of late summer; see 546.

712

Wanting to hang it in his hut, Kukū asked me to write a poem on a portrait of Kenkō

The autumnal hues
     No sign into the bargain
         of a pickling-pot

aki no iro / nukamiso tsubo mo / nakarikeri

Autumn, 1691. The allusion is to passage 98 of *The Tsurezuregusa* (see 303): "One with his thoughts fixed on the world to come should not own so much as a pickling jar" (McKinney, p. 68). *Kukū:* a poet in Kanazawa.

713

Here is lonesomeness
     hung from a peg on the wall
         A creaker-cricket

sabishisa ya / kugi ni kaketaru / kirigirisu

Autumn, 1691. An earlier version reads: *shizukasa ya / e kakaru kabe no / kirigirisu* ("Here is quietness / By the picture on the wall / a creaker-cricket"). The poem refers to the portrait of Kenkō in 712, and was intended as an (oblique) inscription. For *kirigirisu,* the cricket, see 551, 648, 660, 911, 967.

714

The Evening of the Fifteenth

The rice-giving kind
 the friends with me this evening
  my moonviewing guests

yone kururu / tomo o koyoi no / tsuki no kyaku

Autumn, 1691. Bashō alludes to passage 117 of *The Tsurezuregusa* in which Kenkō lists three kinds of good friend: "one who gives gifts, a doctor, a wise man" (McKinney, p. 78). Kenkō's disquisition on good and bad friends derives from Confucius, book 16 of the *Analects*. As with 715, written at a moonviewing party at Gichū-ji on the fifteenth of the Eighth Month (September 7, 1691).

715

Harvest Moon

The Mii-dera gate
 I want to rat-a-tat on
  under tonight's moon

Miidera no / mon tatakabaya / kyō no tsuki

Autumn, 1691. *Mii-dera:* Miidera ("Temple of Three Wells"), at the foot of Mount Hiei in Ōtsu, on the southern shore of Lake Biwa; see 679. The poem was written at a moonviewing party at Gichū-ji (see 606, 644), about 2 km to the southeast of Mii-dera, and is based on lines of the Chinese poet Jia Dao (see 191): "Birds sleep in the trees by the pond / Under the moon a monk knocks on the gate."

716

At Katada, the Night of the Sixteenth

Unlock the door now
   to let the moonlight enter
      Ukimidō

jō akete / tsuki sashiireyo / Ukimidō

Autumn, 1691. *Katada:* see 654, 656. *Ukimidō:* the "floating temple" hall
of Mangetsu-ji, at Lake Biwa in Ōtsu, which can be reached by bridge,
or as Bashō did, by boat. The "sixteenth" is the night after the harvest
moon: see 453, 458, 718, 811, and below.

717

The rising easy
   and yet now hesitating
      the cloud-covered moon

yasu yasu to / idete izayou / tsuki no kumo

Autumn, 1691. *izayou* ("to hesitate," "to dally") refers to the *izayoi no
tsuki:* the moon of the sixteenth night (the sixteenth night of the Eighth
Month of the fourth Year of Genroku: September 8, 1691).

718

The Sixteenth-night moon
   Just enough dark this evening
      to cook these prawns in

izayoi ya / ebi niru hodo no / yoi no yami

Autumn, 1691. *izayoi:* the "hesitating" moon, on the sixteenth night of
the month. On the fifteenth, the moon rises at sunset; on the sixteenth,
it rises about thirty minutes after sunset.

719

With great care Torei tends to the garden of his father's country house,
which is rich with several fruit trees

Grandfather parents
　　　the grandchildren prospering
　　　　　Persimmon mikan

ōji oya / mago no sakae ya / kaki mikan

Autumn, 1691. A greeting poem to Yanase Kakyū (Torei's father), to
whose home Bashō had been invited. *mikan:* a citrus fruit, *Citrus*
unshiu, of Chinese origin but introduced to the West via Japan and
sometimes called the satsuma, after Satsuma Province, the old name for
what is now the western part of Kagoshima Prefecture on the island of
Kyūshū, from where the fruit was first exported.

720

The Harvest Shining
　　　though this one year we've had two
　　　　　The moon at Seta

meigetsu wa / futatsu sugite mo / Seta no tsuki

Autumn, 1691. In 1691 there was an intercalary Eighth Month. Because
twelve lunar months are shorter than one solar year, every few years an
intercalary month (see 871) was added to the calendar. *Seta:* see 415,
609, 627.

721

A rice field's sparrows
　　　with a tea field over there
　　　　　to fly away to

inasuzume / cha-no-ki batake ya / nigedokoro

Autumn, 1691.

722

Now even the eye
of the hawk growing darker
The call of a quail

taka no me mo / ima ya kurenu to / naku uzura

Autumn, 1691. The call of the quail was considered poignant; see 651.

723

At Sanshi's House, Tatsugaoka

Eye the buckwheat too
provoke a fit of envy
the wild bush clover

soba mo mite / kenarigaraseyo / nora no hagi

Autumn, 1691. A greeting poem to Sanshi, a farmer who had invited
Bashō and several of his disciples to his home in Tatsugaoka, Ōtsu.

724

Every now and then
chrysanthemum vinegared
a good sakana

oriori wa / su ni naru kiku no / sakana kana

Autumn, 1691. *sakana*: a dish to eat with sake; a homophone for "fish."

725

Under my thatched roof
as day darkens I'm given
chrysanthemum wine

kusa no to ya / higurete kureshi / kiku no sake

Autumn, 1691. It is the ninth of the Ninth Month, *Chōyō no Sekku:*
the Chrysanthemum Festival; see 108, 458, 582, 909. *kiku no sake*
("chrysanthemum wine"): sake with chrysanthemum is drunk on the
morning of the festival, to wish for long life. Otokuni (see 678), Bashō's
disciple, brought him a cask in the evening.

726

The squirrel's foot fern
by the bridgegirders recalls
the moonlight's traces

hashigeta no / shinobu wa tsuki no / nagori kana

Autumn, 1691. *shinobu* means both "fern" and "to recall"; see 207, 509.
Bashō was visiting Ishiyama-dera (see 672), near the Seta Bridge (see
415), to view the moon of the thirteenth of the Ninth Month, in the
fourth year of Genroku (November 2, 1691), the last full moon of autumn.

727

About the ninth time
awakened and the moon not
four in the morning

kokonotabi / okite mo tsuki no / nanatsu kana

Autumn, 1691. *kokonotabi*: literally, "nine times," but here the meaning
is "many times." In Japanese poetry, the autumn night is often presented
as long, following the short nights of summer.

728

A matsutake
A leaf I do not know clings
tightly to the cap

matsudake ya/ shiranu konoha no/ hebaritsuku

Autumn, 1691. *matsutake* (or *matsudake*): "pine mushroom," so called
because often found under the Japanese red pine, but here the leaf
comes from an unknown tree. "As we trace the evolution of Bashō's
style, we notice that it gradually moved from a style that sought novelty
and dexterity to one that tried to discover a deep meaning in a common
object or scene—the so-called *karumi* style. This poem is one of the
best illustrations of the later style.—*Kobayashi*" (Ueda, p. 323). *karumi*:
see 615, 754, 780, 841, 848, 856.

729

Under the noodles
loading the whittled kindling
against the night cold

nyūmen no / shita takitatsuru / yosamu kana

Autumn, 1691. At Kyokusui-tei, the home of Kyokusui at Zeze (see 629, 630, 652, 658, 880, 881), where in the autumn night the host is cooking *nyūmen*, a dish of noodles in hot soup.

730

The wind of autumn
stirring the paulownia
the frosted ivy

akikaze ya / kiri ni ugokite / tsuta no shimo

Autumn, 1691. Wind moving the paulownia tree (*kiri*) is traditionally associated with the beginning of autumn, and frost on the ivy (*tsuta*) with the end. An earlier version reads: *kiri ugoku / aki no owari ya / tsuta no shimo* ("Paulownia moves / the ending of the autumn / Frost on the ivy").

731

At the rice threshing
the old woman a wonder
Chrysanthemum blooms

inekoki no / uba mo medetashi / kiku no hana

Autumn, 1691. A greeting poem to the Kitamura family, farmers in Hikone with whom Bashō had stayed overnight. Chrysanthemums are emblems of longevity.

732

The Tenth Month of the fourth year of Genroku, staying at the honorable Riyū's place at Menshō-ji. A hundred years have passed since the temple was moved here to the district of Hirata. As related in the records of contributions to the temple, "Bamboo and trees grow densely here, and the earth and rocks are covered with moss." Truly a venerable grove, deeply moving in its aura of age

> They give off the look
> > of a hundred years the leaves
> > > strewn about the lawn

momotose no / keshiki o niwa no / ochiba kana

Winter, 1691. *Riyū:* Kōno Riyū (also Kōno Michikata, 1662–1705), the fourteenth chief priest of Menshō-ji, a temple at Hirata in Hikone, where Bashō was staying on his way to Edo from Zeze, Otsu, in 1691. Riyū had visited Bashō at Rakushi-sha ("House of Fallen Persimmons"; see 703), to become his disciple.

733

> Reverential tears
> > taking on the coloring
> > > of the fallen leaves

tōtogaru / namida ya somete / chiru momiji

Winter, 1691. Written at Menshō-ji; *momiji:* the red leaves of autumn, or more specifically, the leaves of the Japanese maple in autumn.

734

Garden Impromptu

> Tastefully laid out
> > the garden enlivened by
> > > a winter shower

tsukurinasu / niwa o isamuru / shigure kana

Winter, 1691. A greeting poem for Kigai, chief priest of Honryū-ji, in Tarui, Mino Province. Written around the tenth of the Tenth Month of the fourth year of Genroku (November 29, 1691).

735

So deep-rooted the leeks
>   so very white when just washed
>   And then there's the cold

nebuka shiroku / araiagetaru / samusa kana

Winter, 1691. Bashō gave his own drawing of three leeks on a chopping board, which accompanies this hokku, to Kigai of Honryū-ji. *nebuka* (literally, "deep-root"): another name for *negi* (leek, or Welsh onion). The Tarui area was noted for a variety called *Miyashiro nebuka,* which grew up to a foot in length. 6-7-5.

736

A Good Time at Sensen-tei

Now and now again
>   gazing on Mount Ibuki
>   The wintering in

oriori ni / Ibuki o mite wa / fuyugomori

Winter, 1691. *Sensen-tei:* the house of Sensen (Shikin's younger brother, see 480, 796), which had a view of Mount Ibuki (see 580), to the east of Lake Biwa. The word *ibuki* is a homonym for "breath," so Bashō is making a play on words: he is also gazing on breath made visible by the cold; *fuyugomori:* winter seclusion, confinement, isolation, or the hibernation of animals in winter; see 334, 465, 598, 821, 822.

737

Impromptu at Kōsetsu's House

On the withering
>   wind the tinges imbued by
>   late-blooming flowers

kogarashi ni / nioi ya tsukeshi / kaeribana

Winter, 1691. *Kōsetsu:* Bashō's host, of whom nothing is known. *kogarashi:* a withering wind in late autumn and winter; see 140, 223, 662. *nioi:* a word that can mean scent, fragrance, smell, or color.

738

The narcissus blooms
    the white of the shōji
        each each other's hue

suisen ya / shiroki shōji no / tomoutsuri

Winter, 1691. A greeting poem to his host, Baijin, a poet in Atsuta, where he stayed on the twentieth day of the Tenth Month of the fourth year of Genroku (December 9, 1691). *shōji:* a sliding door, window or room divider made of paper within a framework of wood and wooden lattices. "By suggesting an impression of the utmost purity, the poet paid respect to the host and his residence.—*Tosai*" (Ueda, p. 325).

739

A fragrance whiter
    than the whiteness on a peach
        The narcissus blooms

sono nioi / momo yori shiroshi / suisenka

Winter, 1691. A greeting to his host, Ōta Hakusetsu (1661–1735), the head of the village of Shinshiro in Mikawa (see 743). Hakusetsu had two sons, aged fourteen and eleven, to whom Bashō gave pseudonyms, each of which contained the character *tō* ("peach"), an element in his own previous poetic pseudonym, *Tōsei* ("green peach"; see 103). Hakusetsu's name contains the character *haku* ("white").

740

At Suganuma-tei

So tired of Kyoto
    of this the withering wind
        the winter living

Kyō ni akite / kono kogarashi ya / fuyuzumai

Winter, 1691. *Suganuma-tei:* the house of Kōgetsu (Suganuma Gon'emon), in Shinshiro, Mikawa, with whom Bashō stayed on his way back to Edo after the *Oku no Hosomichi* journey. *kogarashi* ("withering wind"); see 140, 737. 6-7-5.

741

At Kōgetsu-tei

The drinkers' faces
　　　anticipating the snow
　　　　　A flash of lightning

yuki o matsu / jōgo no kao ya / inabikari

Winter, 1691. *Kōgetsu-tei*: Kōgetsu's House; see 740.

742

The withering wind
　　　sharpening the rocks and stones
　　　　　between the cedars

kogarashi ni / iwa fukitogaru / sugima kana

Winter, 1691. Written at Hōrai-ji, a temple about 15 km northeast of
Shinshiro on Mount Hōrai; see 743. *kogarashi* ("withering wind"); see
140, 737.

743

*I visited Hōrai-ji in the province of Mikawa. On the way back, my old
illness struck again, and I stayed overnight at an inn at the foot of the
mountain*

A warm covered bed
　　　by praying for now received
　　　　　A traveler's rest

yogi hitotsu / inori idashite / tabine kana

Winter, 1691. The province of Mikawa is the old name for an area
which is today in the eastern half of Aichi Prefecture; see 325, 740. Ōta
Hakusetsu (see 739), who had accompanied Bashō to Hōrai-ji, had
asked the temple for bedclothes when Bashō fell ill.

744

A cold, lonesome rain began to fall, so I sought shelter at a house. I dried my clothes by the burning hearth and my mouth sipped on warm water. The master treated me kindly, easing for a while the troubles of the road. As the dark drew in, I withdrew to do some writing under a lamp, and noticing this he implored, "Of this our one moment of meeting, please leave a memento"

A lodging given
     then the giving of a name
          A passing shower

yado karite / na o nanorasuru / shigure kana

Winter, 1691. A greeting poem to Joshū (Tsukamoto Joshū, 1641–1724), of Shimada-juku, the twenty-third of the fifty-three stations on the Tōkaidō, on the Edo side of the Ōi River (present-day Shizuoka Prefecture). The Tokugawa shogunate forbade the construction of a bridge across the Ōi, and Tsukamoto employed hundreds of *kawagoshi-ninsoku* ("river-crossing carriers") to help travelers reach the other side; see 745. The phrase *ichigo ichie* (literally, "one time, one meeting") is still a commonplace in Japan.

745

The packhorse driver
     unknowing the cold rain on
          the Ōi River

umakata wa / shiraji shigure no / Ōigawa

Winter, 1691. The packhorse driver having brought Bashō to Kanaya on one side of the Ōi River had then departed, not knowing the misery of crossing the river in winter rain.

746

At the end of the Ninth Month, I left the capital and reached Numazu near the end of the Tenth Month. The innkeeper asked for a poem so elegantly, I could not ignore his request

> On leaving Kyoto
> > the gods too count out the days
> > > they'll be traveling

miyako idete / kami mo tabine no / hikazu kana

Winter, 1691. *kami mo tabine: kami no tabi* ("the traveling of the gods"), in Shinto tradition, during the Tenth Month, *kannazuki* (literally, "the month when there are no gods"), it was believed the eight million gods of Japan congregated annually at Izumo Taisha; see 320, 748, 831.

747

With no settled place in this world, these last six or seven years I have traveled, suffering many ailments along the way. With the unforgettable kindnesses of dear friends and disciples in my mind, I have come back to Musashino. Day after day people visit me at my grass cottage, and so I wrote this verse for them

> Anyway somehow
> > not done for just yet the snow
> > > on dry miscanthus

tomokaku mo / narade ya yuki no / kareobana

Winter, 1691. Bashō returned to Edo on the twenty-ninth of the Tenth Month of the fourth year of Genroku (December 18, 1691). The phrase *tomokaku mo naru* ("something happens [to someone]") is often used to refer to the death of someone.

748

While the gods were gone
>the place was overcome with
>>the falling of leaves

rusu no ma ni / aretaru kami no / ochiba kana

Winter, 1691. During the Tenth Month, the gods are said to leave their local shrine and go to the Grand Shrine at Izumo; see 320, 746, 831. A playful metaphor for Bashō's long absence from Edo.

749

The arrowroot leaves
>have turned to show their faces
>>to the morning frost

kuzu no ha no / omote misekeri / kesa no shimo

Winter, 1691. *kuzu* ("arrowroot"): kudzu, a parasitic wild vine, the fluttering leaves of which feature in many classical poems. The underside of the leaf is a whitish color, so on this frost-covered morning both sides of the leaf are white. One of his disciples, Ransetsu (see 286, 309, 759), severely criticized the Fukagawa group of Bashō's followers, angering Bashō. Ransetsu apologized and Bashō forgave him. The poem is said to express the sentiment: "I throw away resentment and show *omote* ('my face')"; the word *urami* ("resentment") contains the element *ura* ("underside").

750

The racket of geese
>across the Toba rice fields
>>The midwinter rain

kari sawagu / Toba no tazura ya / kan no ame

Winter, 1691. Toba (literally, "bird feathers"), in southern Kyoto, is noted for *kari* ("wild geese"); see 41, 654, 658.

751

The fishes and birds
    the heart of their hearts unknown
       Sloughing off the year

uo tori no / kokoro wa shirazu / toshiwasure

Winter, 1691. Written at a *toshiwasure* ("year-forgetting") party at
Sodō's house (see 317, 823), with Ranran (Matsukura Ranran, 1647–93;
see 812) and Shikō (see 432, 755, 881). Based on a passage in the *Hōjōki*
(1212) of Kamo no Chōmei (c. 1153–1216): "Fish never tire of water, a
state incomprehensible to any but the fish. The bird's desire for the for-
est makes sense to none but the birds. And so it is with the pleasure of
seclusion. Who but one who lives it can understand its joys?" (McKin-
ney, pp. 17–18).

752

A spring no one sees
    On the back of a mirror
      blossoms of ume

hito mo minu / haru ya kagami no / ura no ume

Spring, 1692. "Bashō was always attracted to inconspicuous beauty, to
something that showed pure and noble beauty at a place hidden from
people's eyes.—*Ebara*" (Ueda, p. 335).

753

How I envy them
    North of this glib fleeting world
      the mountain cherries

urayamashi / ukiyo no kita no / yamazakura

Spring, 1692. *ukiyo:* "the floating world"; see 164, 206, 344, 455.

754

Here's a bush warbler
        leaving droppings on mochi
            at the porch's edge

uguisu ya / mochi ni fun suru / en no saki

Spring, 1692. *mochi:* mochi is made at New Year by pounding rice with wooden mallets and then left to dry, to make cakes, etc. "In waka and other traditional forms of Japanese poetry, a bush warbler has always been depicted as an elegant bird that sings among the blossoms. In haikai, however, a poet tries to discover new beauty in things familiar and mundane, such as rice cakes and bird droppings. This hokku presents a scene of moldy rice cakes placed in the sunlight on the veranda several weeks after the New Year. Suddenly a bush warbler flew in from the garden and let a dropping fall. This is an idyllic scene filled with spring sunshine.—*Yamamoto*"; "This hokku shows the kind of innovation I am trying to achieve nowadays.—*Bashō*" (Ueda, p. 336). The poem is often cited as an example of Bashō's poetic ideal of *karumi:* see 615, 728, 780, 841, 848, 856.

755

For One Heading East, a Parting Gift

This heart and this mind
        understand through the blossoms
            Take this begging bowl

kono kokoro / suiseyo hana ni / goki ichigu

Spring, 1692. Shikō (see 432, 751, 881) was departing in spring for Michinoku on the same route Bashō took on the *Oku no Hosomichi* journey.

756

The cats' mating ends
  and now into the bedroom
    the hazy moonlight

neko no koi / yamu toki neya no / oborozuki

Spring, 1692. This hokku, "composed by Bashō in 1692 (Genroku 5), juxtaposes the loud caterwauling with the subsequent quiet of the misty moonlight (*oborozuki*), a traditional spring season word, causing the two erotic moods to interfuse.[. . .] If the deer's longing for its mate (*tsuma kou shika*)—expressed by its mournful, lonely cries—was the archetypal seasonal topic on love in classical poetry, then cat's love—with the baby-like crying of the male as it chased the female—embodied the down-to-earth, humorous character of the haikai seasonal topic" (Shirane, *Traces*, p. 197).

757

Sauntering

Counting as I pass
  house after house after house
    ume and willows

kazoekinu / yashiki yashiki no / ume yanagi

Spring, 1692.

758

In the blooming cherry no sleeping place, the heart of the bird among the blossoms in spring

> No sleep mid blossoms
>> a little like that this too?
>>> A nestful of mice

hana ni nenu / kore mo tagui ka / nezumi no su

Spring, 1692. Alludes to a passage in the "Wakana" chapter of *Genji Monogatari* in which Kashiwagi criticizes Hikaru Genji's promiscuity by comparing him to the *uguisu* ("bush warbler") flitting from tree to tree instead of perching on the cherry tree (his wife, Onna San no Miya): "Why should the warbler who flits so from tree to tree among the flowers each time avoid the cherry tree and never perch there at all?" (translated by Royall Tyler, *The Tale of Genji*, p. 622).

759

"The wealth of moon and blossoms," my hut flanked by peach and cherry, me by Kikaku and Ransetsu

> These two at each side
>> one the peach one the cherry
>>> With kusamochi

ryō no te ni / momo to sakura ya / kusa no mochi

Spring, 1692. *kusa no mochi: kusamochi,* a seasonal sweet eaten in spring, made of mochi and Japanese mugwort; see 168, 265. *Kikaku:* see 156, 251, 299, 814. *Ransetsu:* see 286, 309, 749. The expression *ryōte ni hana* ("flowers in both hands") means something akin to "doubly blessed."

760

The first anniversary of Fuboku's death, at a linked-verse gathering hosted by Kinpū

And hear the sound of
    a cuckoo calling and here
        an old inkstone box

hototogisu / naku ne ya furuki / suzuribako

Summer, 1692. Fuboku (see 95) had died on the ninth day of the Fourth Month (May 6) of the previous year. His favorite inkstone was at the gathering; in poetic tradition, the cuckoo's call evokes the past. *Kinpū* (1667–1726) had been a disciple of Fuboku, and later became a disciple of Kikaku.

761

The cuckoo calling
    above the five feet high blades
        of the calamus

hototogisu / naku ya goshaku no / ayamegusa

Summer, 1692. *goshaku* ("five shaku"): shaku is a Japanese unit of length, about 30 cm (see 674). *ayamegusa: Acorus calamus,* calamus or sweet flag; see 96, 513. Based on an anonymous waka in the *Kokinshū: hototogisu / naku ya satsuki no / ayamegusa / ayame mo shiranu / koi mo suru kana* ("A cuckoo calling / amid the Fifth Month blooming / of the calamus / I am as completely lost / in the darkness of my love"). The emperor Go-Toba wrote, "One should write a waka in the same way one pours water over a five-foot calamus."

762

From Kamakura
    still alive on departing?
        The first tuna catch

Kamakura o / ikite ideken / hatsugatsuo

Summer, 1692. *hatsugatsuo:* the highly prized "first catch" of *katsuo* (bonito, or skipjack tuna) in the late spring to early summer. There is a saying, "Eat *hatsugatsuo,* even if you have to pawn your wife."

763

The Sixth of the months
　　albeit there be sea bream
　　　　this salted whale meat

minazuki ya / tai wa aredomo / shiokujira

Summer, 1692. *minazuki:* the traditional name for the Sixth Month in the Japanese lunar calendar; see 155, 524, 706. Sea bream (*tai*) is a delicacy, and because its name forms part of the word *medetai* (auspicious, happy) is served at weddings, birthdays, etc.; Bashō chooses the cold, white whale meat favored by ordinary people in summer as more befitting the season and his temperament.

764

At the curved gable
　　the sunset fading away
　　　　The airish evening

karahafu no / irihi ya usuki / yūsuzumi

Summer, 1692. *karahafu:* a type of undulating curved ornamental gable or bargeboard, initially used only in temples and aristocratic gateways but which, in the Azuchi-Momoyama period (1573–1600), became typical features of feudal lords' mansions and castles. An earlier version refers to a more ordinary style of gable: *hafuguchi ni / hikage ya yowaru / yūsuzumi* ("At the gable end / the light of the sun weakens / The airish evening").

765

To celebrate the seventh day of the Seventh Month and Sodō's mother who was seventy-seven years old, each of us seven poets chose one of the Seven Autumn Flowers as a theme, wishing to live as long as the seven aged poets of China

Bush Clover

These bush clover shrubs
　　　seven into a thousand
　　　　　the stars of autumn

nanakabu no / hagi no chimoto ya / hoshi no aki

Autumn, 1692. *The seventh day of the Seventh Month: Tanabata,* the Star Festival; see 14 (*hoshi no aki* ["the stars of autumn"] refers to *Tanabata*). *the Seven Autumn Flowers* (*aki no nanakusa*): *ominaeshi* (patrinia), *obana* (miscanthus), *kikyou* (Chinese bellflower), *nadeshiko* (blooming pink), *fujibakama* (Eupatorium fortunei), *kuzu* (kudzu, East Asian arrowroot), and *hagi* ("bush clover"), named as typical autumn flowers in a verse in the *Man'yōshū. the seven aged poets of China* include Bai Juyi (Po Chü-i; see 123, 164, 213, 458); all were over the age of seventy. *Sodō:* see 317, 458.

766

On a Painting of Wild Chrysanthemums

The blooming pinks' heat
　　　all forgotten when I see
　　　　　wild chrysanthemums

nadeshiko no / atsusa wasururu / nogiku kana

Autumn, 1692.

767

In crescent moon light
　　　the earth lathered in a haze
　　　　　the buckwheat blossoms

mikazuki ni / chi wa oboro nari / soba no hana

Autumn, 1692.

768

On Transplanting the Bashō

The bashō leaves
    to let hang by the pillar
        The hermit hut moon

bashōba o / hashira ni kaken / io no tsuki

Autumn, 1692. In the haibun from which this poem is taken, he recounts how his third Bashō-an had been built by his disciples, and how bashō trees had been transplanted to enhance the beauty of his view of the moon.

769

The Harvest Moon's light
    surges up to my doorway
        he floodtide cresting

meigetsu ya / mon ni sashikuru / shiogashira

Autumn, 1692. The Bashō-an was located along the banks of the Sumida River.

770

The drizzle-filled sky
    Just the weather wanted by
        the cotton roses?

kirisame no / sora o fuyō no / tenki kana

Autumn, 1692. Written about a painting by Kyoriku (see 776), to whom Bashō taught poetry in return for lessons in painting; see 776.

771

An Evening Party in Fukagawa

As green as ever
  that's how it might have remained
    pod of the pepper

aoku temo / arubeki mono o / tōgarashi

Autumn, 1692. The opening verse of a *kasen* gathering held at the
Bashō-an, to welcome Shadō (?–1737) to Edo; see 623, 773, 822. Shadō
had been the leader of the group that had gathered around Bashō
in Ōmi when he had stayed in the area after his *Oku no Hosomichi*
journey. In the autumn of 1692, Shadō visited Fukagawa and stayed
with Bashō until January. For a time, Shadō played a key role in dis-
seminating the Bashō's new poetic ideal of *karumi*, but his impulsive
personality caused friction within Bashō's circle. The poem is consid-
ered a metaphorical plea to Shadō to temper his behavior. Shadō did
not come to Bashō's deathbed in Osaka, nor did he attend his funeral.

772

At the far end of the Fukagawa district, our boat stopped at Gohonmatsu

On the upper banks
  and on these lower banks too
    the friends of the moon

kawakami to / kono kawashimo ya / tsuki no tomo

Autumn, 1692. *Gohonmatsu* literally means "Five Pine Trees." Gohon-
matsu was located close to the halfway point along the Onagigawa
canal (see 773), a canal running from west to east connecting the Sum-
ida River and the Naka River (the Komatsu River). The Bashō-an was at
the western end of the Fukagawa area; Gohonmatsu, at the eastern end.
tsuki no tomo: moonviewing companions.

773

Enjoying the Onagizawa, visiting Tōkei

Down along the autumn
　　　I'd like to go as far as
　　　　　　Komatsugawa

aki ni soute / yukabaya sue wa / Komatsugawa

Autumn, 1692. *Komatsugawa:* the name of a town and river, about
5 km from Bashō's home in Edo (Tokyo). Bashō was accompanied
by Shadō (see 623, 771, 822) on this trip along the Onagigawa canal
(called Onagizawa in the headnote; see 772), to visit Tōkei who lived at
Komatsugawa.

774

The lingering hopes
　　　of the departing autumn
　　　　　　These green tangerines

yuku aki no / nao tanomoshi ya / aomikan

Autumn, 1692. An earlier version, written as a parting gift for his disci-
ple Otokuni, reads: *yuku mo mata / suetanomoshi ya / aomikan* ("Again
the going / and yet holding out promise / These green tangerines").

775

The year's first hoarfrost
　　　chilling the chrysanthemums
　　　　　　A cotton waistband

hatsushimo ya / kiku hiesomuru / koshi no wata

Autumn, 1692. *koshi no wata:* a waist warmer, made of cotton. To pro-
tect chrysanthemums from frost, a piece of cotton called *kiku no kise-
wata* was placed around them.

776

On the third day of the Tenth Month of the fifth year of Genroku, at a poetry gathering at Kyoriku-tei

For today at least
let us all be the aged
The first winter rains

kyō bakari / hito mo toshiyore / hatsushigure

Winter, 1692. *Kyoriku-tei:* The lodging of Morikawa Kyoriku (1656–1715), a samurai from Ōmi province, who had become Bashō's student that autumn; see 770. The date mentioned in the headnote is November 10, 1692.

777

Hearth reopening
the plasterer growing old
the frost-flecked sideburns

robiraki ya / sakan oiyuku / bin no shimo

Winter, 1692. *robiraki:* the "hearth reopening" refers to the first fire of winter in the sunken hearth, in the floor of a Japanese room. In the Tea Ceremony this was traditionally performed on the first day of winter: the first of the Tenth Month.

778

Opening the tea-jar at the house of Shiryō

Opening the jar
For the garden at Sakai
comes a great longing

kuchi-kiri ni / Sakai no niwa zo / natsukashiki

Winter, 1692. *kuchikiri* (literally, "cut a mouth"): a tea ceremony in November celebrating the breaking of a seal on a jar of new tea. *Sakai no niwa:* the Sakai garden in Sakai, Ōsaka, designed by the most famous of all tea masters, Sen no Rikyū (1522–91).

779

For Omeiko
        here's five shō of sake
            full bodied as oil

Omeiko ya / abura no yōna / sake goshō

Winter, 1692. *Omeiko:* the anniversary of Nichiren's death; see 464.
The word can be pronounced a number of ways, including Omeiku,
Omeko, and Omekō. Bashō uses the four-syllable version in this poem:
O-me-i-ko. shō: a unit of volume, about 1.8 litres: see 186. *abura no yōna
/ sake goshō:* Bashō took these lines from a letter Nichiren wrote in
thanks for a donation of food supplies.

780

The salted sea bream
        even the gums looking cold
            in the fishmonger's

shiodai no / haguki mo samushi / uo no tana

Winter, 1692. Bashō said that this poem was typical of the *karumi*
(lightness) of his late style, comparing it to a poem typical of Kikaku:
koe karete / saru no ha shiroshi / mine no tsuki ("A voice so shrieking /
the monkey's teeth shining white / the moon at the peak"). *karumi:* see
615, 728, 754, 841, 848, 856.

781

Sweeping the garden
        forgetting about the snow
            swishing the besom

niwa hakite / yuki o wasururu / hahaki kana

Winter, 1692. The poem accompanies a portrait Bashō painted of Han-
shan with a broom in his hand. Hanshan ("Cold Mountain") was a Tang
Dynasty Ch'an (Zen) monk and poet, often depicted in painting with
his companion Shide (Jittoku); see 531.

782

A banked charcoal fire
    On the wall the silhouette
        of one invited

uzumibi ya / kabe ni wa kyaku no / kagebōshi

Winter, 1692. Composed on a visit to Kyokusui (see 629, 652, 658, 729, 785, 880, 881) at his lodgings in Minami-Hatchōbori in Edo, therefore the *kyaku* ("guest") is, in fact, Bashō, but in the poem he pretends to be the host.

783

"The moon and flowers"
    Prick such idiocy please
        the coldest season

tsuki hana no / gu ni hari taten / kan no iri

Winter, 1692. *kan* ("the coldest season"): a month-long period considered the coldest of the year, which began in that year on the twenty-ninth of the Eleventh Month (January 5). One of the traditions to prepare for the cold was to receive acupuncture.

784

Impromptu on the twentieth of the Twelfth Month, Mizunoe-Saru

Come closer and see
    on an outing to a vase
        ume camellias

uchiyorite / hanaire sagure / ume tsubaki

Winter, 1692. *Mizunoe-Saru:* the ninth year in the Chinese sexagenary cycle, corresponding to 1692. A greeting poem to his host, Aoji Chōtō, a disciple of Kikaku, in which Bashō wittily uses a term associated with the outdoors: *sagure* comes from the expression *tanbai,* an excursion made in winter to see early *ume* blossoms. See 342 for another *tanbai* poem.

785

How surprisingly
　　gladdened the heart has become
　　　　Last month of the year

nakanaka ni / kokoro okashiki / shiwasu kana

Winter, 1692. Bashō had received a keg of sake from his disciple Kyoku-
sui (see 629, 630, 658, 729, 782, 880, 881), and included this poem in a
letter of thanks. The end of the year (*shiwasu*) is usually a frantic time;
see 283, 344, 607, 665, 677, 668.

786

Thoughts of the Year's End at Sodō's House: Sekizoro

The Sekizoro
　　making the sparrows crack up
　　　　The things they put on

Sekizoro o / suzume no warau / detachi kana

Winter, 1692. *Sodō:* see 121, 317, 458. *Sekizoro:* see 665.

787

The clams and their shells
　　survivors till most valued
　　　　The end of the year

hamaguri no / ikeru kai are / toshi no kure

Winter, 1692. *kai* can mean both "shellfish" and "worth" (e.g., *iki-gai:*
"what makes life worth living"). Clams, eaten in a soup, were an impor-
tant part of the New Year meal.

788

New Year's Day

And year upon year
    on the face of the monkey
        a monkey disguise

toshidoshi ya / saru ni kisetaru / saru no men

Spring, 1693. "Master Bashō said, 'People in general want to be safe in
writing a poem. Experts, however, venture into dangerous territory.
Therefore, experts always produce many bungled poems. My New
Year's hokku on the monkey is a completely bungled poem.'—*Kyoriku*"
(Ueda, p. 350).

789

With konnyaku
    today a selling contest
        the young greens should win

konnyaku ni / kyō wa urikatsu / wakana kana

Spring, 1693. *konnyaku:* konjac, from which a jellylike food is pro-
duced. There is another version of this poem, titled "Nanakusa":
hamaguri ni / kyō wa urikatsu / wakana kana ("With hamaguri / today
a selling contest / the young greens should win"). *hamaguri:* Asian Hard
Clam; see 787; *nanakusa: nanakusa gayu* ("Seven Herb Rice Porridge"),
eaten on January 7, which includes "young greens" not konnyaku, and
not hamaguri; see 262, 263, 354, 840.

790

A little like spring
    The scenery is ready
        the moon the ume

haru mo yaya / keshiki totonou / tsuki to ume

Spring, 1693. Bashō often inscribed this poem on pictures, his own and
others'.

791

On a Portrait of Kensu, the Shrimp Eater

Look at the icefish
   opening their black eyes to
      the net of the Law

shirauo ya / kuroki me o aku / nori no ami

Spring, 1693. *Kensu, the Shrimp Eater:* Xianzi, a legendary *Ch'an* (Zen)
monk of the Five Dynasties period in China, who broke Buddhist
taboos on eating meat by living off clams and shrimp. He is usually
depicted in Zen painting standing in a stream with a net in one hand
and holding a caught shrimp up for inspection with the other. *nori:* the
Law of Nature in Zhuangzi's Taoist philosophy, "dharma" in Buddhism;
see 203, 287, 530. *me* can mean both "eye" and the "mesh" of a net; and
the phrase *me o aku* (literally, "to open the eyes") has the figurative
meaning "to be spiritually awakened."

792

Given to Kyorai

A little bit of
   sashimi-konnyaku
      A sprig of ume

konnyaku no / sashimi mo sukoshi / ume no hana

Spring, 1693. *konnyaku:* see 789; konnyaku was, it is said, one of Bashō's
favorite foods, and *sashimi-konnyaku* (sliced konnyaku in the style of
sashimi) was a specialty of his home province, Iga. The poem is an
offering to the spirit of a recently deceased person. Yamamoto Kenkichi
believes it to be Rogan (also pronounced Romaru), who died at Kyorai's
house on the second of the Second Month.

793

Sadder than homeland
    herbs the violet growing
        upon his grave-mound

tōki yori / aware wa tsuka no / sumiregusa

Spring, 1693. *tōki: Angelica acutiloba,* angelica root, a perennial herb
used medicinally. The kanji for the herb can be read "return home." The
grave is Rogan's, who had died in Kyoto, far from his home province of
Dewa; see 792. *sumiregusa:* see 239.

794

*On an auspicious day in the Second Month, Zekitsu had his head shaved
to enter medical school, and I offered congratulations*

First Day of the Horse
    So you've had your head shaved by
        the Inari Fox?

hatsuuma ni / kitsune no sorishi / atama kana

Spring, 1693. *hatsuuma:* the first day of the horse in the Second Month
of the lunar calendar (in the Chinese zodiacal system, animal signs pre-
side not only over years but also days of the week). On this day, the
Hatsuuma ("First Horse Day") festival is held at Inari (Fox) shrines.
Zekitsu studied medicine under Enomoto Tōjun (see 814), the father of
Bashō's disciple, Kikaku (see 156). The name *Zekitsu* is similar to *kit-
sune* ("fox"). In Japanese folk belief there are tales of shape-shifting
foxes shaving the heads of unsuspecting humans; see 920.

795

Words of Farewell to the Priest Sengin

The crane's black feathers
          the robe around your shoulders
                    The clouds the blossoms

tsuru no ke no / kuroki koromo ya / hana no kumo

Spring, 1693. *Priest Sengin:* a priest and poet in Fukagawa, who was leaving to visit the shrines in Ise and Kumano. Bashō is comparing Sengin's priestly dress (black robe over a white kimono) to a *tsuru* (crane). In the *haibun* "Words of Farewell to the Priest Sengin," from which the poem derives, Bashō and Sengin are standing on the banks of the Sumida River, looking far into the distance at Mount Hakone, over which Sengin would be traveling in cherry blossom season.

796

To a certain Okada, as he departed to Nikkō attending the Lord of the Castle

The sasa grass dews
          dampening your hakama
                    The wayside thickets

sasa no tsuyu / hakama ni kakeshi / shigeri kana

Summer, 1693. *To a certain Okada:* this refers to Sensen; see 736. *Nikkō:* the site of the Tōshō-gū Shrine, and mausoleum of Ieyasu, the first shogun of the Tokugawa shogunate (see 490). In the Edo period, the Tokugawa shogunate held stately processions from Edo to Nikkō along the Nikkō Kaidō, one of the five routes of the Edo period. *sasa:* broad-leafed bamboo grass, the most common variety of which is *kumazasa,* which grows wild in the northern regions of Japan. *tsuyu* means "dew" and forms part of the phrase *tsuyu harai* (literally, "dew sweeper") which refers to a warrior walking ahead of a lord to ensure his safety. *hakama:* traditional formal wear; see 264, 832.

797

1
The cuckoo calling
> That lingering voice stretching
>> over the waters

hototogisu / koe yokotau ya / mizu no ue

2
The cuckoo calling
> That voice lingering stretching
>> over the waters

hototogisu / koe ya yokotau / mizu no ue

3
That lone voice lingers
> stretches across the inlet
>> The cuckoo calling

hitokoeno / e ni yokotau ya / hototogisu

Summer, 1693. In a letter to a disciple, Bashō says that, after his nephew Tōin had died in his hut, in his grief, he had given up writing verses on the *hototogisu* (cuckoo). Sanpū and Sora urged him, to help with his sorrow, to write a verse on "the cuckoo by the water." He wrote three similar verses, inspired by a line ("the gleaming water extends to heaven, and the white mist lies stretched across the river") by the Chinese poet Su Shi (see 128, 160, 534, 823), and wondered which was best. Mizuma Sentoku (1662–1726), Sodō (see 317), and Hara Anteki (?–1716?) chose number 1; Kyoriku preferred number 3.

798

Beyond the wonders
of wind and moon and poem
the tree peony

fūgetsu no / zai mo hanare yo / fukamigusa

Summer, 1693. *fūgetsu* (literally, "wind moon"): the beauties of the natural world and, by association, of the poetic spirit that contemplates them. *fūgetsu no zai:* literary, poetic, or artistic talent. *fukamigusa:* the tree peony, also called *botan,* and sometimes *fūkigusa,* the "plant of wealth"; see 216, 254, 853. The poem was inscribed on a painting of *botan* by Kyoriku; see 776, 799, 800.

799

As Kyoriku sets out on the Kiso Road

The traveler's heart
and mind too please take after
Blossoms of the shii

tabibito no / kokoro ni mo niyo / shii no hana

Summer, 1693. *shii:* pasania; see 629; the pasania opens small, yellow blossoms around June. An earlier version of the poem is included in the haibun "Words Sent to Kyoriku": *shii no hana no / kokoro ni mo niyo / Kiso no tabi* ("The shii tree's blossoms / Imitate their heart upon / the road to Kiso"). Kyoriku (see 776, 798, 800) had been serving his lord in Edo, and was being transferred back to his home province, Ōmi, in June 1693.

800

Learn from their journeys
the griefs of pilgrims of old
The flies of Kiso

uki hito no / tabi ni mo narae / Kiso no hae

Summer, 1693. Addressed to Kyoriku on his journey on the Kiso Road to Ōmi. Bashō composed this and the earlier version of 799 and then asked Kyoriku to choose between the two.

801

Look a moonflower
    I poke my drunken face through
        a hole the window

yūgao ya / yōte kao dasu / mado no ana

Summer, 1693. *yūgao* ("evening face"): the calabash, or white-flowered gourd, whose white flowers bloom in the evening; see 10, 146.

802

You kids over there
    the bindweed's come into bloom
        I'll peel a melon

kodomora yo / hirugao sakinu / uri mukan

Summer, 1693. *hirugao* ("noon face"): the bindweed flower; see 175, 176, 422, 423. There are two earlier versions: *iza kodomo / hirugao sakinu / uri mukan* ("Now then you children / the bindweed's come into bloom/ I'll peel a melon"); *iza kodomo / hirugao sakaba / uri mukan* ("Now then you children / when the bindweed is in bloom / I'll peel a melon").

803

Envying Enmei of Jin

Along the window
    a dais to take a nap
        a bamboo mattress

madonari ni / hirune no dai ya / takamushiro

Summer, 1693. *Enmei* (also known in Japanese as Tou Enmei): Tao Yuanming (also T'ao Ch'ien or Tao Qian, 365?–427; see 238, 458), Jin dynasty poet and scholar recluse, who gave up life as a bureaucrat for the life of a hermit. Ezra Pound ends *Cathay* with "To-Em-Mei's (T'ao Ch'ien) 'The Unmoving Cloud.'" An earlier, slightly different, version reads: *madonari ni / hirune no goza ya / takamushiro. dai:* short for *shindai,* a bedstead or couch. *takamushiro:* a mat of woven bamboo strips, cool to sleep on in summer; *goza:* a light seating mat.

804

In the sixth year of Genroku, the night of the seventh of Fuzuki was so rain-filled and stormy that the whitecaps dashing against the banks of the Milky Way would have washed away that bridge of magpies in the legend of the lovers in the stars, the wind ripping the rudder off their boat, blowing down their house of tryst. As I, thinking the night too long to do nothing, offered a votive candle, someone recited the poems of Henjō and Komachi. And so I wrote down these two poems, to console the spirits of those rain-cursed lovers

Komachi's Song

The flooding waters
    The stars too sleep on their road
        and on a boulder

takamizu ni / hoshi mo tabine ya / iwa no ue

Autumn, 1693. A Tanabata poem: see 14, 97, 675. On this night, Sanpū (see 185, 304, 797, 805) had come to visit Bashō in Fukagawa, and they wrote the two poems mentioned in the headnote. *Fuzuki* ("the month of writing" or "erudition"), the traditional name for the Seventh Month in the Japanese calendar. *Komachi*: Ono no Komachi; see 96, 649, 676, 888. Bashō is referring to a famous poetic exchange between Komachi and the priest Henjō (see 51) at Isonokami Temple. Komachi: *iwa no ue ni / tabine o sureba / ito samushi / koke no koromo o / ware ni kasanan* ("Upon a hard boulder / when I sleep on my journey / it's so very cold / Your flowing robe of mosses / will you not lend that to me"); Henjō: *yo o somuku / koke no koromo wa / tada hitoe / kasaneba utoshi / iza futari nen* ("To stave off the world / with flowing robe of mosses / I've only the one / but callous not to lend it / so let us sleep together"). Bashō borrows the word *tabine* ("a sleep on a journey") from Komachi's poem.

805

Glistening dewdrops
    from bush clover unfallen
        swaying this way that

shiratsuyu mo / kobosanu hagi no / uneri kana

Autumn, 1693. Written at the hut of Sanpū; see 185, 304, 797, 804.

806

A hatsudake
Not so deep into its days
the dews of autumn

hatsutake ya / mada hikazu henu / aki no tsuyu

Autumn, 1693. *hatsutake*: hatsudake, a variety of mushroom, *Lactarius hatsudake Nobuj. Tanaka*. The poem was written at a *kasen* party at the house of Taisui (see 471, 817, 968) in Fukagawa, at which he most probably served hatsudake.

807

In the autumn of the sixth year of Genroku, weary of people, I closed my gate

The morning glory
during the daytime closing up
The hedge by my gate

asagao ya / hiru wa jō orosu / mon no kaki

Autumn, 1693. 5-8-5.

808

When I had shut up my gate in Fukagawa

The morning glory
That too for me yet again
not really a friend

asagao ya / kore mo mata waga / tomo narazu

Autumn, 1693.

809

A stinkyfishsmell
    Exposed on a waterweed
        innards of pale chub

namagusashi / konagi ga ue no / hae no wata

Autumn, 1693. *konagi:* a waterweed common in rice fields and in ponds, which has small purple blooms in late summer and early autumn. *hae: Zacco platypus,* pale chub, a freshwater fish of the carp family.

810

Zansho

The summer has spread
    its heat to the Harvest Moon
        An airish evening

natsu kakete / meigetsu atsuki / suzumi kana

Autumn, 1693. *Zansho:* lingering summer heat; see 546, 711, 841. *suzumi:* an abbreviation of *yūsuzumi* ("going out to take the cool evening breeze"), something usually done in summer rather than in autumn. It was unusually hot on the evening of the harvest moon, and the moonviewing became a *suzumi* as well.

811

The Sixteenth-night moon
    diminishing a little
        The dark beginning

izayoi wa / wazuka ni yami no / hajime kana

Autumn, 1693. *izayoi:* the "hesitating" moon, on the sixteenth night of the month; see 453, 458, 717, 718.

812

Lamenting the Death of Matsukura Ranran

In the autumn wind
    the sorrow in its breaking
        A mulberry stick

akikaze ni / orete kanashiki / kuwa no tsue

Autumn, 1693. *Matsukura Ranran* (see 751): one of Bashō's first students ("like father and son," wrote Bashō in his valediction to Ranran), who had given up a position as a samurai to devote himself to poetry. He died suddenly at age 47; a person's forty-eighth year is known as *sōnen,* the "mulberry age." Bashō habitually used a mulberry stick.

813

The Third Day of the Ninth Month, Visiting His Grave

Have you seen it there
    seven days within your grave
        the Third Night's crescent?

mishi ya sono / nanuka wa haka no / mika no tsuki

Autumn, 1693. *mika no tsuki:* the moon of the third night of the lunar calendar, a crescent moon; see 275, 434. A memorial is held seven days after a person has died.

814

Mourning Tōjun

In the afterwards
    of the moon's setting the four
        corners of his desk

iru tsuki no / ato wa tsukue no / yosumi kana

Autumn, 1693. *Tōjun:* Enomoto Tōjun (1622–93), the father of Bashō's disciple, Kikaku; see 794. In his "Life of Tōjun," Bashō wrote that "[ever since retreating into seclusion, Tōjun] hadn't left his desk for ten-odd years."

815

Speaking of Koshōgen's Wonderful Performance

This moon that putting
     on of *Hachi-no-Ki* of
          his face with no mask

tsuki ya sono / Hachi no Ki no hi no / shitaomote

Autumn, 1693. *Koshōgen:* Hōshō Shigetomo (1619–85), a Noh actor,
the eighth master of the Hōshō school; *Hachi-no-Ki,* a Noh play; see
110. *shitaomote:* a corrupted form of *hitaomote* (also pronounced *hita-
men*), a Noh term for playing a role without a mask in the same manner
as when wearing a mask. Composed when Bashō was invited to the
house of Senpo (see 816); Senpo was the third eldest son of Koshōgen.

816

Three Poets at Hōshō Sadayū's

The bird unknowing
     though its name's shot through with age
          Shijūgara

oi no na no / ari tomo shirade / shijūgara

Autumn, 1693. Hōshō Sadayū's pen name was Senpo (see 815).
shijūgara: the great tit, *Parus major;* in contemporary Japanese it is pro-
nounced *shijūkara* but in Bashō's day it was pronounced with a "g"
sound. *shijū* means "forty," and the line *shijūgara* can be read as "after
forty" (*gara,* or *kara,* meaning "after"), thus the poem can also be read:
"Your name is aged / and yet you don't realize / after you're forty." Based
on a waka by Shōshō-no-Ama (see 604): *ono ga ne ni / tsuraki wakare
wa / ari to dani / omoi mo shirade / tori no nakuran* ("That with its
crowing / it painfully separates / lover from lover / it never realizes /
and thus loudly the cock crows").

817

At Taisui's House

The Sunrise Party
    The scent of chrysanthemum
        on skewered tofu

kagemachi ya / kiku no ka no suru / tōfugushi

Autumn, 1693. *kagemachi* ("Sunrise Party"): an all-night gathering held
at certain times of the year, to watch for the sunrise; see 684 for a *tsuki-
machi* ("waiting for the moon") poem. *Taisui:* see 471, 806; and for
another *kagemachi* at Taisui's house, see 968.

818

The chrysanthemums
    blooming in the stonemason's
        yard between the stones

kiku no hana / saku ya ishiya no / ishi no ai

Autumn, 1693. "A poem like this, which is plain and yet has *yojō* ['sug-
gestiveness'], can be written only by a total amateur or a great master.—
Chikurei" (Ueda, p. 364).

819

Box for a koto
    In back of the used-goods shop
        a chrysanthemum

kotobako ya / furumonodana no / sedo no kiku

Autumn, 1693. *koto:* a Japanese stringed instrument, about 180 cm
long; see 924. They are made of paulownia wood, and played horizon-
tally on the floor. In Bashō's day the instrument was associated with the
daughters of "good families," and when not played was put in a special
lacquered box or case (today, a cloth cover is used). One version of the
poem has the headnote "On Passing Ōmon-dori." Ōmon-dori was the
street leading to Ōmon, the main gate to Yoshiwara, the red-light dis-
trict of Edo.

820

The passing autumn
    behoved sowing the poppy
        but then disappeared

yuku aki no / keshi ni semarite / kakurekeri

Autumn, 1693. The best time for sowing poppy seed is around the time
of the harvest moon.

821

At a haikai gathering with Yaba and three others

The age-old pinetree
    on a gold-leafed folding screen
        A winter retreat

kinbyō no / matsu no furusa yo / fuyugomori

Winter, 1693. *Yaba:* Shida Yaba (1663–1740), one of Bashō's later disci-
ples; see 824. *fuyugomori:* see 334, 465, 736, 822. See 598 for an earlier
version of this poem on *fuyugomori* and a folding screen.

822

For Shadō

*A mudsnail crawling from the lakeside sands should fear the claws of the
crab who lives among the reeds, and the hooves of oxen and horses*

The Naniwa strand
    The mudsnail's shell better close
        a winter retreat

Naniwazu ya / tanishi no futa mo / fuyugomori

Winter, 1693. *Naniwazu:* "Naniwa strand," the sea and port area of the
city known as Osaka today. Shadō (see 623, 771, 773) used to live in
Zeze, a small town near Lake Biwa, before moving to Naniwa, a bustling
city, and a place also famous for reeds; see 75. As with 771, the poem is
a plea to Shadō to temper his behavior.

823

The sixth year of Genroku, on the ninth day of the first month of winter, enjoying the chrysanthemum garden at Sodō's house. The Chrysanthemum Festival was held this day because on the ninth of the Ninth Month the buds remained shut tight. A Chinese poem says, "Whenever the flowers open, that's chrysanthemum festival time," and for the festival to be postponed is not unprecedented. And so we decided, although it is winter, to have this party and write verses on autumn chrysanthemums

Chrysanthemum scent
      In the garden the sole of
         a worn-out sandal

kiku no ka ya / niwa ni kiretaru / kutsu no soko

Autumn, 1693. *Chōyō no Sekku,* the Chrysanthemum Festival, is held on the ninth day of the Ninth Month (see 108, 458, 582, 725, 909). Though as the headnote says, it was written in winter, the season in the poem is autumn. Sodō was particularly fond of chrysanthemums; see 317, 458. The Chinese poem referred to is by Su Shi (also Su Tung-p'o; see 128, 160, 534, 797).

824

Cold chrysanthemums
      coated with dust from rice bran
         beside the millstone

kangiku ya / konuka no kakaru / usu no hata

Winter, 1693. The hokku of a *ryōgin-renku* (two-person linked verse), with Yaba; see 821.

825

The winter chrysanth
      In front of the window where
         sweet sake ferments

kangiku ya / amazake tsukuru / mado no saki

Winter, 1693. *amazake:* a sweetened low-alcohol sake made from fermented rice, often drunk hot on cold winter nights.

826

Fan Li's Eldest Son's Heart, Learning from the Sankashū

The chrysanthemum
    spilling nary a dewdrop
        The frozen flowers

hitotsuyu mo / kobosanu kiku no / kōri kana

Winter, 1693. Fan Li, a semilegendary figure, considered the wealthiest
and most charitable person in Chinese history. He served King Goujian
of Yue. His second son was convicted of murder in Chu and his eldest
son was sent with gold to ransom his life. Rather than pay, the eldest
son kept the gold, and the second son was executed. *Sankashū* ("Moun-
tain Home Anthology"): collection of about fifteen hundred of Saigyō's
poems. The Saigyō poem alluded to: *sute yarade / inochi o kouru / hito
wa mina / chiji no kogane o / mote kaerunari* ("Those who don't throw
off / their love of this world's living / all of those people / with pieces of
gold only / will they travel back homeward").

827

A feathery robe
    enveloping snugly the
        feet of the wild duck

kegoromo ni / tsutsumite nukushi / kamo no ashi

Winter, 1693.

828

On the Subject of Harvesting Daikon

Deep in the saddle
    a little scamp high mounted
        The daikon pulling

kuratsubo ni / kobōzu noru ya / daikohiki

Winter, 1693. *daikohiki*: uprooting daiko(n); daikon is a large, white
Japanese radish. Kon Eizō regards this poem as a splendid example of
karumi: see 615, 728, 754, 780, 841, 848, 856.

829

With the Great Bridge at Fukagawa Nearly Completed

The season's first snow
the yet-to-be-completed
bridge being coated

hatsuyuki ya / kakekakaritaru / hashi no ue

Winter, 1693. The official name of the bridge was the *Shin-Ōhashi* ("*New* Great/Large Bridge"). Construction took five months, from the Seventh Month of the sixth year of Genroku to the Twelfth Month. It was completed on the seventh of the Twelfth Month (January 2, 1694), allowing greater access to the city from the east side of the Sumida River; see 834.

830

Eating the roots of vegetables, talking to a samurai all day long

The conversation
of a warrior the tang
of bitter daikon

mononofu no / daikon nigaki / hanashi kana

Winter, 1693. See 127 and the words of the Sung master Wang Xinmin (Wang Hsin-min): "If a man can chew the roots of vegetables (*caigen*), he can do anything." A greeting hokku for Tōdō Genko (?–1728), a samurai of the Iga Domain, who became a disciple of Bashō in 1693; see 850, 895.

831

The Twentieth of Kannazuki, an Impromptu at Fukagawa

A heart-tearing sight
    at the Feast of Ebisu
        The bird pedlar's geese

furiuri no / gan aware nari / Ebisukō

Winter, 1693. *Kannazuki* (literally, "the month when there are no gods"): traditional name for the Tenth Month; see 320, 746, 748. *Ebisu:* one of the *shichifukujin,* the Seven Gods of Fortune; see 4. *The Feast of Ebisu:* held on the twentieth day of the Tenth Month (in this year, November 17), to wish for prosperity in business. Geese would have been leashed to a pole, with the pedlar walking around hawking his wares.

832

The Ebisu Feast
    forcing the vinegarman
        to hakama up

Ebisukō / suuri ni hakama / kisenikeri

Winter, 1693. *hakama:* traditional formal wear for men, unusual garb for a vinegar pedlar. *Ebisu:* see 4, 831.

833

And seriyaki
    In rice fields in the foothills
        the first of the ice

seriyaki ya / susowa no tai no / hatsugōri

Winter, 1693. *seri:* dropwort; see 113. *seriyaki:* roasted or grilled *seri,* with duck or pheasant, soy and vinegar. *susowa no tai* ("the rice fields in the foothills"), a phrase used in Kamo no Chōmei's *Hōjōki;* see 177, 303, 751, 927, 980, but which dates even further back, to the *Man'yōshū.* A greeting hokku for Jokushi, see 348; the *seri* would have been picked in the rice fields in the foothills.

834

The Shin-Ryōgoku Bridge Completed

Everybody out
    to venerate the new bridge
        The frost untrodden

mina idete / hashi o itadaku / shimoji kana

Winter, 1693. *Shin-Ryōgoku Bridge:* another name for the *Shin-Ōhashi;*
see 829.

835

Alive albeit
    congealed into one by ice
        the sea cucumbers

iki nagara / hitotsu ni kōru / namako kana

Winter, 1693.

836

The Year-End Cleaning
    On his own fixing a shelf
        see the carpenter

susuhaki wa / onoga tana tsuru / daiku kana

Winter, 1693. *susuhaki:* the housecleaning done at the end of the year, to
welcome the New Year, also called *susuharai;* see 344, 668. "Normally a
carpenter is so busy in working at other people's houses that he would
do nothing at his own home. But on the day of the year-end cleaning, he
cannot keep his eyes closed: he is repairing a broken shelf in his house.
Bashō took note of a happening unnoticed by other poets.—*Donto*"
(Ueda, p. 374).

837

The Winter of That Year

The moon at daybreak
    signals the end of the year
      Mochi-making sounds

ariake mo / misoka ni chikashi / mochi no oto

Winter, 1693. *mochi no oto:* "Mochi-making sounds"; at New Year, rice
is pounded using mallets to produce mochi for rice cakes and ozoni
(New Year mochi soup); see 151. *misoka:* "the thirtieth day of the
month"; *misoka ni chikashi* ("near the end of the year"): alludes to a
poem by Yoshida Kenkō: *arito dani / hito ni shirarede / mi no hodo ya /
misoka ni chikaki / ariake no tsuki* ("There are even those / people who
do not notice / being so busy / at the ending of the year / the moon at
the break of dawn").

838

Then there was the night
    a robber came a-calling
      The end of the year

nusubito ni / ōta yo mo ari / toshi no kure

Winter, 1693.

839

At the Hōrai
    I'd love to hear from Ise
      the year's first tidings

hōrai ni / kikabaya Ise no / hatsudayori

New Year, 1694. *Hōrai:* a New Year's decoration named after the legen-
dary Chinese mountain of the immortals, Mount Penglai (Japanese:
Hōrai). *Ise:* the Grand Shrine of Ise, the chief shrine of Shinto.

840

Only once a year
    they get to be harvested
        The shepherd's purses

hitotose ni / ichido tsumaruru / nazuna kana

Spring, 1694. *nazuna*: shepherd's purses. *nanakusa gayu* ("Seven Herb
Rice Porridge," which includes *nazuna*) is eaten on January 7; see 262,
263, 354.

841

A waft of ume
    and out of the blue the sun
        on the mountain path

ume ga ka ni / notto hi no deru / yamaji kana

Spring, 1694. A poem often used to illustrate Bashō's idea of *karumi*:
plain in theme, light in tone, yet evocative; see 615, 728, 754, 780, 828,
848, 856. In contrast to his poems on *zansho* ("lingering summer heat";
546, 711, 810), this is a poem of *yokan* ("lingering winter cold").

842

As if caressing
    an abscess such gentleness
        the willow bending

haremono ni / sawaru yanagi no / shinae kana

Spring, 1694. In an earlier version the word order of the second line is
slightly different: *haremono ni / yanagi no sawaru / shinae kana*.

843

Here's a bush warbler
    behind a weeping willow
        in front of a bush

uguisu ya / yanagi no ushiro / yabu no mae

Spring, 1694.

844

The scent of ume
> that single phrase "the old days"
> > tear at the feelings

ume ga ka ni / mukashi no ichiji / aware nari

Spring, 1694. *mukashi:* the old days, times long past, ancient times. The Japanese version of "Once upon a time" is *mukashi, mukashi.* A poem of condolence to Baigan, a disciple in Ōgaki, on the first anniversary of his son Shinpachi's death. The *bai* in Baigan's name can also be read as *ume.* The phrase *mukashi no ichiji* ("that single phrase the 'old days'") alludes to an old tradition in poetry in which the scent of *ume,* or other flowers, reminds the poet of old days, as in Ki no Tsurayuki's famous waka: *hito wa isa / kokoro mo shirazu / furusato wa / hana zo mukashi no / ka ni nioikeru* ("Well the human heart / one can never truly know / But in my home place / the fragrance of the flowers / smells the same as long ago"); see 980.

845

1

Buddha's Death Day rites
> wrinkled hands joined in prayer
> > The sound of juzu

nehan-e ya / shiwade awasuru / juzu no oto

Spring, 1694. *nehan:* Nirvana, supreme enlightenment, Buddha's Death Day; *nehan-e* (literally "Nirvana assembly or gathering"): a Buddhist ritual held on the fifteenth day of the Second Month, to commemorate the death of Buddha, the day he entered Nirvana; see 373. *juzu:* prayer beads.

2

On Buddha's birthday
> wrinkled hands joined in prayer
> > The sound of juzu

kanbutsu ya / shiwade awasuru / juzu no oto

Spring, 1694. An earlier version of the poem. *kanbutsu:* an abbreviation of *kanbutsu-e,* a Buddhist ritual held on the eighth day of the Fourth Month, to commemorate the birth of Buddha; see 397.

846

With an umbrella
    I part and see my way through
        the willow branches

karakasa ni / oshiwake mitaru / yanagi kana

Spring, 1694.

847

Eight nine lengths of sky
    with a rain-spilling expanse
        of weeping willow

hakkuken / sora de ame furu / yanagi kana

Spring, 1694. *ken:* a traditional unit of length, equivalent to six *shaku* (see 674, 761), a little less than two meters.

848

Spring showers falling
    trickling down through the wasps' nest
        the leak in the roof

harusame ya / hachi no su tsutau / yane no mori

Spring, 1694. "What is original in this hokku lies in the poet's discovery of leaking water running down a wasps' nest. The hokku has captured the essence of spring rain. It is plain and yet has *yojō* —a fine poem written in the karumi style.—*Imoto*" (Ueda, p. 378). *yojō:* "suggestiveness"; see 818. *karumi:* see 615, 728, 754, 780, 828, 841, 856.

849

When I went to Ueno for the blossom viewing, I saw people had raised up bunting and were playing music noisily, singing various popular songs, so I moved away to a quiet place under the shade of a pine

> With an incomplete
> > set of begging bowls how I
> > > go do hanami

yotsu goki no / sorowanu hanami- / gokoro kana

Spring, 1694. *yotsu goki:* a set of four bowls, one within the other, carried by mendicant monks; see 755. *hanami:* blossom-viewing.

850

> Hanami-going
> > Slowly the boat punting down
> > > Yanagihara

hanami ni to / sasu fune ososhi / Yanagihara

Spring, 1694. *Yanagihara:* the southern bank of the Kanda River, between Sujikae-bashi and Asakusa-bashi. Bashō had been invited to the house of Tōdō Genko (see 830, 895), who lived on the northern side, which was called Mukaiyanagihara or Mukōyanagihara.

851

> Now the green willow
> > drooping down into the mud
> > > The tide's lowest ebb

aoyagi no / doro ni shidaruru / shiohi kana

Spring, 1694. One headnote to the poem reads "The third day of the Third Month," which is known as *Jōshi,* the day when the tide is at its lowest; see 72, 153. In the Gregorian calendar, the date was March 28, 1694.

852

The springtime showers
        straightening out the mugwort
                the wayside grasses

harusame ya / yomogi o nobasu / kusa no michi

Spring, 1694. *yomogi*: mugwort, used in the making of *kusamochi* (see 168, 265, 759), and associated in poetry with spring, and the life of recluses.

853

A gift for Tōrin in his new house, written on my own painting

This is not the cold
        of the dew the nectar of
                the tree peony

samukaranu / tsuyu ya botan no / hana no mitsu

Summer, 1694. *Tōrin*: Amano Tōrin; some sources say he was Bashō's cousin, others a friend, from Iga. Dew is associated with the cool of autumn; the tree peony blooms in summer.

854

Hidden in a bush
        Do the tea pickers too hear
                the cuckoo calling?

kogakurete / chatsumi mo kiku ya / hototogisu

Summer, 1694.

855

Deutzia flowers
        Timidly the dark willow
                holds back from touching

unohana ya / kuraki yanagi no / oyobigoshi

Summer, 1694.

856

The hydrangea
    a thicket the small garden
        for a detached room

ajisai ya / yabu o koniwa no / betsuzashiki

Summer, 1694. The hokku at a farewell party for Bashō held at the house
of Shisan (?–1699). Bashō was about to leave on a journey, his final, to
Iga. The poem is an example of the *karumi* of late Bashō: "My thinking
now is as when looking at the sand in a shallow stream, both the shape
of the poem and the mind light. Only when you reach that point, do
things have meaning." *karumi*: see 615, 728, 754, 780, 828, 841, 848.

857

*In the Fifth Month of the seventh year of Genroku, I set off from Edo. For
those who came to see me off, I said*

The ears of barley
    I cling to to give me strength
        such a leavetaking

mugi no ho o / chikara ni tsukamu / wakare kana

Summer, 1694. Written on the eleventh of the Fifth Month (June 3,
1694), as Bashō left on his final journey. Another version of the poem
reads: *mugi no ho o / tayori ni tsukamu / wakare kana* ("The ears of
barley / I grasp to keep me steady / such a leavetaking").

858

Especially when
    you deign to gladden the eye
        Mount Fuji in June

me ni kakaru / toki ya kotosara / satsuki Fuji

Summer, 1694. *satsuki*: the Fifth Month in the lunar calendar (depend-
ing on the year, from late May to June, or from June to early July in the
Gregorian calendar) is the time of the rainy season, when Fuji is only
intermittently visible.

859

The chinaberry
      indistinct the raincloudy
         sky of blossom-time

donmiri to / ouchi ya ame no / hanagumori

Summer, 1694. *ouchi*: the old name for the *sendan, Melia azedarach,* the chinaberry tree, or Persian lilac. *hanagumori:* cloudy weather at the time of cherry blossom viewing in spring.

860

The bush warbler sings
      in a grove of bamboo shoots
         of aging and age

uguisu ya / takenoko yabu ni / oi o naku

Summer, 1694. The *uguisu* ("bush warbler") sings in early spring; *takenoko* ("bamboo shoots") emerge in summer, so the bush warbler in this poem is old and contrasts with the young shoots.

861

Rainy season rains
      the suffering of silkworms
         a mulberry field

samidare ya / kaiko wazurau / kuwa no hata

Summer, 1694. A practice in sericulture was for silk growers to separate silkworms into healthy and ill, throwing the sickly worms into the field.

862

On Entering Suruga Province

The Suruga Road
    even the orange blossoms
        the fragrance of tea

Surugaji ya / hanatachibana mo / cha no nioi

Summer, 1694. Suruga (covering an area that is now the central part of modern-day Shizuoka Prefecture) was noted for both tea and oranges; see 635. Shirane (*Traces*, p. 178) writes that though the poem was probably written for his host, Joshū (see 744, 863, 864), the poem is more a greeting to the land itself.

863

The heavy Fifth Month rains had swollen the Ōi River, and so I had to wait it out at Shimada, staying with Joshū and Jochiku

With the green still on
    leaves of lettuce alongside
        soup with aubergine

chisa wa mada / aoba nagara ni / nasubijiru

Summer, 1694. *the Ōi River*: see 744, 745, 864. *Jochiku*: a haikai friend of Joshū; see 744, 864.

864

Rainy season rains
    blow that sky all the way down
        Ōigawa

samidare no / sora fukiotose / Ōigawa

Summer, 1694. *Ōigawa*: the Ōi River. It is a matter of some debate whether Bashō's command is directed to the wind or to the river. He was held up for three days in Shimada because of the swollen river. Joshū was the river commissioner at Shimada-juku (see 744), and Bashō had at one time worked for the Department of Waterworks in Edo.

865

Already bending
    the bamboo looks like it looks
        forward to the snow

tawamite wa / yuki matsu take no / keshiki kana

Winter, 1694. A poem handwritten on Bashō's own painting of bamboo.

866

In Nagoya, Owari Province

A life traveling
    tilling a small field forward
        and back and forward

yo o tabi ni / shiro kaku oda no / yukimodori

Summer, 1694. *yo* can mean both "world" and "life"; *kaku* can mean both "to write" and "to paint" and also "to till" (a field). A greeting hokku at the house of Kakei (Yamamoto Kakei, 1648–1716), a doctor and poet, the leader of the Nagoya group of Bashō disciples. Bashō was visiting Nagoya in an attempt to heal a rift with the group. Bashō had included few poems by members of the group in *Sarumino* (1691); Kakei had similarly rejected Bashō's new style by including only a few of his poems in the anthology *Arano Ko Shū* (1693), a sequel to *Arano,* the volume he had edited with Bashō; see 445.

867

Yasui, as he was building a hermitage

With coolness in mind
    the carpenter from Hida
        sketches out the house

suzushisa o / Hida no takumi ga / sashizu kana

Summer, 1694. *Yasui:* Okada Yasui, a merchant in Nagoya; see 444. *the carpenter from Hida:* Hida, a province in the northern part of the prefecture now called Gifu, whose carpenters were proverbial for their skills. Bashō wrote two hokku for this occasion. The following is the one he sent in a letter to Yasui (see Shirane, *Traces,* p. 169): *suzushisa no / sashizu ni miyuru / sumai kana* ("It appears to be / a sketched-out plan for coolness / this new residence"), but in a letter to Sanpū, which contains both poems, he said he thought the "carpenter" poem was superior. Both poems allude to *The Tsurezuregusa* of Kenkō (55): "Houses should be built with summer in mind."

868

Stopping over at the house of the hermit Yamada

"The water rail calls there"
    so people say so that's why
        we stop at Saya

kuina naku to / hito no ieba ya / Sayadomari

Summer, 1694. Saya, to the west of Nagoya, was a post town on the Saya Road. The water rail's call is said to be like a knock on a door; see 507, 934. 6-7-5.

869

A calming coolness
    branches growing so as on
        a pine in the wild

suzushisa ya / suguni nomatsu no / eda no nari

Summer, 1694. A greeting poem for his host, Hiro-oka Sesshi (1670–1711), a poet in Iga.

870

They've carried brushwood
    the horses returning with
        rice-planting wine casks

shiba tsukeshi / uma no modori ya / tauedaru

Summer, 1694. Farmers brought brushwood to town to sell for festive
sake, to celebrate the end of rice-planting. This scene took place at the
house of Kubota Ensui (1640–1704), also known as Isen, a merchant in
Iga, who employed tenant farmers.

871

*On the twenty-second of the intercalary Fifth Month, at a rangin party
at the Rakushi-sha*

A shouldered basket
    with coolness the other load
        the year's first melon

yanagigori / katani wa suzushi / hatsumakuwa

Summer, 1694. *intercalary*: see 720. *rangin*: a kind of linked verse in
which there is no set order, and any poet can contribute at any time.
Rakushi-sha: "House of Fallen Persimmons": a cottage owned by Kyorai
(see 424) in Sagano, where Bashō had stayed in the spring of 1691, and
where he wrote *Saga Nikki*; see 696, 699, 703, 732. *yanagigori* (more usu-
ally, *yanagigōri*): a wicker trunk or basket made of willow (*yanagi*).
Among the six poets at the party was Shadō, who had come all the way
from Osaka. The poem expresses Bashō's pleasure at seeing Shadō again.

872

At Yamei's House

Such cooling freshness
    transformed into a picture
        The Saga bamboo

suzushisa o / e ni utsushikeri / Saga no take

Summer, 1694. *Yamei:* Sakai Yamei (?–1713), a samurai of the Fukuoka
Domain in Kyūshū, who had retired and moved to Saga, in western
Kyoto (also known as Sagano; see 694, 703, 871, 874). He was a relative
of Bashō's disciple, Kyorai; see 424, 696, 699.

873

This Kiyotaki
    water drawn up clean and clear
        these jelly noodles

Kiyotaki no / mizu kumasete ya / tokoroten

Summer, 1694. *Kiyotaki:* the name of a river to the west of Kyoto; *kiyo*
means "clean and clear." *tokoroten:* a vegetable gelatine shaped into
noodles, served with vinegar. The dish has been eaten for over a thou-
sand years in Japan. The poem was written in appreciation of Yamei's
hospitality; see 872.

874

Saga

The Sixth of the months
    clouds repose on the top of
        Arashiyama

rokugatsu ya / mine ni kumo oku / Arashiyama

Summer, 1694. Written at Rakushi-sha (see 871). *Saga:* see 694, 703,
871, 872. *Arashiyama* (literally, "storm mountain"): a small mountain to
the west of Kyoto, famous since ancient times for cherry blossoms and
autumn foliage; see 695.

875

The Kiyotaki
       Into its waves dispersing
              bluegreen pine needles

Kiyotaki ya / nami ni chirikomu / aomatsuba

Summer, 1694. The poem is a revision of two poems he had written in
the Sixth Month: *Kiyotaki ya / nami ni chiri naki / natsu no tsuki* ("The
Kiyotaki / not a blemish on its waves / The moon in summer") and
Ōigawa / nami ni chiri nashi / natsu no tsuki ("Ōigawa / not even a
speck of dust / The moon in summer"). Later on, Bashō had written a
poem (see 919) that used the phrase *chiri mo nashi* ("nary a blemish"),
which caused him to be dissatisfied with these earlier poems. On the
ninth day of the Tenth Month, three days before he died, he instructed
Kyorai about the revisions he wanted made to those poems to make
this, in a sense, his last haiku; see 922. *Kiyotaki*: see 873.

876

By the moonflowers
       at a gourd for kanpyō
              playfully peeling

yūgao ni / kanpyō muite / asobikeri

Summer, 1694. *yūgao*: calabash gourd, moonflower; see 10, 146, 421.
kanpyō: the dried shavings of the calabash gourd, used as a food.

877

With the morning dew
       the mud-spattered coolness of
              melons in the field

asatsuyu ni / yogorete suzushi / uri no tsuchi

Summer, 1694.

878

People gathered together, talking about where the best melons come from

The place where I peeled
the makuwa melon's rind
Rendaino

uri no kawa / muita tokoro ya / Rendaino

Summer, 1694. *Rendaino:* a large old cemetery not far from Kinkakū-ji
("The Temple of the Golden Pavilion") in Kyoto; the word *rendaino* is a
common noun meaning "cemetery."

879

The Ogura Mountain Temple

Are these the praises
of the pine and the cedar?
The scents on the wind

matsu sugi o / homete ya kaze no / kaoru oto

Summer, 1694. *The Ogura Mountain Temple* refers to Jōjakkō-ji, at the
foot of Ogurayama (Ogura Mountain) in Saga, Kyoto. It is known as the
site of the villa of the famous waka poet Fujiwara no Teika (also known
as Fujiwara no Sadaie, 1162–1241), and in the temple precincts there
was an old pine called the *shigure no matsu* ("the winter drizzle pine")
said to have been planted by him and about which he composed a poem.
He is also said to have edited the famous anthology *Ogura Hyakunin
Isshu* (a collection of one hundred poems by one hundred poets) here.

880

At Kyokusui's House

A summer evening
the scattering dawn the left-
overs of chilled food

natsu no yo ya / kuzurete akeshi / hiyashimono

Summer, 1694. *Kyokusui's House: Kyokusui-tei,* the home of Kyokusui at
Zeze; see 629, 729.

881

At Kyokusui's House, we chose the theme "farm life"

Fanning steamed rice
> the missus readies the meal
>> The airish evening

meshi aogu / kaka ga chisō ya / yūsuzumi

Summer, 1694. The headnote is not by Bashō himself, but by Shikō (see 432, 751, 755), editor of *Oi Nikki* ("Backpack Diary"), which contains this poem. *Kyokusui:* see 629, 729, 880. *meshi:* boiled (cooked) rice, the more formal word is *gohan; kaka:* more usually pronounced *kakā,* a colloquial term for wife (*kakādenka,* for example, means a house in which the wife "wears the trousers"). *aogu:* "to fan," the word has been most commonly and erroneously transliterated as *augu* due to the complications of switching from traditional Japanese orthography to contemporary orthography.

882

The plates and the bowls
> pale in the darkening cool
>> of the evening air

sarabachi mo / honoka ni yami no / yoisuzumi

Summer, 1694.

883

The seventh year of Genroku, on the twenty-first day of the Sixth Month, at Bokusetsu's hut in Ōtsu

Autumn drawing in
> Our hearts drawing together
>> in a four-mat room

aki chikaki / kokoro no yoru ya / yojōhan

Autumn, 1694. *Bokusetsu:* Mochizuki Bokusetsu, a doctor and poet; see 889. The date is August 11, 1694. *yojōhan:* a tea room, usually four-and-a-half tatami mats in size (about nine feet square).

THE COOL AIR, TWO POEMS

884

The rippling waters
　　To the tapping of the wind's
　　　　musical rhythm

sazanami ya / kaze no kaori no / aibyōshi

Summer, 1694. Both 884 and 885 were composed at the house of the
Noh actor Yūtō at Zeze, on Lake Biwa.

885

On the lake waters
　　the heat of the daytime missed
　　　　by the cloud summits

mizuumi ya / atsusa o oshimu / kumo no mine

Summer, 1694.

886

Enjoying Time at the House of Honma Shume

Flutteringly so
　　a folding fan ascending
　　　　to the cloud summits

hirahira to / aguru ōgi ya / kumo no mine

Summer, 1694. *Honma Shume:* a Noh actor in Ōtsu; his haikai name
was Tan-ya; see 888. Folding fans are often used by Noh actors, particu-
larly as they dance.

887

The scent of lotus
        coming into the eyes through
            the nose of the mask

hasu no ka o / me ni kayowasu ya / men no hana

Summer, 1694. The mask referred to is a Noh mask. Honma Shume had
demonstrated to Bashō how a Noh actor uses the hole for the nose in a
mask to see.

888

*At Honma Shume's house, on the back wall of the Noh stage, there is a
picture of skeletons playing the flute and drums in a Noh performance.
Is human life any different from this skeleton play? Zhuangzi used a
skull for a pillow, said he could not tell reality from dream, telling us thus
that this life is insubstantial*

A flash of lightning
        In the place where the face was
            a miscanthus plume

inazuma ya / kao no tokoro ga / susuki no ho

Autumn, 1694. *Honma Shume:* see 886. In a dream a skeleton told
Zhuangzi (see 150, 172, 173, 203) that man is happier after death, being
freed from the worries of life. Bashō also alludes to the legend that, after
she died, miscanthus plumes grew from the eye sockets of the skull of
Ono no Komachi; see 96.

889

A soothing coolness
    my footsoles against the wall
        napping at noontime

hiyahiya to / kabe o fumaete / hirune kana

Autumn, 1694. Composed early in the Seventh Month, the *zansho* season (see 546, 711, 810), at Bokusetsu's hut in Ōtsu; see 883.

890

A narrow pathway
    through thickets of crowfootgrass
        dew on their flowers

michi hososhi / sumotorigusa no / hana no tsuyu

Autumn, 1694. *sumotorigusa:* scholars differ as to exactly which grass Bashō is referring to; Kon Eizō and Yamamoto Kenkichi say that it is *ohishiba*, also known as *chikaragusa* (literally, "power grass"), *Eleusina indica*, known in English as crowfootgrass, Indian goosegrass, yardgrass, or wiregrass. The poem concerns the pathway to the hut at Gichū-ji at Zeze; see 606.

891

Tanabata here
    The autumn settling in for
        the first of its nights

Tanabata ya / aki o sadamuru / yo no hajime

Autumn, 1694. *Tanabata:* see 14; Tanabata is considered the first day of autumn. An earlier version of the poem, with the headnote "At Yadō's House," had a different word order in the last line: *hajime no yo. Yadō* (?–1701): a disciple from Kyoto.

892

In the seventh year of Genroku, while I was staying at Ōtsu, I received a letter from my older brother asking me to come home for the Bon Festival

The whole house of us
    with walking sticks and white hair
        visiting the grave

ie wa mina / tsue ni shiraga no / hakamairi

Autumn, 1694. *the Bon Festival:* also known as *Obon,* or *Tama Matsuri* (see 440, 545, 644, 893), an annual Buddhist rite to offer prayers to the souls of ancestors. It is a time of family reunion, where the family members visit ancestral graves and places associated with the family. It was held over four days in Bashō's time, and began on the thirteenth of the Seventh Month in the lunar calendar (September 2, 1694). Comparing it with 201 and 346, Kon Eizō sees this poem as a perfect example of *karumi.*

893

On Hearing the Nun Jutei Had Died

As of no account
    never think that of your life
        The Feast of the Souls

kazu naranu / mi to na omoiso / Tama Matsuri

Autumn, 1694. Little is known of Jutei. Some scholars believe her to have been Bashō's mistress at one time; there are letters that indicate that she may have been the wife of Tōin, Bashō's nephew. When Bashō set off for Iga on the eleventh day of the Fifth Month (see 857), he took her son with him, while she and her two daughters moved into the Bashō-an in Fukagawa, where, early in the Sixth Month, she died. Bashō received a letter on the eighth of the Sixth Month telling him the news.

894

A flash of lightning
    Flying into the darkness
        the night herons' calls

inazuma ya / yami no kata yuku / goi no koe

Autumn, 1694.

895

The hues of the wind
     So higgledy-piggledy
          the autumn garden

kazairo ya / shidoro ni ueshi / niwa no aki

Autumn, 1694. A greeting poem to Tōdō Genko; see 830, 850. According to Dohō, Genko's garden was being landscaped when Bashō visited. A different version of the poem, perhaps due to mistranscription, uses *hagi* ("bush clover"): *kazairo ya / shidoro ni ueshi / niwa no hagi* ("The hues of the wind / So higgledy-piggledy / the garden's clovers"). Yet another manuscript uses *ogi* ("common reed"), perhaps again an error of transcription.

896

The village grown old
     Not a single home without
          a persimmon tree

sato furite / kaki no ki motanu / ie mo nashi

Autumn, 1694. Written at the house of Katano Bōsui (?–1705), a merchant in Iga.

897

The winter melons
     Each and every one with change
          written on the face

tōgan ya / tagai ni kawaru / kao no nari

Winter, 1694. *tōgan: Benincasa hispida,* the wax gourd, also called the white gourd, or winter melon. Bashō had returned to Iga after a long time away. The poem was composed in autumn, and there is an implicit comparison between *uri* ("melons") and the less attractive shape of *tōgan.*

898

The Harvest moonlight
    Fog covering the foothills
       mist over the fields

meigetsu ni / fumoto no kiri ya / ta no kumori

Autumn, 1694. Iga Ueno is in a basin surrounded by hills, and fog is common; Bashō's newly built hut overlooked the basin; see 899, 900.

899

The Harvest moonlight
    What I'd taken for blossoms
       a field of cotton

meigetsu no / hana ka to miete / watabatake

Autumn, 1694. As with 898 and 900, written on the fifteenth of the Eighth Month (October 3, 1694) at a moonviewing party at Bashō's newly built hut.

900

The fifteenth of the Eighth Month

And who this evening?
    With the moon of Yoshino
       sixteen ri away

koyoi tare / Yoshino no tsuki mo / jūrokuri

Autumn, 1694. The date is October 3, 1694; see 898, 899. *ri*: a unit of distance, approximately 4 km, so "sixteen ri" is about 64 km. Based on a poem by Genzanmi Yorimasa (Minamoto no Yorimasa, 1104–80): *Koyoi tare / suzu fuku kaze o / mi ni shimete / Yoshino no take no / tsuki o miruran* ("And who this evening / wind blowing through bamboo grass / and through the body / is now looking at the moon / over Yoshino mountain?").

901

The amaranth leaves
　　with the wild geese arriving
　　　　turn a deeper red

keitō ya / kari no kuru toki / nao akashi

Autumn, 1694. *keitō*: cockscomb, *Celosia argentea, var. cristata.* Bashō
seems, however, to be playing on the Chinese characters for the *ha-geitō,*
the *Amaranthus tricolor,* Joseph's coat, or Chinese amaranth. The charac-
ters literally mean "geese come red"; the leaves of the plant turn a deeper
red at the time of year the geese arrive from the north for the winter.

902

Unlike this old face
　　how a poem should emerge
　　　　the year's first blossoms

kao ni ninu / hokku mo ideyo / hatsuzakura

Spring, 1694. The poem was written in autumn with a spring theme, as
an example for his students in Iga. *hatsuzakura*: a term for the first
cherry blossoms of the year; see 375, 929.

903

Here's the new rice-straw
　　out now and already here
　　　　the winter drizzle

shinwara no / desomete hayaki / shigure kana

Autumn, 1694. *shigure*: early winter rain, which, coming in late autumn
in this poem, is a sign of the approaching winter.

904

Tojū of Ise visited my mountain hut

Not soba not yet
    the mountain path welcoming
      with buckwheat blossoms

soba wa mada / hana de motenasu / yamaji kana

Autumn, 1694. Soba ("buckwheat noodles") was one of Bashō's favorite dishes; it was too early in the year for buckwheat as food, so the blooms of the plant would have to serve as a welcome for the guest. Shikō (432, 751, 755, 881, 916, 959) accompanied Tojū on this visit.

905

Autumn departing
    The outspreading of the hand
      burrs on the chestnut

yuku aki ya / te o hirogetaru / kuri no iga

Autumn, 1694. The greeting hokku at Gensetsu's house on October 23, three days before Bashō was scheduled to leave his hometown. Bashō links the opening chestnut burrs and the gesture of the hand made by his family and friends trying to stop him from leaving.

906

A bellowing bawl
    The plaintive deep-bottomed call
      of the deer at night

bii to naku / shirigoe kanashi / yoru no shika

Autumn, 1694. The first use in Japanese poetry of *bii* as onomatopoeia for the belling of a deer (see Shirane, *Traces,* p. 274). According to *Oi Nikki* ("Backpack Diary"), the poem was composed in Nara, on the eighth day of the Ninth Month (October 26, 1694), when Bashō took a walk around Sarusawa Pond at about midnight. For other deer poems, see 40, 98, 180.

907

Chrysanthemum scent
      In Nara all the ancient
            figures of Buddha

kiku no ka ya / Nara ni wa furuki / hotoketachi

Autumn, 1694. Nara served as the capital of Japan from 710 to 784 and
contains some of the most significant Buddhist temples in Japan. The
poem was composed on *Chōyō no Sekku,* the day of the Chrysanthe-
mum Festival (see 108, 458, 582), which fell on October 27, 1694.

908

Chrysanthemum scent
      In Nara so long ago
            that handsome young man

kiku no ka ya / Nara wa ikuyo no / otokoburi

Autumn, 1694. *otokoburi* ("handsome young man"): a reference to the
first story in the *Ise Monogatari,* in which shortly after his *uikōburi*
("Coming of Age") rite, a young nobleman (said to be based on Ariwara
no Narihira; see 28, 71, 101, 403) encounters two beautiful sisters and
presents them with an impromptu waka love poem.

909

On the Kuragari Pass

Amid chrysanth scents
      climbing the dark of the Pass
            Sekku Day today

kiku no ka ni / Kuragari noboru / Sekku kana

Autumn, 1694. *Kuragari:* Kuragari Tōge, the "Dark Pass," on Mount
Ikoma, between Nara and Osaka. *Sekku: Chōyō no Sekku,* the Chrysan-
themum Festival, held on the ninth day of the Ninth Month; see 108,
458, 582.

910

On the ninth, what I felt in my heart leaving Nara

> The Day of Sekku
>> from Nara to Naniwa
>>> the evening crescent

Kiku ni dete / Nara to Naniwa wa / yoizukiyo

Autumn, 1694. *On the ninth/The Day of Sekku: Chōyō no Sekku,* see 108, 458, 582, 458. *Naniwa:* see 75, 640, 822. Bashō stayed the night in Shadō's; see 911.

911

> Even in the lair
>> of the wild boar even there
>>> the creaker-cricket

inoshishi no / toko ni mo iru ya / kirigirisu

Autumn, 1694. Another version of the poem titled "Shadō Snores by My Bedside" reads *toko ni kite / ibiki ni iru ya / kirigirisu* ("Into the bed with / the sound of someone snoring / the creaker-cricket"). *Shadō:* see 623, 771, 773, 822, 910, 914. *kirigirisu* ('creaker-cricket'): see 551, 648, 660, 713, 967.

912

On the thirteenth, visiting the Sumiyoshi Market

Bought a masu box
    had to change my mind alas
        about moonviewing

masu kōte / funbetsu kawaru / tsukimi kana

Autumn, 1694. *masu box:* a *masu* is a box that comes in various sizes
and is used for measuring the amount of a grain or liquid. *the Sumiy-
oshi Market,* which was also known as *Takara no Ichi* ("The Treasure
Market") or *Masu no Ichi* ("The Measure Market"), was famous for sell-
ing these boxes, which were said to bring good fortune. Bashō had been
invited to a moonviewing party to be held on "the thirteenth" (October
31, 1694) at the house of Hasegawa Keishi (?–1695) in Osaka (see 920),
but fell ill after visiting the market earlier that day. At the *kasen* party
held the next day this was his playful excuse.

913

At Kiryū's House

The autumn passing
    behind the scattered showers
        the shape of the moon

aki mo haya / baratsuku ame ni / tsuki no nari

Autumn, 1694. *Kiryū:* a disciple in Osaka.

914

On the twenty-first of the Ninth Month, at Shioe Shayō's House

The autumn darkness
            riven and unraveling
                        with conversation

aki no yo o / uchikuzushitaru / hanashi kana

Autumn, 1694. Bashō had partly come to Osaka to mediate in a dispute
between two disciples, Shidō (see 640) and Shadō (see 623, 771, 773,
822, 871, 911). At the house of Shioe Shayō, a wealthy merchant, a party
was held at which Bashō believed the dispute had been resolved amica-
bly. After seeing him at a few more gatherings, the last being at Keishi's
house on November 15 (see 920), Bashō took ill and never again saw
Shadō, who did not come to his funeral.

915

*The host likes to enjoy himself late into the night, to get up late in the
morning. Going to bed early's mean and miserly, to rise early hurried
and harried*

Yes how sweet it is
            autumn morning rising late
                        the way of the host

omoshiroki / aki no asane ya / teishuburi

Autumn, 1694. The host: Shayō; see 914.

916

Thoughts

Here on a roadway
  where nobody else travels
    The autumn evening

kono michi ya / yuku hito nashi ni / aki no kure

Autumn, 1694. Another version reads: *hitogoe ya / kono michi kaeru / aki no kure* ("Human voices here / on this roadway returning / The autumn evening"). Bashō presented both versions at Deisoku's party, held on the twenty-sixth at *Ukamuse* in Shin-Kiyomizu, Osaka (see 917), and asked the gathered poets to choose between the two. Shikō chose the version beginning *kono michi ya,* with which the day's half-*kasen* began. An earlier version, with the title "Autumn Evening," has a slight variation in its first line: *kono michi o* ("*along* this roadway").

917

The wind in the pines
  comes meddling around the eaves
    The autumn ending

matsukaze ya / noki o megutte / aki kurenu

Autumn, 1694. *matsukaze:* the wind blowing through pine trees is a conventional trope in Japanese poetry and Noh drama. Bashō brings a haikai twist to the genre by using a colloquialism, *megutte* ("going around,""swirling"). The poem was written impromptu for Shirōzaemon, the owner of a restaurant called *Ukamuse* (see 916).

918

Thoughts on a Journey

In this autumntime
  why do I so feel the years?
    In the clouds a bird

kono aki wa / nande toshiyoru / kumo ni tori

Autumn, 1694. Written on the same day (November 13) as 916 and 917. Kon Eizō considers this one of Bashō's finest poems, evoking his life as a wanderer, his awareness of age, and his loneliness.

919

White chrysanthemums
  No matter how close you look
    nary a blemish

shiragiku no / me ni tatete miru / chiri mo nashi

Autumn, 1694. Composed at the house of Sonome (Shiba Sonome), on
November 14. Sonome was the wife of Shiba Ichiyū, a doctor; see 366.
See 875 for the effect of the line *chiri mo nashi* on that earlier poem, and
Shirane and Suzuki, p. 408, for a reading of how this poem illustrates the
social and ritual function (in this case, of complimenting a host) of much
Japanese poetry. The phrase *me ni tatete miru* derives from a waka by
Saigyō: *kumori naki / kagami no ue ni / iru chiri o / me ni tatete miru / yo
to omowabaya* ("Upon a mirror / a cloudlessly clear mirror / the slightest
speck of / dust will be caught by the eye / Such is the way of the world").

920

At Keishi's House, on the topic "In the moonlight, escorting a catamite"

The moon's clarity
  Escorting a catamite
    afraid of foxes

tsuki sumu ya / kitsune kowagaru / chigo no tomo

Autumn, 1694. *Keishi*: a poet in Osaka; see 912, 914. At this gathering,
held on November 15, the poets had been asked to compose poems on
the theme of love: "In the haikai tradition the theme of love covered a
wide range of subtopics, and included homosexual love, which was prev-
alent in Bashō's day. Bashō himself, recalling his youth, once wrote:
'There was a time when I was fascinated with the ways of homosexual
love.' In Japanese folklore, a fox has supernatural powers and often works
mischief on unsuspecting men" (Ueda, p. 409); see 794. *chigo*: see 49. For
a discussion of *nanshoku* ('male love') in Bashō's day, see Introduction.

921

Autumn deepening
    The man next door I wonder
        what is it he does?

aki fukaki / tonari wa nani o / suru hito zo

Autumn, 1694. Bashō was too ill to attend a gathering at the house of Negoro Shihaku (1643–1713) on November 16, and had this hokku sent to the host.

922

Composed on a Sick Bed

On a journey stricken
    Dreams a-wandering around
        stalks and stubble-fields

tabi ni yande / yume wa kareno o / kakemeguru

Winter, 1694. Bashō dictated this poem to his student Donshū in the early hours of the ninth of the Tenth Month, three days before his death (see 875); he died on the twelfth of the Tenth Month (November 28), at around 4 P.M. *kareno* means "withered field."

MISCELLANEOUS POEMS, 1684–1694

923

A Kagekiyo
    blossom viewing turns into
        Shichibyōe

Kagekiyo mo / hanami no za ni wa / Shichibyōe

Spring. *Kagekiyo:* Taira no Kagekiyo (d. 1196), a samurai warrior of the Taira clan, who appears in many Noh and Kabuki plays, and most famously in the *Heike Monogatari.* "Shichibyōe" (sometimes "*Aku*shichibyōe," the prefix *aku* meaning "impressively strong, formidable") was his nickname.

924

The blossoms tumble
        and the birds too astonished
            The koto thrumming

chiru hana ya / tori mo odoroku / koto no chiri

Spring. *koto:* a stringed musical instrument, see 819. The poem was written on a painting of a koto by Kano Tansetsu, owned by Hisamatsu Shukuzan, the chief retainer of the Matsuyama Domain. The poem alludes to the "Wakana 1" ("Spring Shoots 1") chapter of *Genji Monogatari*, in which Hikaru Genji is asked to play the koto and astonish the mountain birds; see 758.

925

Though it may not fall
        on bamboo-planting day sure
            coat and a rainhat

furazu tomo / take uuru hi wa / mino to kasa

Summer. A slightly different version uses *ya* instead of *wa: take uuru hi ya.* "bamboo-planting day": based on a Chinese proverb that says, "A bamboo planted on the thirteenth of the Fifth Month will grow." The Fifth (lunar) Month is the time of the rainy season.

926

When I would hear the words
 "brushwood hut" how unpleasant
the sound and yet how
 wonderful a thing it is
in this world of ours I have found

shiba no io to / kikeba iyashiki / na naredomo / yo ni
 konomoshiki / mono ni zo arikeru

This poem, included in the Sankashū, was composed by the priest Saigyō
when he visited a monk called Amidabō, who lived in the Higashiyama
District in Kyoto. I wonder what kind of person this monk was. I give this
verse to a monk living the same way in a brushwood hut

Over this brushwood
 gate the moon ever the same
  Amidabō

shiba no to no / tsuki ya sono mama / Amidabō

Autumn. *Sankashū:* see 826. Though with little effect on the sense,
Bashō misquotes Saigyō: *shiba no io to / kiku wa iyashiki / na naredomo
/ yo ni konomoshiki / sumai narikeri.*

927

A sight to behold
 chrysanthemums in a field
  after a windstorm

midokoro no / are ya nowaki no / nochi no kiku

Autumn. Based on a line in passage 19 of *The Tsurezuregusa* of Kenkō
(see 177, 303): "The morning after a typhoon has blown through is also
delightful" (McKinney, p. 30). There are three different versions of a
painting by Bashō (signed *Baseo*) of chrysanthemums after an autumn
storm. A slightly different first line of the poem, reading *midokoro mo*
("also"), appears on the version of the painting done in Indian ink. *now-
aki:* an autumn typhoon; see 148, 457, 646.

928

All the long night through
    the freezing of the bamboo
        Frost in the morning

yosugara ya / take kōrasuru / kesa no shimo

Winter.

929

Among a riot
    of fully blossomed peaches
        the year's first cherry

sakimidasu / momo no naka yori / hatsuzakura

Spring. *hatsuzakura*: the first cherry blossoms of the year; see 375, 902.

930

My meal of gruel
    biwa music in the eaves
        a shower of hail

zōsui ni / biwa kiku noki no / arare kana

Winter. *zōsui* (literally, "miscellaneous cooking"): a rice-based vegetable soup. *biwa*: a stringed musical instrument; see 202, 213, 353.

931

The flowers and fruit
    all the one time at the full
        the ripened melon

hana to mi to / ichido ni uri no / sakari kana

Summer. Both the fruit and the flowers of the melon, unlike other plants, appear at the same time.

932

At the old river
    casting her coquettish eyes
        the budding willow

furukawa ni / kobite me o haru / yanagi kana

Spring. *me* is a homophone, and can mean both "eye" and "bud."

933

Hackberries falling
    the beating wings of starlings
        a storm at sunrise

e no mi chiru / muku no haoto ya / asaarashi

Autumn. *Hackberries:* the fruit of the *Celtis sinensis,* the Chinese hackberry (*enoki* in Japanese), a plant of the hemp family, which appears in September and October and is favored by starlings.

934

This country dwelling
    Even the water rail knows
        nothing of its door

kono yado wa / kuina mo shiranu / toboso kana

Summer. The water rail's call is said to resemble a knock on a door; see 507, 868.

935

Out of a snowless
    patch the pale purple sprouts of
        wild asparagus

yukima yori / usumurasaki no / meudo kana

Spring. *meudo:* the sprout (*me*) on an *udo* plant. *udo: Aralia cordata,* Japanese spikenard, or mountain asparagus, the stems of which are edible.

936

Hokaku, For His Folding Fan

Even now the fringe
    of the boy bears the fragrance
        of freshest grasses

maegami mo / mada wakakusa no / nioi kana

Spring. *Hokaku:* little is known of this person. *maegami:* "fringe," or
"forelocks," but also a hairstyle, with partly shaved crown and forelocks
left deliberately long, of a young boy and also, occasionally, women.
maegami more generally referred to any boy before *genpuku* ("coming-
of-age"), but was also used for catamites. The *maegami* stage lasted
from about age ten until the *genpuku* ceremony, which would take
place at some time between the ages of thirteen and seventeen.

937

The long spring nighttime
    in the cherry blossom dawn
        drawn to an ending

haru no yo wa / sakura ni akete / shimaikeri

Spring.

938

All my excuses!
    I've had to empty that bag
        the end of the year

funbetsu no / soko tatakikeri / toshi no kure

Winter. *funbetsu: funbetsu* means "discretion" or "discernment," but
Bashō is invoking a *funbetsubukuro* ("discretion bag"), also known as
chiebukuro ("bag of knowledge"), a term used to denote the originating
source of knowledge and ideas, and here referring specifically to the
excuses used to avoid debts and bill collectors at the end of the year; see
977.

939

A Portrait of Masashige, his loyalty as strong as iron and stone

On the blooming pink
>   tiny teardrops descending
>   The camphor tree dew

nadeshiko ni / kakaru namida ya / kusu no tsuyu

Summer. *Masashige:* Kusunoki Masashige (1294–1336), legendary
samurai considered in the Edo period the epitome of loyalty to a losing
cause, a famous statue of whom, astride a horse, stands outside the
Imperial Palace in Tokyo. The family name Kusunoki means "camphor
tree." Legend says that the emperor Go-Daigo had a dream in which he
took shelter under a camphor tree, which led him to seek Kusunoki's
support. Kusunoki's parting from his young son Masatsura (d. 1348) at
Sakurai (in present-day Osaka Prefecture) before his final battle is one
of the best-known images in Japanese history.

940

Mark this tale of old
>   Even the Lord Chichibu
>   a sumo wrestler

mukashi kike / Chichibu-dono sae / sumōtori

Autumn. *Chichibu-dono* ("Lord Chichibu"): Hatakeyama Shigetada
(1164–1205), a leading warrior under Minamoto no Yoritomo, the first
shogun of the Kamakura shogunate. According to legend, he once
defeated the strongest sumo champion of his time. Chichibu is an area
in the western part of modern-day Saitama Prefecture.

941

The winter cherry
>   the fruit and leaves and the husks
>   in autumn color

hōzuki wa / mi mo ha mo kara mo / momiji kana

Autumn. *hōzuki: Physalis alkekengi,* the bladder cherry, Chinese lan-
tern, Japanese lantern, or winter cherry. Its fruit has a large orange-to-
red papery covering. *momiji:* autumn foliage; see 48, 84, 460.

942

Chrysanthemum dew
        falls and when I pick it up
            in hand a bulbil

kiku no tsuyu / ochite hiroeba / nukago kana

Autumn. *nukago:* a bulbil, most usually of a yam; *nukago* is the older
form of a word pronounced *mukago* in contemporary Japanese.

943

In my hermitage
        a square of light on the floor
            the window-shaped moon

waga yado wa / shikakuna kage o / mado no tsuki

Autumn.

944

*A Motto: Do not speak of the defects of others, do not speak of your own
deserts*

When I say a word
        my lips and mouth grow colder
            The wind in autumn

mono ieba / kuchibiru samushi / aki no kaze

Autumn. The motto is based on a Chinese proverb in the *Wen Xuan*
("Selections of Refined Literature"), one of the earliest and most impor-
tant anthologies of Chinese poetry and prose, compiled in the sixth
century.

945

Urged and encouraged
      to throw a Throw-the-Year-Off
            awaiting the mood

setsukarete / toshiwasure suru / kigen kana

Winter. *toshiwasure:* a "year-forgetting" party, held at the end of the
year; see 669, 678, 751.

946

On a Painting of Bamboo

The roistering wind
      entering the bamboo grove
            suddenly silent

kogarashi ya / take ni kakurete / shizumarinu

Winter.

947

The hydrangeas
      the hemp-kimono season
            shade of greenish blue

ajisai ya / katabiradoki no / usuasagi

Summer. *katabira:* a summer kimono made of hemp; *katabiradoki:* the
time for wearing such a kimono; see 22, 304.

948

In the aftermath
    of chrysanthemums nothing
        only a daikon

kiku no nochi / daikon no hoka / sarani nashi

Winter. *daikon:* a large, white Japanese radish; see 828, 830. Based on
the poem "Chrysanthemum" by the Tang Dynasty poet Yuan Zhen
(Yüan Chen, 779–831), in which he says that though he has no particu-
lar preference for the chrysanthemum, after it blooms there are no
more flowers till spring.

949

The baby sparrows
    exchanging chirrups and squeaks
        the rats in their nest

suzumeko to / koe nakikawasu / nezumi no su

Spring.

950

The squid seller's cries
    mingle-mangling my hearing
        the cuckoo calling

ikauri no / koe magirawashi / hototogisu

Summer.

951

The Nara Seven
          the seven halls of temples
                    the eight-petalled blooms

Nara nanae / shichidō garan / yaezakura

Spring. *Nara nanae* ("Nara Seven"): the Seven Emperors of the period
when Nara was the capital of Japan; *shichidō:* the seven main halls in the
precincts of a Buddhist temple; *yaezakura:* "yae" means "eightfold"; see
620, where the tree is called "the double-petalled cherry tree of Nara."

952

At Lord Rosen's Residence

Saigyō's hut
          somewhere in this garden too
                    amid the blossoms

Saigyō no / iori mo aran / hana no niwa

Spring. *Rosen:* a poet and patron; see 302. See 206 for a poem composed
at a place that was once the site of Saigyō's hut.

953

Is the monkeyman
          beating the monkey's jacket
                    on a fulling block?

saruhiki wa / saru no kosode o / kinuta kana

Autumn. *saruhiki:* the master of a monkey show; *kosode:* a kimono with
short sleeves; *kinuta:* fulling block; see 205, 352.

954

A muttonheaded
      mutt trodden and trampled on
            the mating of cats

matōdona / inu fumitsukete / neko no koi

Spring. *neko no koi* (literally, "the love of cats"): cats mating; see 71, 686, 756.

955

What do they feed on
      in that small house in the shade
            of the fall willow?

nani kūte / koie wa aki no / yanagikage

Autumn.

956

On the strand at Suma
      something needed for New Year
            a bundle of twigs

Suma no ura no / toshitorimono ya / shiba ichiwa

Winter. Written on a painting of brushwood by the sea. *Suma:* see 109, 404. 6-7-5.

957

Here in this temple
      a garden so completely
            full of bashō

kono tera wa / niwa ippai no / bashō kana

Autumn. *bashō:* a pun on his name and the tree from which he took his name, *Musa basjoo,* the Japanese banana tree; see 141, 498, 768.

958

A matsutake
 so pocked and scarred so deeply
  the spit of a pine

matsudake ya / kabureta hodo wa / matsu no nari

Autumn. *matsudake:* a matsutake mushroom, the name of which
means "pine mushroom"; see 728.

959

Come on bat come out
 into the fleet world of birds
  flitting to blossoms

kōmori mo / ideyo ukiyo no / hana ni tori

Spring. According to Shikō (see 432, 751, 755, 881, 916), the poem
had been meant for, but in the end wasn't given to, a priest who was
departing on a journey. *ukiyo:* "the floating world"; see 164, 206, 344,
455, 753.

960

On a Portrait of Hotei

The things I wanted
 he carries in that there bag
  the moon and flowers

monohoshi ya / fukuro no uchi no / tsuki to hana

Miscellaneous, no season word. *Hotei* (also known as Budai): a legen-
dary Chinese monk, familiar as the "fat Buddha," who carries a cloth
sack, from which his name derives. Like Ebisu, one of the *shichifukujin*,
the Seven Gods of Fortune; see 4.

961

Turning away from
    its leaves the camellia's
        coldhearted flowers

ha ni somuku / tsubaki no hana ya / yosogokoro

Spring. When Bashō was told that a disciple of his had already written
a similar poem, he threw this poem away.

962

A springtime shower
    The gusting river willow
        a scratchy raincoat

harusame ya / mino fukikaesu / kawayanagi

Spring. *kawayanagi* ("river willow"): *Salix gilgiana,* a willow usually
found by the banks of rivers.

963

To sleep I'd borrow
    off yonder scarecrow the sleeve
        The frost at midnight

karite nen / kakashi no sode ya / yowa no shimo

Winter. *sode:* sleeve, but it can also stand for the whole robe. The allu-
sion is to a waka by Fujiwara no Yoshitsune, see the note to 87.

964

The scent of ume
    brings back what's been chased away
        the cold of before

ume ga ka ni / oimodosa ruru / samusa kana

Spring.

965

A time for farewell
    the hat lowered in the hand
        the outer coat on

wakareba ya / kasa te ni sagete / natsubaori

Summer. *natsubaori*: literally, "summer *haori*" (see 135, 639, 705), a light
half-coat worn over a kimono; formal wear, worn especially for the
occasion of bidding farewell.

966

The sun occluded
    by cloud the swiftiness of
        migratory birds

hi ni kakaru / kumo ya shibashi no / wataridori

Autumn.

967

Morning after morning
    practicing calligraphy
        the creaker-cricket

asana asana / tenarai susumu / kirigirisu

Autumn. Another name for the *kirigirisu* ("cricket") is the *fudetsu-
mushi* ("the writing brush insect"); see 551, 648, 660, 713, 911. 6-7-5.

968

At Taisui's House, a Sunrise Party

Raining now and again
No need to worry about
the seeds and seedlings

ame oriori / omou koto naki / sanae kana

Summer. *kagemachi* ("Sunrise Party"): an all-night gathering to watch for the sunrise. *Taisui:* see 471, 806; and for another *kagemachi* at Taisui's house, see 817. 6-7-5.

969

Butterflies and birds
in a fluster and tizzy
the blossoms the clouds

chō tori no / uwatsukitatsu ya / hana no kumo

Spring.

970

In Praise of Old Teitoku, On Seeing His Portrait

Bears a childlike name
the old man I never met
in the roundy hood

osanana ya / shiranu okina no / maruzukin

Winter. *Old Teitoku:* Matsunaga Teitoku (1571–1654), founder of the Teimon School of haikai; the poem was inscribed on his portrait. At the age of 63, Teitoku decided to change his name to the more youthful Chozumaru, the suffix *maru* being often appended to the names of children; *maru* can also mean "round." *maruzukin:* a round hood used by an old man or priest.

971

That someone who says
        they're sick and tired of childer
            blossomless now too

ko ni aku to / mōsu hito ni wa / hana mo nashi

Spring.

972

First winter shower
        The character for "first" my
            very own shower

hatsushigure / hatsu no ji o waga / shigure kana

Winter. According to Ippō, this was a greeting poem to a host Bashō
was meeting for the first time, hence the emphasis on first: *hatsushig-
ure:* the first rain shower of winter; see 320, 594, 776; *hatsu no ji:* "the
written (Chinese) character for 'first.'"

973

The world in full bloom
        for the flowers too prayers
            chanted nembutsu

yo ni sakaru / hana ni mo nebutsu / mōshikeri

Spring. *nebutsu:* Nembutsu, a chanted prayer in Pure Land Buddhism,
which entails the ritual incantation of the name of Amida Buddha
(Amitābha); see 211.

974

The wind in the pines
        needles falling the sound of
            water a cooling

matsukaze no / ochiba ka mizu no / oto suzushi

Summer. *matsukaze:* "the wind in the pines"; see 917.

975

In Memory of Senka's Father

The hue on the sleeve
　　darkening to the coldness
　　　　of deepest ashgray

sode no iro / yogorete samushi / koinezumi

Winter. *Senka:* a disciple in Edo.

976

Visiting the private room of the priest Etsudō

The scent lingers on
　　orchided to the curtain
　　　　in the orchid room

ka o nokosu / ranchō ran no / yadori kana

Autumn. Etsudō was a retired priest, about whom little is known. A
ranchō (literally, "orchid curtain") is hung before (or draped over) a
zushi, a sacred cabinet in which an image of Buddha is enshrined.
Though the *ran* in *ranchō* literally means "orchid," it acts as an enhanc-
ing prefix, making *ranchō* a eulogistic term meaning "beautiful curtain."

977

Kohōgen?
　　The pity in how come here
　　　　the year and its end

Kohōgen / dedokoro aware / toshi no kure

Winter. *Kohōgen:* Kanō Motonobu (1476–1559), son of the founder of
the Kanō school of painting, Masanobu, and often credited with estab-
lishing the distinctive characteristics of the school. Bashō had found a
painting by Kohōgen at an end of the year market, and wondered about
the straitened circumstances of the family who had sold it. As the year
ends, it is time to settle debts; see 938.

978

Kine no Ore: "The Broken Kine"

This vase, "The Broken Kine," has been loved by the high and the mighty and is become now a treasured artifact. In what mountains were you born, in what village did you beat upon the cloths of the people? What had been a mallet is now a vase, hanging above the heads of the noble. That which comes down will rise, that which is high, it is said, is bound to come down. The same is true of people. When on top, do not be proud; when down, do not begrudge. This mallet shows the way of the world

This mallet of wood
　　　a camellia one time
　　　　　an ume perhaps

kono tsuchi no / mukashi tsubaki ka / ume no ki ka

Spring. The *Kine no Ore* ("Broken Kine" [pronounced ki-ne]) is a Chinese vase from the fourteenth or fifteenth century (Yuan or Ming Dynasty). A *kine* is a kind of mallet, thin in the middle and round at both ends. The *Kine no Ore* is a *kine* broken in the middle, with each broken half resembling a mallet. It was owned by Toyotomi Hideyoshi (1537–98), who had been born a peasant and rose to become one of the most powerful lords during the Sengoku ("Warring States") period in Japanese history. The *Kine no Ore* was also later owned by Tokugawa Ieyasu, the first shogun of the Tokugawa shogunate (see 490, 796). It is now in the Tokugawa Museum in Nagoya.

979

Tōzan had stayed in Edo for three months on business. I would surprise him by visiting early in the morning when he was still sleeping, and he would wake me at night after I had gone to bed early. We knew each other well, as well as those who live under the same roof. Today he leaves to return home, and to see him off I took up my walking stick and tottered out, to see the last of autumn also departing

Musashino Plain
    with not a thing to hinder
        the hat on your head

Musashino ya / sawaru mono naki / kimi ga kasa

Miscellaneous, no season word. *Musashino Plain:* "the plain of Musashi Province"; see 56. *Tōzan:* see 477.

980

The scent of ume
    With the unmet from worlds past
        communion comes

ume ga ka ya / minu yo no hito ni / gyoi o uru

Spring. A greeting poem for Soshū, whom Bashō was meeting for the first time. In poetic tradition, *ume ga ka* ("the scent of ume") was a conventional phrase meant to evoke the past; see 844. Bashō alludes to two passages in *The Tsurezuregusa* of Kenkō: "It is a most wonderful thing to sit alone beneath a lamp, book spread before you, and commune with someone from the past whom you have never met" (13); "it is above all plum blossom that has the power to carry you back to moments of cherished memory" (19) (McKinney, pp. 27, 30); see also 177, 303.

ACKNOWLEDGEMENTS

I began this book in July 2017, after almost twenty years living in Tokyo, and having started to feel, mistakenly, that I was equipped, linguistically and culturally, to begin the work of understanding what Bashō was doing in his poems. A first draft was done briskly, and by March 2018 I had versions of all the poems. It was then that the work began in earnest. As I added notes and researched more, as I burrowed further within Bashō's Japanese, my English versions fell apart. How could I have believed Bashō was saying *that*? Over time, with the help and advice of friends and colleagues, and standing on the shoulders of many fine scholars and translators of Bashō, and with an ever-deepening sense of Bashō's language and the cultural world out of which the poems emerged, the poems in English took on their present form.

I owe debts of deepest gratitude to Ben Alexander, Jeffrey Angles, Clive Collins, Andrew Houwen, Bernard O'Donoghue, Hamish Macaskill, Maeda Naoko, Manabe Akiko, John McAuliffe, Ohno Mitsuko, Paul Rossiter, Michael Schmidt, Tashiro Naomichi, and Tochigi Nobuaki, and to the late, and dearly missed Diane Takahashi, whose encouragement and support, deep knowledge and experience, and love of Bashō, were invaluable, sustaining, and inspirational. I would like to thank the members of the *renku* group that I (as *Saimon*) have attended on and off for the last fifteen years: *Shoichi, Ange, Jakura, Teina,* and the late *Seiei.* I have learned so much from attending these sessions, not just about the procedures of linked verse, but also about the social experience with which it is so intricately bound. I would like to mark a special thanks to Terence Brown, in whose class in Trinity College Dublin in 1987 I first encountered Bashō. I want to thank Eric Schmidt of the University of California Press for his patient encouragement and his enthusiasm for this book. Most of all, I thank my dear colleague Mano Yasushi for patiently, painstakingly, and with great skill and good humor going through this manuscript, the poems and notes, offering me the benefit of his acumen, erudition, and insight. The book would be far less a thing without his detailed care. All errors are mine, and mine alone.

Acknowledgements are due to the editors of *PN Review* and *RHINO Poetry,* where versions of some of these poems first appeared.

GLOSSARY

aware — sadly beautiful, the pathos produced by the evanescence of things, similar to Virgil's *lacrimae rerum* ("the tears at the heart of things").

awase — (*uta-awase, ku-awase,* etc.), poetry contests/matches. Part of Japanese literary tradition since the Heian period (794–1185), during which *uta-awase* was the most popular variety of this form of literary pursuit. Two teams, "Left" and "Right," composed waka on set themes over a series of rounds. The poems were assessed by one or more judges, and at the end the team with the highest number of winning poems won the competition. Other forms of contest included *renga awase,* a linked-verse contest, and *ku-awase,* a hokku verse contest between poets. Like most poets, Bashō took part in poetry matches and contests, and as part of his work as a *haikai* master served as a judge. Occasionally, the best poems of a contest, including the master's comments, were published in anthologies, such as *Kai Ōi* ("The Seashell Game") and *Haikai Awase* ("Haikai Contests").

dai — ("topic"), the theme of a poem, often set by convention, and a feature of poetry contests. A *daiei* (poem on a set theme) need not stick to the season within which it is composed.

Danrin	("talk forest"), a school of haikai poetry founded by Nishiyama Sōin, which favored plain language, subjects drawn from everyday life, and humor.
dokugin	the solo composition of a linked-verse sequence, as in *Tōsei Montei Dokugin Nijikkasen* ("Twenty Solo Kasen Sequences by Tōsei's Disciples").
engo	("kindred word"), words associated with each other, by context and connotation.
fueki ryūkō	("constancy and change"), *fueki* refers to permanent values, that which never changes, and *ryūkō,* that which changes. For Bashō, both *fueki* and *ryūkō* were fundamental to true art.
fūga	("wind elegance"), poetic elegance, in poetry or prose. Bashō in later life said: "My *fūga* is like a fireplace in summer and a fan in winter."
fūgetsu	("wind moon"), the beauties of the natural world and natural scenery, and by association, of the poetic spirit that contemplates and evokes them. *fūgetsu no zai:* literary, poetic, or artistic talent.
fūkyō	("wind madness"), the dedication to art and experience of the poet or artist, which appears a form of madness to others; it implies deep involvement with the object of aesthetic attention.
fūryū	("drifting on the wind"), a term that originally referred to the pleasure derived from wine and women and song, and later to poetry, painting, music, calligraphy, and activities that reflect and nurture an inclination away from the mundane; implies an aesthetic distancing from the world of things, stylishness of an artistic kind.
hachō	("broken meter"), poems written with more (or fewer) than seventeen syllables.
haibun	("hai[kai] writing"), a narrative "in the haikai spirit" alternating prose and poetry in allusive, complementary arrangement.
haigō	the poetic pen name by which haikai poets were known.
haigon	("hai[kai] words"), vernacular Japanese words, sayings, colloquial phrases, Chinese compounds, Buddhist terms, which were rigorously excluded from the diction of

	Japanese classical poetry but which formed part of the innovations of *haikai* poetry.
haikai	("humorous," "playful"), a word that originally referred to certain poems collected in the Heian period anthology of waka poetry, the *Kokin Wakashū* ("Collection of Ancient and Modern Japanese Poetry"), which were termed *haikai-ka* ("humorous poems"). *Haikai* came eventually to denote a spirit of creative play with tradition and convention; the meaning and significance of a word or phrase derived from its playful relation to, and reinvention of, tradition. Both irreverence and reverence were intermingled in the skillful deployment of *haikai* words. *Haikai* elevated the unorthodox and was a modernizing, rejuvenating impulse in the Edo period.
haikai no renga	("playful linked verse," see "haikai"), comic or unorthodox *renga*.
haiku	the modern term for the *hokku,* which came into use in the late nineteenth century and gained currency through the influence of Masaoka Shiki (1867–1902). Bashō did not use the term *haiku.* The *haiku* is an autonomous poem of (usually) seventeen syllables (5-7-5), and (usually) with a *kigo* ("season word"). See "hokku."
hokku	("opening unit"), the first poem of a *renga* sequence. The seventeen-*on* or "syllable" (5-7-5) *hokku* responds to the specific circumstances of the *renga* gathering, and thus the requirement of a season word developed, as well as other features that led to its stand-alone independence from the rest of the *renga,* and eventually to its reconstitution as *haiku.*
honkadori	an allusion within a poem to an older poem (*honka:* "foundation poem"). In poetry contests, an element in the judging of poems was the skill with which a poet incorporated *honkadori,* and other poetic tropes, into a composition.
ji-amari	("excess characters"), the use of hypermetric *on* ("syllables"), or more than the usual limit of seventeen in *haiku,* or thirty-one in waka.
kana	The Japanese writing system consists of two phonetic *kana* syllabaries, *hiragana* and *katakana,* each of which

	represents all the sounds of the Japanese language; and Chinese characters called *kanji,* which are used for nouns and the "stem" components of verbs.
kakekotoba	("pivot word"), a word written in *hiragana* script rather than *kanji,* to bring out multiple possible meanings in a homonym.
kanji	the Chinese written characters used in Japanese.
karumi	Bashō's late style, plain in theme and light-hearted in tone. Bashō's described *karumi* thus: "My thinking now is as when looking at the sand in a shallow stream, both the shape of the poem and the mind light. Only when you reach that point, do things have meaning."
kasuri	a kind of wordplay in which one syllable of a word is replaced by a different syllable to create a new meaning.
kasen	("poetic saints"), a *renga* sequence of thirty-six verses. Bashō favored this form and helped make it the most popular form of *renga* in his day, and in Japan today. The number thirty-six derives from the *Thirty-Six Poetry Immortals* chosen by Fujiwara no Kintō (966–1041) as exemplars of Japanese poetry.
kigo	("season word"), Japanese poetry, and *haiku* in particular, has been intensely concerned with representing and codifying the seasons. The practice derives out of the composition of poems on set themes (*dai*), and the marking of the season developed into an integral part of the *renga* occasion. As the poetic tradition accumulated, the codification of seasonal representation took the form of manuals, illustrating by explication and example the *kigo* to evoke a specific time of year.
kireji	("cutting word"), a word used for emphasis, or to indicate conjecture, wonder, questioning, or for a heightened end to a verse (*ka, kana*). Other forms of *kireji* include verbal and adjectival suffixes (*-keri, -tsu, -ran, -ramu, -shi*) indicating probability, exclamation, and tenses such as the past and present perfect. When used in the middle of the verse, the *kireji* (*ya*) cuts the stream of thought into almost independent units, with an effect akin to the ambiguity contained in the English verb "to cleave," a word whose meanings point in opposite directions: to

divide; to conjoin. It is often represented in English by a dash, a hyphen, or an exclamation mark. This element in haiku has had a profound influence: on the film editing theories and practice of Sergei Eisenstein; and on English verse through the renovative energies of Imagism. Ezra Pound's imagist poem "In a Station of the Metro" drew on his awareness of the *kireji* to juxtapose, via a semicolon, two (almost) independent images.

kyōka ("mad poem"), a comic form of waka, popular in the Edo period.

on ("sound"), the individual sound units in Japanese poems, in English usually termed "syllable" but the term "mora" is preferred by linguists. The use of *onji,* an obsolete grammatical term in Japan, is erroneous and used only in foreign-language discussions of Japanese poetry.

renga ("linked song"), a collaborative form of poetry. At a *renga* gathering (two or more, and usually up to six people), each person in turn composes a poem, either of seventeen syllables (5-7-5) or fourteen (7-7), according to a set sequence. The *hokku,* the seventeen-syllable initiating poem, composed usually by the guest of honor, developed into the modern *haiku.* The *hokku* is followed by the fourteen-syllable *wakiku,* usually composed by the host of the gathering, and so on, in preordained but fluid sequence, each addition forming a new poetic microcosm with the previous element. The artistry lies in the depth and subtlety of the linking between stanzas.

renku ("linked units"), the term used for modern *renga,* and occasionally used retroactively to refer to *haikai no renga.*

sabi a beauty that emerges out of the old, the faded, the weathered, the unobtrusive, the lonely and tranquil. The noun *sabi* is related to the verb *sabu* ("to wane"), the adjective *sabishii* ("lonely"), and the homophone *sabi,* which means "rust" or "aged in quality."

tanka modern poems in the waka form.

Teimon (sometimes *Teitoku*), an early school of haikai founded by Matsunaga Teitoku (1571–1654).

utamakura ("song pillow"), a place with poetical associations, particularly with Japanese classical poetry.

wabi	a beauty that emerges out of the simple and unadorned, the modest and artless, impoverished and subdued, that rejects material and worldly concerns. The noun *wabi* is related to the verb *wabu* ("to languish"), the adjective *wabishii* ("spiritual loneliness").
waka	the principal form in Japanese Classical poetry, consisting of 31 syllables in 5-7-5-7-7. See *tanka*.
yūgen	mystery and depth, in medieval Japanese poetics a quality of profundity and reverberation produced by a poem's intertextual relationship with existing poems.
za	the *za* is the site and/or the participants (*renju*) in a *renga* session, and also denotes the atmosphere of collaboration and communality of a *renga* gathering.

BIBLIOGRAPHY

PRIMARY SOURCE

Kon, Eizō. *Bashō Ku Shū.* Tokyo: Shinchōsha, 1982.

BASHŌ'S POEMS: ORIGINAL SOURCES

The original sources of Bashō's poems in Kon Eizō's *Bashō Ku Shū,* in chronological order; number in parenthesis indicates an instance of secondary or other publication.

Sayo no Nakayama Shū (1664). In six volumes, compiled by Matsue Shigeyori. 2, 3.

Yoru no Nishiki (1666). Compiled by Fūko. 5, 6.

Zoku Yama no I (1667). Compiled by Koshun, and Kitamura Kigin (Koshun's father). 7–27, 29–33.

Yamato Junrei (1670). Compiled by Okamura Seishin. 36, 37.

Haikai Yabu ni Kō no Mono (1671). Compiled by Yoshida Yūji. 38.

Kai Ōi (1672). 39, 40.

Yamashita Mizu (1672). Compiled by Takase Baisei. 43.

Ise Odori Ondo Shū (1674). Compiled by Gatōan Sokan. 42.

Nyoihōju (1674). Compiled by Ogita Ansei. 28, 34, 35.

Chigiriki (1675). In five volumes, compiled by Hirooka Munenobu. 1, 4, 45–48.

Gojūban Ku Awase (1675). The text of a poetry contest judged by Naitō Rosen. 54, 55.

Zoku Renju (1676). Compiled by Kitamura Kigin. 49–52, 60, 61.

Haikai Imayō Otoko (1676). Compiled by Karakuken Chōchōshi. 56–58.

Edo Ryōgin Shū (1676). A collection by Bashō (under the name Tōsei) and Sodō (under the name Shinshō). 59.

Roppyakuban Haikai Hokku Awase (1677). The text of a poetry contest sponsored by Naitō Yoshimune (Fūko). 68–81, 83, 85, 87–89.

Haikai Edo Tōri-chō (1678). In two volumes, compiled by Shōkaken Jiyōshi. 82, 92, 94, 98, 100.

Haikai Edo Hirokōji (1678). Compiled by Fuboku. 63, 86, 91, 93, 95–97, 99.

Haikai Edo Sangin (1678). A three-hundred-verse (*sanbyakuin*) renga by Bashō (under the name Tōsei), Shintoku, and Sodō (under the name Shinshō), compiled by Shintoku (Itō Shintoku, 1633–98). 90.

Haikai Edo Jikkasen (1678). Compiled by Haruzumi. 101.

Chisoku Edo Shū Saitan o Utsusu (1679). New Year haikai anthology by Edo poets, compiled by Chisoku. 103.

Haikai Tamatebako (1679). Compiled by Karakuken Chōchōshi. 104.

Shirinkingyoku Shū (1679). A collection of twenty thousand poems, compiled by Kōri Muneshige. (5), (6).

Haikai Edo Ja no Sushi (1679). Compiled by Gonsui. 102, 105, 106.

Haikai Bandō Tarō (1679). Compiled by Saimaro. 107, 108, 111.

Shiba Zakana (c. 1680–81). Compiled by Jishun (Konishi Jishun).109.

Haikai Mukai no Oka (1680). Compiled by Fuboku. 64, 112–116, 120, 125.

Sakai Ginu (c. 1680). Compiled by Seison. 132.

Haikai Okure Sugoroku (1681). Compiled by Seifū. 142.

Haikai Azuma no Nikki [*Azuma Nikki*] (1681). In two volumes, compiled by Gonsui. 117, (118), 119, (121n), (122), 127, 128, (136), 137, 138, (139), 140, 143, (144), 145.

Musashiburi (1682). Compiled by Chiharu. 126, 146–148, (152).

Tenna Ninen Saitan Hokku Chō (1682). A collection of New Year hokku, compiled by Bashō and printed by the *hangiya* (block cutter) Matabei. 151.

Minashiguri (1683). In two volumes, compiled by Kikaku, with postscript by Bashō. 149, 150, 155, 156, (157), 159, (160), (161), 163, 164, (165), 166–168.

Fuyu no Hi (1684). Bashō School anthology, compiled by Kakei. 223.

Heiin Kikō (1686). Written by Fūbaku. 189.

Kikaku Saitan Chō (1686). Compiled by Kikaku. (261).

Haikai Hitotsubashi (1686). Compiled by Seifū. 267.

Kawazu Awase ("Frog Contest"; 1686). Compiled by Senka. 270.

Zoku Minashiguri (1687). Compiled by Kikaku. 256, 263, (279), 284, (285), (286), 287, 292, 294, (295), (296), 299, (301), 307, 308, 317–319.

Atsume Ku (1687). Collection of hokku and haibun by Bashō. (142), 165, 172, 222, (229), 258, 260–262, (267), 268, (270), 272, 274, (275), 276, 277, 279, 280, 285, 288, 289, (294), 295, 296, 298, (301), 302, 304, (305), 306, (317).

Hitotsu Matsu (1687). Compiled by Shōhaku. (214), (258), (272), (275), (276), 283.

Jokōshi (1687). Compiled by Jokō. 336.

Kashima Mōde (1687). 310–316.

Tsuzuki no Hara (1688). Compiled by Fuboku. 176, 291.

Sarashina Kikō (1688–89; published in 1709, as part of *Oi no Kobumi*). 445 (1), 448–452, (453), 454–457.

Sarashina Kikō Shinseki Sōkō. Bashō's *Sarashina Kikō* manuscript. (457).

Arano (1689). Compiled by Kakei. (121), 331, 334, (384), 415, (421), (431), 434, 436, 445 (2), (465), 469, 482.

Bashō-ō Tsuki Ichiya Jūgo Ku (1689). A set of fifteen haiku written by Bashō on the fifteenth of the Eighth Month while visiting Tsuruga, as recorded by Keikō, of Ōgaki (one poem is missing). 561, 562n, 563, 564, (565), 566–568, (569), (570), (571), 572, 573, 577.

Haikai Shinobuzuri (1689). Compiled by Sagara Tōkyū. 460, (504).

Haikai Zengo En (1689). Compiled by Gonsui. 419.

Hisago (1690). Bashō School anthology, ed. Shadō. 615.

Amego (1690). Compiled by Shidō. 646.

Sono Fukuro (1690). Compiled by Ransetsu. 374, 562, (608).

Hanatsumi (1690). Haikai diary by Kikaku. 339, 590, 606, 607, 609, 617, 621.

Itsu o Mukashi (1690). Compiled by Kikaku. 303, 309, 418, 479, (603).

Shinsen Miyakoburi (1690). Compiled by Gonsui. 349–352.

Saga Nikki (written in 1691; published in 1753). 694–699, 701–703.

Sarumino (1691). Compiled by Kyorai and Bonchō. 411, 424, 481, 515, 569, 594, (610), 618, (620), 625, (629), 634, 636, (642), (643), 651, 654, 655, 662, 664, 678, 681, 685, 686, 692, 693, 700, 704.

Haikai Kanjinchō (1691). Compiled by Rotsū. 281, 588, 605, 661, 663, 665, 667, 679.

Genroku Yonen Haikai Mitsumonozukushi (1691). Printed by Izutsuya Shōbei. (670).

Nishi no Kumo (1691). Compiled by Besshō, to commemorate his brother, Kosugi Isshō. (707), (715), 720, (721).

Utatsu Shū (1691). Compiled by Hokushi, of Kanazawa. 554, 635.

Iro Sugihara (1691). Compiled by Kanbe Yūkin, of Kanazawa. 677.

Kuzu no Matsubara (1692). A collection of essays on poetry by Shikō (contains the background to Bashō's "frog" poem, 270). 706, 729, (754), 755, (761), 762, 763.

Hairin Ichiji Yūran Shū (1692). Compiled by Sentoku. (300), 757.

Hahasohara Shū (1692). Compiled by Kukū, of Kanazawa. 555, 712.

Kisaragi (1692). Compiled by Sueyori. (749).

Ono ga Hi (1692). Compiled by Shayō. (172), 613, 637, (638), 639, 652, 668, 674, (676), 690, 726, 752, 756.

Zōdan Shū (1692). Written by Kikaku. 727.

Haikai Hakugan (1692). Compiled by Muroga Tetsushi. (743).

Haikai Yaezakura Shū (1692). Compiled by Jiyū. 669.

Kita no Yama (1692). Compiled by Kukū. 753.

Ryokan Nikki (1692–93). Kyoriku's Diary. 766, (790), 791.

Haikai Komojishi Shū (1693). Compiled by Hasui. 576, 673, 780, 783, (787), (788), 789.

Wasure Ume (Preface written in 1692; published in 1777). Compiled by Shōhaku. (464), 682, 728.

Hagi no Tsuyu (1693). Compiled by Kikaku. 810.

Nagaregawa Shū (1693). Compiled by Sawa Rosen. 751, 764.

Haikai Fukagawa. (1693). Compiled by Shadō. 771, 778, 786.

Momo no Mi (1693). Compiled by Sakurai Kōppō. 759.

Sarayama (1693). Compiled by Kōsetsu. (633).

Hirune no Tane (1694). Compiled by Kakei. 565.

Ku Kyōdai (1694). Compiled by Kikaku. (298), 784, 814, (874).

Hari Bukuro (1694). Compiled by Yūō. 929.

Fuji no Mi (1694). Compiled by Sogyū. 583, 797, 802, 818.

Haikai Betsuzashiki (1694). Compiled by Shisan. 853–856, 860, (862).

Ichi no Iori (1694). Compiled by Shadō. 822, 871.

Sono Tayori (1694). Compiled by Deisoku, preface by Kikaku, postscript by Ransetsu. 829, 833, 882, 916, 920.

Sumidawara (1694). One of the most important collections of the Bashō School. Compiled by Yaba, Kooku, and Rigyū. (821), 824, 828, 831, 836, (839), 841, 846, 848, (849), 851.

Kogarashi (1695). Compiled by Kochū and Rokaku. 273, 709, (925n), 931.

Bashō-ō Gyōjōki (1695). Compiled by Rotsū. 857n, 858, 859.

Yahagi Zutsumi (1695). Compiled by Suigin. 932.

Oi Nikki (1695). Compiled by Shikō, as a sequel to *Oi no Kobumi*, and includes an account of Bashō's death. 226, 245, (302), 325, (332), 371, 372, 425, (426), 427, 428, (429), 430, (432), (433), 435, 442, 446, 447, 458, 459, 545, 584, 585, 592, (601), 624, 645, 650, 653, 714, 718, 725, 731, 733, 738–740, 742, 793, 809, 812, 813, (837), 844, (863), (865), (866), 868, 875, 878, 879, 881, 884, 885, (886), 889–891, 900, (906), (907), (910), 913, (916n), 917, 918, 921, 922, (925), 933, 934.

Nochi no Tabi (1695). Compiled by Jokō. 213, 480, 578, (580), 581, 736, 737, 796.

Atsuta Shiwabako Monogatari (Postscript written in 1695, published in 1696). Compiled by Tōtō. 218, 219, 249.

Ariso Umi (1695). Compiled by Rōka. 360, 758, (864), (876), 893, 930.

Sumiyoshi Monogatari (1695–96?). Compiled by Seiryū. 235, 819, (912).

Mutsu Chidori (the journey to Mutsu, 1696; published in August, 1697). Compiled by Tōrin. 760, 773, (857), (867), 947, 948.

Bashō-an Kobunko (1696). Compiled by Fumikuni. 391, 392, 467, 680, 705, 716, 717, (722), 748, 779, 792, (804), (805), 806, (807), 842n, (926), (927), 939–945.

Momo Neburi Shū (1696). Compiled by Rotsū, preface by Chōsui. (248), 476.

Haikai Okinagusa (1696). Compiled by Riho. 134, 675, 815, (923), 935–938.

Hatsusemi (1696). Compiled by Fūkoku. 290, (640), 689.

Ukiyo no Kita (1696). Compiled by Kagin. 767, 774.

Ura Wakaba (1697). Compiled by Kikaku. 266, 794, (924).

Hashimori (1697). Compiled by Kakei. (474).

Hashira Goyomi (1697). Compiled by Kakusei. (262).

Infutagi (1697). Compiled by Riyū and Kyoriku. 423, 461, 671, (732), 770, 776, 777, 799n, 800, 811n, 949, 950.

Tori no Michi (1697). Compiled by Soshōshi Genbai. 53, 883, 946.

Kiku no Ka (1697). Compiled by Fūkoku. 909.

Katami no Dai (1698). Compiled by Shōsei and Kyōshi. 659.

Hentsuki (1698). Compiled by Riyū and Kyoriku. (781).

Zoku Sarumino (1698). In two parts: renga in part one, and part two devoted to hokku by various poets, compiled by Senpo, and (later, partially) Bashō and Shikō. 484, (744), 772, 782, 799, 801, 803, 811, (816), 823, 826, 827, 832, 838, 843, 845, 847, 861, 877, (880), 888, 892, 894, 898, 899, 901, 902, 904, 905.

Zoku Ariso Umi (1698). Compiled by Rōka. 953.

Okurebase Shū (1698). Compiled by Shusetsu. 593.

Hakusen Shū (1698). Six-volume collection of Bashō, ed. Fūkoku. 241, 242, 321, 553, (589), 641, 648, 745, 840, 872, 873, 891n, (908), 951, 952.

Hakusen Shū Kakiire. Supplementary comments by Morikawa Kyoriku on errors in *Hakusen Shū.* 834.

Haikai Dategoromo (1699). Compiled by Sagara Tōkyū. (507).

Kyō no Mukashi (1699). Compiled by Yomoro Shusetsu (Sakamoto Shusetsu). 808.

Haikai Soga (1699). Compiled by Hakusetsu. 492, 957, 958.

Cha no Sōshi (1699). Compiled by Yukimaru (Suya Yukimaru), and Tōsen (Ōta Tōsen 1678–1725). 110, 187, 466, 622, 741, 954–956.

Saika Shū (1699). Compiled by Shikō. 750, 897, 959.

Zoku Betsuzashiki (1700). Compiled by Shisan. 835, 960.

Kusa no Michi (1700). Compiled by Uka and Saryū. 852.

Hadaka Mugi (1700). Compiled by Sobei. 962.

Haikai Sōan Shū (1700). Compiled by Kukū. 713.

Ara Oda (1701). Compiled by Shara. 775, 964.

Hanashidori Shū (1701). Compiled by Banryū. 961.

Shōbikin (1701). Compiled by Kikaku. 293, 602.

Suna Tsubame (1701). Compiled by Sunko, with a preface by Shikō. 386.

Tōzai Yawa (1702). Compiled by Shikō. 708.

Matsu no Nami (1702). Compiled by Shayō. 914, 915.

Uda no Hōshi (1702). Compiled by Riyū and Kyoriku. 842.

Sono Kogarashi (1701). Compiled by Tansai. (478), 963.

Oku no Hosomichi ([1689] 1702). 483, 485, 490, 491, (495), 497, 499, 503, (505), 506, 509–513, (515), 516, 518–520, (521), 522, 523, 526–529, 533, 534, 536, 537, 539, (540), 543, 544, 546–549, 551, 552, 557, (558), 559, 560, (569), 570, 574, 575, 586.

Sora Kakitome (1689). Sora's Notebook from the *Oku no Hosomichi* journey, included in the longer *Sora Tabi Nikki*. 486, (487), 488, (489), 493, 494, 498, (500), 508, 524, 525, 532, (535), 541, (550).

Sora Tabi Nikki (1689). Sora's travel diary from the *Oku no Hosomichi* journey. 501, 502.

Sora-bon Oku no Hosomichi. Sora's copy of Bashō's *Oku no Hosomichi* manuscript, with significant differences from the completed version. 517.

Hakuba (also known by the alternative pronunciation *Shiro Uma*; 1702). Compiled by Shadō and Masahide. 623, 965.

Yawagurui (1703). Compiled by Uchū. 265.

Soba no Furuhata (1703). Compiled by Baiin. 611, 612.

Makitsu-an Iri Nikki (1703). The diary of Makitsu-an Unrei. 967.

Wataridori Shū (1704). Compiled by Kyorai and Ushichi. 966.

Kiso no Tani (1704). Compiled by Taisui. 968.

Asō (1704). Compiled by Hanpu. 672.

Gojūshigun (c. 1704). Compiled by Senchiku. 178–181.

Hōnō Shū (1704). Compiled by Bokusetsu, Teifu and Rikushi. (604).

Yadori no Matsu (1705). Compiled Butsuyo Jokyū. 969.

Senryō Fu (1705). Compiled by Hyakuri. 62.

Sugi Maruta (1705). Compiled by Itō Saetsu. 817.

Kiku no Chiri (1706). Compiled by Sonome. (366), 919, 970.

Haikai Urushijima (1706). Compiled by Urushijima-ken Hakusen. 579.

Ruikōji (1707). In three volumes, compiled by Senshū, Shūshiki (also known as Shūshikijo) and Seiryū. 353, 971.

Shō-ō Ku Shū (1709). Chronological collection of Bashō poems, ed. Dohō. (153), (186), (278), (305), (377), (378), 414, 614, 644, 647, 657, 711, 973–975.

Shō-ō Ku Shū Sōkō (c. 1709). Compiled by Dohō. 359, 361, 710, 895.

Oi no Kobumi (Journey, October 1687 to April 1688; book presumed to have been completed in 1690; published in 1709). Compiled by Otokuni. 320, 322–324, 326, (328), 337, 338, 339n, 340, 342, 344, 345, (346), 357, 358, 362–365, (367), 368–370, (373), (374), (376), 379–383, 385, 387–390, 393–400, 403–410.

Funagura Shū (1710). Compiled by Tōsui. 244.

Haikai Awazuhara (1710). Published to commemorate the seventeenth anniversary of Bashō's death, compiled by Taihakudō Tōō ([Amano] Tōrin). 972.

Sanzan Gashū (1710). Compiled by Tōsui. (530).

Haikai Chidorigake (1712). Compiled by Chisoku. 246, 247, (297), 335, 437, 438, 440.

Hana no Ichi (1712). Compiled by Sunboku. 211.

Shakubikan (1717). In three volumes, compiled by Etsujin. 182, 330.

Haikai Shifukutsui (1719) Compiled by Keikaen Tōjo. 571.

Kako no Watari (1722). Compiled by Tankai. 976.

Yūgao no Uta (1722). Compiled by Saida and Ennyū. 649.

Haikai Bashō Darai (1724). Compiled by Shusetsu and Yūri (the anthology takes its title from 148, *darai* or *tarai* meaning 'tub'). 656.

Mizu no Tomo (1724). Compiled by Kubota Shōhi. 169.

Kamakura Kaidō (1725). Compiled by Senbairin Asei. (333).

Mittsu no Kao (1726). Compiled by Etsujin. 343, 416, 444, 977.

Iga no Ubuyu (1727). Compiled by Ōta Seisei. 666.

Hatsu Nasubi (1728). Compiled by Goten. 487.

Niwakamado Shū (1728). Compiled by Etsujin. 462, 463, 470.

Neko no Mimi (1729). Compiled by Etsujin. 443.

Bashō-an Mikazuki Nikki (1730). Originally compiled by Bashō himself; later compiled by Shikō, before publication. (769).

Haikai Ame no Hikazu (1737). Compiled by Sekishitsu. 746.

Yuki Maruge (1737). Compiled by Sora (revised version: *Yuki Maroge*, ed. Rankō, 1783). (471), 472, (477), 496, (542).

Bashō Ku Sen (1739). Compiled by Kajaku. (591).

Yuki no Mune (Preface, 1743; published in 1744). Compiled by Inoue Kanka. 798.

Yuki no Obana (1744). Compiled by Chosha Yūgo. 747.

Bashō Ku Sen Shūi (1756). Compiled by Kanji. 193, (306), (596), 619, (626), 795.

Ōu no Nikki (1757). Written by Nanreian Baishi. (531).

Karo Ichiro (1757). Compiled by Chōsui. 204.

Tōsen Ichiro (1758). Compiled by Chōsui. 4.

Chishū Hokku Shū (1758). Compiled by Tōshū and Mijin. 600.

Shō-ō Zenden (1762). Biography of Bashō by Kawaguchi Chikujin, based on a manuscript by Dohō. 65–67, 230, 231, 375, 595, 597, 598, 616, 660, (683), 684, 687, 691, (830), 850, 869, 870, 896, 903.

Shō-ō Zenden Furoku. A supplement to *Shō-ō Zenden*, by Chikujin. 514.

Bashō-ō Shinseki Shū (1764). Compiled by Matsumura Tōkyō. (928).

Nozarashi Kikō (Journey, August 1684 to April 1685; the book was completed by 1687; published in 1768). 190–192, 194–203, 205–207, 209, 210, 212, 216, 217, 220, 221, (223), 224, 225, 227–229, 232, 233, 236–240, 243, 250–252, 254, 255, 257.

Nozarashi Kikō Gakan. Illustrated edition of *Nozarashi Kikō* by Nakagawa Jokushi. 348.

Nemu no Ibiki (1769). Compiled by Chiyokura Chyōra. (327).

Aki no Hi (1772). Compiled by Kyōtai. (441).

Atsuta San Kasen (1775). Compiled by Kyōtai. 341.

Sanzōshi ([1702/1703] 1776). Three volumes ("White," "Red," and "Black" book-lets) collecting Bashō's teachings, written by Dohō. The most accurate record of Bashō's ideas about poetry. 730, 911, (911n).

Zoku Kangiku (1780). Compiled by Kyōro. 723, 979, 980.

Bashō Sanpū Ryōgin Hyakuin (1786). A hundred-verse (*hyakuin*) renga by Bashō and Sanpū, compiled by Kanbi. (84).

Kashima Kikō ([1687] 1790). A version of *Kashima Mōde*, with additional poems by Bashō and others, compiled by Baijin. 183, 468.

Kyorai-bumi (1791). A collection of letters on haikai matters, with selections of haikai poetry, compiled by Ganshi. 475.

Zoku Fukagawa Shū (1791). Compiled by Baijin. 123, 124, 135, 141, (162), 170, 184, 185, 188, (268), 354–356.

Katada Shū (1798). Compiled by Kayū. 719.

Yūran Shū (1799). Compiled by Kyōtai. 253, 473.

Kasei Shū (1807). Compiled by Ikuga. 264, 269.

Mitsuwagumi (1833). Compiled by Ippū. (158).

Hana Namasu (1834). Compiled by Tōkan Jakujin. 282.

Haikai Ishizuri Makimono (1842). Compiled by Syōeiken Senshi. 173, (259), 439, 582.

LETTERS

Letter to Bokuin (March 20, 1682). 152–154.

Letter to Jakushō (Spring, 1687). 297.

Letter to Ensui (April 25, 1688). 413.

Letter to Shōhaku (December 5, 1688). 464, 465.

Letter to Tōyō (February 2, 1689). 478.

Letter to Ka-un (late April, 1689). 504, 507.

Letters to Sanpū: (December 13, 1687): (344); (September 22, 1689): 591; (February 7, 1692): 754; (intercalary May 21, 1694): 867; (June 24, 1694): 874, (875n), 876, 880; (September 10, 1694): 906–908.

Letter to Mangikumaru (Tokoku) (Winter, 1689). 599.

Letters to Dosui: (April 10, 1690[?]): 630; (September 27, 1690): 658.

Letter to Shadō (April 16, 1690). 631, 632.

Letter to Koharu (June 20, 1690). 638.

Letter to Kukū (Autumn, 1691). (712).

Letters to Bashidō (Kyokusui): (September 6, 1690): (639), (652); (November 13, 1691): (746); (late December, 1692): 785; (September 25, 1694): (914).

Letters to Kyoriku: (October 9, 1693): 816, 821; (June 15, 1694): (871).

Letters from Kyorai: (May 14, 1694): 820; (January 29, 1694): 842n.

Letters to Keikō: (April 29, 1693): (797); (November 8, 1693): 825, (828).

Letter to Isen (Ensui) and Dohō (September 23, 1694). 910.

Letter to Masahide (September 25, 1694). 911n, 912.

OTHER SOURCES

Awazu Bunko Shō. Yearbook of Gichū-ji, the temple where Bashō is buried. 978.

Bashō-ō Shinseki Shūi. A collection of copies of Bashō manuscripts, ed. Daichū. 412, 556.

Chisoku Denrai Kakitomekō. A collection of notes handed down in the Shimo-zato Chisoku family. 130.

Dohō-bon Shō-ō Zenden. (599), 688.

Futami Bundai Zu (written on the underside of a *bundai*, a small desk of pau-lownia wood, said to have been used by Bashō himself, the top of which features a depiction of the seascape at Futami-ga-ura). (479).

Kaishi ("pocket paper," special sheets of washi paper for writing down poems, originally for waka and for use at renga gatherings). 139 (copy), 149, (150), (151), 160, 174, 175, (196), (197), (202), 208, 234, (236), (237), (238), (239), 248, (258), 259, (260), (266), (267), (270), 271, 278, (280), (294), (295), (298), 300, 301, (302), (306), (317), (320), 327–329, 332, 333, (345), 346, (357), (364), 366, 367, 373, (374), 376–378, 384, (387), (393), (396), 401 (copy), 402 (copy), (410), 417 (copy), (419 [copy]), 420 (copy), 421 (copy), 426, 429, 431–433, (437), 474, 495, 500, 521, 530, 535, 538, (539), (540), 542, (544), (546), (548), (549), 550, 558, (569), 580, (586), (588), 589, (594), 601, (615), 620, (629), 640, 643, 670, 676, (678), 683, 707, 715, 721, 722, 734, 743, 744, 788, 804, 830, 857, 862–864, 866, (868), 926, (944).

Kaishi, by Rotsū (1688). 471.

Kaishi, by Tōsai (1689). (576).

Kaishi, by Chigetsu (1689). 604.

Kasen Kaishi, by Shōhaku (1688). 422.

Kasen Scroll (July 20, 1688), by Kakei. 441.

Kasen Scroll. 477, (847).

Koiya Denrai Yokomono. Scroll handed down in the Sugiyama Sanpū family. 765.

Kugire (a form of manuscript). (150), (151), (167), (168), (199), (270), (346), (477), (499), 642, (655).

Kukō Dankan ("manuscript fragment"). 131.

Matsushima Chōbō Shū. A selection of poems about Matsushima, compiled by Ōyodo Michikaze. 133.

Ōka Bunshū. Compiled by Bokuin. 215.

Omoterokku (a manuscript of six poems, including one of Bashō's). (477).

Miscellaneous Bashō Holographs. (190), (191), (198), (437), (540), 608, (611), (612), (613), 626, 628, (676).

Poems on Drawings/Paintings (*Bashō's own painting; +attributed to Bashō). 118, (121), (121*), 121n*, (142), (156*), (173), (195*), (196*), (214*), (242+), (270*), 275*, (280*), (317*), (317), (320*), (320), (323*), 347, (387*), (387), (393*), (448), (479), 531, (546*), (546), 596, 603*, 627+, 633*, (692*), (700*), (715*), 724*, 732, 735*, 749*, (770), (776*), 781*, 787*, (790), 790*, 805*, 807*, (824), 837*, (839), 839*, (865), 865*, (907*), 924, 925*, 925n, 927*.

Poems on Fans. (267), (294), (615), (823), 923, (927).

Shikishi (a square card, with a poem or painting on it). (156), (280), (282), (314), (320), (477), 489, (540), 587, (594), 610, 849 (copy).

Shō-ō Bun Shū. Compiled by Dohō. 768.

Tanzaku (rectangular cards, usually 36 cm long and 6 cm wide, for the writing down of poems in calligraphic form). (1), 44, 84, (106), 121, (121n), 122, (127), 129, 136, (139), (142), 144, (148), (156), 157, 158, 161, 162, (164), (168), 171, 177, 186, (195), (208), (214), (217), (224), (229), (240), (270), (276), (285), 286, (288), (294), (296), 305, (323), (379), (381), (415), (421), (431), (433), 453, (499), 505, (528), (529), 540, (571), (615), (623), 629, (678), (749), (752), 761, 769, (776), (824), (839), (841), 886, 887, 928, (944).

Tatefuku (a type of hanging scroll). (546).

REFERENCES

Arashiyama, Kōzaburō. *Akuto Bashō.* Tokyo: Shinchosha, 2006.

Akutagawa, Ryūnosuke. *Rashōmon and Seventeen Other Stories.* Translated by Jay Rubin. New York: Penguin, 2006.

Carter, Steven D. "On a Bare Branch: Bashō and the Haikai Profession." *American Oriental Society* 117, no. 1 (January–March 1997): pp. 57–69.

Cooper, Arthur, trans. *Li Po and Tu Fu.* New York: Penguin, 1973.

Dryden, John. *The Works of Virgil: Containing His Pastorals, Georgics and Aeneis* (1697), *Aeneis,* book 6, lines 1173–75.

Fraleigh, Matthew. "At the Borders of Chinese Literature: Poetic Exchange in the Nineteenth-Century Sinosphere." *Oxford Handbook of Modern Chinese Literatures,* edited by Carlos Rojas and Andrea Bachner, pp. 372–98. Oxford: Oxford University Press, 2016.

Hamill, Sam, trans. *Crossing the Yellow River: Three Hundred Poems from the Chinese.* Rochester, NY: BOA, 2000.

Hasegawa Kai. "The Haiku Universe: On Nature." *Modern Haiku* 47, no. 3 (Autumn 2016): pp. 36–44.

Hearn, Lafcadio. *Exotics and Retrospectives and In Ghostly Japan.* Boston: Houghton Mifflin, 1922.

Hinton, David, trans. *The Selected Poems of Tu Fu.* New York: New Directions, 1989.

Katō, Shūichi. *A History of Japanese Literature,* vol. 2. Tokyo: Kodansha, 1979.

Lau, D. C., trans. *Confucius: The Analects.* New York: Penguin, 1979.

McCraw, David R. *Du Fu's Laments from the South.* Honolulu: University of Hawaii Press, 1992.

McCullough, Helen Craig. *Classical Japanese Prose: An Anthology.* Stanford, CA: Stanford University Press, 1990.

———. *Kokin Wakashū: The First Imperial Anthology of Japanese Poetry.* Stanford, CA: Stanford University Press, 1985.

McKinney, Meredith, trans. *Kenkō and Chōmei: Essays in Idleness and Hōjōki.* New York: Penguin, 2013.

Miner, Earl. "Bashō's Laughter and Saikaku's Tears." *Kyoto Conference on Japanese Studies 1994 II* (pub. 1996): pp. 255–64. http://doi.org/10.15055/00003520.

Okada, H. Richard. *Figures of Resistance: Language, Poetry and Narrating in "The Tale of Genji" and Other Mid-Heian Texts.* Durham, NC: Duke University Press, 1991.

Ogata, Tsutomu, et al., eds. *Teihon Bashō Taisei.* Tokyo: Sanseidō, 1962.

Richey, Jeffrey L., ed. *Daoism in Japan: Chinese Traditions and Their Influence on Japanese Religious Culture.* New York: Routledge, 2015.

Rimer, J. Thomas, and Jonathan Chaves, trans. *Japanese and Chinese Poems to Sing: The Wakan rōei shū.* New York: Columbia University Press, 1997.

Schalow, Paul Gordon. "The Invention of a Literary Tradition of Male Love: Kitamura Kigin's *Iwatsutsuji.*" *Monumenta Nipponica* (Sophia University) 48, no. 1 (Spring 1993): pp. 1–31.

Shirane, Haruo, ed. *Early Modern Japanese Literature: An Anthology, 1600–1900.* New York: Columbia University Press, 2002.

———. "Matsuo Bashō and the Poetics of Scent." *Harvard Journal of Asiatic Studies* 52, no. 1 (June 1992): pp. 77–110.

———. *Traces of Dreams: Landscape, Cultural Memory and the Poetry of Bashō.* Stanford, CA: Stanford University Press, 1998.

Shirane, Haruo, and Tomi Suzuki, eds., with David Lurie. *The Cambridge History of Japanese Literature.* Cambridge: Cambridge University Press, 2016.

Shively, Donald H. "Bashō: The Man and the Plant." *Harvard Journal of Asiatic Studies* 16, no. 1/2 (June 1953): pp. 146–61.

Tyler, Royall, trans. *The Tale of Genji.* New York: Viking Penguin, 2001.

———, trans. *The Tale of the Heike.* New York: Viking Penguin, 2012.

Ueda, Makoto. *Bashō and His Commentators: Selected Hokku with Commentary.* Stanford, CA: Stanford University Press, 1992.

Watson, Burton, trans. *The Complete Works of Zhuangzi*. New York: Columbia University Press, 2013.

———, trans. *Po Chü-i: Selected Poems*. New York: Columbia University Press, 2000.

———, trans. *The Selected Poems of Du Fu*. New York: Columbia University Press, 2002.

Yang, Jingqing. *The Chan Interpretations of Wang Wei's Poetry: A Critical Review*. Hong Kong: Chinese University Press, 2007.

BASHŌ: SELECTED ENGLISH TRANSLATIONS

Barnhill, David Landis. *Bashō's Haiku: Selected Poems of Matsuo Bashō*. Albany: State University of New York Press, 2004.

———. *Bashō's Journey: The Literary Prose of Matsuo Bashō*. Albany: State University of New York Press, 2005.

Blyth, R. H. *Haiku*. 4 vols. Tokyo: Hokuseido Press, 1949–52.

———. *The Genius of Haiku*. Tokyo: Hokuseido Press, 1995.

Carter, Steven D. *Matsuo Bashō: Travel Writings*. Cambridge, MA: Hackett, 2020.

Hamill, Sam. *Matsuo Bashō: Narrow Road to the Interior and Other Writings*. Boulder, CO: Shambhala, 2019.

Hass, Robert, ed. *The Essential Haiku: Versions of Bashō, Buson and Issa*. Hopewell, NJ: Ecco Press, 1994.

Miyamori, Asatarō. *Classic Haiku: An Anthology of Poems by Bashō and His Followers*. Mineola, NY: Dover, 2002.

Reichhold, Jane. *Basho: The Complete Haiku*. New York: Kodansha USA, 2008.

Oseko, Toshiharu. *Basho's Haiku*. 2 vols. Tokyo: Maruzen, 1990/1996.

Sato, Hiroaki. *Bashō's Narrow Road: Spring and Autumn Passages*. New York: Stone Bridge Press, 1996.

Stryk, Lucien. *On Love and Barley: Haiku of Basho*. New York: Penguin, 1985.

Ueda, Makoto. *Matsuo Bashō: The Master Haiku Poet*. Tokyo: Kodansha, 1970. (A biographical study of the poet, including some translations of hokku, and renga sequences.)

Yuasa, Nobuyuki. *Matsuo Bashō: The Narrow Road to the Deep North and Other Travel Sketches*. New York: Penguin, 1966.

INDEX OF POEMS IN JAPANESE (ROMAJI)

Numbers refer to poems.

*aa haru haru / ōinaru kana / haru to un
      nun* 112

*achi kochi ya / menmen sabaki / yanagi
      gami* 26

ajisai ya / katabiradoki no / usuasagi 947

ajisai ya / yabu o koniwa no / betsuzashiki
      856

*akaaka to / hi wa tsurenaku mo / aki no
      kaze* 546

*akebono wa / mada murasaki ni /
      hototogisu* 627

akebono ya / shirauo shiroki / koto issun 217

*akeyukuya / nijūshichiya mo / mika no
      tsuki* 275

aki chikaki / kokoro no yoru ya / yojōhan
      883

*aki fukaki / tonari wa nani o / suru hito
      zo* 921

*akikaze ni / orete kanashiki / kuwa no
      tsue* 812

akikaze no / fukedomo aoshi / kuri no iga
      709

*akikaze no / yarido no kuchi ya /
      togarigoe* 13

*akikaze ya / kiri ni ugokite / tsuta no
      shimo* 730

*akikaze ya / yabu mo hatake mo / Fuwa
      no seki* 210

*aki ki ni keri / mimi o tazunete / makura
      no kaze* 79

*aki kinu to / tsuma kou hoshi ya / shika
      no kawa* 98

*aki mo haya / baratsuku ame ni / tsuki no
      nari* 913

*aki ni soute / yukabaya sue wa /
      Komatsugawa* 773

*aki no iro / nukamiso tsubo mo /
      nakarikeri* 712

*aki no kaze / Ise no hakahara / nao
      sugoshi* 590

*aki no yo o / uchikuzushitaru / hanashi
      kana* 914

*aki o hete / chō mo nameru ya / kiku no
      tsuyu* 442

*aki suzushi / tegoto ni muke ya / uri
      nasubi* 547

aki totose / kaette Edo o / sasu kokyō 191

*Akokuso no / kokoro mo shirazu / ume no
      hana* 359

*ama no kao / mazu miraruru ya / keshi
      no hana* 406

*ama no ya wa / koebi ni majiru / itodo
      kana* 655

ame no hi ya / seken no aki o / Sakai-chō 99

ame oriori / omou koto naki / sanae kana
      968

ano kumo wa / inazuma o matsu / tayori
kana 436
ano naka ni / maki-e kakitashi / yado no
tsuki 449
aoku temo / arubeki mono o / tōgarashi
771
aoyagi no / doro ni shidaruru / shiohi
kana 851
aozashi ya / kusamochi no ho ni /
idetsuran 168
ara nani tomo na ya / kinō wa sugite /
fukutojiru 90
arare kiku ya / kono mi wa moto no /
furugashiwa 170
arare majiru / katabirayuki wa / komon
kana 22
arare seba / ajiro no hio o / nite dasan 606
Arashiyama / yabu no shigeri ya / kaze no
suji 695
ara tōto / aoba wakaba no / hi no hikari
490
araumi ya / Sado ni yokotau / Ama-
nogawa 540
ariake mo / misoka ni chikashi / mochi no
oto 837
arigataki / sugata ogaman / kakitsubata
413
arigata ya / yuki o kaorasu / Minamidani
526
asacha nomu / sō shizukanari / kiku no
hana 656
asagao ni / ware wa meshi kū / otoko
kana 156
asagao wa / heta no kaku sae / aware nari
309
asagao wa / sakamori shiranu / sakari
kana 447
asagao ya / hiru wa jō orosu / mon no
kaki 807
asagao ya / kore mo mata waga / tomo
narazu 808
Asamutsu ya / tsukimi no tabi no /
akebanare 562
asana asana / tenarai susumu / kirigirisu
967
asatsuyu ni / yogorete suzushi / uri no
tsuchi 877

asa yosa o / taga Matsushima zo /
kata-gokoro 476
ashi arōte / tsui akeyasuki / marone kana
412
asobi kinu / fuku tsurikanete / shichi ri
made 218
asu no tsuki / ame uranawan / Hina-ga-
dake 564
asu wa chimaki / Naniwa no kareha /
yume nare ya 75
atsuki hi o / umi ni iretari / Mogamigawa
533
Atsumiyama ya / Fukūra kakete /
yūsuzumi 537
awa hie ni / toboshiku mo arazu / kusa no
io 441
ayamegusa / ashi ni musuban / waraji no
o 513
ayame oi keri / noki no iwashi no /
sarekōbe 96
ayu no ko no / shirauo okuru / wakare
kana 484

bashōba o / hashira ni kaken / io no tsuki
768
bashō nowaki shite / tarai ni ame o / kiku
yo kana 148
bashō uete / mazu nikumu ogi no / futaba
kana 141
bii to naku / shirigoe kanashi / yoru no
shika 906
Biwakō no / yo ya samisen no / oto arare 213
botan shibe fukaku / wake izuru hachi no
/ nagori kana 254
bushōsa ya / dakiokosaruru / haru no
ame 685n
bushōsa ya / kakiokosareshi / haru no
ame 685
byōbu ni wa / yama o egaite / fuyugomori
598
byōgan no / yosamu ni ochite / tabine
kana 654

chichi haha no / shikirini koishi / kiji no
koe 394
chidori tachi / fukeyuku shoya no / hieoro-
shi 666

chimaki yū / katate ni hasamu / hitaigami
    704
chi ni taore / ne ni yori hana no / wakare
    kana 269
chiru hana ya / tori mo odoroku / koto no
    chiri 924
chisa wa mada / aoba nagara ni /
    nasubijiru 863
chō mo kite / su o sū kiku no / namasu
    kana 657
chō no ha no / ikutabi koyuru / hei no
    yane 619
chō no tobu / bakari nonaka no / hikage
    kana 245
Chōshō no / haka mo meguru ka /
    hachitataki 603
chō tori no / uwatsukitatsu ya / hana no
    kumo 969
chō yo chō yo / morokoshi no / haikai
    towan 173

Dairi-bina / ningyō tennō no / gyou toka
    ya 93
donmiri to / ouchi ya ame no / hanagu-
    mori 859
dote no matsu / hana ya kobukaki /
    tonozukuri 614

Ebisukō / suuri ni hakama / kisenikeri
    832
edaburi no / higoto ni kawaru / fuyō kana
    593
eda moroshi / hitōshi yaburu / aki no kaze
    83
eiryo nite / nigiwau tami no / niwaka-
    mado 462
en naru yakko / imayō hana ni / Rōsai su
    154
e no mi chiru / muku no haoto ya /
    asaarashi 933

fūgetsu no / zai mo hanare yo /
    fukamigusa 798
Fuji no kaze ya / ōgi ni nosete / Edo
    miyage 65
fuji no mi wa / haikai ni sen / hana no ato
    583

Fuji no yama / nomi ga chausu no / ooi
    kana 62
Fuji no yuki / Rosei ga yume o /
    tsukasetari 88
fuki tobasu / ishi wa Asama no / nowaki
    kana 457
fuku kaze no / naka o uo tobu / misogi
    kana 347
fumi naranu / iroha mo kakite / kachū
    kana 47
fumizuki ya / muika mo tsune no / yo ni
    wa nizu 539
funa ashi mo / yasumu toki ari / hama no
    momo 244
funbetsu no / soko tatakikeri / toshi no
    kure 938
furazu tomo / take uuru hi wa / mino to
    kasa 925
furiuri no / gan aware nari / Ebisukō 831
furuhata ya / nazuna tsumi yuku / otoko
    domo 262
furuike ya / kawazu tobikomu / mizu no
    oto 270
furukawa ni / kobite me o haru / yanagi
    kana 932
furuki na no / Tsunuga ya koishi / aki no
    tsuki 573
furu oto ya / mimi mo sū naru / ume no
    ame 8
furusato ya / heso no o ni naku / toshi no
    kure 346
furusu tada / aware narubeki / tonari
    kana 268
fūryū no / hajime ya oku no / taueuta
    505
futari mishi / yuki wa kotoshi mo /
    furikeru ka 470
futsukaei / monokawa hana no / aru aida
    129
futsuka ni mo / nukari wa seji na / hana
    no haru 357
fuyubotan / chidori yo yuki no /
    hototogisu 216
fuyugomori / mata yorisowan / kono
    hashira 465
fuyuniwa ya / tsuki mo ito naru / mushi
    no gin 597

fuyu no hi ya / bashō ni kōru / kagebōshi
326

fuyu shira nu / yado ya momi suru / oto arare 204

ganjitsu wa / Tagoto no hi koso / koishikere 474

ganjitsu ya / omoeba sabishi / aki no kure 162

geni ya tsuki / maguchi senkin no / Tōri-chō 100

gobyō toshi hete / shinobu wa nani o / shinobugusa 207

go o taite / tenugui aburu / samusa kana 325

guanzuru ni / meido mo kaku ya / aki no kure 120

gu ni kuraku / ibara o tsukamu / hotaru kana 144

hadaka ni wa / mada kisaragi no / arashi kana 374

hafuguchi ni / hikage ya yowaru / yūsuzumi 764n

hagihara ya / hitoyo wa yadose / yama no inu 310

haiide yo / kaiya ga shita no / hiki no koe 520

hakkuken / sora de ame furu / yanagi kana 847

Hakone kosu / hito mo aru rashi / kesa no yuki 340

hamaguri ni / kyō wa urikatsu / wakana kana 789n

hamaguri no / Futami ni wakare / yuku aki zo 586

hamaguri no / ikeru kai are / toshi no kure 787

hana-ayame / ichiya ni kareshi / Motome kana 414

hana mina karete / aware o kobosu / kusa no tane 276

hanami ni to / sasu fune ososhi / Yanagihara 850

hana mukuge / hadaka warawa no / kazashi kana 118

hana ni akanu / nageki ya kochi no / utabukuro 28

hana ni asobu / abu na kurai so / tomosuzume 291

hana ni eeri / haori kite katana / sasu onna 135

hana ni iya yo / sekenguchi yori / kaze no kuchi 44

hana ni nenu / kore mo tagui ka / nezumi no su 758

hana ni ukiyo / waga sake shiroku / meshi kuroshi 164

hana ni yadori / Hyōtansai to / mizukara ieri 114

hana no kage / utai ni nitaru / tabine kana 384

hana no kao ni / hareute shite ya / oborozuki 24

hana no kumo / kane wa Ueno ka / Asakusa ka 294

hana o yado ni / hajime owari ya / hatsuka hodo 377

hana sakite / nanuka tsuru miru / fumoto kana 267

hana to mi to / ichido ni uri no / sakari kana 931

hana wa shizu no / me ni mo miekeri / oniazami 6

hanazakari / yama wa higoro no / asaborake 392

ha ni somuku / tsubaki no hana ya / yosogokoro 961

hanjitsu wa / kami o tomo ni ya / toshiwasure 669

haranaka ya / mono ni mo tsukazu / naku hibari 296

haremono ni / sawaru yanagi no / shinae kana 842

haremono ni / yanagi no sawaru / shinae kana 842n

harinuki no / neko mo shirunari / kesa no aki 130

haritate ya / kata ni tsuchi utsu / karakoromo 55

harukaze ni / fukidashi warau / hana mogana 29

haru mo yaya / keshiki totonou / tsuki to
  ume 790
haru nare ya / na mo naki yama no /
  usugasumi 232
haru no yo wa / sakura ni akete /
  shimaikeri 937
haru no yo ya / komorido yukashi / dō no
  sumi 380
harusame no / koshita ni tsutau / shimizu
  kana 390
harusame ya / futaba ni moyuru /
  nasubidane 611
harusame ya / hachi no su tsutau / yane
  no mori 848
harusame ya / mino fukikaesu /
  kawayanagi 962
harusame ya / yomogi o nobasu / kusa no
  michi 852
haru tachi te / mada kokonoka no /
  noyama kana 358
haru tatsu to / warawa mo shiru ya /
  kazarinawa 38
haru tatsu ya / shinnen furuki / kome
  goshō 186
haru ya koshi / toshi ya yukiken /
  kotsugomori 1
hashigeta no / shinobu wa tsuki no /
  nagori kana 726
hasuike ya / orade sonomama / Tama
  Matsuri 440
hasu no ka o / me ni kayowasu ya / men
  no hana 887
hatake utsu / oto ya arashi no /
  sakura-asa 617
hato no koe / mi ni shimiwataru / iwato
  kana 579
hatsuaki ya / tatami nagara no / kaya no
  yogi 707
hatsuaki ya / umi mo aota no / hitomidori
  438
hatsuhana ni / inochi shichijū- / gonen
  hodo 94
hatsumakuwa / yotsu ni ya tatan / wa ni
  kiran 538
hatsushigure / hatsu no ji o waga / shigure
  kana 972

hatsushigure / saru mo ko mino o /
  hoshigenari 594
hatsushimo ya / kiku hiesomuru / koshi
  no wata 775
hatsutake ya / mada hikazu henu / aki no
  tsuyu 806
hatsuuma ni / kitsune no sorishi / atama
  kana 794
hatsuyuki ni / usagi no kawa no / hige
  tsukure 599
hatsuyuki ya / hijirikozō no / oi no iro 663
hatsuyuki ya / itsu daibutsu no /
  hashiradate 601
hatsuyuki ya / kakekakaritaru / hashi no
  ue 829
hatsuyuki ya / saiwai an ni / makariaru
  279
hatsuyuki ya / suisen no ha no / tawamu
  made 280
hatsuzakura / orishimo kyō wa / yoki hi
  nari 375
hayaku sake / kunichi mo chikashi / kiku
  no hana 582
hebi kū to / kikeba osoroshi / kiji no koe 621
hibari naku / naka no hyōshi ya / kiji no
  koe 481
hibari yori / sora ni yasurau / tōge kana
  381
higashi nishi / awaresa hitotsu / aki no
  kaze 271
hige kaze o fuite / boshū tanzuru wa / ta
  ga ko zo 159
higoro nikuki / karasu mo yuki no / ashita
  kana 673
hi ni kakaru / kumo ya shibashi no /
  wataridori 966
hi no michi ya / aoi katamuku /
  satsukiame 634
hinzan no / kama shimo ni naku / koe
  samushi 149
hirahira to / aguru ōgi ya / kumo no mine
  886
Hira Mikami / yuki sashiwatase / sagi no
  hashi 675
hire furite / mejika mo yoru ya / Oga no
  Shima 180

hirugao ni / hirune shō mono / Toko no Yama 423

hirugao ni / kome tsuki suzumu / aware nari 176

hirugao no / mijikayo neburu / hiruma kana 422

hitobito o / shigure yo yado wa / samuku tomo 595

hitogoe ya / kono michi kaeru / aki no kure 916n

hitogoto no / kuchi ni arunari / shitamomiji 48

hitohi hitohi / mugi akaramite / naku hibari 701

hitokoeno / e ni yokotau ya / hototogisu 797 3

hito mo minu / haru ya kagami no / ura no ume 752

hito ni ie o / kawasete ware wa / toshiwasure 678

hitoone wa / shigururu kumo ka / Fuji no yuki 321

hitori ama / waraya sugenashi / shirotsutsuji 626

hitosato wa / mina hanamori no / shison ka ya 620

hitoshigure / tsubute ya futte / Koishikawa 86

hitotose ni / ichido tsumaruru / nazuna kana 840

hitotsu nuide / ushiro ni oinu / koromogae 396

hitotsuya ni / yūjo mo netari / hagi to tsuki 543

hitotsuyu mo / kobosanu kiku no / kōri kana 826

hi wa hana ni / kurete sabishi ya / asunarō 389

hiyahiya to / kabe o fumaete / hirune kana 889

hokku nari / Matsuo Tōsei / yado no haru 103

hōrai ni / kikabaya Ise no / hatsudayori 839

horohoro to / yamabuki chiru ka / taki no oto 387

Hoshizaki no / yami o miyo to ya / naku chidori 323

hotarubi no / hiru wa kietsutsu / hashira kana 517

hotarumi ya / sendō youte / obotsukana 636

hototogisu / ima wa haikaishi / naki yo kana 183

hototogisu / katsuo o some ni / keri kerashi 171

hototogisu / kieyuku kata ya / shima hitotsu 409

hototogisu / koe ya yokotau / mizu no ue 797 2

hototogisu / koe yokotau ya / mizu no ue 797 1

hototogisu / maneku ka mugi no / muraobana 142

hototogisu / mutsuki wa ume no / hana sakeri 165

hototogisu / naku naku tobu zo / isogawashi 298

hototogisu / naku ne ya furuki / suzuribako 760

hototogisu / naku ya goshaku no / ayamegusa 761

hototogisu / ōtakeyabu o / moru tsukiyo 697

hototogisu / Urami no Taki no / ura omote 492

hōzuki wa / mi mo ha mo kara mo / momiji kana 941

hyakuri kitari / hodo wa kumoi no / shitasuzumi 66

hyoro hyoro to / nao tsuyukeshi ya / ominaeshi 448

ichibito yo / kono kasa urō / yuki no kasa 225

ide ya ware / yoki nuno kitari / semigoromo 304

ie wa mina / tsue ni shiraga no / hakamairi 892

ikameshiki / oto ya arare no / hinokigasa 214

ikauri no / koe magirawashi / hototogisu 950

iki nagara / hitotsu ni kōru / namako kana 835

ikushimo ni / kokorobase o no / matsu kazari 261

imo arau onna / Saigyō naraba / uta yoman 198

imo no ha ya / tsuki matsu sato no / yakibatake 313

imo uete / kado wa mugura no / wakaba kana 369

inasuzume / cha-no-ki batake ya / nigedokoro 724

inazuma ni / satoranu hito no / tattosa yo 652

inazuma o / te ni toru yami no / shisoku kana 308

inazuma ya / kao no tokoro ga / susuki no ho 888

inazuma ya / yami no kata yuku / goi no koe 894

inekoki no / uba mo medetashi / kiku no hana 731

inochi futatsu no / naka ni ikitaru / sakura kana 243

inochi koso / imodane yo mata / kyō no tsuki 46

inochi nari / wazuka no kasa no / shitasuzumi 63

inoshishi mo / tomo ni fukaruru / nowaki kana 646

inoshishi no / toko ni mo iru ya / kirigirisu 911

Iragozaki / niru mono mo nashi / taka no koe 329

iriai no / kane mo kikoezu / haru no kure 489

iri kakaru / hi mo itoyū no / nagori kana 487

irozuku ya / tōfu ni ochite / usumomiji 84

iru tsuki no / ato wa tsukue no / yosumi kana 814

isaribi ni / kajika ya nami no / shita-musebi 554

ishi karete / mizu shibomeru ya / fuyu mo nashi 128

ishi no ka ya / natsukusa akaku / tsuyu atsushi 502

Ishiyama no / ishi ni tabashiru / arare kana 672

Ishiyama no / ishi yori shiroshi / aki no kaze 558

ite tokete / fude ni kumihosu / shimizu kana 391

itoyū ni / musubitsukitaru / kemuri kana 486

itozakura / koya kaeru sa no / ashimot-sure 32

itsutsu mutsu / cha-no-ko ni narabu / irori kana 466

iwatsutsuji / somuru namida ya / hototogishu 11

iza kodomo / hashiriarikan / tamaarare 600

iza kodomo / hirugao sakaba / uri mukan 802n

iza kodomo / hirugao sakinu / uri mukan 802n

iza saraba / yukimi ni korobu / tokoro made 339 1

iza tomo ni / homugi kurawan / kusamakura 250

izayoi mo / mada Sarashina no / kōri kana 453

izayoi no / izure ka kesa ni / nokoru kiku 458

izayoi wa / wazukani yami no / hajime kana 811

izayoi ya / ebi niru hodo no / yoi no yami 718

iza yukan / yukimi ni korobu / tokoro made 339 2

izuku shigure / kasa o te ni sagete / kaeru sō 122

jō akete / tsuki sashiireyo / Ukimidō 716

jōroku ni / kagerō takashi / ishi no ue 363

kachi naraba / Tsuetsukizaka o / rakuba kana 345

kadomatsu ya / omoeba ichiya / sanjūnen 69

Kagekiyo mo / hanami no za ni wa / Shichibyōe 923

kagemachi ya / kiku no ka no suru / tōfugushi 817

kagerō no / waga kata ni tatsu / kamiko kana 477

kagerō ya / saiko no ito no / usugumori 618

kage wa ame no / Shitateruhime ka / tsuki
no kao 16

Kakehashi ya / inochi o karamu /
tsutakazura 450

Kakehashi ya / mazu omoiizu /
umamukae 451

kakitsubata / kataru mo tabi no / hitotsu
kana 403

kakitsubata / nitari ya nitari / mizu no
kage 9

kakitsubata / ware ni hokku no / omoi ari
246

kaki yori wa / nori o ba oi no / uri mo se
de 287

kakurega ya / tsuki to kiku to ni / ta
santan 584

kakurekeri / shiwasu no umi no /
kaitsuburi 677

kakusanu zo / yado wa najiru ni /
tōgarashi 443

Kamakura o / ikite ideken / hatsugatsuo
762

kame waruru / yoru no kōri no / nezame
kana 278

kamigaki ya / omoi mo kakezu / nehanzō
373

kamiginu no / nuru tomo oran / ame no
hana 372

kami haete / yōgan aoshi / satsukiame
301

kanashiman ya / Bokushi seriyaki o / mite
mo nao 113

kanbutsu no / hi ni umareau / kanoko
kana 397

kanbutsu ya / shiwade awasuru / juzu no
oto 845 2

kane kiete / hana no ka wa tsuku / yūbe
kana 349

kane tsukanu / sato wa nani o ka / haru
no kure 488

kangiku ya / amazake tsukuru / mado no
saki 825

kangiku ya / konuka no kakaru / usu no
hata 824

ka ni nioe / uni horu oka no / ume no
hana 360

Kannon no / iraka miyaritsu / hana no
kumo 266

kao ni ninu / hokku mo ideyo /
hatsuzakura 902

ka o nokosu / ranchō ran no / yadori kana
976

ka o saguru / ume ni kura miru / nokiba
kana 342

kapitan mo / tsukubawase keri / kimi ga
haru 92

karahafu no / irihi ya usuki / yūsuzumi
764

karakasa ni / oshiwake mitaru / yanagi
kana 846

Karasaki no / matsu wa hana yori / oboro
nite 240

karazake mo / Kūya no yase mo / kan no
uchi 670

kareeda ni / karasu no tomarikeri / aki no
kure 121

kareeda ni / karasu no tomaritaru ya / aki
no kure 121n

kareshiba ya / yaya kagerō no / ichi nisun
362

kariato ya / wase kata kata no / shigi no
koe 435

karikakeshi / tazura no tsuru ya / sato no
aki 311

kari kiki ni / miyako no aki ni /
omomukan 658

kari sawagu / Toba no tazura ya / kan no
ame 750

karite nen / kakashi no sode ya / yowa no
shimo 963

Kasadera ya / moranu iwaya mo / haru
no ame 297

kasa mo naki / ware o shigururu ka / ko
wa nanto 222

Kasashima wa / izuko satsuki no /
nukarimichi 512

kashi no ki no / hana ni kamawanu /
sugata kana 237

katararenu / Yudono ni nurasu / tamoto
kana 529

katatsuburi / tsuno furiwakeyo / Suma
Akashi 411

katsuouri / ikanaru hito o / yowasu ran
303

Katsura otoko / sumazu nari keri / ame
no tsuki 35

kawakami to / kono kawashimo ya / tsuki no tomo 772

kawakaze ya / usugaki kitaru / yūsuzumi 639

kawauso no / matsuri mite koyo / Seta no oku 609

kazairo ya / shidoro ni ueshi / niwa no aki 895

kazairo ya / shidoro ni ueshi / niwa no hagi 895n

kazairo ya / shidoro ni ueshi / niwa no ogi 895n

kaze fukeba / obosōnaru ya / inuzakura 33

kaze kaoru / haori wa eri mo / tsuku-rowazu 705

kaze no ka mo / minami ni chikashi / Mogamigawa 525

kazoekinu / yashiki yashiki no / ume yanagi 757

kazuki fusu / futon ya samuki / yo ya sugoki 468

kazu naranu / mi to na omoiso / Tama Matsuri 893

kegoromo ni / tsutsumite nukushi / kamo no ashi 827

keitō ya / kari no kuru toki / nao akashi 901

kesa no yuki / nebuka o sono no / shiori kana 111

keshizumi ni / maki waru oto ka / Ono no oku 124

kiku keitō / kiri tsukushikeri / Omeikō 464

kiku ni dete / Nara to Naniwa wa / yoizukiyo 910

kiku no hana / saku ya ishiya no / ishi no ai 818

kiku no ka ni / Kuragari noboru / Sekku kana 909

kiku no ka ya / Nara ni wa furuki / hotoketachi 907

kiku no ka ya / Nara wa ikuyo no / otokoburi 908

kiku no ka ya / niwa ni kiretaru / kutsu no soko 823

kiku no nochi / daikon no hoka / sarani nashi 948

kiku no tsuyu / ochite hiroeba / nukago kana 942

kimi hi o take / yokimono misen / yukimaruge 282

kimi ya chō / ware ya Sōji ga / yume-gokoro 630

kinbyō no / matsu no furusa yo / fuyugomori 821

ki no moto ni / shiru mo namasu mo / sakura kana 615

kinuta uchite / ware ni kikaseyo ya / bō ga tsuma 205

ki o kirite / motokuchi miru ya / kyō no tsuki 82

kirigirisu / wasurene ni naku / kotatsu kana 660

kiri no ki ni / uzura nakunaru / hei no uchi 651

kirisame no / sora o fuyō no / tenki kana 770

kirishigure / Fuji o minu hi zo / omoshiroki 192

kiri ugoku / aki no owari ya / tsuta no shimo 730n

Kisagata ya / ame ni Seishi ga / nebu no hana 534

Kiso no jō / yuki ya haenuku / haru no kusa 680

Kiso no tochi / ukiyo no hito no / miyage kana 455

Kiso no yase mo / mada naoranu ni / nochi no tsuki 459

kite mo miyo / jinbe ga haori / hanagoromo 39

kitsutsuki mo / io wa yaburazu / natsukodachi 495

kiyoku kikan / mimi ni kō taite / hototogisu 166

Kiyotaki no / mizu kumasete ya / tokoroten 873

Kiyotaki ya / nami ni chirikomu / aomatsuba 875

Kiyotaki ya / nami ni chiri naki / natsu no tsuki 875n

kōbai ya / minu koi tsukuru / tamasudare 478

kochira muke / ware mo sabishiki / aki no kure 647

kochō ni mo / narade aki furu / namushi
  kana 578
kodai sasu / yanagi suzushi ya / ama ga ie
  542
kodai sasu / yanagi suzushi ya / ama ga
  tsuma 542n
kodomora yo / hirugao sakinu / uri
  mukan 802
koe sumite / hokuto ni hibiku / kinuta
  kana 362
koe yokuba / utaō mono o / sakura chiru 386
kogakurete / chatsumi mo kiku ya /
  hototogisu 854
kogarashi ni / iwa fukitogaru / sugima
  kana 742
kogarashi ni / nioi ya tsukeshi / kaeribana
  737
kogarashi ya / hōbare itamu / hito no kao
  662
kogarashi ya / take ni kakurete /
  shizumarinu 946
kohagi chire / Masuho no kogai /
  kosakazuki 576
Kohōgen / dedokoro aware / toshi no kure
  977
koke uzumu / tsuta no utsutsu no /
  nebutsu kana 211
kokonotabi / okite mo tsuki no / nanatsu
  kana 727
kome kai ni / yuki no fukuro ya /
  nagezukin 471
komo o kite / tarebito imasu / hana no
  haru 608
komoriite / ki no mi kusa no mi /
  hirowabaya 581
kōmori mo / ideyo ukiyo no / hana ni
  tori 959
ko ni aku to / mōsu hito ni wa / hana mo
  nashi 971
konnyaku ni / kyō wa urikatsu / wakana
  kana 789
konnyaku no / sashimi mo sukoshi / ume
  no hana 792
kono aki wa / nande toshiyoru / kumo ni
  tori 918
kono atari / me ni miyuru mono wa /
  mina suzushi 432

konoha chiru / sakura wa karoshi /
  hinokigasa 208
kono hodo o / hana ni rei iu / wakare
  kana 378
kono hotaru / Tagoto no Tsuki ni /
  kurabemin 416
kono kokoro / suiseyo hana ni / goki
  ichigu 755
kono matsu no / mibae seshi yo ya / kami
  no aki 316
kono michi ya / yuku hito nashi ni / aki
  no kure 916
kō no su mo / miraruru hana no / hagoshi
  kana 292
kō no su ni / arashi no hoka no / sakura
  kana 293
kono tane to / omoikonasaji / tōgarashi 612
kono tera wa / niwa ippai no / bashō kana
  957
kono tsuchi no / mukashi tsubaki ka /
  ume no ki ka 978
kono ume ni / ushi mo hatsune to /
  nakitsubeshi 59
kono umi ni / waranji suten / kasashigure
  219
kono yado wa / kuina mo shiranu / toboso
  kana 934
kono yama no / kanashisa tsuge yo /
  tokorohori 370
kore ya yo no / susu ni somaranu /
  furugōshi 605
kōri nigaku / enso ga nodo o / uruoseri 150
koromo kite / kogai hirowan / iro no tsuki
  577
kotobako ya / furumonodana no / sedo no
  kiku 819
koyoi no tsuki / togi dase Hitomi / Izumo
  no Kami 81
koyoi tare / Yoshino no tsuki mo / jūrokuri
  900
kozue yori / adani ochikeri / semi no kara 78
kuchi-kiri ni / Sakai no niwa zo /
  natsukashiki 778
kuina naku to / hito no ieba ya /
  Sayadomari 868
Kumasaka ga / yukari ya itsu no / Tama
  Matsuri 545

kumo kiri no / zanji hyakkei o /
tsukushikeri 193

kumo nani to / ne o nani to naku / aki no
kaze 116

kumo no mine / ikutsu kuzurete / Tsuki no
Yama 528

kumo o ne ni / Fuji wa suginari no /
shigeri kana 61

kumo oriori / hito o yasumeru / tsukimi
kana 258

kumo to hedatsu / tomo ka ya kari no /
ikiwakare 41

kuniguni no / hakkei sara ni / Kehi no
tsuki 568

kuratsubo ni / kobōzu noru ya / daikohiki
828

kure kurete / mochi o kodama no / wabine
kana 151

kuromori o / nani to iu tomo / kesa no
yuki 181

kusa iroiro / ono ono hana no / tegara
kana 446

kusamakura / inu mo shigururu ka / yoru
no koe 224

kusamakura / makoto no hanami / shite
mo koyo 622

kusa no ha o / otsuru yori tobu / hotaru
kana 418

kusa no to mo / sumikawaru yo zo / hina
no ie 483

kusa no to o / shire ya hotade ni /
tōgarashi 653

kusa no to ya / higurete kureshi / kiku no
sake 725

kusuri nomu / sarademo shimo no /
makura kana 336

kutabirete / yado karu koro ya / fuji no
hana 400

kuwa no mi ya / hana naki chō no /
yosutezake 167

kuzu no ha no / omote misekeri / kesa no
shimo 749

kyō bakari / hito mo toshiyore /
hatsushigure 776

(kyōku) kogarashi no / mi wa Chikusai ni
/ nitaru kana 223

Kyō made wa / mada nakazora ya / yuki
no kumo 322

Kyō ni akite / kono kogarashi ya /
fuyuzumai 740

Kyō nite mo / Kyō natsukashi ya /
hototogisu 638

kyō no koyoi / neru toki mo naki / tsukimi
kana 52

Kyō wa kuman- / kusen kunju no /
hanami kana 5

kyō yori ya / kakitsuke kesan / kasa no
tsuyu 557

machiishi ya / yashikigata yori /
komamukae 54

madonari ni / hirune no dai ya /
takamushiro 803

madonari ni / hirune no goza ya /
takamushiro 803n

maegami mo / mada wakakusa no / nioi
kana 936

Mafukuda ga / hakama yosou ka /
tsukuzukushi

magusa ou / hito o shiori no / natsuno
kana 493

masu kōte / funbetsu kawaru / tsukimi
kana 912

matanu noni / na uri ni kita ka /
hototogisu 74

mata ya tagui / Nagara no kawa no /
ayunamasu 430

matōdona / inu fumitsukete / neko no koi
954

matsudake ya / kabureta hodo wa / matsu
no nari 958

matsudake ya / shiranu konoha no /
hebaritsuku 728

matsu hana ya / Tōzaburō ga / Yoshi-
noyama 104

matsukaze no / ochiba ka mizu no / oto
suzushi 974

matsukaze ya / noki o megutte / aki
kurenu 917

matsu nare ya / kiri eisaraei to / hiku
hodo ni 134

matsu sugi o / homete ya kaze no / kaoru
oto 879

mayuhaki o / omokage ni shite / beni no
    hana 521
mazu iwae / ume o kokoro no /
    fuyugomori 334
mazu shiru ya / Gichiku ga take ni / hana
    no yuki 73
mazu tanomu / shii no ki mo ari /
    natsukodachi 629
medetaki hito no / kazu ni mo iran / oi no
    kure 260
meigetsu ni / fumoto no kiri ya / ta no
    kumori 898
meigetsu no / hana ka to miete /
    watabatake 899
meigetsu no / izuru ya Gojū- / ichi kajō 463
meigetsu no / midokoro towan / tabine
    sen 561
meigetsu wa / futatsu sugite mo / Seta no
    tsuki 720
meigetsu ya / chigotachi narabu / dō no en
    649n
meigetsu ya / hokkoku biyori / sadame-
    naki 570
meigetsu ya / ike o megurite / yomosugara
    272
meigetsu ya / mon ni sashikuru /
    shiogashira 769
meigetsu ya / umi ni mukaeba /
    nana-Komachi 649n
meigetsu ya / za ni utsukushiki / kao mo
    nashi 649n
me ni kakaru / toki ya kotosara / satsuki
    Fuji 858
me ni nokoru / Yoshino o Seta no / hotaru
    kana 417
me no hoshi ya / hana o negai no /
    itozakura 45
meotojika ya / ke ni ke ga soroute / ke
    mutsukashi 40
meshi aogu / kaka ga chisō ya / yūsuzumi
    881
mezurashi ya / yama o ideha no /
    hatsunasubi 532
michi hososhi / sumotorigusa no / hana
    no tsuyu 890
michi no be no / mukuge wa uma ni /
    kuwarekeri 195

midokoro no / are ya nowaki no / nochi
    no kiku 927
Miidera no / mon tatakabaya / kyō no
    tsuki 715
mikazuki ni / chi wa oboro nari / soba no
    hana 767
mikazuki ya / asagao no yūbe /
    tsubomuran 157
mina idete / hashi o itadaku / shimoji
    kana 834
mina ogame / Futami no shime o / toshi
    no kure 473
minazuki wa / fukubyōyami no / atsusa
    kana 706
minazuki ya / tai wa are domo /
    shiokujira 763
mi ni shimite / daikon karashi / aki no
    kaze 454
minomushi no / ne o kiki ni koyo / kusa
    no io 317
miokuri no / ushiro ya sabishi / aki no
    kaze 444
miru kage ya / mada katanari mo /
    yoizukiyo 53
miru ni ga mo / oreru bakari zo /
    ominaeshi 51
mishi ya sono / nanuka wa haka no /
    mika no tsuki 813
misoka tsuki nashi / chitose no sugi o /
    daku arashi 197
miwataseba / nagamureba mireba / Suma
    no aki 109
miyako idete / kami mo tabine no /
    hikazu kana 746
miyamori yo / waga na o chirase /
    konohagawa 215
mizu mukete / ato toi tamae / Dōmyōji 95
mizu no oku / himuro tazunuru / yanagi
    kana 522
mizu samuku / neiri kane taru / kamome
    kana 277
mizutori ya / kōri no sō no / kutsu no oto
    233
mizuumi ya / atsusa o oshimu / kumo no
    mine 885
mochibana ya / kazashi ni saseru /
    yome-ga-kimi 132

mochi o yume ni / orimusubu shida no / kusamakura 136

mochiyuki o / shiraito to nasu / yanagi kana 27

momo no ki no / sono ha chirasu na / aki no kaze 553

momotose no / keshiki o niwa no / ochiba kana 732

mo ni sudaku / shirauo ya toraba / kienu beki 137

mon ni ireba / sotetsu ni ran no / nioi kana 592

mono hitotsu / waga yo wa karoki / hisago kana 274

monohoshi ya / fukuro no uchi no / tsuki to hana 960

mono ieba / kuchibiru samushi / aki no kaze 944

mono kaite / ōgi hikisaku / nagori kana 560

mononofu no / daikon nigaki / hanashi kana 830

mono no na o / mazu tou ashi no / wakaba kana 368

monozuki ya / niowanu kusa ni / tomaru chō 350

moroki hito ni / tatoen hana mo / natsuno kana 427

mugi haete / yoki kakurega ya / Hatake Mura 332

mugimeshi ni / yatsururu koi ka / neko no tsuma 686

mugi no ho o / chikara ni tsukamu / wakare kana 857

mugi no ho o / tayori ni tsukamu / wakare kana 857n

mugura sae / wakaba wa yasashi / yabureie 480

mukashi kike / Chichibu-dono sae / sumōtori 940

Musashino no / tsuki no wakabae ya / Matsushima-dane 133

Musashino ya / issun hodo na / shika no koe 56

Musashino ya / sawaru mono naki / kimi ga kasa 979

musubu yori / haya ha ni hibiku / izumi kana 351

muzan ya na / kabuto no shita no / kirigirisu 551

nabatake ni / hanamigao naru / suzume kana 242

nadeshiko ni / kakaru namida ya / kusu no tsuyu 939

nadeshiko no / atsusa wasururu / nogiku kana 766

nagaki hi mo / saezuri taranu / hibari kana 295

nagamuru ya / Edo ni wa marena / yama no tsuki 67

nakanaka ni / kokoro okashiki / shiwasu kana 785

Nakayama ya / Koshiji mo tsuki wa / mata inochi 567

naki hito no / kosode mo ima ya / doyōboshi 424

namagusashi / konagi ga ue no / hae no wata 809

nami no hana to / yuki mo ya mizu no / kaeribana 34

nami no ma ya / kogai ni majiru / hagi no chiri 575

namo hotoke / kusa no utena mo / suzushi kare 188

nanakabu no / hagi no chimoto ya / hoshi no aki 765

nanigoto mo / maneki hatetaru / susuki kana 355

nanigoto no / mitate ni mo nizu / mika no tsuki 434

nani kūte / koie wa aki no / yanagikage 955

nani ni kono / shiwasu no ichi ni / yuku karasu 607

nani no ki no / hana to wa shirazu / nioi kana 364

Naniwazu ya / tanishi no futa mo / fuyugomori 822

nao mitashi / hana ni akeyuku / kami no kao 393

Nara nanae / shichidō garan / yaezakura 951

nari ni keri / nari ni keri made / toshi no
    kure 68
natsu chikashi / sono kuchi tabae / hana
    no kaze 30
natsugoromo / imada shirami o / tori
    tsukusazu 257
natsu kakete / meigetsu atsuki / suzumi
    kana 810
natsu kite mo / tada hitotsuba no / hitoha
    kana 433
natsukodachi / haku ya miyama no /
    koshifusage 42
natsukusa ni / fūki o kazare / hebi no kinu
    631
natsukusa ya / tsuwamono domo ga /
    yume no ato 515
natsukusa ya / ware sakidachite / hebi
    karan 632
natsu no tsuki / Goyu yori idete / Akasaka
    ya 64
natsu no yo ya / kodama ni akuru / geta
    no oto 699n
natsu no yo ya / kuzurete akeshi /
    hiyashimono 880
natsuyama ni / ashida o ogamu / kadode
    kana 497
natto kiru / oto shibashi mate /
    hachitataki 671
nebuka shiroku / araiagetaru / samusa
    kana 735
nebu no ki no / hagoshi mo itoe / hoshi no
    kage 643
nehan-e ya / shiwade awasuru / juzu no
    oto 845 1
neko no koi / yamu toki neya no /
    oborozuki 756
neko no tsuma / hetsui no kuzure yori /
    kayoikeri 71
nenohi shi ni / miyako e ikan / tomo
    mogana 230
netaru hagi ya / yōgan burei / hana no
    kao 18
niawashi ya / mame no komeshi ni /
    sakuragari 616
nishi ka higashi ka / mazu sanae ni mo /
    kaze no oto 504
niwa haite / idebaya tera ni / chiru yanagi
    559

niwa hakite / yuki o wasururu / hahaki
    kana 781
nomi akete / hanaike ni sen / nishō daru
    688
nomi shirami / uma no shitosuru /
    makuramoto 518
nōnashi no / nemutashi ware o /
    gyōgyōshi 702
no o yoko ni / uma hiki mukeyo /
    hototogisu 499
nōren no / oku monofukashi / kita no ume
    366
norijiru no / tegiwa misekeri / asagiwan 187
nozarashi o / kokoro ni kaze no / shimu
    mi kana 190
nurete yuku ya / hito mo okashiki / ame
    no hagi 550
nusubito ni / ōta yo mo ari / toshi no kure
    838
nyūmen no / shita takitatsuru / yosamu
    kana 729

ochikuru ya / Takaku no shuku no /
    hototogisu 500
ōgi nite / sake kumu kage ya / chiru
    sakura 385
ogi no ho ya / kashira o tsukamu /
    Rashōmon 710
ogi no koe / koya akikaze no / kuchiutsu-
    shi 17
Ō-Hie ya / shi no ji o hii te / hitokasumi
    70
Ōigawa / nami ni chiri nashi / natsu no
    tsuki 875n
oi mo tachi mo / satsuki ni kazare /
    kaminobori 510
oi no na no / ari tomo shirade / shijūgara
    816
ōji oya / mago no sakae ya / kaki mikan
    719
okiagaru / kiku honokanari / mizu no ato
    318
okiyo okiyo / waga tomo ni sen / nuru
    kochō 172
okorago no / hitomoto yukashi / ume no
    hana 365 1
okuraretsu / okuritsu hate wa / Kiso no
    aki 445 2

okuraretsu / wakaretsu hate wa / Kiso no
aki 445 1

Omeiko ya / abura no yōna / sake goshō
779

ōmigaya / ase ya sazanami / yoru no toko
77

omoitatsu / Kiso ya shigatsu no /
sakuragari 253

omokage ya / oba hitori naku / tsuki no
tomo 452

omoshiroki / aki no asane ya / teishuburi
915

omoshiroshi / yuki ni ya naran / fuyu no
ame 335

omoshirōte / yagate kanashiki / ubune
kana 431

omoshiro ya / kotoshi no haru mo / tabi
no sora 475

onoga hi o / kigi no hotaru ya / hana no
yado 637

Onozumi ya / tenarau hito no / haizeseri
125

Oranda mo / hana ni kinikeri / uma ni
kura 105

oriori ni / Ibuki o mite wa / fuyugomori 736

oriori wa / su ni naru kiku no / sakana
kana 724

osanana ya / shiranu okina no /
maruzukin 970

otoroi ya / ha ni kuiateshi / nori no suna
690

Ōtsu-e no / fude no hajime wa / nani
botoke 679

ran no ka ya / chō no tsubasa ni /
takimono su 199

robiraki ya / sakan oiyuku / bin no shimo
777

rokugatsu ya / mine ni kumo oku / Arashi-
yama 874

ro no koe nami o utte / harawata kōru /
yo ya namida 126

rusu ni kite / ume sae yoso no / kakiho
kana 289

rusu no ma ni / aretaru kami no / ochiba
kana 748

ryō no te ni / momo to sakura ya / kusa
no mochi 759

Ryūgū mo / kyō no shioji ya / doyōboshi 72

Ryūmon no / hana ya jōgo no / tsuto ni
sen 382

sabishisa ya / iwa ni shimikomu / semi no
koe 522n

sabishisa ya / kugi ni kaketaru / kirigirisu
713

sabishisa ya / Suma ni kachitaru / hama
no aki 574

Saigyō no / iori mo aran / hana no niwa
952

Saigyō no / waraji mo kakare / matsu no
tsuyu 585

sakarija hana ni / sozoro ukibōshi /
numerizuma 138

sakari naru / ume ni sude hiku / kaze
mogana 25

sakazuki ni / doro na otoshi so /
muratsubame 371

sakazuki ni / mitsu no na o nomu / koyoi
kana 259

sakazuki no / shita yuku kiku ya /
kutsukibon 57

sakazuki ya / yamaji no kiku to / kore o
hosu 108

sake nomeba / itodo nerarene / yoru no
yuki 281

sakenomi ni / kataran kakaru / taki no
hana 383

sakimidasu / momo no naka yori /
hatsuzakura 929

sakuragari / kidoku ya hibi ni / go ri roku
ri 388

sakura yori / matsu wa futaki o / mitsuki
goshi 511

samazama no / koto omoidasu / sakura
kana 376

samidare mo / sebumi tazunenu /
Minaregawa 37

samidare ni / kakurenu mono ya / Seta no
hashi 415

samidare ni / nio no ukisu o / mi ni yukan
302

samidare ni / onmonodō ya / tsuki no
kao 7

samidare ni / tsuru no ashi / mijikaku
nareri 143

samidare no / furinokoshite ya / Hikaridō 516

samidare no / sora fukiotose / Ōigawa 864

samidare o / atsumete hayashi / Mogamigawa 523

samidare wa / taki furiuzumu / mikasa kana 508

samidare ya / kaiko wazurau / kuwa no hata 861

samidare ya / oke no wa kiruru / yoru no koe 300

samidare ya / ryūtō aguru / bantarō 76

samidare ya / shikishi hegitaru / kabe no ato 703

samukaranu / tsuyu ya botan no / hana no mitsu 853

samukeredo / futari nuru yo zo / tanomoshiki 324

sanae toru / temoto ya mukashi / shinobu-zuri 509

sanjaku no / yama mo arashi no / konoha kana 674

sarabachi mo / honokani yami no / yoisuzumi 882

sareba koso / aretaki mama no / shimo no yado 331

saruhiki wa / saru no kosode o / kinuta kana 953

saru o kiku hito / sutego ni aki no / kaze ikani 194

sasa no tsuyu / hakama ni kakeshi / shigeri kana 796

sashikomoru / mugura no tomo ka / fuyuna uri 472

satobito wa / ine ni uta yomu / miyako kana 401

sato furite / kaki no ki motanu / ie mo nashi 896

sato no ko yo / ume orinokose / ushi no muchi 288

satsuki no ame / iwahiba no midori / itsumade zo 115

sazanami ya / kaze no kaori no / aibyōshi 884

sazaregani / ashi hainoboru / shimizu kana 307

sazona hoshi / hijikimono ni wa / shika no kawa 131

sekimori no / yado o kuina ni / toou mono 507

Sekizoro no / kureba fūga mo / shiwasu kana 665

Sekizoro o / suzume no warau / detachi kana 786

seriyaki ya / susowa no tai no / hatsugōri 833

setsukare te / toshiwasure suru / kigen kana 945

shiba no to ni / cha o konoha kaku / arashi kana 123

shiba no to no / tsuki ya sono mama / Amidabō 926

shibaraku wa / hana no ue naru / tsukiyo kana 689

shibaraku wa / taki ni komoru ya / ge no hajime 491

shibashi ma mo / matsu ya hototogi- / su sennen 12

shiba tsukeshi / uma no modori ya / tauedaru 870

shigure o ya / modokashigarite / matsu no yuki 20

shigururu ya / ta no arakabu no / kuromu hodo 659

shihō yori / hana fukiirete / nio no nami 623

shii no hana no / kokoro ni mo niyo / Kiso no tabi 799n

shika no tsuno / mazu hitofushi no / wakare kana 399

shimajima ya / chiji ni kudakite / natsu no umi 514

shimogare ni / saku wa shinki no / hanano kana 23

shimo no nochi / nadeshiko sakeru / hioke kana 661

shimo o funde / chinba hiku made / okurikeri 110

shimo o kite / kaze o shikine no / sutego kana 87

shini mo senu / tabine no hate yo / aki no kure 212

shinobu sae / karete mochi kau / yadori kana 221

shinwara no / desomete hayaki / shigure
kana 903

shiodai no / haguki mo samushi / uo no
tana 780

Shiogoshi ya / tsuruhagi nurete / umi
suzushi 536

shio ni shite mo / iza kotozuten /
miyakodori 101

shiorashiki / na ya Komatsu fuku / hagi
susuki 549

shiore fusu ya / yo wa sakasama no / yuki
no take 21

shiraga nuku / makura no shita ya /
kirigirisu 648

shirageshi ni / hane mogu chō no / katami
kana 252

shirageshi ya / shigure no hana no /
sakitsuran 182

shiragiku no / me ni tatete miru / chiri mo
nashi 919

shiragiku yo shiragiku yo / haji nagakami
yo / nagakami yo 177

shiratsuyu mo / kobosanu hagi no / uneri
kana 805

shirauo ya / kuroki me o aku / nori no
ami 791

shiroato ya / furui no shimizu / mazu
towan 429

shirozumi ya / kano Urashima ga / oi no
hako 89

shizukasa ya / e kakaru kabe no /
kirigirisu 713n

shizukasa ya / iwa ni shimiiru / semi no
koe 522

shizu no ko ya / ine surikakete / tsuki o
miru 312

Shōshō-no- / ama no hanashi ya / Shiga
no yuki 604

shoshun mazu / sake ni ume uru / nioi
kana 234

shūkaidō / suika no iro ni / sakinikeri 708

sō asagao / iku shini kaeru / nori no
matsu 203

soba mo mite / kenarigaraseyo / nora no
hagi 723

soba wa mada / hana de motenasu /
yamaji kana 904

sode no iro / yogorete samushi / koinezumi
975

sode yogosuran / tanishi no ama no /
hima o na mi 153

sōkai no / nami sakekusashi / kyō no tsuki
107

sono katachi / mibaya kareki no / tsue no
take 467

sonomama yo / tsuki mo tanomaji / Ibuki-
yama 580

sono nioi / momo yori shiroshi / suisenka
739

sono tama ya / Haguro ni kaesu / nori no
tsuki 530

Suigaku mo / norimono kasan /
Amanogawa 97

suisen ya / shiroki shōji no / tomo utsuri 738

Sumadera ya / fukanu fue kiku /
koshitayami 408

Suma no ama no / yasaki ni naku ka /
hototogisu 407

Suma no ura no / toshitorimono ya / shiba
ichiwa 956

sumitsukanu / tabi no kokoro ya /
okigotatsu 667

Surugaji ya / hanatachibana mo / cha no
nioi 862

susuhaki wa / onoga tana tsuru / daiku
kana 836

susuhaki wa / sugi no konoma no / arashi
kana 668

suzumeko to / koe nakikawasu / nezumi
no su 949

suzuri ka to / hirou ya kuboki / ishi no
tsuyu 591

suzushisa no / sashizu ni miyuru / sumai
kana 867n

suzushisa o / e ni utsushikeri / Saga no
take 872

suzushisa o / Hida no takumi ga / sashizu
kana 867

suzushisa o / waga yado ni shite / nemaru
nari 519

suzushisa ya / hono mikazuki no /
Haguroyama 527

suzushisa ya / suguni nomatsu no / eda no
nari 869

tabibito no / kokoro ni mo niyo / shii no
   hana 799
tabibito to / waga na yobaren / hatsushig-
   ure 320
tabigarasu / furusu wa ume ni / narini
   keri 231
tabine shite / mishi ya ukiyo no /
   susuharai 344
tabine shite / waga ku o shire ya / aki no
   kaze 348
tabine yoshi / yado wa shiwasu no /
   yūzukiyo 341
tabi ni akite / kyō ikuka yara / aki no kaze
   439
tabi ni yande / yume wa kareno o /
   kakemeguru 922
tachibana ya / itsu no nonaka no /
   hototogisu 635
ta ga muko zo / shida ni mochi ou / ushi
   no toshi 229
ta ichimai / uete tachisaru / yanagi kana 503
taka hitotsu / mitsukete ureshi / Iragozaki
   328
takamizu ni / hoshi mo tabine ya / iwa no
   ue 804
taka no me mo / ima ya kurenu to / naku
   uzura 722
takegari ya / abunaki koto ni / yūshigure
   596
takenoko ya / osanaki toki no / e no susabi
   700
takōna ya / shizuku mo yoyo no / sasa no
   tsuyu 50
takotsubo ya / hakanaki yume o / natsu
   no tsuki 410
Tama Matsuri / kyō mo yakiba no /
   kemuri kana 644
tametsukete / yukimi ni makaru / kamiko
   kana 338
tamukekeri / imo wa hachisu ni / ni taru
   tote 185
Tanabata no / awanu kokoro ya / uchūten
   14
Tanabata ya / aki o sadamuru / hajime no
   yo 891n
Tanabata ya / aki o sadamuru / yo no
   hajime 891

tanda sume / sumeba miyako zo / Kyō no
   tsuki 15
taneimo ya / hana no sakari ni / uri
   aruku 613
tanoshisa ya / aota ni suzumu / mizu no
   oto 402
tare yara ga / katachi ni nitari / kesa no
   haru 286
tawamite wa / yuki matsu take no /
   keshiki kana 865
ta ya mugi ya / naka ni mo natsu no /
   hototogisu 496
tebana kamu / oto sae ume no / sakari
   kana 361
Teikin no Ōrai / ta ga bunko yori / kesa
   no haru 91
tenbin ya / Kyō Edo kakete / chiyo no haru
   58
te ni toraba kien / namida zo atsuki / aki
   no shimo 201
te o uteba / kodama ni akuru / natsu no
   tsuki 699
tera ni nete / makotogao naru / tsukimi
   kana 315
tōgan ya / tagai ni kawaru / kao no nari 897
togi naosu / kagami mo kiyoshi / yuki no
   hana 337
tōkibi ya / nokiba no ogi no / tori chigae
   80
tōki yori / aware wa tsuka no / sumire-
   gusa 793
toko ni kite / ibiki ni iru ya / kirigirisu
   911n
tomokaku mo / narade ya yuki no /
   kareobana 747
tonbō ya / toritsukikaneshi / kusa no ue
   645
to no kuchi ni / yadofuda nanore /
   hototogisu 179
torisashi mo / sao ya suteken / hototogisu
   247
toshidoshi ya / sakura o koyasu / hana no
   chiri 687
toshidoshi ya / saru ni kisetaru / saru no
   men 788
toshi kurenu / kasa kite waraji / haki
   nagara 228

toshi no ichi / senkō kai ni / idebaya na 284

toshi wa hito ni / torasete itsumo / waka-Ebisu 4

tōtogaru / namida ya somete / chiru momiji 733

tōtosa ni / mina oshiainu / go-sengū 589

tōtosa ya / yuki furanu hi mo / mino to kasa 676

tsuka mo ugoke / waga naku koe wa / aki no kaze 548

tsukigane mo / hibiku yōnari / semi no koe 428

tsuki hana mo / nakute sake nomu / hitori kana 482

tsuki hana no / gu ni hari taten / kan no iri 783

tsuki hana no / kore ya makoto no / aruji tachi 249

tsuki hayashi / kozue wa ame o / mochi nagara 314

tsuki izuku / kane wa shizumeru / umi no soko 571

tsuki jūyokka / koyoi sanjūku no / warabe 158

tsuki kage ya / shimon shishū mo / tada hitotsu 456

tsuki ka hana ka / toedo shisui no / ibiki kana 531

tsuki kiyoshi / Yugyō no moteru / suna no ue 569

tsukimachi ya / ume katageyuku / ko-yamabushi 684

tsukimi seyo / Tamae no ashi o / karanu saki 563

tsukimi suru / za ni utsukushiki / kao mo nashi 649

tsuki mite mo / monotarawazu ya / Suma no natsu 405

tsuki ni na o / tsutsumikanete ya / imo no kami 565

tsuki no kagami / koharu ni miru ya / me shōgatsu 19

tsuki nomi ka / ame ni sumō mo / nakarikeri 572

tsuki sabiyo / Akechi ga tsuma no / hanashi sen 588

tsuki shiroki / shiwasu wa Shiro ga / nezame kana 283

tsukishiro ya / hiza ni te o oku / yoi no yado 650

tsuki sumu ya / kitsune kowagaru / chigo no tomo 920

tsuki wa aredo / rusu no yō nari / Suma no natsu 404

tsuki ya sono / Hachi no Ki no hi no / shitaomote 815

tsuki yuki to / nosabari kerashi / toshi no kure 285

tsuki zo shirube / konata e irase / tabi no yado 2

tsukurinasu / niwa o isamuru / shigure kana 734

tsuma koute / nezasa kazuku ya / ————— 628

tsumi ken ya cha o / kogarashi no / aki to mo shirade 140

tsuru naku ya / sono koe ni bashō / yarenubeshi 498

tsuru no ke no / kuroki koromo ya / hana no kumo 795

tsuta no ha wa / mukashi mekitaru / momiji kana 460

tsuta uete / take shi go hon no / arashi kana 200

tsutsuji ikete / sono kage ni / hidara saku onna 241

tsuyu itete / fude ni kumihosu / shimizu kana 343

tsuyu toku toku / kokoromi ni ukiyo / susugabaya 206

ubazakura / saku ya rōgo no / omoiide 3

uchiwa mote / aogan hito no / ushiromuki 248

Uchiyama ya / tozama shira zu no / hanazakari 36

uchiyorite / hanaire sagure / ume tsubaki 784

uguisu no / kasa otoshitaru / tsubaki kana 610

uguisu o / tama ni nemuru ka / taoyanagi 163

uguisu ya / mochi ni fun suru / en no saki
754

uguisu ya / takenoko yabu ni / oi o naku
860

uguisu ya / yanagi no ushiro / yabu no
mae 843

ukarekeru / hito ya Hatsuse no /
yamazakura 31

uki fushi ya / takenoko to naru / hito no
hate 694

uki hito no / tabi ni mo narae / Kiso no
hae 800

uki ware o / sabishigaraseyo / aki no tera 587

uki ware o / sabishigaraseyo / kankodori
698

uma bokuboku / ware o e ni miru /
natsuno kana 169

umakata wa / shiraji shigure no / Ōigawa
745

uma ni nete / zanmu tsuki tōshi / cha no
keburi 196

uma o sae / nagamuru yuki no / ashita
kana 220

ume ga ka ni / mukashi no ichiji / aware
nari 844

ume ga ka ni / notto hi no deru / yamaji
kana 841

ume ga ka ni / oimodosa ruru / samusa
kana 964

ume ga ka ya / minu yo no hito ni / gyoi o
uru 980

ume ga ka ya / Shirara Ochikubo /
Kyōtarō 682

ume koite / unohana ogamu / namida
kana 251

ume mare ni / hitomoto yukashi / Kora no
Tachi 365 2

ume no ki ni / nao yadorigi ya / ume no
hana 367

ume shiroshi / kinō ya tsuru o /
nusumareshi 236

ume tsubaki / hayazaki homen / Hobi no
sato 333

ume wakana / Mariko no shuku no /
tororojiru 681

ume yanagi / sazo wakashu kana / onna
kana 152

umi kurete / kamo no koe / honoka ni
shiroshi 227

umi wa harete / Hie furinokosu / satsuki
kana 420

unohana mo / haha naki yado zo /
susamajiki 299

unohana ya / kuraki yanagi no /
oyobigoshi 855

uo tori no / kokoro wa shirazu /
toshiwasure 751

urayamashi / ukiyo no kita no /
yamazakura 753

uri no hana / shizuku ikanaru /
wasuregusa 353

uri no kawa / muita tokoro ya / Rendaino
878

uri tsukuru / kimi ga are na to / yūsuzumi
306

ūru koto / ko no gotoku seyo / chigozakura
49

ushibeya ni / ka no koe kuraki / zansho
kana 711

utagau na / ushio no hana mo / ura no
haru 479

utsukushiki / sono hime uri ya /
kisakizane 43

uzumibi mo / kiyu ya namida no / niyuru
oto 469

uzumibi ya / kabe ni wa kyaku no /
kagebōshi 782

wabite sume / Tsukiwabisai ga / Naracha
uta 147

waga kinu ni / Fushimi no momo no /
shizuku seyo 238

waga tame ka / tsuru haminokosu / seri
no meshi 184

waga yado wa / ka no chiisaki o / chisō
kana 641

waga yado wa / shikakuna kage o / mado
no tsuki 943

wakaba shite / onme no shizuku /
nuguwabaya 398

wakareba ya / kasa te ni sagete /
natsubaori 965

warau beshi naku beshi / waga asagao no
/ shibomu toki 174

ware mo kami no / hisō ya aogu / ume no hana 60

ware ni niru na / futatsu ni wareshi / makuwauri 640

wase no ka ya / wakeiru migi wa / Arisoumi 544

wasuregusa / nameshi ni tsuman / toshi no kure 102

wasurezuba / Sayo no Nakayama / nite suzume 189

wasuruna yo / yabu no naka naru / ume no hana 290

watayumi ya / biwa ni nagusamu / take no oku 202

wazuraeba / mochi o mo kuwazu / momo no hana 265

yado karite / na o nanorasuru / shigure kana 744

yadori sen / akaza no tsue ni / naru hi made 425

yagate shinu / keshiki wa miezu / semi no koe 642

yakuran ni / izure no hana o / kusa-makura 541

yamabuki no tsuyu / nanohana no / kakochigao naru ya 139

yamabuki ya / kasa ni sasubeki / eda no nari 691

yamabuki ya / Uji no hoiro no / niou toki 692

Yamadera ya / ishi ni shimitsuku / semi no koe 522n

yamadori yo / ware mo kamo nen / yoi madoi

yamagatsu no / otogai tozuru / mugura kana 256

yamaji kite / nani yara yukashi / sumiregusa 239

yamakage ya / mi o yashinawan / uribatake 426

yama mo niwa ni / ugokiiruru ya / natsuzashiki 494

Yamanaka ya / kiku wa taoranu / yu no nioi 552

Yamashiro e / ide no kago karu / shigure kana 602

yama wa neko / neburite iku ya / yuki no hima 178

yamazakura / kawara fukumono / mazu futatsu 624

yamazato wa / manzai ososhi / ume no hana 683

yami no yo to sugoku / kitsune shitabau / tama makuwa 145

yami no yo ya / su o madowashite / naku chidori 693

yanagigōri / katani wa suzushi / hatsu-makuwa 871

yase nagara / warinaki kiku no / tsubomi kana 319

yase sune mo / areba zo hana no / Yoshino-yama

yasu yasu to / idete izayou / tsuki no kumo 717

yogi hitotsu / inori idashite / tabine kana 743

yogi wa omoshi / Go-ten ni yuki o / miru aran 161

yoki ie ya / suzume yorokobu / sedo no awa 437

yoku mireba / nazuna hana saku / kakine kana 263

yomo ni utsu / nazuna mo shidoro / modoro kana 354

yone kururu / tomo o koyoi no / tsuki no kyaku 714

yo ni furu mo / sarani Sōgi no / yadori kana 160

yo ni nioe / baika isshi no / misosazai 235

yo ni sakaru / hana ni mo nebutsu / mōshikeri 973

yo no hito no / mitsukenu hana ya / noki no kuri 506

yo no naka wa / ine karu koro ka / kusa no io 356

yo no natsu ya / kosui ni ukamu / nami no ue 419

yo o tabi ni / shiro kaku oda no / yukimodori 866

yorube o itsu / hitoha ni mushi no / tabine shite 117

yoru hisokani / mushi wa gekka no / kuri o ugatsu 119

Yoshinaka no / nezame no yama ka / tsuki
    kanashi 566
Yoshino nite / sakura mishō zo /
    hinokigasa 379
Yoshitomo no / kokoro ni nitari / aki no
    kaze 209
yosugara ya / take kōrasuru / kesa no
    shimo 928
yotsu goki no / sorowanu hanami- /
    gokoro kana 849
youte nen / nadeshiko sakeru / ishi no ue
    305
yūbare ya / sakura ni suzumu / nami no
    hana 535
yūbe ni mo / asa ni mo tsukazu / uri no
    hana 633
yūgao ni / kanpyō muite / asobikeri
    876
yūgao ni / mitoruru ya mi mo / ukari
    hyon 10
yūgao no shiroku / yoru no kōka ni /
    shisoku torite 146
yūgao ya / aki wa iroiro no / fukube kana
    421
yūgao ya / yōte kao dasu / mado no
    ana 801
yuki chiru ya / hoya no susuki no /
    karinokoshi 664
yukima yori / usumurasaki no / meudo
    kana 935
yuki no ashita / hitori karazake o / kami
    etari 127
yuki no fuku / hidari kachi / minazuki no
    koi 155
yuki no naka wa / hirugao karenu /
    hikage kana 175
yuki o matsu / jōgo no kao ya / inabikari 741
yuki to yuki / koyoi shiwasu no / meigetsu
    ka 226

yuki ya suna / muma yori ochiyo / sake no
    yoi 327
yuku aki no / keshi ni semarite /
    kakurekeri 820
yuku aki no / nao tanomoshi ya / ao-
    mikan 774
yuku aki ya / mi ni hikimatou /
    minobuton 461
yuku aki ya / te o hirogetaru / kuri no iga
    905
yuku haru ni / Waka-no-ura nite / oitsuki
    tari 395
yuku haru o / Ōmi no hito to / oshimikeru
    625
yuku haru ya / tori naki uo no / me wa
    namida 485
yuku koma no / mugi ni nagusamu /
    yadori kana 255
yuku kumo ya / inu no kakebari /
    murashigure 85
yuku mo mata / sue tanomoshi ya / ao
    mikan 774n
yume yori mo / utsutsu no taka zo /
    tanomoshiki 330
yu no hana ya / mukashi shinoban / ryōri
    no ma 696
yu no nagori / ikutabi miru ya / kiri no
    moto 556
yu no nagori / koyoi wa hada no /
    samukaran 555
yu o musubu / chikai mo onaji /
    iwashimizu 501

zatō ka to / hito ni mirarete / tsukimi
    kana 273
zōri no shiri / orite kaeran / yamazakura
    106
zōsui ni / biwa kiku noki no / arare kana
    930

Numbers refer to poems.

A banked charcoal fire 782
A bellowing bawl 906
A bush-warbler's hat 610
A butterfly comes 657
A calming coolness 869
A clam from its shell 586
A cloud of blossoms 294
A cooling freshness 519
A country youngster 312
A creaker-cricket 660
A cuckoo calling 492
A cuckoo flying 298
A debonair young valet 154
A feathery robe 827
A fisherman's face 406
A flash of lightning / Flying 894
A flash of lightning / grasped 308
A flash of lightning / In 888
A flower visible 6
A fragrance whiter 739
A globefish in snow 155
A hatsudake 806
A hay-shouldering 493
A heart-tearing sight 831
A journey's good rest 341
A Kagekiyo 923
A ladder-like bridge 450
A layer taken off 396

A life traveling 866
A little bit of 792
A little like spring 790
A little while to 12
A lodging given 744
A lone butterfly 245
A matsutake / A leaf 728
A matsutake / so 958
A melon flower's 353
A mist-rain in Fall 192
A morning glory 309
A mountain temple's 149
A mountain village 683
A muttonheaded 954
A narrow pathway 890
A night under blossoms 114
A nun all alone 626
A pair of deer rubbing 40
A paulownia 651
A pine-needle fire 325
A pond of lotus 440
A rice field planted 503
A rice field's sparrows 721
A satchel and a sword 510
A scent on the breeze 525
A shaded hillside 426
A shimmer of heat 618
A shimmer rises 477

A shouldered basket 871
A sight to behold 927
A singular treat 532
A small river crab 307
A snowy morning 111
A soothing coolness 889
A spring evening-time 380
A spring no-one sees 752
A springtime shower 962
A stinkyfishsmell 809
A summer evening 880
A Tanabata 14
A temple night's sleep 315
A time for farewell 965
A town with no bell 488
A waft of ume 841
A wandering crow's 231
A warm covered bed 743
A water jar cracks 278
A wayfaring man 320
A Weeping Cherry 32
A whiteness whiter 558
A winter drizzle 659
A winter garden 597
A winter shower 86
A withering wind 662
About a hundred ri's 66
About five meters 363
About the ninth time 727
Above the dead grass 362
Above the meadow 296
Across Mount Hiei 70
Across the wide plain 499
Acupuncturist 55
Again the going 774n
Ah Nakayama 567
Ah the resplendence 490
Aha the spring the spring 112
Akokuso's heart 359
Alive albeit 835
All Kyoto today all 5
All my excuses! 938
All the long night through 928
All these white poppies 182
Allow the sound of 361
Along a byroad 195
Along the window 803

Already bending 865
Although the moon is here 404
Always first to know 73
Amid chrysanth scents 909
Amid the flowers flush 164
Among a riot 929
An ailing wild goose 654
An eyebrow brush forms 521
An octopus pot 410
An old patch of land 262
An olden pond now 270
And after the frosts 661
And even a horse 220
And hear the sound of 760
And I too at the god's 60
And seriyaki 833
And who this evening? 900
And year upon year 788
Anyway somehow 747
Arashiyama 695
Are these the praises 879
Are you a friend to 472
Arouse the gravemound too 548
As cold as it is 324
As green as ever 771
As I knew to fear 331
As if caressing 842
As of no account 893
As the clouds drift apart 41
Asamutsu Bridge 562
At Kasadera 297
At long last it's here 68
At morning glories 156
At Shiogoshi 536
At Suma Temple 408
At the break of day 627
At the Cape of Stars 323
At the curved gable 764
At the gable end 764n
At the Harvest Moon / among 649n
At the Harvest Moon / the temple 649n
At the Harvest Moon / turning 649n
At the homecoming 346
At the Hōrai 839
At the moonviewing 649
At the old river 932
At the rice threshing 731

At Uchiyama 36
At Yamanaka 552
Autumn deepening / A butterfly 442
Autumn deepening / The man 921
Autumn departing / Scrunching 461
Autumn departing / The outspreading 905
Autumn drawing in 883
Autumn's here they say 98
Autumntime coming on 79

Bashō leaves shred in the gale 148
Bears a childlike name 970
Beckon the cuckoo 142
Beginning to rise 318
Belonging neither 633
Beneath the sake 57
Better than a dream 330
Beyond the curtain 366
Beyond the wonders 798
Blossoms at their peak 392
Blossoms of yuzu 696
Bonito seller 303
Bought a masu box 912
Box for a koto 819
Breaking my journey 344
Buddha's Death Day rites 845 1
Buried under moss 211
Butterflies and birds 969
Butterfly Butterfly 173
By noonfaced flowers 423
By the bindweed blooms 176
By the Emperor's 462
By the moonflowers 876
By the white stork's nest 293
By worldly people 506

Calabash flowers 421
Ceremonious 214
Cherry blossoms in full bloom 138
Chōshō's grave 603
Chrysanthemum dew 942
Chrysanthemum scent / In Nara all 907
Chrysanthemum scent / In Nara so 908
Chrysanthemum scent / In the garden 823
Clear sky over the lake 420
Clouds now and now again 258
Cold chrysanthemums 824

Come along children 600
Come closer and see 784
Come listen with me 317
Come on bat come out 959
Come on come and see 39
Come on crawl on out 520
Come on now blossom 582
Coming from all sides 354
Confined for a while 491
Counting as I pass 757
Cranes stalking across 311
Crossing Hakone 340
Cuckoo cuckooing 697
Cuckoo O cuckoo 165
Cuckoo yon cuckoo 409
Curiosity 350
Cut all chrysanthemums 464

Dairi-bina 93
Day after day by day 701
Dear melon-grower 306
Deep in the saddle 828
Deutzia flowers / In 299
Deutzia flowers / Timidly 855
Did Yoshinaka 566
Do not take after me 640
Don't give up those leaves 553
Don't peep at the glee 643
Down along the autumn 773
Dried salted salmon 670
Drinking morning tea 656
Drip down on my robes 238
Dying not yet done 212

Each and every year 687
Each by their own light 637
Eight nine lengths of sky 847
Entering the gateway 592
Especially when 858
Even a long day 295
Even a thatched hut's 483
Even Hollanders 105
Even in the lair 911
Even now the fringe 936
Even the cleavers' 480
Even the Dragon 72
Even the headway 244

Even the three-foot 674
Even the wild boar 646
Even woodpeckers 495
Ever first looked to 629
Every now and then 724
Everybody out 834
Everyone please pray 473
Eye the buckwheat too 723

Falling to the ground 269
Fanning steamed rice 881
Field of bush clover 310
Finally the pine 134
First Day of the Horse 794
First of all rejoice 334
First snow of the year / The leaves 280
First snow of the year / what 279
First winter drizzle 594
First winter shower 972
Fisherman of Suma 407
Five or six of us 466
Flitting among flowers 291
Fluttering her scarf 180 2
Flutteringly so 886
For a little while 689
For my time spent here 378
For Omeiko 779
For the town doctor 54
For this half a day 669
For today at least 776
Forbidden to tell 529
Fragrance of ume 682
Fragrant oranges 635
Friend of mine make the fire 282
From a blade of grass 418
From a white poppy 252
From Atsumiyama 537
From four directions 623
From Kamakura 762
From my summer robes 257
From on high falling 500
From Ōtsu-e 679
From the cherry blooms 511
From the depths of a peony 254
From the herb garden 541
From the topmost bough 78
From the ume tree 367

From the watching them 51
From today the words 557

Gathering mushrooms 596
Gazing at the sawn 82
Gazing on something 67
Glistening dewdrops 805
Go view the moon there 563
Grandfather parents 719

Hackberries falling 933
Had I only walked 345
Hanami-going 850
Has the springtime come? 1
Hatless so I am 222
Have you seen it there 813
Hear the quietness 522
Hearing they eat snakes 621
Hearth reopening 777
Here in this temple 957
Here is lonesomeness / hung 713
Here is lonesomeness / surpassing 574
Here is quietness 713n
Here on a roadway 916
Here's a bamboo shoot 50
Here's a bush warbler / behind 843
Here's a bush warbler / leaving 754
Here's a dragonfly 645
Here's an easterly 26
Here's the new rice-straw 903
Here's where art begins 505
Hibiscus flowers 118
Hidden in a bush 854
Higher than the larks 381
Hira Mikami 675
Hot springs leavetaking / Looking 556
Hot springs leavetaking / Tonight 555
How beautifully 43
How could it be a grief 113
How I envy them 753
How many the frosts 261
How precious the moon 100
How surprisingly 785
How thankful I am 526
How the ring-cupped oak 237
Human voices here 916n

I am in bed sick 265
I am seeing stars 45
I had wanted to ask 531
I scribbled something 560
I washed my feet and then 412
I will hear clearly now 166
I will lodge here till 425
I wish it would hail 606
I'd drunkenly sleep 305
I'd like to sprinkle 449
I'd liken a flower 427
If held in my hands it would melt 201
If you don't forget 189
I'll arise and go 253
I'll pickle it in salt 101
I'm a misery // temple 587
I'm a misery // yon 698
I'm drinking sake 281
I've come and offered 185
In a lightning storm 652
In crescent moon light 767
In early autumn 707
In everybody's 48
In Kisagata 534
In Kyoto too 638
In lonesomeness shine 147
In my hermitage 943
In my sake cup 259
In my tiny hut 641
In priestly garments 577
In setting to plant 49
In the aftermath 948
In the afterwards 814
In the autumn wind 812
In the cattle-shed 711
In the colza field 242
In the combers' folds 575
In the fish-luring 554
In the fisher's house 655
In the midst of our own two 243
In the midst of the snow 175
In the mirror moon 19
In the moonlight his 565
In the night's darkness 693
In the shade of a pail 241
In the strangeness of the nighttime 145
In the summer grass 631

In the summer hills 497
In the summer rains / only 415
In the summer rains / the legs 143
In the winter sun 326
In the withering 737
In the year's first snow 599
In this autumntime 918
Into hiding now 677
Into my sake 371
Into the bed with 911n
Into the gusting 347
Into the skylark's 481
Into this ocean 219
Is it for my sake 184
Is Mafukuda 264
Is that the sound of 124
Is the bush warbler 163
Is the monkeyman 953
Islands and islands 514
It appears to be 867n

Just stay clear and leave 15
Just the way it is 580

Kerria roses / So 691
Kerria roses / The aroma 692
Kids of the village 288
Kiso horse-chestnuts 455
Kohōgen? 977

Leaf-sheathed ears of corn 80
Learn from their journeys 800
Leaves of the ivy 460
Leaves of the taro 313
Leaving this temple 559
Let Saigyō's 585
Let scent fill the world 235
Let the drizzle come 595
Let your fragrance waft 360
Let's get up and go 339 2
Listening to the hail 170
Longing for ume 251
Look a moonflower 801
Look at the icefish 791
Looking all around 432

Make sure to go see 609

Making chimaki 704
Making everybody 4
Mark this tale of old 940
Melancholy nub 694
Millet on millet 441
Missing the wife's love 628
Mochi cakes in my dreams 136
Mochi-like snowflakes 27
Moon do lonesome now 588
Morning after morning 967
Morning and evening 476
Mountain cherry trees 624
Musashino Plain / An inch 56
Musashino Plain / with 979
My body run through 454
My eyes filling with 417
My father mother 394
My friend's not at home 289
My hair growing out 301
My humble opinion 120
My meal of gruel 930
My teeth bite into 690n

Nearing the holy 589
New Year's Day today 162
No simile to 434
No sleep mid blossoms 758
Not letters loose leaves 47
Not only the moon 572
Not soba not yet 904
Not yet a butter- 578
Nothing of the kind close 430
Now a begonia's 708
Now and now again 736
Now even the eye 722
Now for a hokku 103
Now fully in bloom 25
Now I am attired 304
Now I'm surveying 109
Now it's re-polished 337
Now I've got someone to 678
Now pound upon that cloth 205
Now the autumn wind 210
Now the deer's antlers 399
Now the green willow 851
Now then you children / the bindweed
        802n

Now then you children / when 802n
Nowadays cuckoo 183

O dear little snail 411
Of moon and flowers 249
Off to buy the rice 471
Ōigawa 875n
Old bones in a field 190
Ōmi mossie- 77
O-mizutori 233
On a journey stricken 922
On a leafless bough / a crow 121n
On a leafless bough / the perching 121
On a mountain path 239
On Buddha's birthday 845 2
On horseback sleeping 196
On leaving Kyoto 746
On the blooming pink 939
On the folding screen 598
On the lake waters 885
On the scented trail 342
On the strand at Suma 956
On the upper banks 772
On the withering 737
On this New Year's Day 474
Once we've drunk it dry 688
One of its ridges 321
"One of the blind ones?" 273
One ume alone 365 2
Only once a year 840
Ono charcoal-ink 125
Onto snow or sand 327
Opening the jar 778
Ought there be laughter ought there be
        tears 174
Out of a snowless 935
Out there in the world 356
Over this brushwood 926
Overnight the blood 414

Paulownia moves 730n
Petal by petal 387
Picking rice seedlings 509
Pines on a raised bank 614
Pining for blossoms 104
Plovers taking off 666
Plucking out white hairs 648

Praise be to Buddha 188
Priests and morning glories 203

Rabbit-ear iris / looking 9
Rabbit-ear iris / Merely 403
Rabbit-ear iris / stirs 246
Raining now and again 968
Rainy season rains / blow 864
Rainy season rains / Excuse 7
Rainy season rains / gather 523
Rainy season rains / leaving 516
Rainy season rains / outpouring 508
Rainy season rains / testing 37
Rainy season rains / the floating 302
Rainy season rains / the hoop 300
Rainy season rains / the suffering 861
Rainy season rains / The watchman's 76
Rather than oysters 287
Red on red on red 546
Red ume blossoms 478
Reverential tears 733
Rice fields and barley 496
Rise and shine rise and shine 172
Rock-azaleas 11
Rooted to a cloud 61
Ryūmon Falls 382

Sadder than homeland 793
Saigyō's hut 952
Saigyō's inkstone? 591
Scooped into my hands 351
Secluded in here 581
Secretly in the night 119
See how the cuckoo 171
See the slim figure 53
Seeing these ume 59
Shaded by blossoms 384
Shoots of wild bamboo 700
Slivery slender 448
Slumped over bent so low 21
Small bush clover fall 576
Smoothing out wrinkles 338
Snow against the snow 226
Snow on Mount Fuji 88
So alluring indeed 431
So appropriate 616
So deep-rooted the leeks 735

So farewell for now 339 1
So hated on most days 673
So interesting 335
So much harsher than the 44
So now Black Forest 181
So pleasureable 402
So rain-filled today 99
So so many things 376
So spring's really come 232
So the thaw begins 391
So tired of Kyoto 740
So together now 250
So very precious 676
Solitary hawk 328
"Song of the Biwa" 213
Soon I will be included 260
Soon to be dying 642
Sopping wet as they pass 550
Spend nights on the road 348
Spider what is it 116
Spring showers again 611
Spring showers falling 848
Springtime departing 485
Stepping upon the frost 110
Still I wish to see 393
Succumb not to doubt 479
Such a hideaway 584
Such a splendid house 437
Such cooling freshness 872
Such expectations! 475
Such idiocy! 144
Such merrymakers 31
Suigaku please 97
Summer approaching 30
Summer on the breeze 705
Surely those lovers 131
Swaddled by the frost 87
Sweeping the garden 781
Sweet Flags calamus 513
Sweet Flags calamus sprouting 96

Tama Matsuri 644
Tanabata here 891
Tastefully laid out 734
Teikin no Ōrai 91
Tell the mountain's tale 370
Ten autumns it's been 191

That Celestial light 16
That cloudshape a sign? 436
That figure I long 467
That jewel his soul 530
That lone voice lingers 797 3
That someone who says 971
That supine bush-clover 18
That the New Year's here 38
The age-old pinetree 821
The amaranth leaves 901
The arrowroot leaves 749
The August full moon 272
The autumn darkness 914
The autumn passing 913
The autumn wind blows 709
The autumnal hues 712
The autumnal wind / the Ise 590
The autumnal wind / through 13
The azure ocean's 107
The baby sparrows 949
The back and shoulders 444
The barley sprouting 332
The bashō leaves 768
The bashō planted 141
The being-seen-offs / the farewells 445 1
The being-seen-offs / the seeings-off 445 2
The bell at sunset 489
The bird unknowing 816
The birdcatcher too 247
The bitter taste of ice 150
The blooming pinks' heat 766
The blossom-filled day 389
The blossoming wavecrests 34
The blossoms a refuge 377
The blossoms tumble 924
The blossoms unfailing 28
The border guard's house 507
The brazier's banked 469
The Buddha's birthday 397
The bush warbler sings 860
The butterfly's wings 419
The calabash gourd 10
The call of a crane 498
The castle's ruins 429
The Cat of the Mount 178
The cats' mating ends 756
The cherry trees' leaves 208

The cherry's first blooms 375
The chinaberry 859
The chrysanthemum 826
The chrysanthemums 818
The clams and their shells 787
The clapping of hands 699
The clear evening sky 535
The clouds and the mist 193
The clouds as its roots 61
The conversation 830
The cool clear moonlight 569
The cool of autumn 547
The crane's black feathers 795
The creeping ivy 200
The cry of a dove 579
The cuckoo calling / above 761
The cuckoo calling / That lingering 797 1
The cuckoo calling / That voice 797 2
The dawn coming on 275
The Day of Sekku 910
The dew drip-drops drip-drops 20
The dew on mountain roses 139
The dewdrops frozen 343
The drinkers' faces 741
The drizzle-filled sky 770
The drowsy noddings- 702
The dyeing begins 84
The early summer rain 115
The ears of barley / I cling 857
The ears of barley / I grasp 857n
The east and the west 271
The Ebisu Feast 832
The Eight Sights of so 568
The elegance of 187
The emperor's tomb grown old 207
The end of the month moonless 197
The end of the year 228
The end of year ends 151
The faces of blossoms 24
The fernstalks withered 221
The firefly at noon 517
The first called upon 629
The first of autumn 438
The first of springtime 234
The first to the blooms 94
The fishes and birds 751
The fleas and the lice 518

The flooding waters 804
The flowers and fruit 931
The flowers blooming 267
The full moon shining 463
The futon pulled up 468
The genteelness of 549
The grassy pillow / Go 622
The grassy pillow / that 224
The hailstones commingling 22
The harvest half done 435
The Harvest Moon night 570
The harvest moon tonight 81
The Harvest Moon's light 769
The Harvest moonlight / Fog 898
The Harvest moonlight / What 899
The Harvest Shining 720
The heat of the day 533
The horse ambling along 169
The hot waters scooped 501
The house that knows no 204
The hue on the sleeve 975
The hues of the wind // the autumn
    garden 895
The hues of the wind // the garden's clovers
    895n
The hydrangea 856
The hydrangeas 947
The icefish shoaling 137
The Irago cape 329
The journeying horse 255
The kadomatsu 69
The Kapitan too 92
The Karasaki 240
The Katsura Gallant 35
The Kiso spirit 680
The Kiso swing bridge 451
The Kiyotaki / Into 875
The Kiyotaki / not 875n
The life source and seed 46
The life that's given 63
The light of sunrise 217
The light of the moon 456
The lingering hopes 774
The long spring nighttime 937
The Mii-dera gate 715
The miscanthus plumes 710
The mochi flowers 132

The moon and blossoms 482
"The moon and flowers" 783
The moon at crescent 157
The moon at daybreak 837
The moon now a signpost 2
The moon of the Fourteenth night 158
The moon's clarity 920
The moon's whereabouts? 571
The morning after 129
The morning after snow 127
The morning glories 447
The morning glory / during 807
The morning glory / That 808
The Mount of Fuji 62
The mountain itself too 494
The mulberry's fruit 167
The Musashino 133
The name of these things 368
The Naniwa strand 822
The Nara Seven 951
The narcissus blooms 738
The nests of white storks 292
The noonfaced flowers 422
The old nest emptied 268
The olden name of 573
The packhorse driver 745
The paper-pulp cat 130
The passing autumn 820
The path of the sun 634
The pickers of tea leaves the 140
The pity of it 551
The place where I peeled 878
The plates and the bowls 882
The poor woodcutter 256
The racket of geese 750
The Rainy Season 703
The rice-giving kind 714
The rippling waters 884
The rising easy 717
The riverside breeze 639
The robes of the dead 424
The roistering wind 946
The rooftiles of the 266
The rosebud cherry 3
The sake-filled cup 108
The salted sea bream 780
The sasa grass dews 796

The scent lingers on 976
The scent of lotus 887
The scent of orchid 199
The scent of ume / brings 964
The scent of ume / that 844
The scent of ume / With 980
The scudding of clouds 85
The sea has darkened 227
The season's first snow 829
The Sekizoro 786
The shape of the tree 593
The sheen of the moon 283
The shii tree's blossoms 799n
The Shōshō- 604
The Shrine Maidens' House 365 1
The shriveling frost 23
The Sixteenth-night moon / and 453
The Sixteenth-night moon / diminishing 811
The Sixteenth-night moon / Just 718
The Sixteenth-night moon? / Or 458
The Sixth of the months / albeit 763
The Sixth of the months / clouds 874
The smacking of these oars upon the waves 126
The snow falling now 664
The snows we have seen 470
The sound so cleanly 352
The sounds of downpour 8
The sounds of tilling 617
The spring arisen 358
The spring arising 186
The spring departing 625
The spring rain trickling 390
The springtime breezes 29
The springtime showers 852
The squid seller's cries 950
The squirrel's foot fern 726
The Star Festival 539
The stench of the stone 502
The stones have dried up 128
The summer evening 699n
The summer grasses 515
The summer has spread 810
The summer sward it's 42
The summertime moon 64
The summit-like clouds 528
The sun about to 487

The sun occluded 966
The Sunrise Party 817
The Suruga Road 862
The swelter of June 706
The taro-seed man 613
The temple bell fades 349
The temple bell too 428
The things I wanted 960
The thinning at Kiso 459
The tomcat's molly 71
The traveler's heart 799
The traveling moon 314
The tubers planted 369
The turbulent sea 540
The various grasses 446
The venerable 413
The vestigial trace 452
The village grown old 896
The villagers here 620
The villagers sing 401
"The water rail calls there" 868
The water so cold 277
The weakening years 690
The weight of these bedclothes 161
The white of charcoal 89
The white of the moon 650
The whiteness of the moonflowers 146
The whole house of us 892
The willowing bow 202
The wind from Mount Fuji 65
The wind in the pines / comes 917
The wind in the pines / needles 974
The wind of autumn 730
The winter cherry 941
The winter chrysanth 825
The winter drizzle 20
The winter melons 897
The withering of flowers 276
The withering wind / makes 223 2
The withering wind / sharpening 742
The world in full bloom 973
The world in summer 419
The worry-not herb 102
The year-end bazaar 284
The Year-End Cleaning / On 836
The Year-End Cleaning / Through 668
The year's first hoarfrost 775

The year's first melon 538
The year's first snowfall / And 601
The year's first snowfall / The color 663
The youngster sweetfish 484
Then there was the night 838
There at Yoshino 379
These bluegreen crackers 168
These bush clover shrubs 765
These flitting fireflies 416
These minuscule seeds 612
These natto-slicing 671
These tiny sea bream // the fisherman's
    house 542
These tiny sea bream // the fisherman's
    wife 542n
These two at each side 759
They give off the look 732
They're muddying up their sleeves 153
They've carried brushwood 870
Thief Kumasaka 545
Thin at the same time 319
Thin from boiled barley 686
This country dwelling 934
This Day of the Rat 230
This heart and this mind 755
This house doesn't hide 443
This is not the cold 853
This Kiyotaki 873
This mallet of wood 978
This moon that putting 815
This pine a seedling 316
This the world has left 605
This year's second day 357
Those places famous 561
Though I see the moon 405
Though it may not fall 925
Though my paper robes 372
Though summer has come 433
Though unwaited for 74
Threads of heated air 486
Through the aroma 544
Through the summer grass 632
Tipsy from the blossoms 135
Tired of journeying 439
To drink medicine 336
To have a good time 218
To hear the wild geese 658

To live is to fall 160
To my brushwood door 123
To see the blossoms 388
To sleep I'd borrow 963
To the "capital" 322
To the west? Or to the east? 504
To walk naked now? 374
To whatsoever 355
To Yamashiro 602
Today comes the nighttime 52
Tomorrow chimaki 75
Tomorrow night's moon 564
Tossing and turning 457
Try not to forget 290
Turn your face this way 647
Turning away from 961
'Twas Yoshitomo's 209

Ume and willow 152
Ume and young greens 681
Ume winter rose 333
Under my thatched roof 725
Under the noodles 729
Under this one roof 543
Underneath the tree 615
Unlike this old face 902
Unlock the door now 716
Upon the inn door 179
Upon the stones of 672
Upstream a little 524
Urged and encouraged 945
Utter laziness / being 685
Utter laziness / shaken 685n

Voices in the reeds 17

Waiting for the Moon 684
Wandering heartmind 667
Warden of the shrine 215
Watching the fireflies 636
Water offerings 95
Weakening branches 83
Wearied travelling 400
Weighed upon the scales 58
Well so anyway no ado 90
Were my voice better / I would 386n
Were my voice better / I'd 386

What cooling freshness 527
What do they feed on 955
What tree is this that 364
When I look closer 263
When I say a word 944
When Sekizoro 665
When the breezes blow 33
When to reach safe haven? 117
Where the winter shower? 122
Where's Kasashima? 512
Wherefore and what for 607
While the gods were gone 748
White chrysanthemum white
    chrysanthemum 177
White chrysanthemums 919
White ume blossoms 236
Who is this person 286
Whose bridegroom is this 229
Winter peonies 216
Wintering indoors 465
Wisteria beans 583
With a flick of fin 180 1
With a folding fan 248
With an incomplete 849
With an umbrella 846

With coolness in mind 867
With fan unfolded 385
With hamaguri 789n
With his beard blowing in the wind 159
With konnyaku 789
With my drinking friend 383
With the fleeing spring 395
With the freshest leaf 398
With the green still on 863
With the morning dew 877
With the only thing 274
With tucked-in sandal-backs 106
With witty waka in the wind 223 1
Within the shrine's bounds 373
Wrapped in a straw mat 608
Writing "moon" and "snow" 285

Yes how sweet it is 915
Yo marketgoers 225
You kids over there 802
You the butterfly 630
You who listen to monkeys 194
You will know my hut 653
You women scrubbing potatoes 198
Your name is aged 816n

INDEX OF NAMES

Except where indicated, numbers refer to poems.

Abe no Yasuchika, 502
Ajiro Minbu, 367
Akashi Genzui, 235
Akokuso. *See* Ki no Tsurayuki
Akutagawa Ryūnosuke, 710
Amidabō, 10
Aoji Chōtō, 784
Arakida Moritake, 209, 249
Arashiyama Kōzaburō, Introduction,
  p. xvi
Ariwara no Motokata, 1
Ariwara no Narihira, 28, 71, 101, 403, 908
Ashikaga Takauji, 207
Ashino Minbu Suketoshi (Kohō-bō), 503
Asukai Masaaki, 322

Bai Juyi (also Bo Juyi; Po Chü-i),
  Introduction, p. xxii; 123, 164, 213, 458,
  525, 765
Baigan, 844
Baijin, 738
Baiken, 397, 399
Bansai (Katō Bansai), 248
Benkei, 510
Biji (Takayama Biji), Introduction, p. xxiv
Blyth, R. H., Introduction, p. xxxiv

Bokuin (Tani Bokuin; also, Boku'in), 212,
  215, 584
Bokusetsu (Mochizuki Bokusetsu), 883,
  889
Bokushi (Mozi, also Mo Tzu), 113
Bonchō, Introduction, p. xxxi
Bōsen, 342
Buddha, 188, 203, 211, 297, 363, 370, 373,
  379, 397, 506, 530, 601, 679, 845, 907,
  973, 976
Bunrin (Torii Bunrin), 188
Butchō (Butchō Kanan), Introduction, p.
  xx; 314, 495

Carter, Steven D., Introduction, pp. xix,
  xxi, xxii, xxv, xxix, xxx, xxxi
Chang Tu (Zhang Du; Chōdoku), 122
Chen Yuyi, 175
Cheng Hao (Cheng Mingdao), 263, 291,
  295, 317
Chichibu-dono ("Lord Chichibu";
  Hatakeyama Shigetada), 940
Chikusai, 223
Chine, 424
Chiri (Naemura Chiri), 187, 202
Chōkō, 441

Chōmei (Kamo no Chōmei), 177, 303, 751, 833, 927, 980
Chōsetsu, 340
Chōshō (Kinoshita Chōshōshi), 603, 624
Chuang Tzu. *See* Zhuangzi
Confucius, 112, 158, 283, 714

Daiten, 251
Deikin, 471
Deisoku, 916
Dewa no Kami Ujikumo (Okajima Sasuke), 335
Dōen, 467
Dohō (Hattori Dohō), Introduction, pp. xiv, xxvi, xxxiii; 199, 231, 243, 288, 615, 683, 895
Dokukai, 355
Donshū, 922
Dosui, 630, 658
Dryden, John, Introduction, p. xxx
Du Fu (Tu Fu), Introduction, pp. xx, xxii, xxiii, xxx–xxxi; 126, 159, 160, 184, 194, 215, 485, 515, 688
Du Mu, 196

Ebisu, 4, 831, 832, 960
Ekaku (Priest Ekaku), 526
Emperor Go-Daigo, 207, 939
Emperor Go-Horikawa, 604
Emperor Gomizuno-o, 409
Emperor Go-Toba, 240, 761
Emperor Nintoku, 462
Emperor Shōmu, 370
Emperor Takakura, 694
Emperor Toba, 502
Empress Ichijō, 620
En no Gyōja, 393, 497
Enmei (Tou Enmei; Tao Yuanming, T'ao Ch'ien or Tao Qian), 238, 458, 803
Ensui (Kubota Ensui, also Isen), Introduction, p. xxx; 397, 399, 870
Etsudō, 976
Etsujin (Ochi Etsujin, Jūzō), Introduction, p. xxviii; 324, 327, 329, 340, 447, 453, 459, 470

Fan Li, 826
Fenggan (Bukan), 531, 781
Fleming, Ian, Introduction, p. xxxiv
Fu Wen, 119
Fūbaku, 189, 358
Fuboku (Ichiryūken Okamura), 95, 760
Fūjin, 30
Fujiwara no Kintō, 119, 352, 676
Fujiwara no Sanekata, 512
Fujiwara no Sanesada (Tokudaiji Sanesada), 409
Fujiwara no Teika (Fujiwara no Sadaie), Introduction, p. xxii; 879
Fujiwara no Toshiyuki, 79, 130, 546
Fujiwara no Yoshitsune, 87, 210, 963

Ganjin (Jianzhen, or Chien-chen), 398
Genki (Priest Genki), 277
Genji (Hikaru Genji), 80, 758, 924
Gensetsu, 905
Genzanmi Yorimasa (Minamoto no Yorimasa), 105, 900
Gichiku (Tōzaburō), 73, 104
Gyōki (Priest Gyōki), 394, 506
Gyōson, 297

Hairiki (Sugino Kanbei), 595
Hamada Chinseki. *See* Shadō
Hanshan (Kanzan), 531, 781
Hara Anteki, 797
Hasegawa Kai, Introduction, p. xxvii
Heaney, Seamus, Introduction, p. xxxvi
Hearn, Lafcadio, Introduction, p. xxxiii
Heiu (or Heiuemon), 483
Henderson, Harold Gould, Introduction, p. xxxiv
Henjō (Priest Henjō), 51, 804
Higuchi Jirō, 551
Hikoboshi (Altair, *Tanabata* star), 14, 97, 98, 539, 540, 643, 675, 765, 804, 891
Hiro-oka Sesshi, 869
Hisamatsu Shukuzan, 924
Hitokotonushi, 393
Hitomi Iwami no Kami, 81
Hitomi Izumo-no-Kami, 81
Hitomi Sado no Kami, 81
Hōgetsu, 225

Hokushi, 560

Hong Zicheng (Hong Yingming), 127

Honma Shume (Tan-ya), 886, 887, 888

Hōshō Sadayū (Senpo), 815, 816

Hotei (Budai), 960

Huangdi ("The Yellow Emperor"), 117

Huo Di, 117

Hyūganokami (Akechi Mitsuhide), 588

Ichiyū (Shiba Ichiyū), 366, 919

Ieyasu. See Tokugawa Ieyasu

Ihara Saikaku, Introduction, pp. xviii, xix, xxi, xxiii

Ikari Sakuboku, 419

Ikkyū, 70

Inkei, 622

Inoue Yasushi, 398

Ippō, 972

Isen. See Ensui

Ishikawa Hokukon, 184

Ishikawa Santen, 184

Issei, 341

Issen, 547

Isshō (Kosugi Isshō), 548

Isshō (Yasukawa Yaemon), 403

Isui, 471

Itō Fugyoku, 537

Jia Dao, 191, 715

Jidō (also Kikujidō; Makura-Jidō), 57, 108, 234, 442, 552.

Jirōbei, Introduction, p. xxxii

Jiyū (Ogurusu Yūgen), 669

Jō Magodayū, 41

Jochiku, 863

Jokō, 340

Jōkō (Priest Jōkō), 676

Jokushi (Nakagawa Jokushi), 348, 833

Joshū (Tsukamoto Joshū), 744, 862, 863, 864

Jōsō, 705

Josui (Toda Gondayū), 581

Jōzan (Ishikawa Jōzan), 705

Jutei, Introduction, pp. xvi, xxxii; 893

Jūzō. See Etsujin

Ka Shi, 161

Kaemon (Kae'mon), 513

Kagekiyo (Taira no Kagekiyo), 923

Kakei (Yamamoto Kakei), Introduction, p. xxvi; 340, 445, 455, 866

Kamo no Chōmei. See Chōmei

Kanamori Atsuko, Introduction, p. xxv

Kan'ami (Kanze Kiyotsugu), Introduction, p. xxvi; 117, 676

Kano Tansetsu, 924

Kansei, 550

Kanze Nobumitsu, 710

Kashima, 432

Kashin, 506

Kashiwagi, 758

Katano Bōsui, 896

Katō Shuichi, Introduction, pp. xx, xxi

Ka-un, 507

Kawai Chigetsu ("the Nun Chigestu"), 604, 678

Keishi (Hasegawa Keishi), 912, 914, 920

Kenkō (Yoshida Kenkō), 177, 303, 713, 714, 927, 980

Kensu (Xianzi), 791

Ki no Tsurayuki (Akokuso), Introduction, p. xxviii; 6, 16, 359, 844

Kigai, 734, 735

Kigin (Kitamura Kigin), Introduction, pp. xvi, xvii; 121

Kihaku, 425

Kikaku (Takarai Kikaku; Enomoto Kikaku), Introduction, pp. xix, xxv, xxvi, xxvii; 156, 251, 299, 759, 760, 780, 784, 794, 814

Kikujidō. See Jidō

Kinpū, 760

Kiryū, 913

Kiso Yoshinaka (also Yoshinaka; Minamoto no Yoshinaka), 566, 644, 680

Kōgetsu (Suganuma Gon'emon), 740, 741

Kogō no Tsubone, 694

Kohōgen (Kanō Motonobu), 977

Kon Eizō, Introduction, pp. xxxiv, xxxvii, xxxviii

Konishi Jin'ichi, Introduction, p. xxx

Kōno Shōha, 353

Konoe-dono (Konoe Sakihisa), 413

Konohana Sakuya Hime, 486

Kosen (Fujimura Izu), 549
Kōsetsu, 737
Koshōgen (Hōshō Shigetomo), 815
Kubota Ensui. *See* Ensui
Kukai, 394
Kukū, 712
Kumagai Naozane, 408
Kumasaka (Kumasaka Chōhan), 545
Kumenosuke (Tōyō), 552, 553, 555
Kurosawa Akira, 549, 710
Kusunoki Masatsura, 939
Kyōboku (Tōdō Shuri), 614
Kyohaku, 511
Kyokusui (Suganuma Kyokusui),
    Introduction, p. xxii; 629, 630, 652,
    658, 729, 782, 785, 880, 881
Kyorai (Mukai Kyorai), Introduction, pp.
    xxvi, xxxi; 424, 603, 625, 703, 705, 792,
    871, 872, 875
Kyoriku (Morikawa Kyoriku), 770, 776,
    788, 797, 798, 800
Kyōtarō, 682

Lady Jōruri, 682
Lady Tokiwa ("Hotoke Gozen," "Lady
    Buddha"), 209
Li Bai (Li Po), Introduction, p. xx; 194,
    259, 383, 538
Lin Hejing (also Lin Bu), 236
Liu Yuan-shu, 352

Mafukuda (Mafukudamaru), 264
Mahon, Derek, 338
Makura-Jidō. *See* Jidō
Mangikumaru. *See* Tokoku
Masaoka Shiki, Introduction, pp. xxxix–xl;
    240
Masashige (Kusunoki Masashige), 939
Matsukura Ranran. *See* Ranran
Matsunaga Hisahide, 601
Matsunaga Teitoku. *See* Teitoku
Matsuo Tōsei (Bashō), 103
Matsuo Yozaemon (Bashō's father),
    Introduction, p. xv
Mi Fu (Mi Fei), 112
Minamoto no Sanetomo, 672
Minamoto no Tokiwa, 610

Minamoto no Tomonaga, 211
Minamoto no Toshiyori, 31
Minamoto no Yorimasa, 105, 900
Minamoto no Yoritomo, 209, 211, 566,
    940
Minamoto no Yoshihira, 211
Minamoto no Yoshinaka. *See* Kiso
    Yoshinaka
Minamoto no Yoshitomo, 209, 211
Minamoto no Yoshitsune, 209, 510, 515,
    545, 682
Miner, Earl, Introduction, pp. xxiv, xxx,
    xxxi
Mitsui Shūfū, 236, 237
Miura-no-suke, 502
Mizuma Sentoku, 797
Mojie. *See* Wang Wei
Moritake of Ise. *See* Arakida Moritake
Mozi. *See* Bokushi
Munemori (chief of the Heike), 3
Murasaki Shikibu, 627, 672
Musashi-no-Kami Yasutoki (Hōjō
    Yasutoki), 463
Myōmuni (Kikaku's mother), 299

Nagayama Shigeyuki, 532
Naitō Yoshimune (Fūko), 302
Nakagawa Jokushi, 348
Negoro Shihaku, 921
Newman, Randy, Introduction, p. xxx
Nichiren, 464, 540, 779
Ninigi no Mikoto, 486
Ninkō Shōnin, 238
Nishiyama Sōin. *See* Sōin
Nōin (Priest Nōin), Introduction, p. xxxi;
    504
Nokiba no Ogi, 80

Ochikubo, 682
Oda Nobukatsu, Introduction, p. xv
Oda Nobunaga, Introduction, p. xv
Ogurusu Yūgen. *See* Jiyū, 669
Okamoto Taiso, 377
Ōmiya Gyokushi, 538
Onna San no Miya, 758
Ono no Komachi, 96, 649, 676, 804, 888
Ono no Tōfū (Michikaze), 125

Orihime (Vega, *Tanabata* star), 14, 97, 98, 539, 540, 643, 675, 765, 804, 891
Ōta Hakusetsu, 739, 743
Otokuni (Kawai Otokuni), 604, 631, 678, 681, 725, 774

Po Chü-i. *See* Bai Juyi
Pound, Ezra, Introduction, pp. xxxiii–iv, xl
Prince Amewaka, 6
Princess Otohime, 201
Princess Shitateru, 16

Rakugo (Yasukawa Suke'emon), Introduction, p. xix; 426, 427, 469
Ranran (Matsukura Ranran), Introduction, p. xix; 751, 812
Ransetsu (Hattori Ransetsu), Introduction, p. xix; 286, 309, 749, 759
Rika, Introduction, p. xxiii; 141, 308, 468
Risetsu, 397, 399
Riyū (Kōno Riyū; Kōno Michikata), 732
Roboku, 200
Rogan, 792, 793
Rosei (Lu Sheng), 88
Rosen (Naitō Yoshihide), 302, 952
Rosō, 372
Rotsū (Inbe Rotsū), 250, 471, 605, 622
Ryōbon (Tomoda Kakuzaemon), 600
Ryūkyo, Introduction, p. xxxiii
Ryū no Shōsha (Tatsuno Hirochika), 368
Ryūjin, 76

Saburōzaemon, 437
Saichō, 70
Saigyō, Introduction, pp. xx, xxii, xxv, xxx, xxxi; 63, 121, 160, 198, 206, 258, 297, 306, 343, 364, 390, 429, 435, 503, 567, 576, 577, 585, 587, 590, 591, 608, 698, 826, 919, 926, 952
Saikaku. *See* Ihara Saikaku
Saitō Bettō Sanemori, 3, 551
Sakuei, 231
Sanpū (Sugiyama Sanpū), Introduction, pp. xix, xxiii, xxxii; 185, 304, 459, 797, 804, 805, 867
Sanshi, 723

Satō Hiroaki, Introduction, pp. xxi, xxxvi
Schalow, Paul Gordon, Introduction, p. xvi
Sei Shōnagon, 116, 248, 317, 380, 562
Seishi (Hsi Shih), 534
Seishin (Shibuya Kurobei, or Kurōbei), 525
Seishū (Priest Seishū), 587
Sekidō, 339
Sekigiku, 471
Sen no Rikyū, Introduction, p. xxx; 778
Sengin (Priest Sengin), 795
Sengin (Tōdō Yoshitada), Introduction, p. xv, xvi, xxix; 376
Senka, 975
Senpo. *See* Hōshō Sadayū
Senpū (Sugiyama Senpū), 185
Sesshū, Introduction, p. xxx
Sensen, 736, 796
Setsudō (Ajiro Hirokazu), 367
Shadō (Hamada Shadō; Hamada Chinseki), Introduction, p. xxi; 623, 771, 773, 822, 871, 910, 911, 914
Shayō (Shioe Shayō), 914, 915
Shen Jiji, 88
Shichibyōe (Kagekiyo), 923
Shichirobei, 259
Shide (Jittoku), 531, 781
Shidō (Emoto Tōko; Tōko), 640, 648, 914
Shikin, 480, 736
Shikō (Kagami Shikō), 188, 432, 751, 755, 881, 916, 959
Shimosato Chisoku, 437
Shirane Haruo, Introduction, pp. xxviii, xx, xxi, xxii, xxviii, xxxi, xxxiii, xxxvi, xxxix
Shirara, 682
Shiro (Zilu, or Zhong You), 283
Shirōzaemon, 916, 917
Shisan, 856
Shōdō Shōnin, 490
Shōhaku, 625
Shōheki, 338
Shōkei, 343
Shōshō-no-Ama (the Nun of Shōshō), 604, 816
Shūa (Jōbōji Zusho Takakatsu), 493, 494

Shūson, 404

Sodō (Yamaguchi Sodō), Introduction, p. xviii; 121, 263, 317, 458, 751, 765, 786, 797, 823

Sōgi (Iio Sōgi), Introduction, p. xxxi; 160, 345, 583

Sogyū (Hirose Gennojō; also Izen), 583

Sōha, Introduction, p. xxviii; 268

Sōin (Nishiyama Sōin, Introduction, p. xviii

Sonome (Shiba Sonome), 366, 919

Sora (Kawai Sora; also Sōgorō), Introduction, pp. xxviii, xxxii; 282, 471, 557, 587, 705, 797

Sosei, 108

Sōshichi, Introduction, p. xxx

Soshū, 980

Su Shi (Su Tung-p'o), 128, 148, 160, 534, 797, 823

Su Tung-p'o. See Su Shi

Sugawara no Michizane (Tenjin), 59, 60, 69

Sugino Kanbei. See Hairiki

Suigaku (Suigaku Sōho), 97

Suitō (Kanokobata Toyoakira), 493

Suzuki Seifū, 519

Taa Shōnin, 569

Taira no Atsumori, 408

Taira no Chikamune, 74

Taira no Kiyomori, 209, 694

Taisui, 471, 806, 817, 968

Takahata Shiin, 65

Takano Ichiei, 523

Takemikazuchi (Kashima-no-kami), 316

Takutai, 397, 399, 684

Tamakazura, 53

Tamano-no-Mae, 502

Tandō (Priest Tandō), 269

Tangan, 376

Tao Yuanming. See Enmei

Teitoku (Matsunaga Teitoku; also, Chozumaru), Introduction, p. xvi; 249, 970

Tenjin. See Sugawara no Michizane

Tenyū, 530

Terajima Hikosuke, 533

Terashima Bokugen, 322

Tōdō Genko, 830, 850, 895

Todō Yoshikiyo, Introduction, p. xv

Tōdō Yoshitada. See Sengin

Tōin (Bashō's nephew), Introduction, pp. xix, xxxii

Tojū, 904

Tōjun (Enomoto Tōjun), 794, 814

Tōkei, 773

Tōko. See Shidō

Tokoku (Tsuboi Tokoku), Introduction, p. xxi; 226, 252, 328–332, 379, 599

Tokudaiji Sanesada. See Fujiwara no Sanesada

Tokugawa Ieyasu, Introduction, p. xxx; 490, 796, 978

Tōkyū (Sagara Tōkyū), 505, 507

Torei, 719

Tōrin (Amano Tōrin), 853

Tōsai, 561

Tōsetsu, 541

Tōyō. See Kumenosuke

Tōyō (Hayashi Tōyō), 219, 220, 254

Toyotomi Hideyoshi, 978

Tōzaburo. See Gichiku

Tōzan, 477, 979

Tsuchiya Shiyū, 110

Tsunuga Arashito, 573

Tu Fu. See Du Fu

Tu Mu. See Du Mu

Ueda Makoto, Introduction, pp. xxv, xxvi, xxxv

"Urashima Tarō," 72, 76, 89, 201, 218

Ushiwakamaru. See Minamoto no Yoshitsune

Usō, 443

Utsusemi, 80

Virgil, Introduction, p. xxx

Wang Ji, 522

Wang Wei (Mojie), 175

Wang Xinmin (Wang Hsin-min), 127, 830

Watanabe no Tsuna, 710

Wordsworth, William, Introduction, p. xxv

Xianzi. *See* Kensu
Xu You, 150

Yaba (Shida Yaba), 821, 824
Yadō, 891
Yamabe no Akahito, 118
Yamagishi Hanzan, 597
Yamaguchi Sōdo. *See* Sōdo
Yamamoto Kenkichi, 319, 792, 890
Yamato Takeru, 345
Yamazaki Sōkan (Shina Norishige, or
    Noringa), 249, 413
Yamei (Sakai Yamei), 872, 873
Yanase Kakyū, 719
Yao, 150
Yaoya Oshichi, Introduction, p. xxiii
Yasuda, Kenneth, Introduction,
    p. xxxiv
Yasui (Okada Yasui), 340, 444, 867
Yasunobu, 323

Yeats, W. B., Introduction, p. xxi
Yoshida Kenkō. *See* Kenkō
Yoshioka Motome, 414
Yoshinaka. *See* Kiso Yoshinaka
Yoshitsune. *See* Minamoto no Yoshitsune
Yuan An, 175
Yuan Zhen (Yüan Chen), 948
Yūgen (of Ise), 588
Yūgo, 471
Yukihira (Counsellor Yukihira), 404
Yūtō, 884

Zeami Motokiyo, 3, 540
Zekitsu, 794
Zhang Ji, 410
Zhuangzi (Chuang Tzu, also Chuang-tzu,
    Zhuang Zhou; Japanese: Soshi),
    Introduction, p. xx; 143, 144, 150, 163,
    172, 173, 203, 235, 578, 630, 791, 888
Zōga Hijiri, 374

Founded in 1893,
UNIVERSITY OF CALIFORNIA PRESS
publishes bold, progressive books and journals
on topics in the arts, humanities, social sciences,
and natural sciences—with a focus on social
justice issues—that inspire thought and action
among readers worldwide.

The UC PRESS FOUNDATION
raises funds to uphold the press's vital role
as an independent, nonprofit publisher, and
receives philanthropic support from a wide
range of individuals and institutions—and from
committed readers like you. To learn more, visit
ucpress.edu/supportus.